THE
MATERIA MEDICA
OF THE HINDUS

THE

MATERIA MEDICA

OF THE HINDUS,

COMPILED FROM SANSKRIT MEDICAL WORKS,

UDOY CHAND DUTT,

WITH A GLOSSARY OF INDIAN PLANTS,

GEORGE KING, M. B., F. L. S.

GYAN

Published by

Gyan Publishing House
5, Ansari Road
Daryaganj, New Delhi-110002
Phone: 011-47034999, 9811692060
E-mail: books@gyanbooks.com

Distribution Network
gyanbooks.com
India, USA, Canada, UK, Australia, France

ISBN : 978-81-212-9546-8 (PB)
First Published, 1877

2nd Impression 2023

Printed at: Gyan Press, Delhi.

THE MATERIA MEDICA OF THE HINDUS,
Author: UDOY CHAND DUTT, GEORGE KING

THE

MATERIA MEDICA

OF THE HINDUS,

COMPILED FROM SANSKRIT MEDICAL WORKS,

BY

UDOY CHAND DUTT,

Civil Medical Officer.

WITH A GLOSSARY OF INDIAN PLANTS,

BY

GEORGE KING, M. B., F. L. S.

SUPERINTENDENT, ROYAL BOTANICAL GARDEN, CALCUTTA.

AND THE AUTHOR.

1877.

PREFACE.

THIS work is not a literal translation of any particular treatise, but a compilation from standard Sanskrit medical works, arranged somewhat upon the plan of Waring's Manual of Therapeutics, and intended to give a concise exposition of the Materia Medica of the Hindus. Dr. Wise, in his Commentary on the Hindu system of Medicine, has given a pretty full and accurate account of the Anatomy, Surgery and Pathology of the Hindus. With regard to his work I may here repeat what I have stated in the preface to my translation of the Nidána, "That the natives of India cannot be too grateful to him for the trouble he has taken in bringing to light the contents of their ancient medical works, and establishing their right position in the history of Medicine." The scope and plan of his book did not, however, admit of his treating of Sanskrit Materia Medica in the manner of modern works on the subject. I have, therefore, undertaken to publish this work under the impression that it will prove an acceptable contribution to the history of drugs, and will form a basis for further researches on indigenous medicines.

In the first part of the work I have given an account of the mineral medicines used by the Hindus, the mode in which they are prepared for use, their chemical composition, and the principal combinations in which they are employed in different diseases. With regard to the Vegetable Materia Medica, I have endeavoured to give the correct scientific names of the plants described, by procuring the drugs through practising kavirajas or native physicians, and having them identified in the Royal Botanic Gardens.

In describing the general properties of individual articles I have not followed the Sanskrit texts literally. Sanskrit writers, under this head, after recounting their sensible properties, enter into minute details regarding their cooling or heating effects on the system, and their special influence on the humours which are supposed to support the machinery of life, namely, air, bile, phlegm and blood. These details are not so much the result of observation and experience as the outcome of an erroneous system of pathology and therapeutics. I have, therefore, selected for notice such portions of the texts as relate to the practical use of the drugs and their tangible effects on the system. This latitude in departing from the texts, has enabled me to bring together in one place, useful hints regarding the uses of particular drugs from different Sanskrit treatises on therapeutics. I have occasionally added remarks on their history and economic uses where I thought I had new or additional information to afford on the subject. These remarks are for the most part based on personal knowledge.

In describing the preparation and uses of medicines employed in different diseases I have confined myself strictly to the texts of the authors whom I have quoted, and have given the original Sanskrit verses in foot-notes. I have not incorporated with them the results of modern researches on indigenous drugs, or my personal experience of their use. These I have reserved for a future essay. My object here has been to show the extent of knowledge attained by Hindu physicians by their own practice and observation.

In the selection of the prescriptions for illustrating the uses of medicines in individual diseases I have, as a rule, given preference to such recipes as are commonly used by native physicians. Where there are several well-known medicines of similar composition and use, I have described in detail only one, and given under it the names of the others with a brief allusion to their composition. My main object in including the names of the principal or generally known preparations of the Hindu Materia Medica in the text and index, is to enable the practitioner of European Medicine to get an idea of their nature and composition when he comes to hear of their having been used by patients who had been under native treatment before coming under his care, as is very often the case. The list is by no means an exhaustive one, nevertheless I have, at the risk of being tedious, endeavoured to include under some head or other most of the combinations which were pointed out to me by experienced native physicians, as generally used in practice.

In detailing the uses of particular combinations of medicines, Sanskrit writers are, sometimes, in the habit of indulging in exaggerated statements. Thus for example a medicine, which is really used in a special disease, say jaundice, is described in the chapter devoted to the treatment of this disease, but a host of other diseases may also be recited as cured by it. Native physicians who regard these writings as sacred, explain these irrelevant statements by saying that they are secondary uses. I have, for the most part, omitted them in my translations of the texts, hence their English renderings will sometimes appear deficient or incomplete.

The names of the works given below the Sanskrit texts merely shew that those texts are to be found in them, and not that they were originally composed by the authors or compilers of those books The combinations or formulæ generally used, are to be found in most compilations, and it is not always practicable to trace them to their original sources. In quoting these authorities I have, as a natural consequence of the principle upon which the prescriptions were selected, had to give preference to works that are used as text books by native physicians.

The number of Sanskrit medical works, and especially of small compilations on the treatment of diseases, is too numerous and indefinite to admit of detailed enumeration here. The enquirer after them is sure to find, in different parts of the country or seats of learning, many little manuals, essays and digests of which he did not hear before. It would seem that in the absence of printing, teachers of medicine used to prepare small compilations containing such prescriptions as they were in the habit of using, for the guidance of their pupils, who copied them for personal use. These manuals are often dubbed with fancy names, and have more or less circulation according to their merit or the extent of influence of their authors. There are however a few works which owing to their comprehensive character, ancient date, or real merit, are well known throughout India. I will here notice them briefly.

The two works called Charaka Sanhitá and Susruta A'yurveda are the oldest and most celebrated treatises on Hindu medicine now extant. An older work called A'yurveda is mentioned in both these works as having formed a part of the Atharva Veda. It is said to have been originally composed by Brahmá, the creator, and to have consisted of a thousand chapters and a hundred-thousand *slokas.* Afterwards, in consideration of the short lives and small intellects of human beings, it was abridged into eight chapters as follows :—

1. *Salya* or surgical treatment.
2. *Sálakya* or diseases of the head, eyes, ears and face.
3. *Káyachikitsá* or treatment of general diseases.
4. *Bhutavidyá* or diseases caused by evil spirits.
5. *Kaumára-bhritya* or the treatment of infants and of the puerperal state.
6. *Agada* or antidotes to poisons.
7. *Rasáyana* or medicines which promote health and longevity.
8. *Vájikarana*, or aphrodisiacs.

The A'yurveda with a hundred thousand *slokas* is probably a myth, but the abridged A'yurveda with its eight divisions seem to have had a real existence, although it is not available in the present day. It probably became obsolete after the works of Charaka and Susruta were composed.

Charaka is generally believed to be older than Susruta and consequently to be the oldest work on Sanskrit Medicine now extant. In the introduction to this work it is said that A'treya, a learned devotee, taught the holy A'yurveda to six pupils ; namely, Agnivesa, Bhela, Játukarna, Parásara, Hárita and Kharapáni. Agnivesa first wrote a treatise on medicine, and afterwards Bhela and others followed, each producing a separate work and thereby acquiring great renown. The work of Agnivesa was regarded as the best. It was edited or corrected by Charaka in whose name it is now current. At the end of each book of this work it is said, that this *tantra* or scientific treatise was composed by Agnivesa and corrected by Charaka. A later writer Vágbhatta in his introduction to his Ashtánga-hridaya-sanhitá says, that that work had been compiled from the treatises of Agnivesa, Hárita, Bhela, Sásvata, Susruta, Kavala, and others. From this it would seem that the six disciples of A'treya, mentioned in Charaka, were not mythical beings, but authors of books, for two of them, namely, Agnivesa and Bhela are mentioned by Vágbhatta. It would appear also that at the time Vágbhatta lived, Agnivesa's work was not called by the name of Charaka, and Susruta had also been written. Hence it follows that Charaka's edition of Agnivesa, that is the work now called Charaka, was probably edited after Susruta had been written. A'treya is said to have lectured somewhere near the Himalaya, and his name occurs very frequently in the Vedas. His father Atri was a renowned sage, and the author of a law treatise which is current in his name. There is no clue to the nativity of Charaka, but Dridhabala, who added some chapters to his work, calls himself a native of Panchanada or the Panjab.* Susruta, on the other hand, is said to have been written in Benares. From the facts detailed above it is clear that the work called Charaka was composed at a very early age. I will not attempt to hit at the century before Christ in which it was probably written as it is a question which can be best discussed by professed antiquarians. I may notice, however, that the book is composed in an antiquated style and appears to have been written before the spread of the Puranic form of Hinduism, as the names of modern gods and goddesses do not occur in it, and the author does not, at the commencement of the work, offer his salutations to any mythological deity, as is usual with later writers. Beef was not then, apparently, a forbidden food, for Charaka speaks of it as an article of diet that should not be taken daily.†

---

* अखण्डार्थं दृढबलो जातः पञ्चनदे पुरे। कृत्वा बहुभ्यस्तन्त्रेभ्यो विशेषाञ्छ शिलोच्चयम्। सप्तदशौषधाध्यायैः सिद्धिकल्पैरपूरयत्।

शेषाध्यायचरक सिद्धिस्थान।

† कूर्च्चिकांश्च किलाटांश्च शौकरं गव्यमाहिषे। मत्स्यान् दधि च माषांश्च यवकांश्च न शीलयेत्।

चरकसूत्रस्थान मात्राशितीयाध्यायः।

The work next in point of age, namely, Susruta, is more systematic in its arrangement, contains better details of anatomy and pathology, and shews on the whole a more advanced state of knowledge, both of general principles and of details of treatment.

The origin of the Susruta A'yurveda is thus described in the introduction to that work. Dhanvantari, the surgeon of heaven, descended upon earth in the person of Diva dása, king of Benares, for the purpose of teaching surgery along with the other branches of medical knowledge by which the gods preserve themselves from decline, disease and death. Susruta and other pupils besought him for instruction in surgical knowledge. Dhanvantari asked them what they wished to learn. The pupils replied "you will be pleased to make surgical knowledge the basis of your instruction, and to address your lectures to Susruta, who will take notes." Dhanvantari replied, "be it so. For surgery is the first and most important part of the A'yurveda, inasmuch as the healing of wounds was the first necessity for the medical art among the gods on account of their battles with the demons. Besides surgical treatment effects rapid cures, has recourse to instruments, mechanical appliances,caustics and the actual cautery and is intimately connected with the other branches of medical porscience." Accordingly we find that Susruta devotes the greater portion of his work to such subjects as anatomy, surgical instruments and operations, inflammation and surgical diseases, care of the king and his troops in the battle-field, obstetrical operations, poisons, etc.

The general diseases such as fever, diarrhœa, chest diseases, etc., are treated of in the last book called "Uttara-tantra," but there are reasons for believing, that this portion did not originally form a part of the work, but was subsequently added by some writer with the object of giving completeness to it. This is evident from several reasons. The very name *Uttara* "supplemental" is enough to suggest the idea of its being an after thought, if not a subsequent work. Had it been an integral part of the original treatise, it would have been included in the original scheme. But at the end of the first chapter of the first book an analysis of the contents of the entire work is given wherein it is said that this work consists of five parts containing 120 chapters in all.* This is followed by a line to the effect that in the Uttará-tantra the remainder of the subject will be described. This last line, however, is evidently an interpolation, for if the original writer of the work had divided his book into six parts, he would not have said that it consisted of five parts. Besides the Uttara-tantra has a separate introduction in which the writer says it is compiled from the works of learned sages on the six divisions of *Káyachikitsá* or the treatment of general diseases, and from the work of Videhidhipa on Sálakya Sástra or diseases of the head, eyes, ears and nose.

If therefore we leave out of consideration the Uttara-tantra of Susruta, the work resolves itself mainly into a treatise on the principles of medicine as bearing on surgical diseases. It would thus appear that from a very early age, Hindu medical practitioners were divided into two classes, namely, Salya chikitsaka or surgeons and Káyachikitsaka or physicians. The surgeons were also called Dhanvantaryia sampradáya after Dhanvantari the reputed teacher of Susruta, or from Dhanvantari the mythological surgeon of the gods. This division existed before the work of Charaka was compiled, for as pointed out by Kaviràja Brajendrakumar Sen Gupta, Charaka, like our modern physicians, refers his readers to surgeons when surgical aid is necessary, as for example in the passage quoted below. † We may conclude, therefore, that Charaka is the oldest treatise on Medicine and Susruta the oldest treatise on Surgery now extant.

These two works, namely, Charaka and Susruta mark the highest phase of development of the Hindu system of Medicine

---

* बीजं चिकित्सितस्यैतत् समासेन प्रकीर्त्तितं। सविंश मध्याय शतमस्य व्याख्या भविष्यति। तच्च सविंशमध्याय शतंपञ्चसु स्थानेषु। तत्र सूत्रस्थान निदान शारीर चिकित्सित कल्पेष्वर्थ वशात् संविभज्योत्तरे तन्त्रे शेषानर्थान् व्याख्यास्याम। सुश्रुतः प्रथमाध्यायः।

† तत्र धन्वन्तरीयानामधिकाः क्रियाविधौ वैद्यानां कृतयोग्यानां व्यधशोधन रोपणे। चरकचिकित्सितस्थाने गुल्माधिकारः।

in ancient times. Their comprehensive character and superior merit probably led, in course of time, to the extinction of th manuscripts of authors who had preceded them. Succeeding writers and practitioners came to regard these works as of divine origin and beyond the criticism of man. Accordingly they dared not add to or amend what these ancient sages had recorded regarding the general principles of medicine and special pathology, but confined their labours to making better arranged and more compendious compilations for the use of students, and to explaining or dilating upon the texts of Charaka and Susruta, while in the matter of surgical practice, there has been a gradual decline in knowledge and experience till at the present day an educated surgeon of the Dhanvantariya sampradáya is a phenomenon unknown in Hindustan.

The next compilation on Hindu Medicine is said to be the Ashtánga-hridaya-sanhitá by Sinha Gupta Sena Vágbhatta. This work is a mere compilation from Charaka and Susruta methodically arranged. It contains little or nothing that is original or that is not to be found in the works from which it was compiled. This circumstance, together with the fact of Vágbhatta being always mentioned by later writers as an old authority, seems to show that his work was compiled not long after those of Charaka and Susruta. Like these two writers he does not mention the use of mercury in the treatment of diseases.

Next in point of age, are the two works called respectively the Nidána by Mádhava Kara and Chakradatta-sangraha by Chakrapáni Datta. The first is a concise treatise on the causes, symptoms and prognosis of diseases, compiled from various authors, and has been used from a long time as the text-book on pathology by students of Hindu Medicine throughout India. Professor Wilson is of opinion that "the Arabians of the eighth century cultivated the Hindu works on Medicine before those of the Greeks; and that the Charaka, the Susruta, and the treatise called Nidána were translated and studied by the Arabians in the days of Harun and Mansur (A. D. 773), either from the originals, or more probably from translations made at a still earlier period into the language of Persia."

The treatise called Chakradatta-sangraha, describes in detail the treatment of diseases arranged in the order in which they are described in the Nidána of Mádhava Kara, and to which it is a companion volume. Its author deals chiefly with vegetable drugs. He gives a few prescriptions containing mercury, in which this metal is mixed with sulphur and vegetable substances, but the preparations of mercury produced by sublimation and chemical combination with salts, etc., were unknown to him. It would appear, therefore, that mercury was just coming into use in his time. He does not mention opium, so that his work, and consequently the Nidàna, must have been composed before the introduction of this drug into India by the Mussulmans.

The last great work on Hindu Medicine is that called the Bhávaprakása, compiled by Bháva Misra. It is a comprehensive treatise, compiled from the works of preceding authors, with much additional information on the properties of drugs, accounts of new drugs, and of some new diseases, as for example the syphilis introduced into India by the Portugeese and described in this work under the name of Phiringi-roga. By the time this work was composed, opium had been largely employed in practice, the use of mercury had extended to almost all diseases, various preparations of gold, silver, tin, copper, orpiment, arsenic, etc., had come into fashion, superseding to a considerable extent the vegetable drugs of the older writers ; in short Hindu pathology and therapeutics had reached their acme. Dr. Wise says that the Bhávaprakása was composed about three hundred years ago. It cannot, at any rate, be a much older work. China root, called Chob-chini in the vernacular, is described in it. According to Fluckiger and Hanbury the use of this drug as a remedy for syphilis was made known to the Portugueese at Goa by Chinese traders, about (A. D. 1535). Hence the Bhávaprakása must have been compiled after this period.

Besides the systematic treatises on the description and treatment of diseases above noticed, there are several works in Sanskrit devoted especially to the description of the synonyms and properties of individual medicines and articles of diet. The oldest treatise on this subject is the one called Rájanirghantu. It is generally ascribed to Dhanvantari, but Pundit Madhusúdan Gupta estimated the age of this work at 600 years. As both mercury and opium are mentioned in this treatise, it cannot be older. Some later compilations on this subject are in general use at the present day. In the North-West Provinces, the Nirghantu, compiled by Madanapála, is generally perused by students. In Bengal, a very superficial compilation, under the name of Rájavallabha, is in currency. In Orissa, a superior work, called Satkantha-ratnábharana, is used.

The progress of chemistry or rather of the art of calcining, subliming and of otherwise preparing mineral substances for medical use, was comparitively slow in the early ages. Susruta used the natural salts, such as chloride of sodium, impure carbonates of potash and soda, borax, etc.; he employed iron in anæmia, and briefly referred to the supposed properties of silver, copper, tin, lead and the precious stones, but he gave no detailed instructions regarding their calcination, preparation or administration in special diseases. Chakradatta gives some processes for reducing to powder iron, copper and talc, and a few prescriptions containing these remedies. The oldest work containing a detailed account of the calcination or preparation of the different metals (such as gold, silver, iron, mercury, copper, tin and lead), for internal use, with formulæ for their administration, is I believe a concise treatise on medicinal preparations by Sárangadhara. Opium and pellitory root are mentioned in this work, hence it must have been compiled during the Mussulman period. Since then a host of works on metallic preparations and combinations have been prepared both in Bengal and the North-West Provinces, and mineral medicines have been largely adopted in the treatment of diseases. The more important parts of the information contained in these works are embodied in the Bhávaprakása and the two works on inorganic medicines generally used in Bengal, namely, Rasendra-chintámani and Rasendra-sárasangraha. As observed on page 54, most of the mineral medicinal preparations of the Hindus consist of their few metallic remedies combined or mixed together in an endless variety of forms. Nevertheless we cannot help admiring the ingenuity and boldness of the Hindu physicians, when we find that they were freely and properly using such powerful drugs as arsenic, mercury, iron, etc., while the Mussulman Hakims around them, with imperial patronage and the boasted learning of the west, recording such remarks regarding them as the following :—

" Soomboolkhar, 'the white oxide of arsenic.' There are six kinds of this, one named Sunkia, the third Godanta, the fourth Darma, the fifth Huldea. The Yunani physicians do not allow this to form a part of their prescriptions, as they believe it destroys the vital principle. The physicians of India, on the contrary, find these drugs more effectual in many disorders, than others of less power, such as the calx of metals. For this reason too I am in the habit of seldom giving these remedies internally, but I usually confine my use of them to external application and as aphrodisiacs which I prescribe to a few friends, who may have derived no benefit from Yunáni prescriptions. It is better however to use as few of them as possible." [1]

" Para, 'Mercury.' It is very generally used throughout India in many ways, both in its native and prepared state, but in the latter we ought to be very cautious, for it is seldom sufficiently killed or removed from its native state, in which it is a dangerous drug." [2]

" Loha, 'iron.' It is commonly used by physicians in India, but my advice is to have as little to do with it as possible." [3]

At the end of the present work is appended a glossary of Indian plants described by Sanskrit writers. In the body of the work I have selected for notice only such drugs and plants as have some definite use in a particular disease, or class of diseases. Numerous other plants used in medicine incidentally, or for economic purposes, are mentioned by Sanskrit writers, but these are not of sufficient importance in a medicinal point of view to deserve detailed notice in a work of this sort. I had prepared an alphabetical list of these plants with their vernacular and scientific names for my personal use. Dr. King kindly undertook to revise this glossary for me, and, at his suggestion, it is printed as an appendix to this work.

---

1. Taleef Shareef, translated by George Playfair, page 99.
2. Idem, page 26.
3. Idem, page 146.

The Bengali equivalents of the Sanskrit terms in the glossary have been taken mainly from Sir Rájá Rádhákánta Deva's Encyclopædia of Sanskrit learning entitled the Sabdakalpadruma. The Hindi names have been obtained from the vernaculars given in the Bhávaprakása ; the Amrita-ságar, a Hindi translation of a treatise on Sanskrit medicine ; and the Kesava-binoda-bhásá Nirghantu, a Hindi treatise on therapeutics translated from the Sanskrit by Pandit Kesava-prasáda Dvivedi of the Agra College.

The scientific equivalents of these Sanskrit and vernacular terms have been gleaned chiefly from Roxburgh's Flora Indica, Jameson's Report on the Botanical garden of the North-West Provinces for 1855, O'Shaughnessy's Bengal Dispensatory, Powell's Report on Panjab Products, etc. The translations of these writers have been verified, whenever it was practicable to do so, by identifying the plants in the Royal Botanic Gardens. The rest have been given chiefly on the authority of Roxburgh after carefully comparing his descriptions with the characters assigned to them by Sanskrit writers. Some plants, the identification of which was doubtful, have been omitted from the list. The scientific names of many of these plants have been ascertained for the first time, by Dr. King, after examination of specimens procured by me. Dr. King has also furnished the recent botanical names of numerous plants the old names for which have now become obsolete. With regard to the spelling of the Sanskrit and vernacular terms, I should mention that professor H. H. Wilson's system of transliteration, or as it is now sometimes called the Hunterian System, has been adopted, so far as is necessary to arrive at the correct pronunciation of the words, but the minute distinctions between the two varieties of the dental and palatal S, the four varieties of N, and the long and short sounds of some of the vowels, which are not always practically observed in pronouncing them, have not been insisted upon in correcting the proof-sheets. The vernacular terms have been for the most part, spelt as they are written in standard Bengali and Hindi dictionaries. The spoken language varies so much in different parts of the country and among different classes of people, that it would be hopeless to attempt any thing like a complete vocabulary of names as pronounced by the people of the different provinces of which Hindi and Bengali are the vernaculars.

One great peculiarity of the Sanskrit language consists in its having numerous synonyms for material objects, and medicines form no exception to this rule. Almost all well-known plants have several synonyms, and some have as many as twenty to forty names; gulancha has thirty-nine, chebulic myrobalan thirty, the lotus thirty-eight, with half as many for its varieties, and so on. Native physicians learn these synonyms by rote, just as they do their grammars and dictionaries. Sanskrit medical works, like most other works in the language, are composed in rhyme, and any one of the numerous synonyms of a drug may be used to designate it in prescriptions containing the article according to the fancy of the writer and the necessities of metrical composition. Many names again are common to numerous articles, and it is often impossible without the help of annotations to make out which drug is meant by a particular term. In the absence of any scientific description of plants, however, these synonyms sometimes serve to describe their prominent characters, and thus prove an aid to their identification. In the glossary appended to this work, I have not attempted to give a complete list of all these synonyms. As a general rule I have given only the principal or current name of each plant. Some plants have however more than one well-known and currently-used names. In such instances I have given those names in the first column only, with a reference to the synonyms under which their vernacular and Sanskrit equivalents have been given.

I avail myself of this opportunity, publicly to tender my cordial thanks to those gentlemen who have assisted me in carrying this work through the press. To Dr. George King, Superintendent of the Royal Botanic Gardens, I feel myself particularly beholden. He has helped me most materially in a variety of ways, and has thereby enabled me to avoid many errors and mistakes. On many occasions he has spent hours in identifying various drugs for me; and he has revised nearly all the last proofs, before the sheets were printed. The recent names of plants in the glossary are entirely due to his pen, and they entailed on him considerable and tedious labour. Without these names I should have been obliged to content myself with the old names, gleaned from the works of Roxburgh and others, which are now only tolerated as synonyms, and which would have seriously impaired the usefulness of the glossary as a work of reference. I am indebted to him, likewise, for his permission to allow Babu Prasanna Kumar Sen, overseer of the Royal Botanic Gardens, to assist me in my enquiries, and this has enabled me to solve many a doubtful point in the translation of the scientific names of plants into the vernacular. During the absence of Dr. King from the Gardens, Mr. S. Kurz cordially helped me whenever I had occasion to seek his aid in identifying native medicines.

Dr. Norman Chevers kindly corrected for me some of the forms, and put me in the proper way of doing this work. Rai Kánái Lál Dey Bahadur has, at considerable sacrifice of his valuable time, analyzed the mineral substances and preparations, the chemical composition of which has been described in the first part of this work. Most of these preparations have now for the first time been analyzed by him. To Dr. Rájendralála Mitra, I am indebted for valuable advice regarding the plan of getting up this work, and for explanations of some obscure questions regarding the history of Indian medical works.

To Kaviráj Binod Lál Sen, my grateful acknowledgments are due for the very liberal manner in which he has furnished me with lists of medicines generally used in practice, supplied me with specimens of native medicines, and practically shewn and explained to me the processes by which metallic medicines are prepared in the dispensary under his charge. His cordial assistance has enabled me to bring out this work with greater confidence than if I had had to depend upon my knowledge of Sanskrit books alone.

Kaviráj Brajendra Kumár Sen Gupta, son of the late learned Háráddhan Sen Gupta, the leading native physician of his time in Calcutta, and latterly physician to his Highness the Maharaja of Kashmere, has interpreted for me the meanings of many obscure passages in Sanskrit, furnished me with specimens of drugs from his dispensary, supplied me with a list of the preparations ordinarily used by him in practice, and cordially rendered me such other assistance as I had occasion to seek from him.

THE

MATERIA MEDICA

OF THE HINDUS.

INTRODUCTION.

MATERIAL OBJECTS AND CLASSIFICATION OF MEDICINES.

CHARAKA divides material objects into three classes, namely, mineral, animal and vegetable. Minerals consist of gold, silver and other metals; diamond, emerald and other gems; realgar, orpiment and other ores; and the various sorts of earths. Vegetables are divided into four classes, namely, *Vanaspati*, *Vriksha*, *Virudh* and *Oshadhi*. Those plants which produce fruits, without first showing their flowers, are called *Vanaspati*. Plants which produce fruits from flowers, which are known by their flowers and fruits, and which wave small branches from their trunks, are called *Vriksha*. Plants which during their growth are supported by other plants, are called *Virudh*, *Pratánavatya* or *Valli*. Lastly, those grasses, etc., which die after maturing their fruits, are called *Oshadhi*. Animals are divided into four classes, namely, *Jaráyuja* or mammalia, *Andaja* or oviparous, *Svedaja* or those produced from animal excretions, as parasites, etc., and *Udbhijja* or those produced under ground or from vegetable matter, as for example *Indragopa*, a sort of red insect.

All parts of vegetables may be used in medicine, namely,

Root, as of *Chitraka* (*Plumbago Zeylanica*).
Underground stem, as of *Surana* (*Amorphophallus campanulatus*).
Leaves, as of *Vásaka* (*Justicia Adhatoda*).
Fruits, as the three Myrobalans.
Flowers, as of *Dhátaki* (*Woodfordia floribunda*).
Extract, as Catechu, Opium, etc.
Bark, as of *Kurchi* (*Holarrhena antidysenterica*).
Wood, as of *Dárvi* (*Berberis Asiatica* or *aristata*).

Gum, as Myrrh, Assafœtida, etc.

Sometimes the entire plant is used as *Kanṭakári* (*Solanum Xanthocarpum*).

The skin, hair, wool, nails, horns, hoofs, milk, bile, honey, fat, marrow, blood, flesh, urine, fæces, semen, bones and nerves of animals are all used in medicine.

Susruta divides remedial agents into two classes, namely, *Párthiva* or material and *Kálakrita* or effected by time, such as wind, sun-shine, shade, moon-light, darkness, heat, cold, rain, day and night, changes of the moon, months and seasons of the year, etc. These are all said to affect the humours of the body, and, through them, the diseases caused by their derangement. The influence of these agents, if properly regulated or availed of, sometimes cures diseases, without the aid of material remedies.

Sanskrit writers do not agree in the mode in which they classify medicines when describing their properties. Charaka divides medicines into fifty classes, according to their supposed action on the different organs of the system, or on particular symptoms of disease. These classes are as follows :—

1. जीवनीय *Jívaníya*—Medicines which prolong life.
2. बृंहणीय *Vrinhaníya*—Medicines which promote nutrition and increase corpulency.
3. लेखनीय *Lekhaníya*—Medicines which thin the tissues, or reduce corpulency.
4. भेदनीय *Bhedaníya*—Promote excretions.
5. सन्धानीय *Sandhániya*—Promote the union of fractured or divided parts.
6. दीपनीय *Dípaníya*—Increase the appetite and digestive power.
7. बल्य *Balya*—Increase strength. Tonics.
8. वर्ण्य *Varnya*—Improve the complexion.
9. कण्ठ्य *Kanṭhya*—Improve the voice, or cure hoarseness.
10. हृद्य *Hridya*—Promote cheerfulness or relish.
11. तृप्तिघ्न *Triptighna*—Remove a supposed phlegm which causes a sense of satiety.
12. अर्शोघ्न *Arsoghna*—Cure piles.
13. कुष्ठघ्न *Kushṭhaghna*—Cure skin diseases.
14. कण्डुघ्न *Kanḍughna*—Cure pruritus.

15. क्रिमिघ्न *Krimighna*—Cure worms.
16. विषघ्न *Vishaghna*– Act as antidotes to poisons.
17. स्तन्यजनन *Stanyajanana*—Promote secretion of milk.
18. स्तन्यशोधन *Stanyasodhana*—Improve the quality of milk.
19. शुक्रजनन *Sukrajanana*—Increase the secretion of semen.
20. शुक्रशोधन *Sukrasodhana*—Purify the semen.
21. स्नेहोपयोग *Snehopayoga*—Emollients.
22. स्वेदोपयोग *Svedopayoga*—Diaphoretics.
23. वमनोपयोग *Vamanopáyoga*—Emetics.
24. विरेचनोपयोग *Virechanopayoga*—Purgatives. [enemas.
25. आस्थापनोपयोग *A'sthápanopayoga*—Medicines for use in
26. अनुवासनोपयोग *Anuvásanopayoga*—Medicines for oily enemas. [from the nose.
27. शिरोविरेचनोपयोग *Sirovirechanopayoga*—Promote discharge
28. छर्द्दिनिग्रहण *Chhardinigrahana*—Relieve vomiting.
29. तृष्णानिग्रहण *Trishnánigrahana*—Relieve thirst.
30. हिक्कानिग्रहण *Hikkánigrahana*—Relieve hiccup.
31. पुरीषसंग्रहणीय *Purishasangrahaníya*—Render the fæces consistent. [fæces.
32. पुरीषविरजनीय *Purishavirajaníya*—Alter the colour of the
33. मूत्रसंग्रहणीय *Mutrasangrahaníya*—Reduce secretion of urine.
34. मूत्रविरजनीय *Mutravirajaníya*—Alter colour of urine.
35. मूत्रविरेचनीय *Mutravirechaníya*—Increase secretion of
36. कासहर *Kásahara*—Cure cough. [urine.
37. श्वासहर *Svásahara*—Cure difficult breathing or asthma.
38. शोथहर *Sothahara*—Cure anasarca or swellings.
39. ज्वरहर *Jvarahara*—Febrifuges.
40. श्रमहर *Sramahara*—Remove fatigue. [body.
41. दाहप्रशमन *Dáhaprasamana*—Relieve burning or heat of
42. शीतप्रशमन *Sítaprasamana*—Relieve sense of coldness.
43. उदर्द्दप्रशमन *U'darddhaprasamana*—Cure urticaria. [limbs.
44. अङ्गमर्द्दप्रशमन *Angamarddaprasamana*—Relieve pain in the
45. शूलप्रशमन *Sulaprasamana*—Cure pain in the bowels.
46. शोणितस्थापन *Sonitasthápana*—Styptics.
47. वेदनास्थापन *Vedanásthápana*—Anodynes.
48. संज्ञास्थापन *Sanjnásthápana*—Restore consciousness.

49. प्रजास्थापन *Prajásthápana*—Cure sterility.

50. वयःस्थापन *Vayahsthápana*—Prevent the effects of age.

Susruta divides medicines into thirty seven classes, named after the first article of each class. The medicines included in each class have certain common properties, such as acidity, sweetness, astringency, etc., are often used in combination, and can be substituted for one another. This has the advantage of bringing analogous substances under one head, but numerous medicines come to be written under two or more heads. The *Nighanṭu* and some other works on the properties of medicines adopt the following classification in describing them :—1. Strongly scented substances. 2. Moderately scented substances. 3. Weak scented substances. 4. Extracts. 5. Precious stones. 6. Metals. 7. Sweet plants. 8. Acid plants. 9. Potherbs. 10. Bitter herbs. 11. Flower plants. 12. Fruit-bearing creepers. 13. Root-stocks. 14. Large trees. 15. Middle sized trees. 16. Small trees or shrubs. 17. Creepers. 18. Corn and Pulses. 19. Cooked food. 20. Different sorts of water. 21. Fluids as milk, honey, etc. 22. Necessaries of life, such as baths, dress, ornaments, etc. 23. The influence of the elements and imponderables, etc.

THE PROPERTIES OF MATERIAL OBJECTS AND THE ACTION OF MEDICINES ON THE HUMAN SYSTEM.

MATERIAL objects, according to Sanskrit writers, have six sorts of tastes, twenty sorts of qualities, and two sorts of forces in them. The six tastes are sweet, acid, salt, bitter, acrid and astringent. The twenty qualities of objects are as follows :—Heavy, light, soft, dull, oily, consistent, watery, hot, fixed, sharp, tremulous, delicate, demulcent, smooth, harsh, transparent, hard, pungent, coarse and cold. The two forces are heating and cooling. All substances are supposed, after digestion, to assume one or other of three sorts of properties : thus sweets and salts are supposed to be turned after digestion into sweets ; acids, into acids ; and bitters, acrids and astringents, into acrids. Besides the above properties, each medicine has a special action of its own. It is that quality which shews itself superior to the usual properties of taste, force, and result of assimilation ; as for example, *Danti* (*Baliospermum Montanum*), which though similar in properties to *Chitraka* (*Plumbago*

Zeylanica), yet, unlike the latter, acts as a purgative. This result is owing to its special action, the nature or ultimate cause of which is beyond the comprehension of the Gods themselves.

The various actions of medicines on the human system are described in considerable detail. All diseases being supposed to be caused by derangement of the humours, namely, wind, bile, phlegm, blood, etc., all medicines are likewise supposed to have some influence upon one or other of these humours. Susruta divides medicines into two classes, with reference to their action on the humours, namely, *Sansamana* and *Sansodhana*. *Sansamana* are medicines which rectify the deranged state of the humours and calm their excited action, without promoting the excretions. *Sansodhana* are medicines which remove collections of bad humours and discharge them by the excretions. The first is subdivided into three orders, namely, medicines influencing wind, bile and phlegm, respectively. The second includes emetics, purgatives, errhines and other depuratories. Sárangadhara and other writers describe the actions of medicines in further detail and mention the following classes :—

दीपन *Dípana* are medicines which promote appetite, but do not aid in digesting undigested food.

पाचन *Páchana* are medicines which assist in digesting undigested food, but do not increase the appetite. Some medicines have both these properties, that is, they are appetizers as well as digestives.

अनुलोमन *Anulomana* are medicines which digest the humours and set them free, that is, promote excretions and favour their discharge.

विरेचक *Virechaka* or purgatives are described under three heads, namely, स्रंसन *Sransana*, भेदन *Bhedana*, and रेचक *Rechaka*. Those medicines which hurry the chyle or materials for digestion, without allowing them to be properly digested, are called *Sransana*, as for example the pulp of *Cassia fistula*. Those medicines which set free scybala and other contents of the intestines, and discharge them from the bowels, without producing watery stools, are called *Bhedana*, as for example *Katuki* (*Pricorrhiza Kurroa*). Those medicines which cause the discharge of the digested or undigested contents of the intestines in a liquid form, are called *Rechaka*, as for example, *Trivrit (Ipomœa Turpethum)*. These last again are subdivided into three orders, namely, *mridu* or mild, *madhyama* or intermediate, and *krura* or drastic.

वमन *Vamana* or emetics are medicines which cause emesis of bile, mucus and other contents of the stomach.

छेदन *Chhedana* are medicines which remove by force as it were and discharge from the body adherent phlegm or other humours. Emetics, expectorants, errhines, caustics, etc. would probably come under this head. Black pepper and alkaline ashes are given as examples of this class of medicines.

लेखन *Lekhana* or attenuants remove bad humours and altered constituents of the body by thinning them gradually and thus clearing the system of them. Warm water, honey, barley, etc. are examples of this class.

Medicines which promote the secretion of perspiration, urine, and milk are called, respectively, स्वेदन *Svedana*, मूत्रल *Mutrala* and स्तन्यजनन *Stanyajanana*.

प्रमाथि *Pramáthi* are medicines which facilitate the exit of collected secretions from their tubes or receptacles, as for example *Vacha* (*Acorus Calamus*).

ग्राहि *Gráhi* or inspissants are medicines which from their stomachic, digestive and heating qualities, dry the fluids of the body.

स्तम्भन *Stambhana* or constipators are medicines which from their drying, astringent and cooling qualities, and from their easy digestibility, increase the air and retain the secretions, as for example *Indrayava* (seeds of *Holarrhena antidysenterica*).

अभिष्यन्दि *Abhishyandi* are substances which from their emollient qualities or heaviness, retain the secretions and cause heaviness and fulness of the body, as for example, *Dadhi* or curdled milk.

रसायन *Rasáyana* or alternative tonics are medicines which prevent or remove the effects of age, increase the vigour of healthy persons and cure the ailments of the sick.

बल्य *Balya* or tonics are medicines which increase strength.

बृंहण *Vrinhana* are medicines which promote nutrition and increase the bulk of the body.

वाजीकरण *Vájí'karana* or aphrodisiacs are medicines which increase the sexual powers.

विष *Visha or* poisons are said to be endowed with the following qualities, namely, व्यवायी *Vyaváyí*, that is affecting the entire system, as for example, opium and hemp. सूक्ष्म *Sukshma* that is, penetrating into the minutest pores of the body. विकाशि *Vikási*, that is drying the humours, depressing the system and causing relaxation of the joints, as for example betel-nuts. आग्नेय *A'gneya*, that is, heating or stimulant. मदावह *Madávaha*, that is, depriving men of their senses and enveloping their minds in darkness as spirituous liquors. Taken in large doses, poisons destroy life, but, judiciously used, they act as curatives and restore health, even in dangerous diseases.

Nine active or virulent poisons are mentioned by most writers, namely *vatsanábha*, *háridra*, *saktu*, *pradipana*, *saurásht̤rika sringi*, *kálakut̤a*, *haláhala*, and *brahmaputra*. These cannot all be identified at present. Most of them are apparently varieties of aconite, (see page 97). The following seven drugs are described, as minor poisons, viz., opium, *gunjá* (seeds of *Abrus precatorius*), *datura*, roots of *Nerium odorum* (*karavirá*), and *Gloriosa superba lánguli*) and the milky juices of *Calotropis gigantea* (*arka*) and *Euphorbia neriifolia* (*snuhi*). The mineral poisons mentioned in Susruta are *phenásma bhasma* or white arsenic, and *haritála* or orpiment. Of animal poisons, the poison of the serpent is the only one used in medicine.

WEIGHTS AND MEASURES.

THE scales of weights and measures used in ancient days differed in different parts of the country. Separate scales are described by modern compilers, under the names of *Mágadhi*, *Kálinga*, *Cháraka*, *Sausruta*, etc. The number of *gunjás* making a tolá varies in these scales from forty to ninety-six. The scale of weights and measures in ordinary use in Bengal, at the present day, has the *gunjá* (seed of *Abrus precatorius*) for its lowest weight. The *gunjá*, however, is divided into fractional parts by other seeds, thus eighteen mustard seeds, four grains of paddy, three grains of barley and two grains of wheat are respectively said to be equal to one *gunjá* गुञ्जा. This scale is as follows :—

6 *Gunjás* make one *áná*.
12 *Gunjás* make one *máshá* माषा.
8 *Máshás* or 16 *ánás* make one *tolá* तोलक.
8 *Tolás* make one *pala* पल.
8 *Palas* or 64 *tolás* make one *seer* शराव.
2 *Seers* make one *prastha* प्रस्थ.
8 *Seers* make one *áḍhaka* आढ़क.
32 *Seers* make one *drona* द्रोण.
100 *Palas* or 12½ *seers* make one *Tulá* तुला.

In the scale above described ninety-six *gunjás* make one tola. It would seem, however, that in ancient days Susruta's scale of forty *gunjás* to a tolá was in general use, for the doses of powders, confections, decoctions, etc. given in the older works, are considered monstrous for the present age, and much smaller doses are given in practice. Orthodox physicians explain the large doses by saying that they were intended for a superior race of men of ancient days. The subject is involved in much obscurity and this is scarcely the place to discuss it thoroughly. In giving the doses of medicines described in this work, I will state the quantities now prescribed by native physicians in current weights, hence they will differ from the Sanskrit texts from which the prescriptions will be translated.

There is a peculiarity in fluid measures which must also be noticed in order to prevent misapprehension of the Sanskrit texts. When a fluid article is ordered in measures of a *prastha* or two *seers* and upwards, twice the quantity mentioned should be taken. Thus if in a preparation it is stated, take of solid paste of certain substances one seer, oil two seers, and water eight seers, the quantities actually taken are solid paste one seer, oil four seers and water sixteen seers. In measures below two seers or in those indicated by *pala* such as eighty *palas*, sixty *palas* etc, the quantities are not doubled.

The doses of medicines are not fixed. They are regulated by the age, strength, and digestive power of the patient, the nature of the illness, the state of the viscera and humours, and lastly by the properties of individual drugs.

Supposing the full dose of a medicine for adults to be two tolás, the doses for children of different ages would be as follows :— For infants a month old, one *gunjá*, and an additional *gunjá* for each additional month. For children a year old, the dose would be one *máshá* or twelve *gunjás*, and an additional *máshá* for every year, till the full dose of sixteen *máshás* or two tolás is reached at the sixteenth year. From sixteen to seventy the full dose should be used, after which it should be again gradually reduced. When infants are unable to take decoctions and other bulky medicines, their nurses are made to take them. Sometimes small quantities of medicines are applied to the nipples, and the infants made to suck them.

Medicines may be administered during four periods of the day, namely, sunrise, mid-day, evening and night. Sometimes they are administered frequently. Morning is regarded as the best time for administering such medicines as purgatives, emetics, decoctions and pills which are generally given once daily. When no specific direction is given regarding the time of administration, morning must be taken for granted. Very often one sort of medicine is given in the morning and another in the afternoon. Some medicines for dyspepsia are given before, along with, and after meals.

FORMS OF MEDICINES.

चूर्ण *Churna* or powders are prepared by pounding dry substances in a mortar with a pestle and passing the powder through cloth.

स्वरस *Svarasa* or expressed juice is prepared by pounding fresh vegetables in a mortar, expressing the juice and straining it through cloth.

कल्क *Kalka* or paste is prepared by grinding dry or fresh vegetable substances on a stone with a muller, and then making a thin paste, with the addition of water when necessary.

क्वाथ *Kvátha* or decoctions are, as a general rule, prepared by boiling one part of vegetable substances with sixteen parts of water, till the latter is reduced to one-fourth. The medicines should first be pounded small, then boiled over a slow fire, and the decoction strained through cloth. When decoctions are prepared with dry substances, eight parts of water are recommended to be used. Decoctions are administered with the addition of salt, honey, sugar, treacle, alkalies, clarified butter, oil, or some medicinal powders.

फाण्ट *Phánṭa* or infusions are prepared by steeping one part of powdered herbs in eight parts of hot water, for twelve hours during the night. They are administered in the same way as decoctions.

शीतकषाय *Sítakasháya* or cold infusion is propared by steeping one part of a drug in six of water for the night, and straining the fluid in the morning.

पानीय *Páni'ya* is a weak form of decoction prepared by boiling one part of medicinal substances in thirty-two of water till the latter is reduced to one-half. This preparation is usually taken *ad libitum* for appeasing thirst or some such object.

प्रमथ्या *Pramathyá* is a sort of decoction in which the medicines are first reduced to a pulp and then boiled in eight parts of water till the latter is reduced to one-fourth. It is administered with the addition of honey.

मन्थ *Mantha* is an emulsion of medicines in fine powder with four parts of cold water.

क्षीरपाक *Kshi'rapáka* or decoction in milk. The proportions in this preparation, are one part of medicine, eight of milk and thirty-two of water. The materials are boiled together, till the water is evaporated and the milk alone remains; the decoction is then strained.

यवागु *Yavágu.* Sometimes medicines are added to powdered rice, wheat, barley, etc., and boiled with water into a gruel which is taken as aliment. The proportion of water in this preparation is six to one of solid materials. This preparation is called *Kalkasádhya-yavágu* or gruel made with medicinal paste, in contradistinction to another form called *Kvátha-sádhya-yavágu* or gruel made with a decoction of medicines, for which last see *Oryza sativa.*

अवलेह *Avaleha* or extract. To prepare it, decoctions, after being strained, are again boiled down to the consistence of a thick extract. This extract, when properly made, does not readily dissolve in water, can be drawn out into wires, and will receive impressions of coins on its surface. Extracts are administered with the addition of sugar, decoctions, or powders.

वटिका *Vaṭiká* and गुड़िका *Guḍiká* or pills and boluses. These are usually prepared by reducing a decoction of vegetable substances to a thick consistence and then adding some powders for making a pill-mass. Sometimes pill-masses are made of powdered medicines with the addition of treacle or honey.

मोदक *Modaka* are boluses prepared by adding powders to cold syrup and stirring them together till uniformly mixed. No boiling is required in this preparation.

खण्डपाक *Khanḍapáka* or confections. These are made by adding to syrup medicines in fine powder and stirring them over the fire till intimately mixed and reduced to proper consistence. Honey is often subsequently added to confections. Syrup may be made with sugar and water or milk or the strained decoction of some medicinal substance. Confections should be of the same consistence as extracts above described.

भावना *Bhávaná* or maceration of powders in fluids. Powders, and especially mineral substances, are often soaked in various fluids, such as expressed juice of herbs, decoctions, etc., and then dried. For this process the quantity of fluid added to the powder should be sufficient to cover it. The mixture is then allowed to dry in the sun. A single operation of this sort is completed in twenty-four hours, but the process is generally repeated from three to seven times, and often with a variety of fluids, so that the resulting mass combines in it the active principles of various drugs.

पुटपाक *Puṭapáka* or roasting. In this process vegetable drugs are reduced to a paste which is wrapped up in *jamvu* or *vaṭapaṭra* (leaves of *Eugenia Jambolona* and *Ficus Bengalensis*), firmly tied with fibres of some sort, covered with a layer of clay from half to one inch in thickness and roasted in cowdung fire. When the layer of clay assumes a brick-red colour on the surface, the roasting is known to be completed. The ball should now be withdrawn from the fire and broken, and the juice of the roasted drug expressed and administered, with the addition of honey or such other adjuncts as may be directed. Sometimes the roasted drug itself is given in the form of a powder or pill.

सन्धानवर्ग *Sandhánavarga* or products of acetous fermentation.

काञ्जिक *Kánjika.* This is a sour liquid produced from the acetous fermentation of powdered paddy. Two seers of powdered *áus dhán* (paddy grown in rainy season), are steeped in eight seers of water and laid aside in an earthen pot for fifteen days and upwards, when the mixture undergoes acetous fermentation. The resulting fluid is called *Kánjika* or *Dhányámla*, that is, the acid produced from paddy. *Kánjika* is a clear transparent fluid with an acid taste and vinous smell. It is cooling, refrigerent, and useful as a drink in fever, burning of the body, etc. It is sometimes applied externally upon the principle of wet-sheet packing, cloth steeped in the fluid being wrapped round the body for relief of high fever and heat of body. It is also used as a vehicle for other medicines and for preparing decoctions, oils, etc. Other grains besides paddy are sometimes used for acetous fermentation. If mustard or the seeds of *Raphanus sativus* (*mulaka*) *are* added to paddy, the resulting fluid is called *Sinṭáki.* If the husked grains of barley are boiled and steeped in water, the resulting acid liquor is called *Sauvira.* When the husks of fried *máshakaláya* (pulse of *Phaseolus Roxburghii*) and barley are boiled together for acetous fermentation, the acid is called *Tushámvu. A'rnála* is a sour gruel made from fermentation of boiled rice. A mixture called *Sukta* or *Chukra* is thus prepared :—Take of treacle one part, honey two parts, *kánjika* made as above described, four parts, whey eight parts, mix together in a clean earthen pot, and bury the pot in a heap of paddy for three days. The properties of these preparations are similar, they being regarded as cooling, refrigerent, diuretic, and useful in nervous diseases, rheumatism, dyspepsia, indigestion, urinary diseases, intoxication from spirituous drinks, etc. What is ordinarily spoken of as conjee water in English, is a decoction of rice and not the *kánjika* of Sanskrit Materia Medica.

द्रावक *Drávaka* or distilled mineral acids. Several formulæ are given in different works for the preparation of mineral acids. A number of mineral substances or salts are heated in a retort and the distilled fluid collected in a glass receiver. The test of acids is said to be their property of dissolving a cowrie or shell thrown into them. The following are two examples of the compositions used for preparing mineral acids.

स्वल्पद्रावक *Svalpadrávaka.* Take of alum, chloride of ammonium, borax, sulphide of antimony, impure carbonates of potash and soda called *yavakshára* and *svarjikákshára*, and rock salt, each eight tolás, nitre six tolás, orpiment four tolás ; powder, mix and rub them together repeatedly with lemon juice and dry. Introduce the mixture into the receptacle of a distilling apparatus, and distill over the fire. The dose of the acid thus distilled is two drops. It should be taken with six grains of long pepper. One week's use of this medicine is said to cure spleen disease, dyspepsia, etc.

शङ्खद्रावक *Sankhadrávaka.* For this preparation take of sulphate of iron thirty-two tolás, alum and rock salt sixteen tolás each, nitre one hundred and twenty-eight tolás, powder, mix and distill the mixture from a glass retort. The dose of this acid is said to be twelve minims. The tongue should be anointed with clarified butter before using this medicine. It should not also touch the teeth.

आसवारिष्ट *Asava* and *arishṭa* or medicated spirituous liquors. These are prepared from honey and treacle, with the addition of various medicinal substances. They are all steeped in water and aid aside in earthen jars for vinous fermentation. The proportion of the different ingredients, as a general rule, is as follows :—Water thirty-two seers, treacle twelve seers and a half, honey six seers and a quarter, medicinal substances one seer and a quarter, in powder or decoction. When raw vegetables are used for fermentation, the resulting fluid is called *A'sava.* When the decoction of drugs only is added, the fermented liquor is called *Arishṭa.* These preparations combine the properties of spirituous drinks and those of the drugs used in preparing them. They are heating, stimulant, easily digested and stomachic. The preparation called *Drákshárishṭa* is made with honey, sugar and decoction of raisins, with the addition of a few aromatics, (see *Vitis vinifera*). Its action must be analogous to that of wines. It is used as a stimulant in exhausting diseases.

घृत तैलयोर्विधिः Medicated oils and *Ghritas.* These are decoctions of vegetable drugs in oil or *ghrita* (clarified butter) and form a prominent feature of native practice. They are prepared in great varieties and are extensively used in almost all sorts of diseases. The *ghritas* are chiefly used internally, and the oils are rubbed on the body. They are prepared by boiling vegetable drugs in *ghrita* or oil, with the addition of water or other fluids such as *kánjika*, milk or a decoction of drugs, etc. As a general rule, the proportion of the different ingredients used is as follows :— Medicinal substances, in form of paste, one part, *ghrita* or oil four parts, water or other menstruum sixteen parts. When the fluids used are thick, such as decoctions or the expressed juice of vegetables, the proportion of solid paste is reduced from one-fourth to one-sixth and one-eighth respectively of the oil or *ghrita*. Sometimes no solid paste is used at all.

If more than one variety of fluid is ordered, then up to four sorts the usual proportion of four of fluid to one of *ghrita* or oil is observed, and these are boiled separately with each fluid ; but, when the number of fluids exceeds four, each of the fluids ordered is taken in quantity equal to the oil or *ghrita*, and the whole boiled together.

घृतपाक *Ghritapáka* or preparation of medicated *ghrita*. The *ghrita* or clarified butter is first of all heated on a fire so as to deprive it of any water that may be mixed with it. A little turmeric juice is then added to purify it, as it is said, but the object, I suppose, must be to colour it. *Ghrita* thus purified is placed on a fire in an earthen, copper, or iron pan and melted with a gentle heat. Then the medicinal paste and fluids to be used are added, and the whole boiled together till the watery parts are all evaporated and the *ghrita* is free from froth. It is then strained through cloth and preserved for use. *Ghrita* thus prepared should be imbued with the colour, taste and odour of the medicines with which it has been boiled. It is recommended that the preparation of *ghrita* by boiling be not completed in one day, and that the medicines be allowed to remain in contact with the butter for some time, so that their active principles may be thoroughly extracted. The boiling process is carried on to three degrees, called, respectively, *mridu*, *madhyama* and *khara páka*. In the first, the boiled paste is somewhat soft ; in the second, it is dry and just soft enough to be made into pills with the fingers. In the third form, it is turned hard and dry. The intermediate form is preferred for internal administration and injection into the rectum, while the over-boiled form is used for external application. The under-boiled form is said to be suitable for use as snuff.

तैलपाक *Tailapáka* or medicated oils. In preparing these, sesamum oil should be used unless otherwise specified. Sesamum oil, before being boiled with medicinal substances, is coloured and purified as follows :—First of all it is heated to deprive it of any water that may be mixed with it; then the following substances are steeped in it for twenty-four hours, viz., madder one sixteenth part in weight of the oil, turmeric, wood of *Symplocos racemosa* (*lodhra*), tubers of *Cyperus rotundus* (*mustaka*), a bark called *naliká*, the three myrobalans, root of *Pavonia odoráta* (*bálá*) and the tender shoots of *Pandanus odoratissimus* (*ketaki*), each one sixty-fourth part in weight of the oil. These ingredients in fine powder should be soaked in the oil, with the addition of an equal quantity of water for a day. The mixture should then be boiled till the water is evaporated, and finally strained. To the oil thus prepared, medicinal substances, in the form of paste, decoction, etc., are added in the same proportions as for the preparation of *ghritapáka*. They are then boiled together till the watery parts are all evaporated. When cool, the oil is strained through cloth so as to separate the solid particles. Some medicinal oils, and especially those used in the treatment of nervous diseases, rheumatism, etc., are subjected to a third process of boiling with various aromatic and fragrant substances. This is called the *Gandha páka* or boiling for rendering the oil fragrant. The following substances, or as many of them as are available, are used for scenting medicated oils, namely, cardamoms, cinnamon, cloves, fenugreek seeds, saffron, leaves of *Cinnamomum Tamala*, white sandal wood, aloes wood, *jatámansi* root, *Curcuma Zedoaria* (*sati*), *Cyperus rotundus* (*mustaka*), *kakkola* (an aromatic seed,) resin of *Pinus longifolius* (*gandhavirajá*), storax, long pepper root, root of *Andropogon muricatus* (*usira*), *nakhi* (*Unguis odoratus*),* pouch of civet cat (*khaṭṭási*), camphor,

* This *nakhi* according to Rumphius who describes ten kinds of the odoriferous onyx which serve as the basis of the principal perfumes in the Indian Islands, (Herb. Amb. ii. c. 17) is the operculum or lid of the shells of *Purpura* and *Murex*, This being flat and something like a nail explains the origin of its name.—*Royle's Antiquity of Hindu Medicine, page* 144.

musk, *Permelia perlata* (*saileya*,) root of *Aplotaxis auriculata* (*kushṭa*), seeds of *Abelmoschus moschatus* (*latákasturi*), etc.

For four seers of oil, one tola of each of the above ingredients should be taken, with the exception of camphor which should be four tolas. These ingredients, with the exceptions noticed below, are reduced to a paste with water and added to the oil, which is then boiled with an equal quantity of water till the latter is evaporated, and lastly strained. Camphor, musk, storax and the substance called *nakhi* should be added after the process of boiling is finished, and the oil strained. Oils for rheumatism and nervous diseases, are sometimes rendered fragrant by the addition of camphor alone.

Castor oil and mustard oil are sometimes used in the preparation of medicated oils. The proportions of oil, medicinal substances and fluids are the same as with sesamum oil, but the preliminary preparation of these oils is different. Mustard oil is purified by being boiled with the following ingredients, namely, emblic myrobalan, turmeric, tubers of *Cyperus rotundus* (*mustaka*), root-bark of *Ægle Marmelos* (*vilva*), pomegranate bark, flowers of *Mesua ferrea* (*nágakesara*), Nigella seeds, root of *Pavonia odorata* (*bálá*), the bark called *naliká*, and belleric myrobalan, two tolás each, and madder sixteen tolás, for four seers of oil. These should be boiled together with sixteen seers of water, till the latter is all evaporated, and the oil should then be strained. It is now fit for being boiled with medicinal substances, the process for which is the same as for sesamum oil above described.

For purifying castor oil, the following ingredients are used, namely, madder, tubers of *Cyperus rotundus* (*mustaka*), coriander, the three myrobalans, leaves of *Sesbania aculeata* (*vaijayanti*), *Pavonia odorata* (*hrivera*), wild dates, tender red buds of *Ficus Bengalensis* (*vaṭasunga*), turmeric, wood of *Berberis Asiatica* (*dáruharidrá*), the bark called *naliká*, ginger and the shoots of *Pandanus odoratissimus* (*ketaki*), each half a tolá for four seers of oil. Castor oil should be boiled with equal parts of whey and *kánjika* (fermented paddy water) along with the above ingredients.*

---

* The processes above described, for the preliminary purification of oils before being boiled with medicinal substances are not adopted by the physicians of upper India. They are not mentioned by the ancient writers and are the inventions of recent Bengali authors.

ON THE DIFFERENT MODES IN WHICH MEDICINES ARE APPLIED.

Besides being taken internally, medicines are applied in various other ways, such as by injections into the rectum, urethra and female organs ; application to the nose ; to the mouth ; to the eyes ; to the skin in the shape of plasters, ointments, oils and fumigations, and to the lungs by inhalation.

वस्तिकर्म *Vastikarma* or injections into the rectum, were thrown in by means of a tube with a membranous bag tied to its end. The bag was recommended to be made of the bladder of some animal, such as bull, goat, etc. It was filled with the fluid to be injected and tied to one end of a tube, about eight inches long and with a tapering rounded extremity for introduction into the rectum. Injections into the urethra and vagina were thrown in by similar contrivances, the tubes being adapted in length and thickness to the passages for which they were intended.

फलवर्त्ती *Phalavarti* or suppositories were recommended to be made of the size of the patient's thumb. They were smeared with clarified butter and introduced into the rectum. The following is an example of a suppository. Take of assafœtida and rock-salt equal parts and make a suppository with honey, for use in tympanitis.

नस्य *Nasya* or the application of medicated substances to the nose, forms a prominent feature of native therapeutics. Two primary classes of medicines for this organ are recognized, namely *Sirovirechana* or medicines causing a flow of secretion from the nose and thus relieving cerebral congestion, and *Vrinhana* or medicated oils applied to the nose with the object of cooling the head and relieving affections of the neck and chest. For clearing the head and promoting discharge from the nose, the expressed juice of pungent drugs is poured into the nose, drop by drop, or powders are blown into the nostrils by means of a tube. The former process is called *Avapiḍa* and the latter, *Pradhamana*. For cooling the head and relieving affections of the upper part of the body, various medicated oils are used. In one form of snuff called *Pratimarsha*, two or three drops of medicated oil are directed to be snuffed up the nostril till they reach the throat, when they should be expectorated and not swallowed. In another form of application called *Marsha* about a drachm of oil is recommended to be gradually poured into each nostril from a spoon or shell.

कवल *Kavala*. Liquids used as gargles are so called. Sometimes a mixture of liquid and solid substances or solid balls of medicine are taken into the mouth and retained in it till they bring on a discharge from the nose and eyes. This mode of application is called गण्डूष *Gaṇḍusha.* When powders or thick solutions are applied to the teeth and gums with the finger, the process of medicament is called प्रतिसारण *Pratisárana.*

शिरोवस्ति *Sirovasti*, etc. or applications to the head. Oils or other fluids are applied to the head in four different ways. The first form called *Sirovasti*, consists in tying a piece of leather four and a half inches in breadth all round the head, luting its lower margin to the skin by a paste of the pulse called *máshakaláya* and then filling the cavity thus formed on the top of the head with lukewarm oil. The oil is directed to be retained till relief of pain, or till there is discharge from the eyes and nose. It should then be removed and the head washed with warm water. This sort of medication is said to be useful in severe headache and shaking of the head. In the second form, oil or other fluid is poured in a stream on the head. This is called *Parisheka.* In the third form, called *Pichu*, cotton soaked in oil is applied to the scalp ; and in the fourth, called *Avyanga*, the oil is simply rubbed on the head.

Applications of liquids and medicated oils to the ears are used in diseases of the head as well as of the ears. The external meatus is filled with the fluid which is allowed to remain in it from one to twenty minutes and is then withdrawn.

नेत्रकर्म *Netrakarma* or applications to the eyes receive various names according to the nature of the substances used and the manner in which they are applied. Pouring of drops into the eyes is called *A'schotana.* A poultice enclosed within a piece of cloth and applied over the lids is called *Piṇḍa.* A paste applied to the lids is called *Viḍálaka.* Medicines applied to the margin of the lids or to the conjunctiva with the finger or a metallic probe are called *Anjana.* These last may be in the shape of powder or liquid or they may be made into sticks or pills which are rubbed with water before use. The probe for applying medicines to the margin of the lids should be six inches long with a rounded bulbous end. It may be made of gold, silver, copper, iron or stone. For habitual use of collyria a lead probe is preferred. When medicines are applied not only to the lids but also to the conjunctiva up to the margin of the cornea, the finger is recommended to be used, as it is soft and safe.

Applications to the skin. These consist of *ghritas*, oils, plasters, poultices, baths and hot applications for inducing perspiration. Medicated *ghritas* and oils have been already described. They are for the most part rubbed all over the body, except those intended for local ailments. Plasters called प्रलेप *Pralepa* are applied moist and cold. प्रदेह *Pradeha* or poultices are applied moist and hot. They are also thicker than plasters.

स्वेदन *Svedana* or application of heat to the skin for inducing perspiration is carried out in four different ways, namely :—

1. तापस्वेद *Tápasveda* or the application of dry heat by means of heated plates, bricks, sand, cloth or the palm of the hand only. These are recommended to be heated by catechu-wood fire.

2. उष्मस्वेद *Ushmasvéda* or the application of hot steam. This is effected in various ways. The part to be heated is covered with wet cloth. Bricks, stones or iron plates are made red hot and sprinkled over with *kánjika* or some decoction, and are then applied to the part to be heated; or an earthen pot with a small opening in the side is filled with hot water or decoction of some drugs, a tube is adjusted to the hole in the pot and the steam is applied to the covered body through it. A third method consists in heating the ground by burning catechu-wood over it, and after removing the fire, sprinkling some decoction over the spot and making a bed of castor oil leaves on it. The patient is to lie on this bed and cover himself with a blanket. Or the ground may be covered with a thick layer of boiled pulse such as *máshakaláya* and a bed made over it for the patient.

3. उपनाहस्वेद *Upanáhasveda.* This means the application of heat by hot medicinal substances in the form of decoctions, pastes, or plasters, or of fomentation by cloth wrung out of hot fluids ;

or heat may be applied by enclosing hot medicinal substances or pastes within a cloth bag and applying the latter to the skin.

4. द्रवस्वेद *Dravasveda*. This means the hot hip-bath and hot bath with warm water or decoctions. Milk, broth, oil, *kánjika* etc. may also be used for baths. The patient should sit in a tub with the fluid up to his navel, and which should also be poured over his body from above the shoulders, so as to bathe him thoroughly. The tub should be made of wood, silver, copper or iron, of square form and twenty-six fingers in measurement in all directions, that is in height, length and breadth. After the application of heat, the patient should take a hot bath, eat light food and keep himself covered in bed. If too much heat has been applied, and the patient suffers from pain in the joints, thirst, langour or giddiness, then he should be treated by cooling applications. The region of the heart, scrotum and eyes should be heated with great care and to a mild degree only.

धूमपान *Dhumapána* or inhalations. Tapers or pastilles made of medicinal substances are set fire to, and their fumes inhaled through a tube by the mouth or nose. Pastilles for inhalation are thus prepared: a reed, half a cubit in length, is smeared or laid over with a paste of the drugs to be used, to two-thirds of its extent and is dried in the shade. When dry, the reed is withdrawn from the paste, leaving it in the form of a hollow tube. This is smeared with clarified butter and lighted. The lighted extremity is introduced into one end of the inhaling tube and the fumes drawn in by the other end through the mouth or nose, as the case may be, and emitted again through the mouth. In affections of the throat and chest, inhalation through the mouth is recommended, while in diseases of the head, eyes or nose, the fumes are drawn in through the nose. The tube for inhalation may be metallic or made of wood or ivory. Its length varies from two cubits to half a cubit, and its calibre should be sufficient to allow a large pea to pass through. The shorter tubes are used in administering expectorant and emetic fumes. Inhalations are useful in cough, asthma, catarrh, pain in the neck or head, etc. They may be used for soothing the air passages, for promoting discharge from them, for the relief of cough, or for inducing vomiting. Another form of inhalation, called *Samana*.

is recommended to be used daily after washing the face, bathing, breakfast, etc. The pastille for this was made of cardamoms and other aromatic substances. This sort of smoking is not seen in the present day. Probably it was in vogue before the introduction of tobacco and has been displaced by the latter.

धूपन *Dhupana* or fumigations were employed for ulcers and skin diseases. The pastilles for these are made as for inhalation. They are lighted and placed inside two earthen pots, placed face to face. A hole is made in the upper pot and a tube adjusted to it. The free or open end of the tube is now directed to the affected part and the fumes allowed to spread over it. Incenses and tapers composed of various medicinal substances are also burnt in rooms occupied by the sick, for removing unpleasant smells and supposed evil spirits.

क्षारकर्म्म *Ksharakarma* or caustic applications. The ancient physicians of India, like their modern representatives, preferred opening abscesses by caustics, to incising them with the lancet. Hence caustics were described as superior to the lancet, inasmuch as, in addition to opening abcesses, they purified them by removing the derangement of the humours. The ashes of the following plants were used for the preparation of caustics, namely :—

पाटला *Páṭalá.—Stereospermum suaveolens.*

कुटज *Kuṭaja.—Holarrhena antidysenterica.*

पलाश *Palása.—Butea frondosa.*

अश्वकर्ण *Asvakarna.—Shorea robusta.*

पारिभद्र *Páribhadra.—Erythrina Indica.*

विभितक *Vibhitaka.—Terminalia Bellerica.*

आरग्वध *A'ragvadha.—Cassia fistula.*

लोध्र *Lodhra.—Symplocos racemosa.*

अर्क *Arka.—Calotropis gigantea.*

स्नुहि *Snuhi.—Euphorbia neriifolia.*

अपामार्ग *Apámárga.—Achyranthes aspera.*

करञ्ज *Karanja.—Pongamia glabra.*

वासक *Vásaka.—Justícia Adhatoda.*

कदलि *Kadali.—Musa sapientum.*

चित्रक *Chitraka.—Plumbago Zeylanica.*

पूतिक *Putika.—Cæsalpinia Bonducella.*

देवदारु *Devadáru.—Cedrus Deodara.*

आस्फोता *A'sphotá.—Vallaris dichotoma.*

करवीर *Karavira.—Nerium odorum.*

सप्तपर्णी *Saptaparni.—Alstonia scholaris.*

गम्भारि *Gambhári.—Gmelina arborea.*

गुञ्जा *Gunjá.—Abrus precatorius.*

कोषातकी *Koshátaki.—Luffa pentandra.*

The roots, stems and leaves of these plants or of such of them as are available, are cut into pieces and burnt in a pit. The ashes are then collected and boiled in six times their weight of water till the solution becomes transparent, red, pungent and soapy to the feel. It should then be strained and again put on fire and the following substances added, namely, ashes of *Euphorbia neriifolia (snuhi)*, and the burnt powders of bivalve and conch shells. The mixture should be constantly stirred and boiled till it is of a thick consistence. The proportion of shell-lime added varies from one fourth to one-eighth or one-sixteenth part of the solution. Caustics of three strengths are thus obtained. Sometimes orpiment and realgar are added to increase their strength.

The part where the caustic is to be applied, should first be cleaned and rubbed. The caustic should then be applied with a probe. It should be allowed to remain in contact with the skin for such time as is occupied in uttering a hundred words and then removed. The skin becomes black from the application, when it is dressed with a paste of acids, clarified butter and honey. For hastening the removal of the slough, a paste or poultice composed of sesamum seeds, liquorice root, lemon juice and *kánjika* should be applied. Caustics are applied to external piles, sinuses, fistulæ in ano, abscesses, warts, tumours, leprous patches, etc.

THE

MATERIA MEDICA OF THE HINDUS.

PART I.

INORGANIC MATERIA MEDICA.

GENERAL REMARKS ON MINERAL MEDICINES.

MINERAL or inorganic medicines are generally described under five heads, namely, *Rasa* or mercury which forms a class by itself; *Uparasa* or metallic ores and earths, *Dhátu* or metals, *Lavana* or salts, and *Ratna* or precious stones. The metals used in Sanskrit medicine are mercury, gold, silver, copper, tin, zinc, lead, iron, bell-metal, and brass. The *Uparasas* used are sulphur, talc or mica, two sorts of iron pyrites called *Svarnamákshika* and *Táramákshika*, loadstone, orpiment, realgar, sulphate of copper, sulphate of iron, cinnabar, minium or red lead, sulphuret of lead, calamine (*kharpara*), *Silájatu* (a bituminous substance containing iron), alum, borax, chalk, calcined cowries and conch shells, *Gairika* a sort of red mountain earth or ochre, *Kankushṭa* a sort of mountain earth, *Sauráshṭri* a fragrant earth from Surat, sand, clay, etc.

The precious stones described are, 1 *Hiraka*, diamond; 2 *Gárutmat*, emerald; 3 *Pushparága*, topaz; 4 *Mánikya*, ruby; *Indranila*, sapphire; 6 *Gomeda*, a yellow gem of the colour of fat; 7 *Vaidurya*, a gem of a dark blue colour, the lapis lazuli; 8 *Mauktika*, pearls; 9 *Vidruma*, corals. Collectively they are called *Navaratna* or the nine gems. *Rájavarta*, an inferior kind of diamond from Virat, and *Vaikránta*, another inferior kind of diamond, are sometimes used instead of diamond.

Salts.—Of these the following are noticed by most writers, viz., *Saindhava*, rock salt; *Sámbara*, Sambar lake salt; *Sauvarchala*, sonchal salt; *Bit*, black salt; *Sámudra*, sun-dried sea salt, commonly known as *Karkach*; *Audbhida*, a saline efflorescence on *reh* lands; *Pánsuja* or salt obtained from saline earth; *Yavakshára*, impure carbonate of potash; *Sarjikákshára*, impure carbonate of soda; *Sarvakshára,* mixed ashes of several plants; *Narasára* chloride of ammonium; *Soraka,* nitrate of potash, and *Tankana,* borax. The term *Ushara* is applied to saline earth.

Metals and metallic compounds are subjected to a so-called process of purification in order to get rid of their impurities or deleterious qualities. If used in an unpurified state, they are supposed to induce certain diseases or morbid symptoms. The metals, for the most part, are purified by repeatedly heating their plates and plunging them in the following fluids, namely, oil, whey, sour conjee, cow's urine and the decoction of a pulse called *kulattha* (*Dolichos uniflorus*). Another method of purification consists in soaking the plates of heated metals in the juice of the plantain-tree.

Metals and metallic compounds are reduced to powder by various processes. The operation is called *márana,* which literally means killing or destruction of metallic character but practically a reduction to powder, either in the metallic state, or after conversion into an oxide or a sulphide. Various processes for the calcination of different metals are described in Sanskrit works on the subject. I will not burden these pages with a detailed account of these but shall only describe modes of preparation followed at the present day.

Although the Hindus had made some successful efforts in preparing a certain number of chemical compounds such as perchloride of mercury, sulphides of copper and silver, oxide of tin, some acids, alkalies, etc., yet their chemical operations were of a very rude and primitive character. The apparatus employed by them consisted of crucibles of different sorts, glass bottles and earthen pots arranged for sublimation of volatile compounds, retorts for distillation, sand and vapour baths, etc. The furnace for heating metals is usually a pit in the ground called **गजपुट** *Gajaputa.* It is made one and a quarter cubits in depth, length and breadth. This is filled with dried balls of cowdung. The metals or metallic compounds to be roasted are enclosed in a covered crucible and placed in the centre of the pit within the balls of cowdung, which are then set fire to and allowed to burn till consumed to ashes.

मुषायन्त्र. *Musháyantra* or crucibles, are recommended to be made of husks of rice two parts, earth from ant-hills, iron rust, chalk and human hair cut into small bits, one part each. These are rubbed together into a paste with goat-milk, and made into crucibles which are dried in the sun. Practically, however, goldsmith's crucibles or common earthen cups are used. The compounds to be roasted are placed in one crucible, this is covered with a second, and the two are luted together with clay.

वालुकायन्त्र. The sand-bath called *Váluká yantra* is made by filling an earthen pot with sand and heating it over the fire. Metalic preparations sublimed within glass bottles are heated in sand-baths.

दोलायन्त्र. When medicines, tied in a piece of cloth or other material, are suspended and boiled in a pot of water, the apparatus is called *Dolá yantra.* The steam-bath called *Svedana yantra* is got up by covering the mouth of a pot of boiling water with a piece of cloth, placing the medicines to be heated by steam on this cloth, and then covering them with another pot.

For the sublimation of metals and metalic preparations, two sorts of apparatus are used. The first, called ऊर्द्धपातनयन्त्र *Urddha-pátana yantra,* consists of two earthen pots placed one above the other with their rims luted together with clay. The lower pot containing the medicine is put on fire while the upper one is kept cool with wet rags. The sublimate is deposited in the interior of the upper pot. Sometimes the lower pot is covered with a concave dish and water poured into its hollow to keep it cool and changed as often as it gets hot. The second plan consists in placing the medicines to be sublimed in the bottom of a glass bottle which has been strengthened with layers of clay and cloth wrapped round it, and then exposing it to heat in a sand-bath. The sublimate is deposited in the neck of the bottle, whence it is extracted by breaking the latter.

तिर्य्यक्पातनयन्त्र *Tiryak pátana yantra.* This apparatus means the adjustment of retorts and receivers for sublimation and distillation. At the present day glass retorts of European manufacture are used. Country-made glass retorts are also available.

SULPHUR.

Sans. गन्धक *Gandhaka.*

Four varieties of sulphur are mentioned by Sanskrit writers, namely, red, yellow, white and black. Of these the red and black are not now available. The yellow variety or vitreous sulphur is called *ámlá-sár*, because its semi-transparent crystals resemble the translucent ripe fruits of the *ámalaki* (*Phyllanthus emblica*). It is preferred for internal use in combination with mercury. The white variety or ordinary roll sulphur is inferior to the yellow, and used for external application in skin diseases.

Sulphur is purified by being washed in milk. It is first dissolved in an iron ladle smeared with butter and then gradually poured into a basin of milk. When cool and solidified it is fit for use. Dose twelve to twenty-four grains with milk or other vehicle.

Sulphur is described as of bitter, astringent taste, with a peculiar strong smell. It increases bile, acts as a laxative and alterative, and is useful in skin diseases, rheumatism, consumption, enlarged spleen etc. In combination with mercury it is used in almost all diseases. The circumstance of its readily combining with and fixing metalic mercury, has led to its extensive use in combination with that metal.

In skin diseases sulphur is used both internally and externally. Internally it is given with milk or in the shape of a sulphurated butter, prepared from milk boiled with the addition of sulphur. The butter thus obtained is called *Gandha taila*, and is taken internally, and applied externally, in skin diseases.[1] Sulphur and *yavakshára* (an impure carbonate of potash), mixed with mustard oil, is applied in pityriasis psoriasis etc.[2] Sulphur enters into the composition of a large number of applications for skin diseases, the following is an example.

---

1. गन्धतैलम्। आवर्त्तमाने पयसि दत्वा गन्धकजं रजः। तज्जातदधिजं सर्पिर्गन्धतैलं वदन्ति हि। गन्धतैलं गलत्कुष्ठं हन्ति लेपाच्च भक्षणात् ॥ सन्देहभञ्जनी।

2. गन्धपाषाणचूर्णेन यवक्षारेण मेषितम्। सिध्मनाशं व्रजत्याशु कटुतैलयुतेन वा ॥ चक्रः।

A'dityapáka taila.[1] Take of sesamum oil four seers, madder, the three myrobalans, lac, turmeric, orpiment, realgar and sulphur equal parts, in all one seer. Mix and expose to the sun. This oil is useful in eczema, scabies etc.

In rheumatism it is used in combination with bdellium, as in the following, called *Sinhanáda guggulu.*[2] Take of sulphur eight tolás, bdellium eight tolás, decoction of the three myrobalans seventy-two tolás, castor oil thirty-two tolás, mix and boil together in an iron vessel till reduced to the consistence of a confection. Dose about one drachm twice daily. It is useful in chronic rheumatism, lameness, cough, asthma, and skin diseases.

MERCURY.

Sans. पारद *Párada.* रस *Rasa.*

Mercury, though not mentioned by Charaka* and Susruta, has in later days come to be regarded as the most important medicine in the Hindu Pharmacopœia. *Párada* literally means that which protects, and mercury is so called because it protects mankind

---

1. आदित्यपाकं तैलम्। मञ्जिष्ठा त्रिफला लाक्षा निशा शिलालगन्धकैः। चूर्णितैस्तैलमादित्यपाकं पामाहरं परम्॥ चक्रः।

2. सिंहनादगुग्गुलुः। पलत्रयं कषायस्य त्रिफलायाः सुचूर्णितम्। सौगन्धिक पलञ्चैकं कौशिकस्य पलन्तथा॥ कुडवं चित्रतैलस्य सर्व्वमादाय यत्नतः। पाचयेत् पाकविद्वैद्यः पात्रे लौहमये दृढ़े॥ हन्ति वातं तथा पित्तं स्लेष्मानं खञ्ज-पङ्गुताम्। श्वासं सुदुर्जयं हन्ति कासं पञ्चविधं तथा॥ कुष्ठानि वातरक्तञ्च गुल्म-शूलोदराणि च। आमवातं जयेद्देतदपि वैद्यविवर्जितम्॥ चक्रः।

* There is a passage in Charaka in the chapter on *Kushtha* or skin diseases which some physicians construe into a recommendation for the use of mercury. It is this सर्व्वव्याधिविनाशन मदद्यात कुष्ठी रसञ्चनिष्टद्योतम. It may be translated as follows. Reduced mercury which cures all diseases should be taken by those affected with skin diseases. The term *rasa*, however, signifies mercury as well as many other things, such as myrrh, sulphur, gold etc., and since Charaka does not mention *párada*, the principal name for mercury, it is doubtful if he really meant mercury by the term *rasa*. Supposing, however, he did mean mercury, its use was at all events, in his time, confined to skin diseases only.

from all sorts of diseases. It is said that the physician who does not know how to use this merciful gift of God is an object of ridicule in society.

Good mercury is said to be bright like the mid-day sun externally, and of a bluish tinge internally. Mercury of a yellowish-white, purple, or variegated colour should not be used in medicine. Mercury, as met with in commerce, contains several sorts of impurities, such as tin, lead, dirt, stone, etc. If administered in an impure state it is said to bring on a number of diseases; hence it is purified before use. Various processes for purifying mercury are described in books. At the present day the following is generally adopted by *Kavirájas.* Mercury is first rubbed with brick-dust and garlic, then tied in four folds of cloth and boiled in water over a gentle fire for three-hours in an apparatus called *Dolá yantra.* When cool, it is washed in cold water and dried in the sun. Some practitioners use betle-leaves instead of garlic for rubbing the mercury with. Mercury obtained by sublimation of cinnabar is considered pure and preferred for internal use.[1] Cinnabar is first rubbed with lemon juice for three hours, and then sublimed in the apparatus called *Urddhapátana yantra.* The mercury is deposited within the upper pot of the apparatus, in form of a blackish powder. This is scraped, rubbed with lemon-juice and boiled in water, when it is fit for use. A peculiar form of mercury called *Shadguna bali járita rasa*[2] is thus prepared. A little sulphur is placed in an earthen pot, and over it some mercury. The pot is heated in a sand-bath, and, as the sulphur begins to melt, cautiously and gradually more of it is added to or placed over the mercury, altogether to the extent of six times the weight of the

---

1. हिङ्गुलोत्थरसः। जम्बीरनिम्बुनीरेण मर्द्दितं हिङ्गुलं दिनम्। ऊर्द्ध्वपातन-यन्त्रेण ग्राह्यः स्यान्निर्म्मलो रसः। कञ्चुकैर्नागवङ्गाद्यै र्निर्मुक्तो रसकर्म्मणि॥
रसेन्द्रसारसंग्रहः।

2. षड्गुणबलिजारितरसः। क्षुद्रभाण्डे रसं कृत्वा वालुकायन्त्रमध्यगं। षड्गुणं गन्धकं तत्र क्षिपेदल्पाल्पकं शनैः। तैलरूपो यदा गन्धस्ततोऽवतारयेत् द्रुतं। स्वाङ्गशीते दृढ़े गन्धे स्फोटयित्वा रसं नयेत्। सर्व्वरोगेषु दातव्यो रसो व्याधिनिसूदनः॥ रसेन्द्रसारसंग्रहः।

mercury. When the whole is melted like oil the pot should be quickly removed from the fire, and cooled till the mass is consolidated. It should then be broken, and the mercury extracted from within the mass. Mercury thus obtained is said to be superior to all other forms, but it is not much used at present.

The purified metal obtained by the processes above mentioned is employed for the preparation of mercurial compounds. Four preparations of mercury are described in books, namely, black, white, yellow, and red, called respectively, *krishna*, *sveta*, *pita* and *rakta bhasmas*.

1. *Krishna bhasma*. The black preparation is the black sulphide of mercury, made by rubbing together and dissolving over the fire three parts of mercury with one of sulphur.[1]

2. *Rasakarpura*. The white preparation is the *Rasakarpura* or perchloride of mercury. Several processes are given for preparing it; one is as follows.[2] Take of mercury and chalk equal parts, and rub them together till the globules disappear. Rub this mixture of chalk and mercury with *pánsu* (salt obtained from saline earth) and the juice of *Euphorbia nereifolia* (*snuhi*) repeatedly. Enclose in a covered crucible and heat it within a pot full of rock salt. The perchloride of mercury will be deposited in the shape of a pure white powder under the lid of the crucible. The *Bhávaprakása* gives the following process for its preparation.[3] Take of purified

---

1. कृष्णभस्म। लौहपात्रेऽथवा ताम्रे पलैकं शुद्धगन्धकम्। वह्निना द्रुते तस्मिन् शुद्धसूतं पलत्रयम्॥ क्षिप्त्वाथ चालयेत् किञ्चित् लौहदार्व्या पुनः पुनः। गोमये कदलीपत्रं तस्योपरि च चालयेत्॥ रसेन्द्रसारसंग्रहः।

2. श्वेतभस्म। पिष्टं पांशुपटु प्रगाढ़ममलं वज्र्यम्बुना नैकधा सूतं धातुगतं खटीकवलितं तत् संपुटे रोधयेत्। अन्तःस्थं लवणस्य तस्य च तले प्रज्वाल्य वह्निं हठात् भस्मं ग्राह्यमथेन्दुकुन्दधवलं भस्मोपरिस्थं शनैः॥ रसेन्द्रसारसंग्रहः।

3. अथ कर्पूररसस्य विधिः। तत्र पारदस्य संक्षिप्तशोधनं कर्त्तव्यम्। शुद्धसूतसमं कुर्य्यात् प्रत्येकं गैरिकं सुधीः। इष्टिकां खटिकां तद्वत् स्फटिकां सिन्धुजन्म च। वल्मीकं क्षारलवणं भाण्डरञ्जकमृत्तिकाम्। सर्व्वाण्येतानि संचूर्ण्य वाससा चापि शोधयेत्। एभिश्चूर्णैर्युतं सूतं यावद्यामं विमर्द्दयेत्। तच्चूर्णसहितं सूतं स्थालीमध्ये परिक्षिपेत्। तस्याः स्थाल्या मुखे स्थालीमपरां धारयेत् समाम्।

mercury, *gairika* (red-ochre), brick dust, chalk, alum, rock salt, earth from ant-hill, *kshári lavana* (impure sulphate of soda) and *bhánda-ranjaka*, or red earth used in colouring pots, in equal parts, rub together and strain through cloth. Place the mixture in an earthen pot, cover it with another pot, face to face, and lute the two together with layers of clay and cloth. The pots so luted are then placed on fire, and heated for four days, after which they are opened, and the white camphor-like deposit in the upper pot is collected for use.

3. *Pita bhasma.* The yellow preparation called *Pita bhasma*[1] is directed to be prepared as follows. Take of mercury and sulphur equal parts, rub them together for seven days with the juice of *bhumyámalaki* (*Phyllanthus neruri*) and *hastisundi* (*Heliotropium Indicum*). Place the mixture in a covered crucible, and heat it in a sand-bath for twelve hours. The result will be a yellow compound.

4. *Rakta bhasma.* The red preparation called *Rakta bhasma* or *Rasa sindura*[2] is prepared in a variety of ways. The following is one of them. Take of mercury and sulphur equal parts, rub together with the juice of the red buds of *Ficus Bengalensis* (*vata*) for three days successively, introduce the mixture within a bottle and heat it in a sand-bath for twelve hours. A red deposit will adhere below

---

सवस्त्रकुट्टितम्रदा मुद्रयेदनयोर्मुखम्। संशोष्य मुद्रयेद्भूयो भूयः संशोष्य मुद्रयेत्। सम्यक् विशोष्य मुद्रां तां स्थालीं चुल्यां विधारयेत्। अग्निं निरन्तरं दद्यात् यावद्दिनचतुष्टयम्। अङ्गारोपरि तद्यन्त्रं रक्षेद्यत्नादहर्निशम्। शनैरुद्घाटयेद् यन्त्रमूर्द्ध्वस्थालीगतं रसम्, कर्पूरवत् सुविमलं गृह्णीयाद् गुणवत्तरम्॥ भावप्रकाशः।

1 पीतभस्म। रसगन्धौ समौ कृत्वा हस्तिशुण्डीद्रवैर्दृढम्। भूधात्रिकरसैः पिष्ट्वा पर्यन्तं दिनसप्तकम्। विशोष्य वालुकायन्त्रे मूषायां सन्निवेश्य तत्। दिनमेकं ददेदग्निं मन्दं मन्दं निशावधि। एवं निष्पाद्यते पीतः शीतः सूतस्तु भस्मते॥ रसेन्द्र सारसंग्रहः।

2 रक्तभस्म वा रससिन्दूरः। पलमात्रं रसं शुद्धं तावन् मात्रन्तु गन्धकम्। विधिवत् कज्जलीं कृत्वा न्यग्रोधाङ्कुरवारिभिः॥ भावनां त्रितयं दत्त्वा स्थालीमध्ये निधापयेत्। विरच्य कवची यन्त्रं वालुकाभिः प्रपूरयेत्॥ दत्त्वा तदन्ते मन्दाग्निं पचेद्यामचतुष्टयम्। जायते रससिन्दूरं तरुणारुणसन्निभम्॥ अनुपानविशेषेण करोति विविधान् गुणान्॥ रसेन्द्रसारसंग्रहः।

the neck of the bottle. It is taken out in the shape of dark red shining scales.

The four preparations of mercury above mentioned, though described in most works on metalic medicines, are not, practically used in the treatment of disease under these names. In the present day the yellow preparation is not in use. The white form called *Rasakarpura* is now prepared, not according to the processes described in Sanskrit works, but by subliming the black sulphide of mercury with common or rock salt. In this form it is largely manufactured and sold in all the bazars. The red preparation is better known as *Rasa sindura* ; and the black one as *Rasa parpati*. In fact, practically, prepared mercury means the red preparation or *Rasa sindura* and this is the form in which it is largely used. Besides this, the black and red sulphides of mercury are also used internally. The black sulphide is prepared by rubbing together equal parts of sulphur and mercury till the globules disappear. It is called *Kajjali*.[1] The red sulphide or cinnabar is called *hingula*. These four preparations, namely, cinnabar, the black sulphide called *Kajjali*, the red preparation called *Rasasindura*, and the *Rasakarpura* of the bazar, are the four principal forms in which mercury is used in Hindu medicine; that is, they constitute the basis of all the formulæ containing mercury.

Mercury is said to be imbued with the six tastes, and capable of removing derangements of all the humours. It is the first of alterative tonics. Combined with other appropriate medicines it cures all diseases, acts as a powerful tonic and improves the vision and complexion.

In fevers of all descriptions, mercury is extensively used in combination with aconite, croton seed, *datura*, and other medicines. The following are a few illustrations.

Hingulesvara. Take of cinnabar, aconite, and long pepper, equal parts, rub together in a mortar and make into pills about

---

1 कज्जलिका। शुद्धं सूतं तथा गन्धं खल्वे तावद्विमर्दयेत्। सूतं न दृश्यते यावत् किन्तु कज्जलवद्भवेत्॥ एषा कज्जलिका ख्याता बृंहणी वीर्यवर्द्धिनी। नानानुपानयोगेन सर्व्वव्याधिविनाशिनी॥ रसेन्द्रसारसंग्रहः।

four grains each. They are given, beaten up with a little honey, in ordinary remittent fever.[1]

Taruna jvarári.[2] Take of mercury, sulphur, aconite and croton seeds, equal parts, rub together with the juice of *Aloe Indica* and make into four grain pills. These pills act on the bowels and relieve fever. They are administered with sugar and water.

In diarrhœa and dysentery, mercury is used in a great variety of forms. The following are a few examples.

Vajrakapáta rasa.[3] Take of mercury, sulphur, opium, *mocha-rasa,* (gum of *Bombax Malabaricum*), the three myrobalans, ginger, black pepper, and long pepper, in equal parts, powder and mix. Soak the powder in the juice of the leaves of *Cannabis sativa* (*Vijayá*) and *Verbesina calendulacea* (*bhringarája*) seven times and make into six grain pills. This medicine is administered with honey in obstinate chronic diarrhœa. Dose grains four to twenty-four.

Rasa parpati.[4] This is prepared by melting together a mixture of equal parts of sulphur and mercury in an iron ladle, smeared with *ghee* (clarified butter). The melted fluid is poured on a piece of plantain leaf, placed on a ball of cowdung. It is then pressed

---

1 हिङ्गुलेश्वरः। तुल्यांशं मर्द्दयेत् खल्ले पिप्पलीहिङ्गुलं विषम्। द्विगुञ्जं मधुना देयं वातज्वरविमुक्तये॥ भैषज्यरत्नावली।

2 तरुणज्वरारिः। जयपाल गन्धं विष पारदञ्च तुल्यं कुमारीस्वरसेन पिष्टम्। अस्य द्विगुञ्जा हि सितोदकेन ख्यातो रसोऽयं तरुणज्वरारिः। दातव्य एषोऽह्नि पञ्चमे वा षष्ठेऽथवा सप्तम एव वापि। जाते विरेके विजितज्वरः स्यात् पटोलमुद्गाम्बुनिषेवनेन॥ भैषज्य रत्नावली।

3 वज्रकपाटरसः। पारदं गन्धकं चैवाहिफेन सह मोचकम्। त्रिकटु त्रिफलाञ्चैव सममेकत्रकारयेत्। भङ्ग भृङ्ग द्रवैश्चैतत् भावयेच्च पुनः पुनः। रक्ति-त्रयं ततश्चैव मधुना सह भक्षयेत्। असाध्यां ग्रहणीं हन्ति रसो वज्रकपाटकः॥ भैषज्यरत्नावली।

4 रसपर्प्पटी। पूर्व्वोक्तौ द्विविधशुद्धौ समानौ रसगन्धकौ। सम्मर्द्य कज्जलाभन्तु चूर्णं कुर्य्याद्दृढाशये॥ ततो वदरवह्निस्थे लौहपात्रे द्रवीकृतम्। गोमयोपरि सन्न्यस्तकदलीपत्रपातनात्। कुर्य्याच्च पर्पटाकारं तस्यरक्तीद्वयं क्रमात्॥ द्वादश-रक्तिका यावत् प्रयोगः प्रहरार्द्धतः॥ चिकित्सारत्नः।

by another ball of cowdung, enclosed in plantain leaf. When cool, the black sulphide of mercury is obtained in the shape of round disks. It is much used alone, or with the addition of other medicines, in chronic diarrhœa. Other varieties of *Parpati* or mercurial preparations in shape of disks are prepared with the addition of iron, gold, copper etc, and used in this complaint, as for example, *Svarna parpati*, *Panchámrita parpati* etc. The preparation of the former will be described under the head gold. The latter is thus prepared.

Panchámrita parpati.[1] Take of sulphur eight tolás, mercury four tolás, prepared iron two tolás, prepared talc one tolá, prepared copper half a tolá. Rub together in an iron mortar, melt in an iron ladle and prepare disks like those of *Rasa parpati*, above described. Dose four grains with honey and *ghee*, to be gradually increased to sixteen or eighteen grains. *Parpatis* of different sorts when given in cases of diarrhœa with anasarca are conjoined with a milk diet, water and salt being prohibited.

Mahágandha rasa.[2] Take of mercury and sulphur each two tolás, and make a *Parpati* as before described. Take of nutmegs, mace, cloves, and *nim* leaves, each two tolás, powder them well, mix together, and inclose the mixture within bi-valve shells. Cover the shells with a layer of clay and roast in fire. When cool, extract

---

1 पञ्चामृतपर्प्पटी। अष्टौ गन्धकतोलका रसदलं लौहं तदर्द्धं शुभम्। लौहार्द्धञ्च वराभ्रकं सुविमलं ताम्रं तदभ्रार्द्धिकम्॥ पात्रे लौहमये च मर्द्दनविधौ चूर्णीकृतञ्चैकतः। दर्व्यां वादर वह्निनातिमृदुना पाकं विदित्वा द्रुते॥ रम्भायां लघु ढालयेत् पटुरियं पञ्चामृता पर्प्पटी। ख्याता क्षौद्रघृतान्विता प्रतिदिनं गुञ्जाद्वयं वर्द्धितः॥ लौहे मर्द्दनयोगतः सुविमलं भक्ष्य क्रिया लौहवत्। गुञ्जाष्टावथवा त्रिकं त्रिगुणितं सप्ताहमेवं भजेत्॥ भैषज्यरत्नावली।

2 महागन्धकम्। रसगन्धकयोर्ग्राह्यं कर्षमेकं सुशोधितम्। ततः कज्जलिकां कृत्वा मृदुपाकेन शोधयेत्॥ जातीफलं तथा कोषं लवङ्गारिष्टपल्लवे। एतेषां कर्षमात्रेण चूर्णेन सह मर्द्दयेत्॥ शुक्ता श्टहे पुनः स्थाप्यं पुटपाकेन साधयेत्। गुञ्जाद्वयप्रमाणेन वटिकां कारयेद्बुधः॥ एतत् प्रोक्तं कुमाराणां रक्षणाय महौषधम्। अग्नेर्ज्ञं दीपनञ्चैव बलवर्णप्रसादनम्॥ दुर्व्वारग्रहणीरोगं जयेच्चैव मनाह्निकाम्। सूतिकाख्यं जयेदेतदपि वैद्यविशक्षितम्॥ रसेन्द्रसारसंग्रहः।

the medicine from the shells. It is administered in doses of about four grains in the acute diarrhœa of children.

Pándusudana rasa.[1] In jaundice, mercury is used along with other alteratives and purgatives, as in the following, called *Pándusudana rasa.* Take of mercury, sulphur, prepared copper, croton seeds and bdellium, equal parts, rub them together with *ghee* and make into two-grain pills. They are given with the juice of *nim* bark and honey in jaundice. Acids and cold water for drinking should be avoided.

In affections of the lungs mercury is used in a variety of combinations. The following are a few illustrations.

Rasendra gudiká.[2] Take of purified mercury two tolás. Add to it one tolá of the juice of *jayanti* leaves (*Sesbania Ægyptica*) and of fresh ginger, rub together till the mixture thickens, then soak it in the juice of *Jussiœa repens* (*kanchata*) and *Solanum Indicum (vrihati)* respectively for twenty-four hours. Take of purified sulphur eight tolás and soak in the juice of *Verbesina calendulacea* (*bhringarája*). When dry, mix the sulphur with the mercury, and rub together with sixteen tolás of goat-milk till the mass is fit for being made into pills. Dose about four grains, to be taken with goat-milk and juice of ginger. This pill is useful in bronchitis and cough generally.

Rájamrigánka rasa.[3] Take of *Rasa sindura* three parts, prepared gold and copper one part each, realgar, orpiment and sulphur

---

1 पाण्डुसूदनरसः। रसं गन्धं मृतं ताम्रं जयपालञ्च गुग्गुलुम्। समांशमाज्यसंयुक्तां गुड़िकां कारयेद्भिषक्॥ एकैकां खादयेन्नित्यं पाण्डुशोथोपशान्तये। शीतलञ्च जलं चाम्लं वर्ज्जयेत् पाण्डुसूदने॥ रसेन्द्रसारसंग्रहः।

2 रसेन्द्रगुड़िका। कर्षं शुद्धरसेन्द्रस्य स्वरसेन जयार्द्रयोः। शिलायां खल्वयेत्तावद्यावत् पिण्डं घनं ततः॥ जलकणा काकमाची रसाभ्यां भावयेत् पुनः। सौगन्धिकपलं भृङ्गस्वरसेन विभावितम्॥ चूर्णितं रससंयुक्तमजाक्षीरपलद्वये। खल्लितं घनपिण्डन्तु गुड़ीं सिद्धकलायवत्॥ कृत्वादौ शिवमभ्यर्च्य द्विजातीन् परितोष्य च। जीर्णान्नोभक्षयेदेकां क्षीरमांसरसाशनः॥ सर्व्वरूपं क्षयं कासं रक्तपित्तमरोचकम्। अपि वैद्यशतैस्त्यक्तमम्लपित्तं नियच्छति॥ चक्रः।

3 राजमृगाङ्करसः। रसभस्मत्रयो भागा भागैकं हेमभस्मकम्। मृतताम्रस्य

two parts each and mix. Introduce the mixture into the cavities of *couries*, close their openings with borax reduced to a paste with goat-milk, roast the shells in closed crucibles and take out the medicine when cold. Dose about four grains, with two grains of long and two of black pepper, honey and clarified butter. It is said to be useful in phthisis, and chronic bronchitis with fever.

In diseases of the nervous system, several combinations of mercury with gold, iron, talc, etc. are used, such as, the *Chaturmukha rasa*, *Chintámani chaturmukha*, *Yogendra rasa* etc. They are all similar in composition, with but slight variation in the proportions of the active ingredients and their adjuncts.

Chintámani chaturmukha[1] is thus prepared. Take of the red preparation of mercury called *Rasa sindura* two tolás, prepared talc two tolás, prepared iron one tolá, prepared gold half a tolá, rub them together with the juice of *Aloe Indica* and make into two-grain pills. This medicine is said to be useful in nervous diseases, insanity, cephalalgia, deafness, noise in the ears, paralysis of the tongue, diseases of the female and urinary organs, phthisis, fever etc. It improves nutrition, increases the appetite and strength, and brightens the complexion.

As an alterative tonic the red preparation of mercury, or *Rasasindura* already described, is much used in a variety of diseases.

भागैकं शिलागन्धकतालकम् ॥ प्रतिभागद्वयं शुद्धमेकीकृत्य विमर्द्दयेत्। वराटीं पूरयेत्तेन अजक्षीरेण टङ्कणम् ॥ पिष्ट्वा तेन मुखं रुद्ध्वा मृद्भाण्डे तत् निधापयेत्। शुष्कं गजपुटे पाच्यं चूर्णयेत् स्वाङ्गशीतलम् ॥ रसो राजमृगाङ्कोऽयं चतुर्गुञ्जः क्षयापहः। दशपिप्पलिकं क्षौद्रैर्मरिचैकोनविंशतिम् ॥ सघृतैर्द्दापयेद् वैद्यो वातश्लेष्मभवे क्षये॥ भैषज्यरत्नावली।

1 चिन्तामणिचतुर्मुखः। कर्षैकं रससिन्दूरं तत्समं मृतमभ्रकम्। तदर्द्धं मृतलौहञ्च स्वर्णं शाणं क्षिपेद् बुधः ॥ कन्यारसेन सम्मिश्य गुञ्जामानां वटीञ्चरेत्। अनुपानादिकं दद्यात् बुद्ध्वा दोषबलाबलम् ॥ हन्ति पित्तात्मकं वायुं केवलं पित्तसंयुतम्। हृल्लासमरुचिं दाहं वान्तिभ्रान्तिं शिरोग्रहम् ॥ प्रमेहं कर्णनादञ्च जड़गद्गदमूकताम्। वाधीर्यं गर्भिणीरोगमश्मरीसूतिकामयम् ॥ प्रदरं सोमरोगञ्च यक्ष्माणं ज्वरनाशकं। बलवर्णाग्निदः सम्यक् कान्तिपुष्टिप्रदायकः ॥ चिन्तामणिरसश्चायं चिन्तामणिरिवापरः ॥ रसेन्द्रसारसंग्रहः।

Two other forms of this medicine in common use are called *Shadguna balijárita rasa sindura* and *Svarna sindura* respectively.

Shadguna balijárita rasa sindura is thus prepared. Take of mercury and sulphur equal parts, and prepare *Rasa sindura* as already described by sublimation in a glass bottle. On the second day, mix this *Rasa sindura* with an equal quantity of sulphur and again sublime the compound. Repeat the process in this way, six times. This preparation is considered superior to the ordinary *Rasa sindura*.

Svarna sindura[1] is thus prepared. Take of fine leaf gold one tolá, purified mercury eight tolás, mix together by rubbing in a mortar, add twelve tolás of sulphur and again rub together, till the mass is of a dark colour. Sublime in a glass bottle on the sand-bath. The three forms of *Rasa sindura* above mentioned are said to cure all sorts of diseases, but are particularly used in chronic fever, catarrh and cough of children, mental and bodily debility, anæmia etc.

Mercury is used in syphilis both externally and internally. Syphilis and its treatment by mercury are described only in recent compilations, such as the Bhavaprakása. The following are a few illustrations of its use in this disease.

Saptasáli vati.[2] Take of mercury and catechu each half a tolá, pellitory root one tolá, honey one and a half tolá. Rub together till the globules of mercury disappear, and divide into seven pills or boluses. One pill is administered every morning with

---

1. स्वर्णसिन्दूरः। सूक्ष्मपत्रं सुवर्णस्य सुशुद्धं कोलसम्मितम्। शुद्धसूतपलैकेन मेलयेद्यत्नतो भिषक्॥ सार्द्धं पलं गन्धकञ्च कृत्वा कज्जलिकां ततः। निवेश्य काचकूप्याञ्च दृढायां परिवेष्टयेत्॥ तां कर्पटैर्मृदा चैव खटिकाभिः समन्ततः। सम्यङ्निरुध्य यत्नेन संपूज्येशं सहोमया॥ वालुकायन्त्रमध्ये तां सन्निरुध्य समाहितः। पचेद्द्वादशयामांस्तु निःसम्पाते सुनिर्जने॥ एकाकी पाकविद्वैद्यः स्वाङ्गशीतं समुद्धरेत्। स्वर्णसिन्दूरमित्येतत् सर्व्वरोगनिसूदनम्॥ संक्षिप्तसारः।

2. सप्तशालिवटी। पारदष्टङ्कमानः स्यात् खदिरष्टङ्कसंमितः। अकरा-करभस्यापि ग्राह्य ष्टङ्कद्वयोन्मितः। टङ्कत्रयोन्मितं चौद्रं खल्वे सर्वञ्च निक्षिपेत्। संमर्द्य तस्य सर्वस्य कुर्य्यात् सप्तवटीर्भिषक्। स रोगी भक्षयेत् प्रातः एकैकां अम्बुना वटीम्। वर्ज्जयेदम्ललवणं फिरङ्गस्तस्य नश्यति॥ भावप्रकाशः॥

water in primary syphilis. Acids and salt should not be taken after the use of this medicine.

Rasa karpura[1] or corrosive sublimate as sold in the bazars is recommended to be given in a single dose of eight grains. The medicine is enclosed in a ball of wheat-flour and covered with powdered cloves. It is swallowed with water so as not to touch the teeth. Salts and acids are forbidden to be taken after the use of this medicine. As the *Rasa karpura* of the bazars is not a pure perchloride of mercury, but is a mixture of calomel and corrosive sublimate in indefinite proportions, the patient sometimes escapes after this dose. When, however, it contains more of corrosive sublimate than of calomel, intense salivation, gastritis and even death may result. When such doses of poisonous remedies are recommended in standard works it is no wonder that we should occasionally come across cases of dreadful salivation, induced by native treatment. The circumstance of wheat-flour being used as a covering to the poison may act as an antidote to some extent. In secondary syphilis *Rasa karpura* is given in small doses in combination with cloves, saffron, sandal wood, and musk.

For external application, about a drachm of mercury is recommended to be rubbed between the palms with the juice of the leaves of *Sida cordifolia* (*bátyálaka*) till the globules of mercury are no longer visible. The palms are then to be warmed over the fire till perspiration breaks out from them.[2]

---

1. रसकर्पूरप्राशनेविधिः। फिरङ्ग संज्ञकं रोगं रसः कर्पूर संज्ञकः। अवश्यं नाशयेदेतदूचुः पूर्वचिकित्सकाः॥ लिख्यते रसकर्पूरप्राशनेविधिरुत्तमः। अनेन विधिना खादेन्मुखे शोथं न विन्दति॥ गोधूमचूर्णं सन्नीय विदध्यात् सूक्ष्मकूपिकाम्। तन्मध्ये निक्षिपेत्सूतं चतुर्गुञ्जमितं भिषक्॥ ततस्तु गुटिकां कुर्य्याद्यथा न दृश्यते वहिः। सूक्ष्म चूर्णे लवङ्गस्य तां वटीमवधूलयेत्॥ दन्तस्पर्शो यथा न स्यात् तथा तामम्भसा गिलेत्। ताम्बूलं भक्षयेत् पश्चाच्छाकाम्ललवणान् त्यजेत्। श्रममातपमध्वानं विशेषात् स्त्रीनिषेवनम्॥ भावप्रकाशः।

2. पीत पुष्प वलापत्ररसैष्टङ्कमितं रसम्। हस्ताभ्यां मर्दयेत्तावद्यावत् स तो न दृश्यते। ततः संस्वेदयेद्धस्तावेवं वासरसप्तकम्। त्यजेल्लवणमम्लञ्च फिरङ्गस्तस्य नश्यति॥ भावप्रकाशः।

For fumigation in primary syphilis, about half a drachm of the black sulphide, mixed with one fourth part of wheat-flour, is employed daily for seven days in succession.[1] In secondary syphilitic eruptions the following composition is used for fumigation. Take of cinnabar one tolá, realgar half a tolá, powder and mix. About fifteen grains of this is used at a time. Powders for fumigation are heated over a fire of jujube tree wood, and the vapour is applied to the skin under cover in a closed room.

Mercury enters into the composition of several applications for skin diseases, as in the following. Take of cinnabar, sulphur, red oxide of lead, rock salt, seeds of *Cassia tora* (*chakramarda*), *baberung*, *Cleome felina* (*svarnakshiri*), and the root of *Aplotaxis auriculata* (*kushta*) in equal parts. Powder them, and reduce to a thin paste with the juice of *datura*, *nim* or betle leaves. This application is said to cure ringworm, eczema, prurigo, psoriasis etc.[2]

For lice in the hair, mercury rubbed with *datura* or betle leaf is recommended to be applied to the scalp.[3]

ARSENIC.

THREE compounds of arsenic are used in Hindu medicine, namely, arsenious anhydride or white arsenic, red sulphide of arsenic or realgar, and the yellow sulphide or orpiment. Of these three, orpiment and realgar have been used in medicine from a very remote period, and are indigenous to India. Native white arsenic is not met with in India. It is brought from Burmah, China and

---

1. धूमप्रयोगः। पारदः कर्षमात्रः स्यात्तावानेव हि गन्धकः। तण्डुलाश्चाष्टमात्राः स्युरेषाः कुर्वंति कज्जलीम्।। तस्याः सप्तवटीः कुर्य्यात्ताभिर्धूमं प्रयोजयेत्। दिनानि सप्त तेन स्यात् फिरङ्गान्तो न संशयः॥ भावप्रकाशः।

2. हेमक्षीरी विडङ्गानि दरदङ्गन्धकं तथा। दद्रुघ्नः कुष्ठ सिन्दूरं सर्वाण्येकत्र मर्दयेत्। धत्तुरनिम्बताम्बूलीपत्नानाम् स्वरसैः पृथक्। अस्य प्रलेपमात्रेण यामाद्दद्रुविचर्चिकाः। कण्डूस्वरकसश्चैव प्रशमं यान्ति वेगतः॥ शार्ङ्गधरः।

3. रसेन्द्रेण समायुक्तो रसो धुस्तूरपत्रजः। ताम्बूलपत्रजो वापि लेपो यूकविनाशनः॥ चक्रः।

the Persian gulf. It is not mentioned in the more ancient Sanskrit works, neither in the list of metallic ores, where orpiment, realgar etc. are described, nor in any prescription for the treatment of diseases. In compilations of a later date, however, such as the Bhávaprakása, and the Tantras, it is recommended as a powerful medicine for fever, and is now much used as such.

In these later works white arsenic is called by several names, such as शङ्खविष *Sankha visha*, साम्बलक्षार *Sámbala kshára*, फेनाश्मभस्म *Phenásma bhasma*, and दारुमुच् *Dárumuch*. None of these terms, however, is to be found in standard lexicons, such as Wilson's Sanskrit-English Dictionary, or Sir Rájá Rádhákanta Deva's Sabdakalpadruma. *Phenásma bhasma* is mentioned by Susruta in his chapter on poisons, where he says, it and *haritála* (orpiment) are the two mineral poisons,* but it is very doubtful if Susruta meant any native white arsenic by it. The derivation of the term implies that it was obtained by roasting some sort of stone or ore. White arsenic was obtained artificially in ancient days by roasting orpiment (see orpiment), and probably this preparation was called *Phenásma bhasma*. At a later period imported white arsenic had been used in medicine under the designations of *sambalakshára*, *dárumuch*, and *sankha visha*.

WHITE ARSENIC.

Sans. शङ्खविष *Sankha visha.* दारुमुच *Dárumuch.* साम्बलक्षार *Sámbala kshára.*

White Arsenic is sold in the bazars under the names of *Sunka bish*, *Suffed sambul* and *Darumuch*. It is purified by being soaked in lemon juice or the juice of the plantain tree. It is chiefly used in fever, for which it is now preferred to the other compounds of arsenic, and is employed alone as also in a great variety of combinations. The following are a few illustrations.

Jvara brahmástra.[1] Take of white arsenic two tolás, soak it in cow's urine for three days, and afterwards in the juice of

---

* फेनाश्मभस्म हरितालञ्च द्वे धातुविषे। Susruta. kalpasthàna. chapter II.

1 ज्वरब्रह्मास्त्रः। विपनीञ्च समागम्य शुभ्रवर्णं सुशोभनम्। आनीय सम्यक्

Celsia Coromandeliana (*kokasima*), for one day, and then wash in cold water. Take a small quantity, the weight of a mustard, (about one-ninth of a grain), and administer within a lump of sugar in intermittent fever before the paroxysm comes on. Thus taken for three days, it cures recent and chronic fevers, ague and remittent fever. It is called *Jvara brahmástra* or the weapon which infalliably destroys fever.

Dárubrahma rasa.[1] Take of white arsenic, cinnabar, *datura* seeds and long pepper, equal parts, and make into four-grain pills with lemon juice. They are given with the juice of *tulsi* (leaves of *Ocimum sanctum*) in remittent fever with shivering, incoherent speech or wandering, profuse perspiration or much heat of body, difficult breathing, etc. The dose of arsenic in this medicine is very large and may induce unpleasant symptoms.

Chandesvara rasa.[2] Take of mercury, sulphur, aconite, prepared copper and white arsenic, equal parts, rub together with the juice of fresh ginger for six hours, then soak in ginger-juice and dry, successively for seven days. Afterwards soak in the juice of *Vitex nigundo* (*nirgundi*) for seven days, make into pills about a grain each, and administer with the juice of fresh ginger. Along with this medicine, inunction with oil, cold bathing and nourishing animal food should be used.

देवि तोलक द्वय सम्मितम् ॥ स्वच्छगोमूत्रमानीय शरावेस्थापयेद्बुधः सम्बलं तत्र संक्षिप्य दिवसत्रयमेवच ॥ तत उद्धृत्य देवेशि कुकशिम्बारसेषुच । स्थापयेद्दिनमेकन्तु ततः स्वच्छजलेनच । संशोध्य स्थापयेद्देवि निर्म्मलेकाचपात्रके । एकसर्षपमानं तत् ज्वरागमनपूर्ब्बतः ॥ फेणीमध्यगतं कृत्वा भक्षेत्सुस्थिरमानसः । अथवा शर्कराद्रावैः पीत्वारोगी सुखीभवेत् । एवं दिनत्रयं भुक्तामुच्यतेज्वरसङ्कटात् जीर्णज्वरे तथावाते कम्पज्वरे विशेषतः निश्चितं ज्वरमुक्तः स्यात् सत्यं सत्यंन संशयः । तन्त्रोक्तः।

1 दारुब्रह्म वा कर्णिकरसः । रसजं शङ्खविषञ्चैव कृष्णा धुस्तूरवीजकैः। जम्बीराणां द्रवैर्मर्द्दं द्विगुञ्जं परिमाणतः । गन्धपत्रानुपानेन कर्णिकाणां कृतान्तकृत् ॥ संक्षिप्तसारः ।

2 चण्डेश्वररसः रसं गन्धं विषं ताम्रं साम्बलं क्षारमेवच। आर्द्रकस्य रसे नैव

ORPIMENT.

Sans. हरिताल, *Haritála.*

Orpiment occurs in two forms, namely, in smooth shining gold-coloured scales called *Vansapatri haritála,* and in yellow opaque masses called *Pinda haritála.* *Vansapatri haritála* is preferred for internal use as an alterative and febrifuge. *Pinda haritála* is chiefly used as a colouring ingredient in paints, and for sizing country paper. Most of the older Sanskrit MSS. are written on paper prepared with *haritála,* to preserve them from the ravages of insects, and this it does most effectually.*

मर्द्दयेद् याममात्रकम् ॥ रसेनापि च तेनास्य भावयेत् सप्तवारकम् । निर्गुण्डीस्वर-सेनापि भावयेत् सप्तधा पुनः ॥ गुञ्जार्द्धमाना वटिका गुडार्द्रकरसेन वै । मूत्रादेव ज्वरं हन्ति तैलाभ्यङ्गं समाचरेत् ॥ सुशीतलजले स्नानं तैलमत्स्यादि भोजनम् । चण्डेश्वरो रसो नाम सर्व्वरोगकुलान्तकृत् ॥ संक्षिप्तसारः ॥

* Babu Rájendralála Mitra gives the following interesting account of arsenicised paper in his report on Sanskrit manuscripts, published in the Proceedings of the Asiatic Society, for March 1875.

"The manuscripts examined have mostly been written on country paper sized with yellow arsenic and an emulsion of tamarind seeds, and then polished by rubbing with a conch-shell. A few are on white Kásmiri paper, and some on Palm-leaf. White arsenic is rarely used for the size, but I have seen a few codices sized with it, the mucilage employed in such cases being acacia gum. The surface of ordinary country paper being rough, a thick coating of size is necessary for easy writing; and the tamarind-seed emulsion affords this admirably. The paper used for ordinary writing is sized with rice gruel; but such paper attracts damp and vermin of all kinds, and that great pest of literature, "the silver-fish" thrives luxuriantly on it. The object of the arsenic is to keep off this insect, and it serves the purpose most effectually. No insect or worm of any kind will attack arsenicised paper, and so far the MSS. are perfectly secure against its ravages. The superior appearance and cheapness of European paper has of late induced many persons to use it instead of the country arsenicised paper in writing puthis; but this is a great mistake, as the latter is not near so durable as the former, and is liable to be rapidly destroyed by insects. I cannot better illustrate this than by referring to some of the MSS. in the Library of the Asiatic Society. There are among them several volumes written on foolscap paper, which dates from 1820 to 1830, and they already look decayed, mouldering, and touched in several places by silver-fish. Others on John-letter paper which is thicker, larger and stouter, are already so far injured that the ink has quite faded, and become in many places illegible, whereas the MSS. which were originally copied on arsenicated paper for the College of Fort William in the first decade of this century, are now quite as fresh as they were when first written. I

Haritála is purified for internal use by being successively boiled in *kánjika*, the juice of the fruit of *Benincasa cerifera* (*kushmánda*), sesamum oil, and a decoction of the three myrobalans, for three hours in each fluid. Some physicians, probably to save time, mix all these fluids together, and boil the orpiment in the mixture for three hours only. The dose of orpiment thus purified is from two to four grains.

Several methods of roasting orpiment are described. The Bhávaprakása recommends that orpiment should be powdered and made into a ball with the juice of *Boerhaavia diffusa* (*punarnavá*) and placed in the centre of a pot full of the ashes of that plant. The pot should be now covered with a dish, luted with clay, and heated over a fire for twenty hours. When cool the ball of roasted orpiment is taken out from the pot and reduced to powder. Another process is as follows. Take of purified orpiment and *yavakshára*, equal parts, rub them together with the juice of *Vitex Negundo* (*nirgundi*), and roast the mixture in a closed crucible. The resulting compound from both these processes is described as a white camphor-like substance.

A specimen of roasted orpiment supplied to me by an up-country physician was analized and found to contain but a small proportion of white arsenic. Bengali physicians do not prepare this drug from a superstitious notion that the man who roasts orpiment dies very soon. They purchase it from *Fakirs* or religious mendicants. It is said that some specimens of roasted orpiment are highly poisonous, and contain a large proportion of white arsenic. The quality of the drug would no doubt vary according to the method in which it is prepared.

Orpiment is said to cure fevers and skin diseases, to increase strength and beauty, and to prolong life. In fever it is used in combination with mercury, aconite, etc. The following is an illustration.

---

have seen many MSS. in private collections which are much older, and still quite as fresh. This fact would suggest the propriety of Government records in Mofussil Courts being written on arsenicised paper instead of the ordinary English foolscap, which is so rapidly destroyed both by the climate and also by white-ants. To guard against mistake I should add here that the ordinary yellow paper sold in the bazars is dyed with turmeric, and not at all proof against the attack of insects."

Vetála rasa.[1] Take of purified mercury, sulphur, orpiment, aconite, and black pepper, equal parts. First rub the mercury and sulphur together, then add the other ingredients in fine powder, and make into two-grain pills. They are given with the juice of fresh ginger in remittent fever with affection of the brain.

Vidyádhara rasa.[2] Take of mercury, sulphur, prepared copper, iron pyrites, realgar and orpiment equal parts, rub them together and soak the mixture in a decoction of long pepper and in the milky juice of *Euphorbia nereifolia* (*vajri*). Make into pills about six grains each. These pills are given with honey in enlarged spleen and other enlargements of the abdominal viscera.

Tálakesari rasa.[3]—Orpiment forms the active ingredient of several pills for skin diseases, of which this is an example. Take of orpiment, realgar, iron pyrites (*svarnamákshika*), mercury, borax, and rock salt, one part each, sulphur and burnt conch-shell two parts each, rub them together for a day with lemon juice, then add to the mass one-thirtieth part of its weight of aconite, and mix. Dose, five to ten grains with butter. After it, powdered seeds of *Vernonia anthelmintica* (*vákuchi*), two drachms should be taken with honey and *ghee*. This medicine is useful in all sorts of chronic skin diseases. The above formula is taken from the Bhávaprakása. Sárangadhara gives a similar prescription under the name of *Mahátálesvara.*

---

1. वेतालरसः । रसं गन्धं विषं तालं मरिचञ्च समांशिकम् । शिलायां मर्द्दयेत्तावत् यावत् कज्जलसन्निभम् ॥ गुञ्जामात्रं प्रयोक्तव्यं हरेद्‌द्वादशसंज्ञकम् । साध्यासाध्यं निहन्त्याशु सन्निपातं सुदारुणम् ॥ ध्यानेषु खिन्नदेहेषु मोहयस्तेषु देहिषु । दातुमर्हति वेतालं यमदूतनिवारणम् ॥ भैषज्यरत्नावली ।

2. विद्याधररसः । गन्धकं तालकं ताप्यं मृतं ताम्रं मनःशिला । शुद्धसूतस्य तुल्यांशं मर्द्दयेत् भावयेद्दिनम् ॥ पिप्पल्याः स्वकषायेण वज्रीक्षीरेण भावयेत् । निष्कार्द्धं भक्षयेत् क्षौद्रैः प्लीहगुल्मादिकं जयेत् ॥ रसेन्द्रसार संग्रहः ।

3. तालकेश्वरी । तालताप्यशिला सूतटङ्कणाः सिन्धुसंयुताः । गन्धको द्विगुणः सूतात् शङ्खचूर्णञ्च तत्समम् ॥ जम्बीराद्भिर्दिनं घृष्ट्वा त्रिंशदंशं विषं क्षिपेत् । अस्य माषद्वयं खादेन्माहिषीघृतसंयुतम् ॥ मध्वाज्यैर्वाकुचीबीजकर्षं लिह्यात् ततः परम् । तालकेश्वरनामायं सर्व्वकुष्ठहरो रसः ॥ भावप्रकाशः ।

Orpiment forms an ingredient of several external applications for skin diseases. Thus, take of orpiment, wood of *Berberis lycium* (*dáruharidrá*), seeds of *Raphanus sativus* (*mulaka*), wood of *Pinus Deodara* and betle leaves, each two tolás, burnt conch-shell half a tolá, beat them together with water into a thin paste. This paste is an useful application in psoriasis.[1]

The use of orpiment as a depilatory was known to the ancient Hindus. It enters into the composition of numerous formulæ for the removal of hair. The following are examples.[2] Take of conch-shell-lime, soaked in the juice of plantain tree, and of orpiment, equal parts, make them into a paste with the aid of water, and apply it to the part from which the hair is to be removed. Or take of conch-shell-lime two parts, orpiment one part, realgar half a part, *sarjikákshára* (impure carbonate of soda) one part, rub together with water, and apply.

REALGAR.

Sans. मनःशिला, *Manahsilà.*

Realgar is purified by being rubbed with the juice of lemons, or of ginger. It is used internally in fever, skin diseases, cough, asthma, etc, and externally in skin diseases. In fever, it is generally used in combination with mercury, orpiment etc. The following is an illustration.

Chandesvara rasa.[3] Take of realgar, mercury, sulphur, and aco-

---

1. दार्व्वीमूलकबीजानि तालकं सुरदारु च। ताम्बूलपत्रं सर्व्वाणि कार्षिकाणि पृथक् पृथक्॥ शङ्खचूर्णं शाणमात्रं सर्व्वाण्येकत्र चूर्णयेत्। लेपोऽयं वारिणा पिष्टः सिध्मानां नाशनः परः॥ शार्ङ्गधरः।

2. शङ्खचूर्णस्य भागौ द्वौ हरितालस्य भागैकम्। मनःशिलार्द्धभागा सर्जिका चैक भागिका॥ लेपोऽयं वारिपिष्टस्तु केशानुत्पाट्य दीयते। अनया लेपयुक्त्या च सप्तवेलं प्रयुक्तया। निर्मूलकेशस्थानं स्यात् क्षपणस्य शिरो यथा॥
शार्ङ्गधरः।

3 चण्डेश्वर रसः। समांशं योजयेत् खल्ले रसं गन्धं शिलां विषम्। निर्गुण्डी सरसै र्भाव्यं त्रिवारं चार्द्रक द्रवैः। गुञ्जैकं भक्षयेत् प्रतिः ज्वरं हन्ति महोद्धतम्॥ रसेन्द्रसारसंग्रहः।

nite, equal parts, soak in the juice of *Vitex Negundo (nirgundi)*, and of fresh ginger, three times respectively, and make into two-grain pills. This medicine is useful in remittent fever.

Svása kuthára rasa.[1] Take of realgar, mercury, sulphur, aconite, borax, each one part, black pepper seven parts, ginger, and long pepper, three parts each, rub them together with water, and make into four-grain pills. They are said to be useful in asthma with cough, and in remittent fever with cerebral complications. In coma from remittent fever, these pills are powdered and used as snuff for rousing the patient. They are also used in this manner in cephalalgia, hemicrania, ozæna, etc.

Realgar enters into the composition of numerous applications for skin diseases. Realgar mixed with the ashes of *Achyranthes aspera* (*apámárga*) is applied to patches of leucoderma or white lepra. In leprous ulcers a liniment composed of realgar, orpiment, black pepper, sesamum oil and the juice of *Calotropis gigantea* is used.[2]

Chandraprabhá varti.[3] Realgar enters into the composition of several applications for the eye : the following is an example. Take of realgar, galena, conch-shell lime, seeds of *Moringa pterygosperma* (*sveta maricha*), long pepper, liquorice and the kernel of belleric myrobalan, equal parts, rub them together with water, dry the mixture and make into small pastils or pencils. These are rubbed with a little honey and applied to the eyes as a collyrium in affections of the internal tunics, tumors or other growths, night-blindness etc.

---

1 श्वासकुठाररसः। सूतं गन्धं विषञ्चैव टङ्कनञ्च मनःशिला। एतानि टङ्कमात्राणि मरिचं तच्चतुर्गुणम्॥ त्रिकटु त्रिगुणञ्चैव खल्ले पिष्ट्वा विचूर्णयेत्। रसः श्वासकुठारोऽयं श्वाससर्व्वज्वरापहः॥ रसेन्द्रसारसंग्रहः।

2. मनःशिलाल मरिचानि तैल मार्कं पयः कुष्ठहरः प्रदेहः॥ चक्रः॥

3 चन्द्रप्रभावर्त्तिः। अञ्जनं श्वेतमरिचं पिप्पली मधुयष्टिका। विभीतकस्य मध्यन्तु शङ्खनाभि मनःशिला॥ एतानि समभागानि अजाक्षीरेणपेषयेत्। छायाशुष्कां कृतां वर्त्तिं नेत्रेषु च प्रयोजयेत॥ अर्व्बुदं पटलं काचं तिमिरं रक्तराजिकाम्। अधिमांसं मलञ्चैव यश्चरात्रौ न पश्यति॥ वर्त्तिश्चन्द्रप्रभा नाम जातान्ध्यमपि शोधयेत्॥ चक्रः॥

An oil for application to fistulous sores is prepared as follows. Take of sulphur, realgar and turmeric, eight tolas each, mustard-oil one seer, juice of *datura* leaves one seer, water four seers; boil together in the usual way.[1]

IRON.

Sans, लौह, *Lauha.*

THREE varieties of iron are used in Hindu Medicine, namely, *Kánta lauha* or cast-iron, *Mandura* or iron rust, and *Lauhasára* or salts of iron produced by iron being kept in contact with vegetable acids. The form of cast iron used in the manufacture of pans for boiling milk is considered superior to all others for medicinal use. The small particles of iron which are scattered around when hot iron is beaten on the anvil, are called *mandura.* They are allowed to remain in contact with the earth till they become very rusty and brittle, when they are considered fit for use. The properties of *mandura* are said to be analogous to those of cast iron. *Lauhasára* or the granules produced on iron plates, smeared with vegetable acids, are also used in medicine. This variety of iron is said to be especially useful in diarrhœa, chronic bowel-complaints, dyspepsia and nervous diseases.

Cast iron is purified by beating it into thin plates, heating the plates in fire and sprinkling them with cow's urine, sour conjee, oil, and a decoction of the pulse of *Dolichos uniflorus* (*kulattha*), seven times in succession. The plates are reduced to powder by pounding them in an iron mortar, rubbing them with cow's urine, and roasting the powder in a covered crucible repeatedly till it is reduced to a fine impalpable powder, that will float on water and will not irritate the eyes when applied to them. It is usual to rub the iron with cow's urine and roast it about a hundred times in succession. In some cases it is recommended that iron should be thus roasted repeatedly for a thousand times. *Mandura* is purified and prepared for uselike cast iron. Prepared iron is a fine impalpable

---

1 चूर्णेन गन्धकशिला रजनीभवेन मुष्टंशकेन कटुतैलपलाष्टकं तु । धत्तूरपत्ररसतुल्यमिदं विपक्वं नाडीं जयेत् चिरभवामपि कर्णजाताम् ॥ भावप्रकाशः ।

powder of a reddish grey or brick-dust colour. On chemical analysis it is found to be a mixture of the proto and peroxide of iron. Dose grains six to twelve.

Iron, it is said, increases strength, vigour and longevity, cures all sorts of diseases and is the best of tonics. When gold and silver are not available, iron is substituted for them. It is used in painful dyspepsia, chronic fever, phthisis, anasarca, piles, enlarged spleen and liver, anæmia, jaundice, obesity, urinary diseases, diseases, of the nervous system, skin diseases etc. When iron is administered, the following articles of diet should be avoided, namely, *kushmànda* (fruit of *Benincasa cerifera*), sesamum oil, *kulattha* (pulse of *Dolichos uniflorus*), mustard, wines and acids.

In chronic fever with anæmia, debility, emaciation, enlarged spleen or other complications, several preparations of iron are used, such as the *Vrihat sarvajvara hara lauha*, *Chandanádya lauha*, etc.

Vrihat sarvajvara hara lauha.[1] Take of purified mercury and sulphur, prepared copper, iron pyrites, talc, gold and orpiment,

---

1. वृहत्सर्व्वज्वरहर लौहम्। पारदं गन्धकं शुद्धं ताम्रं माक्षिकमभ्रकम्। हिरण्यं हरितालञ्च कर्षमेकं पृथक् पृथक्॥ मृतकान्तं पलं देयं सर्व्वमेकीकृतं शुभम्। वक्ष्यमानौषधैर्भाव्यं प्रत्येकं दिनसप्तकम्॥ कारवेल्ल रसेनापि दशमूल रसेन च। पर्पटस्यकषायेन क्वाथेन त्रैफलेनच॥ गुडूच्याः स्वरसेनापि नागवल्ली रसेन च। काकमाचीरसेनैव निर्गुण्ड्याः स्वरसेनच। पुनर्नवार्द्रकाम्भोभिर्भावनां परिकल्पय च॥ रक्तिकादिक्रमेणैव वटिकां कारयेद्भिषक्। पिप्पली गुडसंयुक्ता वटिका वीर्य्यवर्द्धिनी॥ ज्वरमष्टविधं हन्ति चिरकालसमुद्भवम्। विविधं वारिदोषोत्थं नानादोषोद्भवन्तथा॥ सततादि ज्वरं हन्तिसाध्यासाध्यमथापि वा। चयोद्भवञ्च धातुस्थं कामशोकभवं तथा॥ भूतावेश ज्वरं हन्ति कृच्छ्र-दोषभवन्तथा। अभिघात ज्वरञ्चैव अभिचार समुद्भवम्॥ अभिन्यासं महाघोरं विषमञ्च त्रिदोषजम्। शीतपूर्व्वं दाहपूर्व्वं विषमं शीतलं ज्वरम्॥ प्रलेपकज्वरं घोरं अर्द्धनारीश्वरं तथा। प्लीहज्वरं तथाकाशं चातुर्थकविपर्य्ययम्॥ पाण्डु रोगान् गणान सर्व्वान् अग्निमान्द्यं महागदम्। एतान् सर्व्वान् निहन्त्याशु पथ्याद्नेनालसंशयः॥ शाल्यन्नं तक्रसहितं भोजयेद्द्विजसंयुतम्। ककारपूर्व्वकं सर्व्वं वर्ज्जनीयं विशेषतः॥ मैथुनं वर्ज्जयेत्तावत् यावन्न बलवान् भवेत्। सर्व्वज्वर हरं स्वेष्ठमनुपानं प्रकल्पयेत्॥ भैषज्यरत्नावली।

each two tolás, prepared iron eight tolás, mix them together, and soak the mixture for seven days, in each of the following fluids, *viz*, fresh juice of the leaves of *Momordica Charantia* (*káravella*), decoction of *dasamula* or ten roots (see *Hedysarum Gangeticum*), decoction of *parpata* (*Hedyotis biflora*), and of the three myrobalans, fresh juice of *guruchi*, (*Tinospora cordifolia*), of betel leaves, of *kákamáchi* (*Solanum nigrum*), of *nirgundi*, (*Vitex Negundo*), of *punarnavá* (*Boerhaavia diffusa*) and of ginger. Divide the mass into two-grain pills, and administer with long pepper and treacle. The dose of the medicine may be gradually increased. It is used in all sorts of intermittent fevers, in emaciation, wasting, hectic fever, enlarged spleen, anæmia, loss of appetite etc. A light diet consisting of fine rice and poultry meat should be adopted during the use of this medicine, and all undigestible food should be avoided.

Chandanádya lauha.[1] Take of red sandal wood, *Pavonia odorata* (*bálá*), *Cissampelas hernandifolia* (*páthá*), *Andropogon muricatus* (*usir*), long pepper, chebulic myrobalan, emblic myrobalan, ginger, *Nymphæa cyanea* (*nilotpala*), *Chavica officinarum* (*chai*), *Plumbago Zeylanica*, (*chitraka*), and *baberung* seeds, each one part, prepared iron twelve parts, rub them all together. Dose about ten grains to be taken with the fresh juice of *Tinosphora cordifolia* (*guruchi*) and *Hedyotis biflora* (*parpati*). This medicine is said to cure all sorts of chronic intermittent fever and fever with enlarged spleen.

Vishamajvarántaka lauha.[2] This is another compound metallic preparation containing iron and much used in chronic fever. To

---

1. चन्दनाद्यलौहम् । रक्तचन्दनह्रीवेरपाठोशीरकणाशिवा । नागरोत्पलधात्रीभिस्त्रिमदेन समन्वितः । लौहं निहन्ति विविधान् समस्तान् विषमज्वरान् ॥
रसेन्द्र सारसंग्रहः ।

2. विषमज्वरान्तकलौहम् । हिङ्गुलसम्भवं सूतं गन्धकेन सुकज्जलीम् । पर्पटीरसवत्पाच्यं सूतांशमिश्रहेमभस्मकम् ॥ लौहं ताम्रमभ्रकञ्च रसस्य द्विगुणं तथा । वङ्गकं गैरिकञ्चैव प्रवालञ्च रसार्द्धकम् ॥ मुक्ता शङ्खं शुक्तिभस्म प्रदेयं रसपादिकम् । मुक्ताण्डहे च संस्थाप्य पुटपाकेन साधयेत् ॥ भक्षयेत् प्रातरुत्थाय द्विगुञ्जाफलमानतः ॥ अनुपानं प्रयोक्तव्यं कणाहिङ्गुससैन्धवम् । ज्वरमष्टविधं हन्ति वातपित्तकफोद्भवम् ॥ प्लीहानं यकृतं गुल्मं साध्यासाध्यमथापि वा । सन्ततं सतताख्यञ्च विषमज्वरनाशनम् ॥
भैषज्यरत्नावली ।

prepare it, take of mercury obtained by sublimation of cinnabar, and sulphur, each one tolá. Rub them together and melt over the fire in an iron ladle as in the preparation called *Rasaparpati*, described under mercury. Then take of prepared gold, one quarter of a tolá, prepared iron, copper, and talc, two tolás each, prepared tin, red ochre, and corals, half a tolá each, roasted pearls, conch-shell and bi-valve shell, each a quarter of a tola. Beat all these ingredients together into a mass with the aid of water. Inclose the mass within bi-valve shells, cover the shells with a layer of clay and roast them lightly in cow-dung fire. This medicine is given in doses of four grains with the addition of long pepper, rock salt and assafœtida, each four grains, and a little honey. It is taken once daily in the morning and is said to be useful in chronic fever, spleen and liver diseases etc.

Several preparations of iron are used in piles, such as the *Mána suranádya lauha*, *Arsàri lauha*, *Agnimukha lauha* etc. The first mentioned compound is prepared as follows.

Mána suranádya lauha.[1] Take of the root-stocks of *Colocasia Indica* (*mána*) and *Amorphophallus campanulatus* (*surana*), of the roots of *Ipomœa Turpethum* (*trivrit*) and *Baliospermum montanum* (*danti*), marking nuts, the three myrobalans, black pepper, long pepper, ginger, seeds of *Embelia Ribes* (*baberung*), root of *Plumbago Zeylanica* (*chitraka*) and the tubers of *Cyperus rotundus* (*mustaka*), equal parts, prepared iron in quantity equal to all the above ingredients. Powder and mix. Dose about a scruple. This medicine is said to be useful in piles with constipation.

Lauhásava.[2] Take of powdered iron, of the three myrobalans,

---

1. मानसूरणाद्यलौहम्। मानसूरणभल्लातत्रिवृद्दन्तीसमन्वितम्। त्रिकत्रयसमायुक्तमयोदुर्नामनाशनम्॥ भैषज्यरत्नावली

2. लौहासवम्। लौहचूर्णं त्रिकटुकं त्रिफलाञ्च यमानिकाम्। विडङ्गं चित्रकं मुस्तं चतुःपलमितं पृथक्। चूर्णीकृत्य ततः क्षौद्रं चतुःषष्टिपलं क्षिपेत्। दद्यात् गुडतुलां तत्र जलद्रोणद्वयं तथा। घृतभाण्डे विनिक्षिप्य निदध्यात् मासमात्रकम्। लौहासवमिदं मर्त्त्यः पिवेदग्निकरं परम्। पाण्डुश्वयथुगुल्मानि जठराण्यर्शसां रुजम्। कुष्ठप्लीहामयं कण्डु कास श्वासं भगन्दरम्। अरोचकञ्च ग्रहणीं हृद्रोगञ्च विनाशयेत्॥ शार्ङ्गधरः।

ginger, long pepper and black pepper, *ajwain*, *baberung* seeds, plumbago root, and tubers of *Cyperus rotundus* (*mustaka*), each thirty-two tolas, honey eight seers, treacle twelve and a half seers, water one hundred and twenty-eight seers. Powder the solid ingredients and steep them in the honey and water in an earthen jar smeared with *ghee*, for a month, or till complete fermentation takes place. This iron-wine is said to be tonic and stomachic, and useful in anæmia, spleen, anasarca, ascites, enlargements of the abdominal viscera, piles etc.

A'malakádya lauha.[1] Iron enters into the composition of several medicines for hæmorrhagic diseases, such as the *Khandakádya lauha*, *Sudhánidhi rasa*, *A'malakádya lauha* etc. We will here transcribe the mode of preparing the last which is the simplest and shortest. Take of emblic myrobalan and long pepper, each one part, sugar two parts, prepared iron four parts, powder and mix them together. Dose six to twelve grains in hæmoptysis, hæmaturia etc., with suitable adjuncts.

Guda mandura.[2] A preparation nearly similar to the above and called *Guda mandura* is used in dyspepsia. It is composed of old treacle, emblic and chebulic myrobalans one part each, and iron rust three parts. These are rubbed together with honey and *ghee*, and made into boluses about a drachm each. One of these is taken in divided doses before, along with, and after meals, in dyspepsia with pain after digestion.

Vidyádharábhra.[3] Take of *baberung* seeds, tubers of *Cyperus rotundus* (*mustaka*), the three myrobalans, *gulancha*, root of

---

1. आमलकाद्यलौहम्। आमलापिप्पलीचूर्णं तुल्यया सितया सह। रक्तपित्तहरं लौहं योगराजमितिस्मृतम्। हृष्याग्निदीपनं बल्यं चाम्लपित्तविनाशनम्। पित्तोत्थानपि वातोत्थान् निहन्ति विविधान् गदान्। रसेन्द्रसारसंग्रहः।

2. गुड़मण्डूरम्। गुड़ामलकपथ्यानां चूर्णं प्रत्येकशः पलम्। त्रिपलं लौहकिट्टस्य तत्सर्वं मधुसर्पिषा॥ समालोड्य समश्नीयादक्षमात्रप्रमाणतः। आदिमध्यावसानेषु भोजनस्य निहन्ति तत्॥ अन्नद्रवं जरत्पित्तमम्लपित्तं सुदारुणम्। परिणाम समुत्थञ्च शूलं संवत्सरोत्थितम्॥ भावप्रकाशः।

3. विद्याधराभ्रः। विड़ङ्गमुस्तत्रिफला गुड़ूची दन्ती त्रिवृच्चित्रककटुत्रयञ्च। प्रत्येकमेषां पिचुभागचूर्णं पलानिचत्वार्य्यय सोमलस्य। गोमूत्रशुद्धस्य पुरातनस्य

Baliospermum montanum (danti), of *Ipomœa Turpethum (trivrit)*, of *Plumbago Zeylanica (chitraka)*, ginger, long pepper and black pepper, each two tolás, prepared iron thirty-two tolás, old iron rust thirty-two tolás, prepared talc eight tolás, purified mercury one tolá and a half, sulphur two tolás. Rub together the sulphur and mercury, then mix them with the other ingredients, add sufficient *ghee* and honey, and rub them together for twelve hours. Preserve the confection in an earthen pot smeared with *ghee*. Dose from ten to thirty grains with milk or cold water. This medicine is used in chronic dyspepsia, especially in that form of the disease in which the pain comes on after digestion is completed, and in chronic fever, diarrhœa, phithisis etc.

Naváyasa lauha.1 In anæmia iron is much used in a variety of forms. The following compound powder called *Navâyasa lauha* is a popular and well known medicine. To prepare it take of ginger, long pepper, black pepper, the three myrobalans, *baberung* seeds, tubers of *Cyperus rotundus (mustaka)* and plumbago root, each one part, prepared iron nine parts, powder the ingredients and mix. Dose four grains, gradually increased to eighteen grains, to be taken with honey and *ghee*. This medicine is used in anæmia, jaundice, piles, heart disease etc. It is given on the first day in four-grain dose. Every second day the dose is increased

---

यड्भागयुक्तानि शिराटिकायाः। कृष्णाभ्रचूर्णस्य पलं विशुद्धमिन्द्रकस्य स्त्वच्छ-
मतीव सूतात्। पादोनकर्षं खरसेन खल्ले शिलातले मन्युमनोदलस्य।
विशोध्य पश्चादतिशुद्धगन्धपाषाणचूर्णेन पिचून्मितेन। युक्त्या ततः पूर्व्वर-
जांसि दत्त्वा सर्पिर्मधुभ्यां परिमर्द्द्य यत्नात्। निधापयेत् स्निग्धविशुद्धभाण्डे ततः
प्रयोज्योऽस्य रसोत्तमस्य। माङ्माषकोद्वावथ वालयो वा गवां पयो वा शिशिरं जलं
वा। पिबदयं योगवरः प्रभूतकालप्रनष्टानलदीपनेषु। योगेषु हन्यात् परि-
णामशूलं शूलं तथान्नद्रवसंज्ञकञ्च। यश्माम्लपित्तं ग्रहणीं प्रवृद्धां जीर्णज्वरं
लोहितपित्तकुष्ठम्। न सन्ति ते यानि निहन्ति रोगान् योगोत्तमः सम्यगु-
पास्यमानः।

रसेन्द्रसार संग्रहः।

1. नवायसंलौहम्। त्र्यूषणत्रिफलामुस्तविडङ्गचित्रकाः समाः। नवायो-
रजसो भागास्तच्चूर्णं मधुसर्पिषा। भक्षयेत् पाण्डुहृद्रोगकुष्ठार्शः काम-
लापहम्॥

चक्रः।

by two grains till the maximum quantity is reached. The above preparation with the addition of one part of the watery extract of *gulancha* is called *Guduchyádi lauha*,[1] and is given in burning of hands and feet and in diseases supposed to be caused by deranged air.

Mahásvásári lauha and *Pippuládi lauha*[2] are the two forms in which iron is used in asthma. They are similar in composition. The former is thus prepared. Take of prepared iron four tolás, prepared talc one tolá, honey and sugar four tolás each, the three myrobalans, liquorice root, raisins, long pepper, kernel of jujube fruits, bamboo-manna, *tálisapatri* (leaves of *Pinus Webbiana*), *baberung* seeds, cardamoms, root of *Áplotaxis auriculata* (*kushtha*), and flowers of *Mesua ferrea* (*nágakesara*), each one tolá, powder and rub them together in an iron mortar. Dose about one scruple, to be taken with honey two or three times a day.

In enlarged spleen *Rohitaka lauha* is the favourite form in which iron is used. It will be described under *Rohitaka* (*Amoora Rohitaka*). In enlarged liver the following called *Yakridari lauha*[3] is used. Take of prepared iron, talc and copper, each four tolás, root of *Citrus Bergamia* (*limpáka*) eight tolás, burnt deer-skin eight tolás,

---

1. गुडूच्यादिलौहम्। गुडूचीसारसंयुक्तं त्रिकत्रयमयो रजः। वातरक्तं निहन्त्याशु सर्व्ववातहरं परम्॥ रसेन्द्रसारसंग्रहः।

2 महाश्वासारिलौहम्। कर्षद्वयं लौहचूर्णं कर्षार्द्धमभ्रमेव च। सिताकर्षद्वयञ्चैव मधुकर्षद्वयं तथा। त्रिफला मधुकं द्राक्षा कणा कोलास्थिवंशजा। तालीशपत्रं वैड़ङ्गमेला पुष्करकेशरम्॥ एतानि सर्व्वचूर्णानि कर्षार्द्धञ्च समांशिकम्। लौहे च लौहदण्डेन मर्द्दयेत् प्रहरद्वयम्। ततो मात्रां लिहेत् क्षौद्रैर्बुद्ध्वा दोषबलाबलम्। इदं श्वासारि लौहञ्च महाश्वासं विनाशयेत्॥ कासं पञ्चविधञ्चैव रक्तपित्तं सुदारुणम्। एकजं द्वन्द्वजञ्चैव तथैव सान्निपातिकम्। निहन्ति नात्र सन्देहो भास्करस्तिमिरं यथा॥ भैषज्यरत्नावली।

3. यकृदरिलौहम्। द्विकर्षं लौहचूर्णस्य अभ्रञ्चापि तथैव च। कर्षद्वयं मृतं ताम्रं लिम्पाकाङ्घ्रित्वचः पलम्। मृगाजिनं पलं भस्म सर्व्वमेकत्र कारयेत्। नवगुञ्जा प्रमाणेन वटिकां कारयेद्भिषक्। यकृत्प्लीहोदरं हन्ति कामलाञ्च हलीमकम्। कासं श्वासं ज्वरं हन्याद्बलवर्णाग्निवर्द्धनम्। यकृदरिस्त्विदं लौहं सालगुल्मविनाशनम्॥ रसेन्द्रसारसंग्रहः।

rub them together with water and prepare a pill-mass. Dose grains nine to eighteen in enlarged liver, spleen, jaundice etc.

In anasarca, iron is given in combination with carbonate of potash, as in the following called *Tryushanádi lauha.*[1] Take of *yavakshára* (impure carbonate of potash), ginger, long pepper and black pepper, one part each, iron four parts. Make into six-grain pills with water.

In erysipelas, carbuncles and boils the following called *Kálágnirudra rasa*[2] is recommended. Take of mercury, sulphur, prepared talc, iron, iron rust, and iron pyrites, each one part, rub them together with water, and roast the mixture within a covered crucible; when cool add to it one-tenth part of its weight of aconite, mix intimately, and divide the mass into twenty-two grain pills.

In urinary diseases the following, called *Meha mudgara rasa*,[3] is used. Take of *rusot*, black salt, wood of *Berberis Asiatica* (*dáruharidrá*), root of *Ægle Marmelos* (*bilva*), *Tribulus terrestris* (*gokshura*), pomegranate seeds, chiretta, long pepper-root, long pepper, black pepper, ginger, the three myrobalans and root of *Ipomœa Turpethum* (*trivrit*), each one tolá, prepared iron fifteen tolás, bdellium eight tolás, mix them together and beat into a uniform mass with *ghee.* Dose twenty-two grains with water or goat's milk. This medicine is said to be useful in gonorrhœa, strangury, chronic fever, anæmia, jaundice etc.

---

1 त्र्यूषणादिलौहम्। अयोरजस्त्र्यूषणयावशूकं चूर्णं सुपीतं त्रिफलारसेन शोथं निहन्यात् सहसा नरस्य यथाशनिर्वृक्षसदीर्णवेगम्॥ रसेन्द्रसारसंग्रह।

2 कालाग्निरुद्ररसः। सूतकान्ताभ्रलौहानां भस्म माक्षिकगन्धकम्। भूधराख्ये पुटे पश्चादहिनैकं तद्विपाचयेत्। दशमांशं विषं योज्यं माषमात्रन्तु भक्षयेत्। रसः कालाग्निरुद्रोऽयं दशाहेन विसर्पनुत्॥ रसेन्द्रसारसंग्रहः

3 मेहमुद्गररसः। रसाञ्जनं विडं दारुबिल्वगोक्षुरदाडिमाः। भूनिम्ब पिप्पलीमूलं त्रिकटु त्रिफला त्रिवृत्॥ प्रत्येकं तोलकं देयं लौहचूर्णन्तु तत्समम्। पलैकं गुग्गुलुं दत्वा घृतेन वटिकां कुरु॥ माषैकप्रमिताचेयं मेहमुद्गरसंज्ञिनी। श्रीमद्गहननाथेन लोकनिस्तारकारिणी॥ अनुपानं प्रयोक्तव्यं छागीदुग्धं जलञ्च वा। विंशन्मेहं निहन्त्याशु मूत्रकृच्छ्रं हलीमकम्॥

रसेन्द्रसारसंग्रहः।

Vrihat Somanátha rasa.[1] Take of mercury obtained by subliming cinnabar and purified with the juice of *Erythrina Indica* (*páribhadra*), and of sulphur, rubbed with the juice of *Salvinia cucullata* (*Leandá*) each one part, prepared iron four parts, prepared talc, tin, silver, *kharpara* or calamine, iron pyrites, and gold, each half a part. Rub them together with, and soak in the juice of *Aloe Indica* (*ghritakumári*) and *Hydrocotyle Asiatica* (*mandukaparni*) and divide into four-grain pills. They are administered with honey in diabetes and other urinary diseases, female complaints etc. A preparation similar to the above in composition, and called *Somesvara rasa* is given in leucorrhœa and other female complaints. Besides the preparations mentioned above numerous other combinations of mercury, iron and talc with the addition of gold, silver, copper etc, in varying proportions and combinations, are described under different names. In fact the three first mentioned drugs constitute the basis of the great majority of the pills used by *Kavirájas.*

Iron forms an ingredient of hair dyes. The following is an illustration. Take of powdered iron two tolás, mangoe stones five tolás, chebulic and emblic myrobalans two tolás each, belleric myrobalan one tolá, rub them together with water in an iron vessel and steep for one night. This paste is applied to grey hairs for turning them into black.[2]

---

1 बृहत्सोमनाथरसः। हिङ्गुलात् सम्भवं सूतं पालिधारस मर्द्दितम्। रण्डा-शोधित गन्धञ्च तेनैव कज्जली कृतम्॥ तद्द्वयद्विगुणं लौहं कन्यारसवि मर्द्दितम्। अभ्रकं वङ्गकं रौप्यं खर्परं माक्षिकं तथा॥ सुवर्णञ्च समं सर्वं प्रत्येकञ्च रसार्द्ध-कम्। तत्सर्व्वं कन्यकाद्रावैर्मर्द्दयेद्भावयेत्तथा। भेकपर्णीरसेनैव वटीं गुञ्जाद्वयां कृताम्। मधुना भक्षयेच्चापि सोमरोग निवृत्तये। प्रमेहं विंशतिं हन्ति बहुमूत्रञ्च सोमगम्। मूत्रातिसारकृच्छ्रञ्च मूत्राघातं सुदारुणम्। मूत्रदोषं बहु-विधं प्रमेहं मधुसञ्ज्ञकम्। हस्तिमेहमिक्षुमेहं लालामेहं विनाशयेत्। स्वेच्छे यस्य शतं स्त्रीणां विद्यते च व्यवायिनः। न तस्य लिङ्गशैथिल्यं शुक्रक्षयो न जायते। अग्निञ्च कुरुते दीप्तिमम्लपित्तञ्च नाशयेत्। वातिकं पैत्तिकं चैव श्लैष्मिकं सोमनामकम्। नाशयेत् बहुमूत्रञ्च प्रमेहमविकल्पतः॥ रसेन्द्रसारसंग्रहः।

2 लौहचूर्णस्य कर्षन्तु दद्यात् चूतमज्जतः। धात्रीफलद्वयं पथ्ये द्वे तथैकं विभी-

SULPHATE OF IRON.

Sans. काशीश *Kásisa.*

NATIVE sulphate of iron is indigenous to India, and has been used in medicine from a very ancient age. Two sorts of sulphate of iron are mentioned, namely, *Dhátukásis* or green variety and *Phushpa kásis* or yellowish variety. The latter is evidently sulphate of iron, covered with the basic sulphate of the sesquioxide from absorption of oxygen. It would seem that the ancient Hindus did not know sulphate of iron, as an iron compound. It is neither described as a tonic nor used in combination with iron like iron pyrites and iron rust. It is seldom used internally. I have met with only one prescription by Chakradatta, who recommends a linctus composed of sulphate of iron and pulp of wood apple, in hiccup.[1]

Externally, it is used in skin diseases along with other medicines. Thus take of sulphate of iron, gall-stone of cows (*gorochaná*). *rusot* and orpiment, equal parts and beat into to a paste with *kánjika.* It is useful in intertrigo, pruritis etc.[2]

Kásisádyataila.[3] Take of sesamum oil four seers, water sixteen seers, sulphate of iron, wood of *Withania somnifera* (*asvagandhá*), bark of *Symplocos racemosa* (*lodhra*), root of *Pothos officinalis* (*gajapippali*) each sixteen tolás. Beat the solid ingredients into a paste and boil it with the oil and water in the usual way. This oil is recommended to be applied to the genitals and the breasts with the view of strengthening these parts.

तकम्। पिष्ट्वालोहमये भाण्डे स्थापयेन्निशि वासयेत्। लेप्योयमचिराद्धन्ति पलितं नात्र संशयः। भावप्रकाशः।

1. हिक्काश्वासे अवलेहः। काशीशं दधिनामच हिक्काघ्ना मधुसंयुताः। चक्रः

2. काशीशं रोचनातुल्यं हरितालं रसाञ्जनम्। अम्लपिष्टैः प्रलेपोयं दृपपाच्छुहि पूतयोः॥ चक्रः।

3. काशीशाद्यतैलं। काशीशतुरगगन्धा शावरगजपिप्पलीविपक्वेन। तैलेन यान्ति वृद्धिं स्तनकर्णवराङ्गलिङ्गानि॥ चक्रदत्तः।

IRON PYRITES.

Sans. स्वर्णमाक्षिक *Svarnamákshika,* तारमाक्षिक *Táramákshika.*

IRON pyrites is met with in many parts of India, and has been used in medicine from a very remote period. It occurs in two forms, namely, in dark yellow nodules with a golden lustre, and in silvery radiated crystals. The former is called *Svarnamákshika* and the latter *Táramákshika.* The ancients supposed that they contained gold and silver respectively, in combination with other ingredients, and possessed in part the properties of those precious metals.* Chemically iron pyrites consists of bisulphide of iron. It is purified by being boiled in lemon juice with one-third of its weight of rock-salt in an iron vessel, till the pot turns red hot. It is reduced to powder by being rubbed with oil or goat's urine and then roasted in a closed crucible. Iron pyrites thus prepared has a sweetish bitter taste. It is considered as tonic, alterative and useful in anæmia, urinary diseases, ascites, anasarca, prurigo, eye diseases etc. As an alterative tonic it is generally used in combination with other medicines of its class, such as iron, talc, mercury etc. The following is an example. Take of prepared iron, sesamum seeds, long pepper, black pepper and ginger, each one part, iron pyrites five parts. Beat into a mass with honey. Dose about half a drachm in advanced anæmia.[1]

In diseases of the pregnant state the following called *Garbha-vinoda rasa*[2] is much used, as an alterative tonic. Take of iron pyrites and cinnabar, each four tolás, ginger, long pepper and black pepper, each three tolás, cloves and mace, each six tolás, beat them

---

* न केवलं स्वर्णरूप्यगुणास्तापिजयोर्मता द्रव्यान्तरस्य संसर्गात् सन्त्यन्योऽपि गुणास्तयोः॥ भावप्रकाशः।

1. स्वर्णमाक्षिकं अयस्तिलत्र्यूषणकोलभागैः सर्व्वैः समं माक्षिकधातुचूर्णम्। तैर्मोदकः क्षौद्रयुतोऽनुतक्रः पाण्ड्वामये दूरगतेऽपि शस्तः॥ चक्रः।

2. गर्भविनोदरसः। त्रिभागं त्रिकटुर्देयं चतुर्भागञ्च हिङ्गुलम्। जातीकोषं लवङ्गञ्च प्रत्येकञ्च त्रिकार्षिकम्। सुवर्णमाक्षिकञ्चैव पलार्द्धं प्रक्षिपेद्बुधः। जलेन मर्द्दयित्वा च चणमात्रा वटी कृता। निहन्ति गर्भिणी रोगं भास्करस्तिमिरं यथा॥ रसेन्द्रसारसंग्रहः।

together with water and divide into pills about four grains each. One pill to be taken twice daily.

GOLD.

Sans. सुवर्ण, *Suvarna.*

GOLD enters into the composition of a large number of medicines for various diseases. Pure leaf-gold is used. It should be free from admixture of copper and silver, of a red colour when exposed to heat, and of saffron colour when rubbed on touchstone. It is purified by heating its leaves and cooling them alternately with *kánjika*, oil, cow's urine, butter-milk and a decoction of horse-gram. Gold is reduced to powder by being rubbed with mercury and exposed to heat in a covered crucible with the addition of sulphur. Two parts of mercury and one of leaf-gold are rubbed together into a mass with lemon juice and placed in a crucible with three parts of sulphur. The crucible is then covered and exposed to heat. This process of mixing the gold with mercury and exposing to heat is repeated fourteen times, when the gold completely loses its metallic character. In books it is stated that the gold should be rubbed with mercury only the first time, and that in roasting it afterwards sulphur alone should be placed in the crucible with the gold, but *Kavirája* Binod Lál Sen tells me that he reduces gold to powder by mixing it with mercury every time it is roasted, and that he repeats the process till the gold is reduced to a dark brown impalpable powder. This powder of gold appears to undergo little change from its metallic state, for on being rubbed on an agate mortar it produces a brilliant yellow stain like that of massive gold, when it is rubbed on touchstone for ascertaining its purity.

Gold thus prepared for medicinal use is considered a valuable tonic and alterative. It is said to increase strength and beauty, to improve the intellect and memory, to clear the voice and to increase the sexual powers. It is used in fever, consumption, insanity, diseases of the nervous system and urinary organs, impotence, etc. Dose, one to two grains.

Jayamangala rasa.[1] Take of mercury obtained by sublimation, of cinnabar, sulphur, borax, prepared copper, tin and iron pyrites, rock-salt, and black pepper, prepared iron and silver, each one part, prepared gold two parts, powder them well, mix and soak the mixture three times respectively in the juice of *datura* leaves, and leaves of *Nyctanthes Arbor-tristis (sephálíká)*, in the decoction of the ten roots, called *dasamula*, and of chiretta. Divide the mass into four-grain pills. They are taken with cumin-seed powder and honey. This medicine is used in old chronic fevers of all sorts and is said to be a powerful tonic and alterative, that may be administered with suitable adjuncts in many diseases.

Mrigánka rasa.[2] Take of mercury one part, prepared gold one part, sulphur and pearls each two parts, borax one-fourth part, rub them together and beat into a ball with *kánjika*. This is dried, enclosed in an earthen crucible and exposed to heat within a pot of rock-salt in the manner of a hot sand-bath for twelve hours. When cool the ball is taken out from the crucible and reduced to powder. It is administered in doses of one to four grains with about a scruple of black pepper in phthisis. Two other preparations used in this disease, and called *Pottali hemagarbha rasa*, and *Ratnagarbha pottali rasa*, respectively, are similar in composition to the *Mrigánka rasa*. They contain mercury, sulphur, gold, pearls, borax etc, in varying proportions.

---

1 जयमङ्गलरसः। हिङ्गुलसम्भवं सूतं गन्धकं टङ्कणं तथा। ताम्रं वङ्गं माक्षिकञ्च सैन्धवं मरिचं तथा। सर्व्वं समं समाहृत्य द्विगुणं स्वर्णभस्मकम्। तदर्द्धं कान्तलौहञ्च रूप्यभस्मापि तत्समम्। एतत्सर्व्वं विचूर्ण्याथ भावयेत् कनकद्रवैः। शेफालिदलजैश्चापि दशमूलरसेन च। किराततिक्तकाथैः त्रिवारं भावयेत् सुधीः। भावयित्वा ततः कार्य्या गुञ्जाद्वयमिता वटी। अनुपानं प्रयोक्तव्यं जीरकमधुसंयुतम्। जीर्णज्वरं महाघोरं चिरकालसमुद्भवम्। ज्वरमष्टविधं हन्ति साध्यासाध्यमथापि वा। पृथक् दोषांश्च विविधान् समस्तान् विषमज्वरान्।

रसेन्द्रसारसंग्रहः।

2 मृगाङ्करसः। स्याद्रसेन समं हेमं मौक्तिकं द्विगुणं भवेत्। गन्धकस्तु समस्तेन रसपादस्तु टङ्कणः॥ सर्व्वं तद्गोलकं कृत्वा काञ्जिकेन विशोधयेत्। भाण्डे लवणपूर्णे च पचेद्यामचतुष्टयम्॥ मृगाङ्कसञ्ज्ञको ज्ञेयं रोगराज निकृन्तनः॥

रसेन्द्रसारसंग्रहः।

Svarna parpati.[1] Take of mercury eight tolás, gold one tolá, rub them together, then add sulphur eight tolás and mix. Melt the mixture over the fire in an iron ladle smeared with *ghee*, and press the melted fluid between cow-dung balls enclosed in plantain-leaves in the manner described under *Rasa parpati*, so as to make thin round disks of it. This medicine is used like *Rasa parpati* in chronic diarrhœa, and anasarca. Milk diet is enjoined, and water and salt are prohibited. Dose grains two, gradually increased to grains ten in the course of twenty-one days, to be again gradually reduced to the original dose of two grains in another three weeks. Another preparation of the sort called *Vijayaparpati* contains diamond, pearls, silver, copper, and talc, in addition to gold, sulphur and mercury. It is used in the same cases as the *Svarna-parpati* above described.

Gold is much used as an alterative tonic. Prepared gold in doses of two grains daily with the addition of honey, *ghee* and emblic myrobalan, or root of *Acorus Calamus* (*vacha*) is recommended to be taken for a lengthened period.[2] It is also given to infants under an impression that it will impart strength and beauty to their frames. The following composition is recommended for them. Take of powdered gold, root of *Acorus Calamus* (*vacha*) and *Aplotaxis auriculata* (*kushtha*), chebulic myrobalans, and leaves of *Herpestes Monniera* (*brimhi*) equal parts, powder and mix. Dose two grains with honey and *ghee*. It is recommended to be given to feeble infants a few days after birth.

The principal alterative tonic of the Hindu Materia Medica is the preparation popularly called *Makaradhvaja*. To prepare it, take

---

1 स्वर्णपर्प्पटी। रसोत्तमं पलं शुद्धं हेमतोलकसंयुतम्। शिलायां मर्द्दयेत् तावत् यावदेकत्वमागतम्॥ गन्धकस्य पलञ्चैकमयःपात्रे ततो द्रवे। मर्द्दयेद्दृढपाणिभ्यां यावत् कज्जलतां भजेत्॥ ततः परं विधानज्ञः पर्प्पटीं कारयेत् सुधीः। रक्तिकादिक्रमेणैव योजयेदनुपानतः। ग्रहणीं विविधां हन्ति दृष्या सर्व्वज्वरापहा॥ रसेन्द्रसारसंग्रहः।

2 मध्वामलकचूर्णञ्च सुवर्णञ्चेति तत्त्रयम्। प्राश्यारिष्टगृहीतोऽपि मुच्यते प्राणसंशयात्। वचाघृतं सुवर्णञ्च मधुना सह संलिहेत्। सम्वत्सरं प्रयुञ्जानः श्रुतिधारो भवेन्नरः॥ सन्देहभञ्जनी।

of leaf-gold one tolá, mercury eight tolás, beat into a mass, then add sulphur sixteen tolás, and rub together till the mass becomes black. Rub this mass repeatedly with the juice of the red cotton flower and of *Aloe Indica*, and dry. Now take a bottle with a flat bottom, wrap it with layers of cloth and clay to strengthen it, and dry. Place the mixture of gold, mercury and sulphur at the bottom of the bottle, insert it in a sand-bath up to its neck and cover the mouth lightly with a piece of chalk. Apply heat gently at first. When the process of sublimation commences the heat should be increased, and the chalk-stopper removed. The sulphur now burns with its characteristic blue flame at the mouth of the bottle and a red sublimate collects below its neck. The narrow neck of the bottle is apt to be closed with sulphureous deposits and when there is this tendency, it should be cleared with an iron rod. The sublimation is over in the course of about nine hours. When done the bottle is broken, and the sublimate extracted from its neck in the shape of shining dark red scales. In this process the sulphur and mercury are sublimed in the form of red sulphide, and the gold remains at the bottom of the bottle. The latter may be used again in the preparation of *Makaradhvaja* or converted into powdered gold. *Makaradhvaja* is administered in doses of one grain daily with honey or other suitable adjuncts in nervous debility, weakness of brain from excessive mental labour, habitual costiveness, general debility, female complaints after delivery, spermatorrhoea etc.

Chandrodaya makaradhvaja.[1] When *Makaradhvaja* is adminis-

---

1 चन्द्रोदयमकरध्वजः। पलं मृदुस्वर्णदलं रसेन्द्रात् पलाष्टकं षोड़श गन्धकस्य। शोणैः सुकार्पासभवैः प्रसूनैः सर्व्वं विमर्द्याथ कुमारिकाद्भिः। तत्काचकूपे निहितं प्रगाढ़ं मृत्कर्पटैस्तद्दिवसत्रयञ्च। पचेत् क्रमाग्नौ सिकताख्ययन्त्रे ततो रजः पल्लवरागरम्यम्। निगृह्य चैतस्य पलं पलानि चत्वारि कर्पूररजस्तथैव। जातीफलं शोषणमिन्द्रपुष्पम्। कस्तूरिकाया इह शाण एकः। चन्द्रोदयोऽयं कथितोऽस्य माषो भुक्तोऽहिवल्लीदलमध्यवर्त्ती। मदोन्मदानां प्रमदाशतानां गर्व्वाधिकत्वं श्लथयत्यवश्यम्। घृतं घनीभूतमतीवदुग्धं गुरूणि मांसानि समण्डकानि। माषान्नपिष्टानि भवन्ति पथ्यान्यानन्ददायीन्य पराणि चात्र। वलीपलितनाशनस्तनुभृतां वयस्तम्भनः समस्तगदनाशनः प्रबलरोगपञ्चाननः।

रसेन्द्रसारसंग्रहः।

tered as an aphrodisiac, it is usual to mix it with some stimulant drugs, the resulting preparation being called *Chandrŏdaya makara-dhvaja.* Thus take of *Makaradhvaja*, one part, camphor, nutmegs, black pepper, and cloves, each four parts musk one-sixteenth part, mix together and make into pills about ten grains each. These pills are enclosed or wrapped in betle leaves and chewed. Along with this medicine a generous diet consisting of meat, *ghee*, milk, pulses, etc, should be taken. It is used in nervous debility, impotence, premature old age etc.* A preparation similar in appearance to *Makaradhvaja* and called *Ashtavaktra rasa*, is sublimed from a mixture of mercury, sulphur, gold, silver, lead, copper, zinc and tin in equal parts. It is used as a nervine tonic, in general debility.

SILVER.

Sans. रूप्य, *Rupya.* तार, *Tára.*

PURE silver, according to Sanskrit writers, should be soft, white, brilliant and ductile. It should not be discoloured by fire. Impure silver, that is, silver mixed with other metals, is discoloured by fire, of a reddish or yellowish colour, and not ductile. Silver is purified in the same way as gold. It is converted into a black oxide by thin silver leaves being mixed with twice their weight of cinnabar, and heated in the subliming apparatus, called *Urddhapátana yantra.* This process is repeated fourteen times. The resulting compound is a fine greyish black powder with minute shining white particles intermixed with it. On chemical analysis it is found to consist of the black oxide of silver. The properties of silver thus prepared are said to be allied to those of gold but somewhat inferior. It is generally used in combination with other metals, such as gold, iron,

* *Makaradhvaja* is regarded as a preparation of gold, which is supposed to be the active principle of the medicine. The gold used in its preparation however remains below, and the mercury and sulphur only are sublimed in the form of red sulphide. as in the preparation of mercury called *Rasasindura.* Properly speaking, therefore, it is but a preparation of mercury, although the gold may possibly exercise some catalytic influence during the process of sublimation. some physicians use the preparation called *Sadgunabalijarita rasa-sindura* (see page 36) under the name of *Makaradhvaja.*

etc. Dose, grains one to two. The following is an example of a complex prescription containing silver.

Vrihat váta gajánkusa.[1] Take of mercury, prepared talc, iron, gold, copper and silver, orpiment, sulphur, ginger, coriander, root of *Sida cordifolia* (*balá*), bark of *Myrica sapida* (*katphala*), *Rhus succedanea* (*sringi*), aconite, long pepper, black pepper, and borax, each one part, chebulic myrobalans, two parts, powder, mix and rub with the juice of *Sphæranthus mollis* (*mundi*) and *Vitex Negundo* (*nirgundi*) for one day. Divide the mass into four grain-pills. They are said to be useful in various nervous diseases. Silver enters into the composition of several other remedies in common use, such as the *Yogarája* (see *silájatu*), *Jayamangala rasa* (see gold) etc.

COPPER.

Sans. ताम्र, *Támra. Vern. Támá.*

THIN plates of copper such as can be pierced by thorns are used in medicine. They are purified by being boiled in cow's urine for three hours. Copper is reduced to powder by smearing its thin leaves with a paste of sulphur and lemon juice, beating them into a mass, and exposing to heat in a covered crucible within a sand-bath for twelve hours. The powder thus produced is rubbed with *kánjika* and made into a ball, which is introduced into a tuber of *Amorphophallus campanulatus* (*ola*), as in a crucible and roasted. This last process is said to render the copper innocuous and prevent it from causing purging and vomiting when taken internally.

Copper thus prepared is a dark coloured powder, somewhat gritty to the feel. On chemical analysis it is found to consist of sulphide

---

1 बृहत्वातगजाङ्कुशः। सूताभ्रतीक्ष्णताम्राग्नितारतालकगन्धकम्। स्वर्णं शुण्ठी बलाधान्यं कट्फलश्चाभयाविषम्॥ पथ्याश्टङ्गी पिप्पली च मरिचं टङ्कणन्तथा। तुल्यं खल्ले दिनं मर्द्यं मुण्डीनिर्गुण्डीजैर्द्रवैः। द्विगुञ्जां वटिकां खादेत् सर्ववातप्रशान्तये। साध्यासाध्यं निहन्त्याशु रसोवातगजाङ्कुशः॥
रसेन्द्रसारसंग्रहः।

of copper. It is described as an alterative, emetic and purgative, and is used in poisoning, dyspepsia, fever, enlarged liver and spleen, anæmia, skin diseases, diarrhœa etc. Dose, as an alterative, grains two to four. In poisoning prepared copper is given in doses of about twenty-four grains with sugar or honey to cause vomiting.[1]

Copper enters into the composition of several medicines for ague, remittent fever, enlarged spleen etc. The following are a few illustrations.

Sitabhanji rasa.[2] Take of orpiment, mercury, sulphur and realgar, two, one, half and quarter parts, respectively, rub them together into a thin paste with the juice of *Momordica Charantia* (*káravella*). Apply this paste on copper plates equal in weight to the other ingredients, enclose the plates in a covered crucible, and roast in a sand-bath over a strong fire for twelve hours. When cool extract the copper plates from the crucible and powder them. Dose, four grains with four black peppers enclosed in a betel leaf. This packet should be chewed. It is given in intermittent fever with shivering fits, followed by burning and heat of skin. A preparation very similar to the above in composition is called *Pliha panchánana rasa*, and used in enlarged spleen.

Svachchhanda bhairava rasa.[3] Take of prepared copper and aconite equal parts, rub together with the juice of *datura* leaves and make into one-grain pills. They are given with ginger juice, sugar and rock salt in fevers complicated with cerebral symptoms.

---

1 क्षौद्रलीढं ताम्ररजोवमनं गरदोषनुत् । चक्रः ।

2 शीतभञ्जिरसः । तालकोदरदोद्भूतो पारदोगन्धकः शिला । क्रमाद्भागार्द्धं विहितं कारवेल्या प्रमर्द्दितम ॥ अनेनास्य प्रमाणेन ताम्रपत्रं प्रलेपयेत् । अधोमुखो दृढे भाण्डे तान्निरुध्याथ पूरयेत् ॥ चुल्यां वालुकापात्राध अग्निं प्रज्वालयेद्दृढम् । शीरां संचूर्ण्य माषोऽस्य नागवल्ली दले स्थितः ॥ भक्षितो मरिचैः सार्द्धं समस्तान् विषमज्वरान् । शीतदाहादिकान् हन्ति पथ्यञ्चास्यौदनं पयः ॥
रसप्रदीपः ।

3 स्वच्छन्दभैरवरसः । ताम्रभस्मविषं हेम्नः शतधा भावितं रसैः । गुञ्जार्द्धं सन्निपातादिनवज्वरहरं परम् । आर्द्राम्बुशर्करासिन्धुयुतः स्वच्छन्दभैरवः । क्षौद्र द्राक्षासिताश्चापि दधिपथ्यं दचौददेत् । रसेन्द्रसारसंग्रहः ।

Mahámritunjaya lauha.[1] Take of mercury, sulphur, talc, orpiment and realgar, each one part, iron two parts, copper four parts, *yavakshára* and *sarjikákshára* (impure carbonates of potash and soda), borax, black salt, burnt couries, and conch-shells, plumbago-root, assafœtida, root of *Picrorrhiza Kurroa* (*katuki*), *Amoora rohitaka* (*rohitaka*,) and *Ipomœa Turpethum* (*trivrit*); tamarind pulp, colocynth root, root bark of *Anogeissus latifolius* (*dhava*), root of *Alangium decapetalum* (*ankota*), *Achyranthes aspera* (*apámárga*), ashes of the spikes of the palm-tree, turmeric and wood of *Berberis Asiatica* (*dáruharidrá*), croton seeds, sulphate of copper, *rusot* and *Oxalis corniculata* (*amlaloniká*), all in equal parts, with the exception of *rohitaka* bark, which should be two parts. Powder the ingredients, mix, soak the mixture in the fresh juice of ginger and *gulancha* and add to it thirty-two tolás of honey. Make into six grain pills with honey. One pill is given every morning in enlarged liver, spleen disease, ascites etc.

In enlargements of the abdominal viscera, designated by the term *gulma*, copper is used in a variety of forms. Thus, prepared copper in doses of two grains rubbed with ginger juice and enclosed in betel leaf may be given, or the following composition may be used.[2]

---

1 महामृत्युञ्जयलौहम्। शुद्धसूतं समं गन्धं जारिताभ्रं समं तथा। गन्धकाद्द्विगुणं लौहं मृतताम्रं चतुर्गुणम्। द्विक्षारं टङ्कणविड़ं वराटीमथशङ्खकम्। चित्रकं कुनटीं तालं रामठं कटुकीं तथा। रोहितकं त्रिवृत् चिञ्चा पिशाला धवमङ्कठम्। अपामार्गं तालखण्डमल्लिका च निशायुगम्। कांनकं तुत्थकञ्चैव यत्नमर्द्दं रसाञ्जनम्। एतानि समभागानि चूर्णयित्वा विभावयेत्। आर्द्रकस्य रसेनैव गुडूचीस्वरसेन च। मधुनः कुडवैर्भाव्यं वटिकां माषमात्रकम्। भक्षयेत् प्रातरुत्थाय सर्व्वोदरकुलान्तकृत्। प्लीहानं ज्वरहृद्यञ्च कासञ्च विषमज्वरम्। कासं श्वासं शिरोरोगं कर्णरोगं सशोथकम्। चिरजं कुष्ठकञ्चैव श्लीपदं हन्ति दारुणम्। रोगानीकविनाशाय धन्वन्तरिकृतं पुरा। मृत्युञ्जयमिदं लौहं सिद्धिदं शुभदं नृणाम्॥ रसेन्द्रसारसंग्रहः।

2 केवलं जारितं ताम्रं शृङ्गवेररसैः सह। दातव्यं पर्णखण्डेन सर्व्वगुल्मं निवारणम्॥ रसेन्द्रसारसंग्रहः।

Gulma kálánana rasa.[1] Take of mercury, sulphur, copper, orpiment, borax, and *yavakshára* (impure carbonate of potash), each two tolás, tubers of *Cyperus rotundus* (*mustaka*), black pepper, ginger, long pepper, fruit of *Pothos officinalis* (*gajapippuli*), chebulic myrobalans, *Acorus Calamus* (*vacha*) and *Aplotaxis auriculata* (*kushtha*), each one tolá. Powder them all, mix and soak the mixture in the juice of *Hedyotis biflora* (*parparti*), *Heliophytum Indicum* (*hastisundi*), *Achyranthes aspera* (*apámarga*) and *Trichosanthes dioica* (*patala*) respectively and dry. This medicine is given in the form of a powder in doses of eight grains with the decoction of chebulic myrobalans.

Several preparations of copper are recommended for use in asthma and heart disease, as for example, *Suryávarta rasa*, *Hridayárnava rasa* etc.

Suryávarta rasa.[2] This preparation of copper is recommended for use in asthma by Sárangadhara and other writers of note. It is thus prepared. One part of mercury and one of sulphur are rubbed together with the juice of *Aloe Indica* for six hours. Two parts of copper leaves are pasted with the above mixture, and roasted within a closed crucible in a sand-bath for twelve hours. When cool the copper leaves are taken out from the crucible and powdered. Dose four grains with the addition of honey and the juice of *Adhatoda Vasica* (*vásaka*).

---

1 गुल्मकालाननरसः। सूतकं गन्धकं ताम्रं तालकं टङ्कणं समम्॥ तोलद्वयमितं भागं यवक्षारश्च तत्समम्॥ मुस्तकं मरिचं शुण्ठी पिप्पली गजपिप्पली। हरीतकी वचाकुष्ठं तोलैकं चूर्णयेत् सुधीः॥ सर्व्वमेकीकृतं पात्रे भावना क्रियते ततः। पर्पटी वारणशुण्डीमपामार्गपटोलकैः॥ ततः पुनः चूर्णयेत् पश्चात् सर्व्वगुल्मविनाशनम्। गुञ्जामात्रमिदं खाद्यं हरीतक्यनुपानतः॥ वातिकं पैत्तिकं गुल्मं श्लैष्मिकं च त्रिदोषजम्। द्वन्द्वजां च निहन्त्याशु वातगुल्मं विशेषतः॥ श्रीमद्गहननाथेन निर्म्मितो विश्वसम्पदे। गुल्मकालानलो नाम्ना रसोयं भुविदुर्लभः॥ रसेन्द्रसारसंग्रहः।

2 सूर्य्यावर्त्तरसः। सूतकं गन्धकञ्चैव यामैकं कन्यकाद्रवैः। द्वयोस्तुल्यं ताम्रपत्रं

Hridayárnava rasa.[1] Take of purified mercury and sulphur, each one part, prepared copper two parts, rub them together for twelve hours with the decoction of the three myrobalans, and with the fresh juice of *Solanum nigrum* (*kákamáchi*). Make into pills about four grains each. These pills are administered with a decoction of the fruits of *Solanum nigrum* and the three myrobalans, prepared with two tolás, in all of the drugs and thirty-two tolás of water, which is boiled down to one-eighth, or four tolás. They are said to be useful in heart disease.

Támresvara.[2] Take of prepared copper, mercury, borax, and iron, sulphur, and long pepper, equal parts, soak in the decoction of the leaves, bark, fruit, root, and flowers of *Azadirachta Indica* (*nimba*), of the pulp of *Cassia fistula* and of the three myrobalans. Dose four grains, in skin diseases of various sorts. During the administration of this medicine a cooling regimen should be observed.

SULPHATE OF COPPER.

Sans. तुत्थ, *Tuttha. Vern. Tutia.*

Sulphate of copper was known in India from a very remote period. It is prepared by roasting copper pyrites, dissolving the roasted mass in water and evaporating the solution to obtain crystals of the sulphate. It was known as a salt of

---

कन्याकल्केन लेपयेत् । दिनैकं क्रौञ्चिकायन्त्रे पचेत् शीतं समुद्धरेत् । सूर्य्यावर्त्तौ रसोनामाद्विगुञ्जः श्वासकासजित् । रसरत्नावली ।

1 हृदयार्णवरसः। शुद्धसूतं समं गन्धं मृतताम्रं तयोः समम्। मर्द्दयेत् त्रिफला क्वाथे काकमाचीद्रवैर्दिनम्॥ चनमात्रां वटीं खादेद्रसोयं हृदयार्णवः। काकमाचीफलं कर्षं त्रिफलाफलसंयुतम्॥ द्वात्रिंशत्तोलकं तोयं क्वाथमष्टावशेषिकम्। अनुपानं पिवेच्चात्र हृद्रोगेहि कफात्मके॥ रसेन्द्रसारसंग्रहः।

2 ताम्रेश्वरः। ताम्रं रसं टङ्कनगन्धलौहं भस्मीकृतं मागधिका समेतम्। पञ्चाङ्गनिम्बेन फलत्रयेण विभावितं राजतरोस्तथैव॥ नियोजयेद्वल्लयुगं प्रमाणं कुष्ठेषु सर्व्वेष्वपि रोगसंघे॥ उपाचरेत् कुष्ठ जुष्टं नान्यथा सिद्धिमिच्छति॥ रुक्षो स्निग्धा क्रियाकार्य्या विपरीतो विपर्य्यये॥ रसेन्द्रसारसंग्रहः।

copper, for the Bhávaprakása says it contains some copper and therefore possesses some of the properties of that metal.* It is described in this work as astringent, emetic, caustic, and useful in eye diseases, skin diseases, poisoning etc. It is purified for internal use, by being rubbed with honey and *ghee* and exposed to heat in a crucible. It is then soaked for three days in whey, and dried. Sulphate of copper thus prepared is said not to produce vomiting when taken internally. Dose, one to two grains.

Sulphate of copper dissolved in hot water is administered in insensibility from poisoning to excite vomiting. It enters into the composition of some medicines for remittent fever, such as the *Jvaránkusa* mentioned in Bhávaprákása, but arsenic is the active ingredient in these preparations. In quartan fever the following, called *Cháturthakàri*,[1] is recommended by many writers. Take of orpiment, realgar, sulphate of copper, burnt conch-shell and sulphur, equal parts, rub them together with the juice of *Aloe Indica* and roast in a covered crucible. When cool extract the powder and make into four-grain pills with the juice of *Aloe Indica*. They are administered with powdered black pepper and *ghee*. Butter-milk should be taken before these pills which relieve the fever by inducing vomiting.

Grahanikapáta rasa.[2] Sulphate of copper is used in chronic bowel complaints along with other medicines, as for example in the following called *Grahanikapáta rasa*. Take of sulphate of

---

*तुत्थं वितुन्नकञ्चापि शिखिग्रीवं मयूरकम् । तुत्थन्ताम्रोपधातुर्हि किञ्चित्ताम्रेण तद्भवेत् ॥ किञ्चित्ताम्रगुणं तस्माद्वक्ष्यमाणगुणञ्च तत् । भावप्रकाशः ।

1 चातुर्थकारिरसः । हरितालं शिलातुत्थं शङ्खचूर्णञ्च गन्धकम् । समांशं मर्द्दयेत् प्राज्ञः कुमारीरसभावितम् । शरावसंपुटे कृत्वा लिप्त्वा गजपुटे पचेत् । कुमारिकारसेनैव वल्लमात्रा वटीकृता । दत्वा शीतज्वरं हन्ति चातुर्थकं विशेषतः । मरिचघृतयोगेन तक्रं पीत्वा चरेद्वटीम् । एतया वमने जाते ज्वरः सद्यो विनश्यति ॥ भैषज्यरत्नम् ।

2 ग्रहणीकपाटः । तुत्थं तालं रसं कान्तं माक्षिकं टङ्कणं तथा । प्रपादनिष्कं प्रत्येकं षड्निष्का वराटिका । द्विनिष्कं गन्धकं सर्व्वं पिष्ट्वा जम्बीरजैर्द्रवैः । अर्द्ध-

copper, orpiment, mercury, iron, iron pyrites and borax, each five *máshás*. Prepared couries two and a half tolás and sulphur one tolá. Rub them all together with lemon juice and roast the mass lightly. This medicine is given in chronic bowel complaints, consumption etc.

Garbhavilása rasa.[1] Sulphate of copper enters into the composition of some medicines for diseases of the pregnant and puerperal state, such as, the *Sutikàvinoda* or *Garbhavilása rasa.* To prepare it take of mercury, sulphur and sulphate of copper, each one part, rub them together with lemon juice for three days. Then take of cumin seeds, *kálájirá,* long pepper, black pepper and ginger each one part, mix and make into eight-grain pills. They are used in bowel complaints and indigestion during the puerperal and pregnant state.

Sulphate of copper is applied to sinuses and fistula-in-ano with the object of stimulating and healing them. It is added to ointments for foul ulcers.[2] A solution of sulphate of copper is poured into the eyes in opacity of the cornea.[3] The following compound powder is applied to chancres. Take of mercury, sulphur, sulphate of copper, cinnabar, and sulphate of iron, equal parts, powder and mix. This composition may be used in the form of powder or paste.

TIN.

Sans. वङ्ग, *Vanga. Vern. Ráng.*

TIN, though not indigenous to India, has been known from a very ancient period, and is mentioned by Susruta. Dr. Royle

भाग करीषेण पुटितं भस्मशोभनम्। योजितं ग्रहणीगुल्मक्षयकुष्ठप्रमेहजित्॥

1 गर्भविलासरसः। रस गन्धकतुत्थञ्च त्र्यहं जम्बीरमर्द्दितम्। द्विजीरकं त्रिकटुना देयं गुञ्जाचतुष्टयम्। गर्भिण्याः सूतविष्टम्भ ज्वराजीर्णेषु केवलम्॥

रसेन्द्रसारसंग्रहः

2 व्रणविशोधने। कुष्ठं त्रिवृत्तिलादन्तीमागध्यः सैन्धवं मधु। रजनी त्रिफला तुत्थं हितं व्रणविशोधनम्॥ चक्रः

3 चक्षुःरोगे। तुत्थकं वारिणायुक्तं शुक्लं हन्त्यक्षिपूरणात्॥ चक्रः।

observed "But the Hindoos like the Egyptians have employed tin for various purposes from very ancient times. And though there is no proof of its being found in the present day in the peninsula of India yet it is abundant on the opposite coast of the Bay of Bengal, as in Burma, Tenasserim, Junkseylon and Malacca. There must in very ancient times have been a trade between India and these places."

Tin is purified by melting it over the fire and pouring the melted fluid into the milky juice of *Calotropis gigantea* (*arka*). It is prepared for medicinal use by melting it in an iron cup, adding to it one-fourth part of its weight of *yavakshára* (impure carbonate of potash) and powdered tamarind shells, and agitating with an iron rod till the mass is reduced to a fine powder. It is then washed in cold water and dried over a gentle fire. The resulting product is a greyish white powder consisting chemically of oxide of tin with some impurities. It is chiefly used in urinary disorders in a variety of forms. Thus the simple powder may be given in four-grain dose every morning with honey, or one of the following preparations may be used.

Trinetra rasa.[1] Take of prepared tin, mercury and sulphur equal parts, rub them together in an iron mortar and soak seven times respectively in the juice of *Cynodon dactylon* (*durvá*) and the decoctions of liquorice root, gum of *Bombax Malabaricum* (*Mocharasa*), and *Tribulus terrestris* (*gokshura*). Then roast in a covered crucible, again soak in the above mentioned fluid medicines and make into four-grain pills. This medicine is given with a decoction in milk of the above named vegetable drugs, in painful micturition.

Vangesvara rasa.[2] Take of the preparation of mercury called

1 त्रिनेत्ररसः। वङ्गं सूतं गन्धकं भावयित्वा लौहपात्रे मर्द्दयेदेकवक्रम्। दूर्व्वायष्टी शाल्मलीगोक्षुरैस्तु मुषामध्ये भूधरे पाचयित्वा। तत्तद्द्रवैर्भावयित्वा-स्ववल्लं दद्याच्छीतं पायसं वक्ष्यमाणम्। दूर्व्वायष्टी शाल्मलीवल्कतुल्यैर्दुग्धैः कुर्य्यात् पायसं तद्ददीत। प्रातःकालेऽशीत पानीयपानात् मूत्रे जातेऽस्मात् सुखी-चंक्रमेण॥ रसेन्द्रसारसंग्रहः।

2 वङ्गेश्वरः। रसभस्मसमायुक्तं वङ्गभस्म प्रकल्पयेत्। अस्य माषद्वयं हन्ति प्रमेहान् क्षौद्रसंयुतम्। रसेन्द्रसारसंग्रहः।

Rasasindura, and of prepared tin, equal parts and mix. Dose about four grains with honey in urinary diseases and diabetes.

Vrihat Vangesvara rasa.[1] Take of prepared tin, mercury, silver and talc, sulphur and camphor each two tolas, prepared gold and pearls, each half a tola, mix them together, soak the mixture in the juice of *Eclipta prostrata* (*kesarájá*), and make into four-grain-pills. This medicine is said to cure all sorts of urinary diseases, and to act as an alterative tonic. It is given in diabetes with the juice of the ripe fruit of *Ficus glomerata* (*udumbara*).

Svarnavanga.[2] Take of mercury, sulphur and tin, equal parts, and rub them together, then take sal-ammoniac in quantity equal to all the above ingredients and rub together in a mortar. Introduce the mixture in a glass bottle and expose to heat in a sand-bath. The resulting powder called *Svarna Vanga* or golden preparation of tin has a beautiful golden lustre and flaky texture. It is given in urinary complaints in doses of five to ten grains with honey and the juice of emblic myrobalans. This preparation is the bisulphuret of tin or mosaic gold "used in the arts as a bronze powder especially for the manufacture of paper hangings." It is noticed by Pereira. The Sanscrit text for its preparation quoted below, is taken from a manuscript compilation in the possession of Kavi-

---

1 वृहद्वङ्गेश्वरः। वङ्गभस्मरसं गन्धं रौप्यं कर्पूरमभ्रकम्। कर्षं कर्षं मानमेषां मुक्ताद्धं हेममौक्तिकम्। केशराजरसैर्भाव्यं द्विगुञ्जाफलमानतः। वृहद्वङ्गेश्वरोनाम सोमरोगं निहन्त्यलम्। बहुमूत्रं बहुविधं मूत्रमेहं व्यपोहति। मूत्रातीसारकृच्छ्रञ्च चीणानां पुष्टिवर्द्धनम्। ओजस्तेजस्करं स्त्रीषु सम्यक्चापि वृषायते। बलवर्णकरं रुच्यं शुक्रसञ्जनकं परम्। छागं वा यदि वा गव्यं पयो वा दधिनिर्म्मितं अनुपानं प्रयोक्तव्यं बुध्वा दोषगतिं भिषक्। दद्यात् बालेच प्रौढ़े च सेवयेच्च रसायनम्॥ भैषज्यरत्नावली।

2 स्वर्णवङ्गः। सूतेन मर्द्दितं वङ्गो गन्धकेन सुकज्जली। नरसारेण तत् पश्चात् सर्व्वतुल्येन खल्लयेत्। पश्चात् तं वालुका यन्त्रे काच कूप्याम् निधापयेत्। पाकं कुर्य्याद्भिषक प्राप्य स्वर्णवर्ण्णं यदा भवेत्। तदासिद्धं विजानियात् सर्व्वमेहेषु योजयेत्। वातिकं पैत्तिकं चैव श्लैष्मिकं सान्निपातिकं। सर्व्वव्याधि विनाशाय महादेवेन निर्म्मितः॥

raja Benod Lal Sen. It is evidently a recent innovation if not an imitation of the European preparation.

ZINC.

Sans. यशद्, *Yasada. Vern. Dastá.*

Zinc is not mentioned by the older writers, such as Susruta, nor does it enter into the composition of many prescriptions. The Bhávaprakása mentions it in the chapter on metallic preparations, and directs it to be purified and reduced to powder in the same way as tin. It is said to be useful in eye diseases, urinary disorders, anæmia and asthma.

Kharpara. This mineral is mentioned in most works. It enters into the composition of a number of prescriptions both for internal and external use. The article used under this name by the physicians of Upper India is a sort of calamine or zinc ore. Most of the physicians in Bengal are not acquainted with this ore, and substitute zinc for *kharpara*, that is, they consider *kharpara* as a mere synonym of zinc or *yasada.* They accordingly direct that *kharpara* should be reduced to powder by being melted over a fire and rubbed with rock salt. Zinc thus prepared is a fine yellowish grey powder consisting of carbonate of zinc mixed with chloride of sodium. In the works of the physicians of Upper India, this preparation is not described. There they use the zinc ore, which does not dissolve on the application of heat. It is simply purified by being boiled in cow's urine or soaked in lemon juice and then powdered. The Bengali physicians who substitute zinc for *kharpara* are evidently wrong, for the description of some of the preparations of this drug, as for example of the collyrium mentioned below, can not apply to metallic zinc.

Kharpara, as sold by Hindustani medicine vendors, occurs in greyish or greyish black porous earthy masses composed of agglutinated granules. On chemical analysis it was found to consist of carbonate and silicate of zinc with traces of other metals as iron, baryta, etc. *Kharpara* is described as tonic and alterative and useful in skin diseases, fevers etc. It is also much used as a collyrium in eye diseases. Dose, grains six to twelve.

Vasanta málati rasa. Take of leaf gold one part, pearls two parts, cinnabar three parts, black pepper four parts, purified *kharpara* eight parts, and rub them together. Then add some butter and lemon juice and rub together till intimately mixed and no separate particles are visible. Dose two to four grains with honey and long pepper. This medicine is much used by Up-country physicians in chronic fever, secondary syphilis, chronic gonorrhœa, leucorrhœa etc.[1]

A collyrium is prepared as follows. Rub some *kharpara* in a stone mortar with water, take the dissolved watery portion, rejecting any solid particles that may have subsided to the bottom. Evaporate this solution, powder the residue and soak it three times in a decoction of the three myrobalans. When dry add one tenth part of powdered camphor and mix intimately. This collyrium is said to be useful in various sorts of eye diseases.[2]

LEAD.

Sans. सीसक, *Sisaka. Vern. Sisá.*

Lead is produced abundantly in India in the shape of the sulphide called galena. Galena is sold in the bazars under the name of *surma*, and is much used by the natives as a collyrium.

---

1 सुवर्णं मुक्ता दरद मरिचं भागवृद्ध्या प्रदिष्टं खर्परात्ष्टौ प्रथम मखिलं मर्द्दयेत् म्रक्षणेन। यावत् स्नेहो व्रजति विलयं निम्बनीरेण तावत् गुञ्जाद्वन्द्वं मधुचपलया मालतीप्राग्वसन्ता॥ सेवितेयं हरेत्तूर्णं जीर्णञ्च विषमज्वरम्। व्याधीनन्यांश्च कासादीन् प्रदीप्तं कुरुते ऽनलम्। वैद्यविनोदः।

2 खर्परवर्त्तिः। शिलायां रसकं पिष्टा सम्यगाप्लाव्य वारिणा। गृह्णीयात् तज्जलं सर्व्वं त्यजेच्चूर्णं मधोगतम्। शुष्कञ्च तज्जलं सर्व्वं पर्पटी सन्निभं भवेत्। विचूर्ण्य भावयेत् सम्यक् त्रिवेलं त्रिफलारसैः। कर्पूरस्य रजस्तत्र दशमांशेन निक्षिपेत्। अञ्जयेत् नयनेतेन सर्व्वदोषहरं हितम्। सर्व्वरोगहरं चूर्णम् चक्षुषः सुखकारि च॥ शार्ङ्गधरः।

The red oxide of lead, or minium, was manufactured by the ancient Hindoos. It is known by the name of *sindura*, and is used by all married Hindu women as a paint for the forehead. Litharge or massicot, called *murdasang* in Hindustani, has no proper Sanskrit name and was unknown to the ancients. In some recent compilations it is occasionally introduced as a component of some compound preparations. Carbonate of lead, called *saffedá*, now common in the bazars and extensively used as a paint, is not mentioned by the ancient writers. The name *saffedá* is of Persian origin, and the article itself is an imported one.

Lead is purified and reduced to powder in the same way as tin. Lead thus prepared is a gritty powder of a greyish red colour. Chemically it is an impure carbonate of lead. Its properties are said to be similar to those of tin. It is seldom used internally except as a component of compound medicines containing a number of other metals. A probe made of lead is preferred for applying collyria to the eyelids.

The red oxide of lead, called *sindura*, is used externally in eruptive skin diseases in the form of ointment or liniment. Thus *sindura* and powdered black pepper mixed with butter is recommended to be applied in chronic eczema. An oil called *Sindurádya taila*[1] is thus prepared. Take of mustard oil one seer, water four seers, minium four tolás and cumin seeds eight tolás. Boil together in the usual way. This oil is used in eczema and other eruptive skin diseases.

GALENA.

Sans. अञ्जन, *Anjana.* सौविराञ्जन, *Sauviránjana.*

Galena or sulphide of lead is called *anjana* or *sauviránjana* in Sanskrit, and *krishna surmá* in Vernacular. It is called *anjana*, which literally means collyrium or medicine for the eyes, from the

1 सिन्दुराद्यं तैलम् । सिन्दुरार्द्धपलं पिष्ट्वा जीरकस्य पलं तथा । कटुतैलात् पचेन्मानीं सद्यः पामाहरं परम् ॥ चक्रः ॥

circumstance of its being considered the best application or cosmetic for them. The other varieties of *anjana* mentioned are *srotonjana*, *pushpánjana* and *rasánjana*.

सौवीराञ्जन *Sauviránjana* is said to be obtained from the mountains of Sauvira, a country along the Indus, whence it derives its name. The article supplied under its vernacular name *surma* is the sulphide of lead ore. *Surmá* is usually translated as sulphide of antimony, but I have not been able to obtain a single specimen of the antimonial ore from the shops of Calcutta and of some other towns. The sulphide of antimony occurs in fine streaky, fibrous, crystalline masses of a radiated texture. The lead ore on the contrary, occurs in cubic masses destitute of rays and is tabular in its crystalline arrangement.

स्रोतोञ्जन *Srotonjana* is described as of white colour, and is said to be produced in the bed of the Jamuná and other rivers. It is called *saffed surmá* in the vernacular, and the article supplied under this name by Hindustani medicine vendors is calcareous or Iceland spar. It is used as a collyrium for the eyes, but is considered inferior to the black *surmá* or galena.

पुष्पाञ्जन *Pushpánjana* is described as an alkaline substance. I have not met with any vernacular translation of this word, nor with any person who could identify or supply the drug. Wilson, in his Sanskrit-English Dictionary, translates the term as calx of brass, but I know not on what authority.[1]

रसाञ्जन *Rasánjana* is the extract of the wood of *Berberis Asiatica* called *rasot* in the vernacular. It will be noticed in its place in the Vegetable Materia Medica.

Sauviránjana or galena is chiefly used as a cosmetic for the eyes, and is supposed to strengthen these organs, improve their appearance and preserve them from disease. It enters into the composition

1 सौवीराञ्जनं कृष्णं कालनीलं सुवीरजम्। स्रोतोञ्जनं तु स्रोतोजं नदीजं यामुनं वरम्। सौवीरं स्याद्धि मधुरं चक्षुष्यं कफवातजित्॥ सिध्माक्षयास्रनुच्छीतं स्रोतोञ्जनमपीदृशम्॥ पुष्पाञ्जनं पुष्पकेतु रीतिजं कुसुमाञ्जनम्। पुष्पाञ्जनं क्षारसूक्ष्मं काचार्मपटलापहम्॥ मदनपालः।

of some collyria for eye diseases. Galena, heated over a fire and cooled in a decoction of the three myrobalans for seven times in succession, is rubbed with human milk and used in various eye diseases.[1] Another collyrium prepared with lead is as follows. To one part of purified and melted lead, add an equal portion of mercury and two parts of galena, rub them all together and reduce to powder. Now add camphor, equal in weight to one-tenth part of the mass and mix intimately. This preparation is said to be useful in eye diseases.[2] From the composition and uses of lead and galena above described it would seem that by the term *surmá* the Hindus meant sulphide of lead, and not sulphide of antimony as is generally supposed.

BELL METAL AND BRASS.

Bell metal, (कांस, *Kánsa*), as used in medicine, is an alloy of copper and tin. Brass, (पित्तल, *Pittala*) is an alloy of copper and zinc. They are sometimes used in combination with other metals, and are regarded as tonic and alterative. They are purified and reduced to powder in the same way as copper. The following is an example of a preparation containing bell metal.

Nityánanda rasa.[3] Take of mercury, prepared copper, iron, bell-metal and tin, purified orpiment, sulphate of copper and calcined

---

1 अग्नितप्तञ्च सौवीरं निषिञ्चेत् त्रिफलारसैः। सप्तवेलन्तथास्तन्यैः स्त्रीणां सिक्तं विचूर्णितम्। अञ्जयेन्नयनेतेन प्रत्यहञ्चक्षुषोर्हितम्। सर्वानक्षिविकारांस्तु हन्यादेतन्नसंशयः॥ शार्ङ्गधरः।

2 शुद्धे नागे द्रुते तुल्यं शुद्धं सूतं विनिक्षिपेत्। कृष्णाञ्जनं तयोस्तुल्यं सर्वमेकत्र चूर्णयेत्। दशमांशेन कर्पूरं तस्मिन् चूर्णे प्रदापयेत्। एतत् प्रत्यञ्जनं नेत्रगदाजिन्नयनामृतम्। शार्ङ्गधरः।

3 नित्यानन्दरसः। हिङ्गुलात् सम्भवं सूतं गन्धकं मृततामकम्। कांस्यं वङ्गं हरितालं तुत्थं शङ्खं वराटकम्। त्रिकटु त्रिफलालौहं विडङ्गं पटुपञ्चकम्। चविकापिप्पलीमूलं हवुषाच वचातथा। शटीपाठादेवदारु एलाच

conch-shell and couries, sulphur, ginger, long pepper and black pepper, the three myrobalans, *baberung* seeds, the five salts, namely, rock, sun-dried sea, black, *sonchál* and Sambar Lake salts, *Chavica officinarum(chavika)*, long pepper root, *havusa* (an aromatic substance), *Acorus Calamus* (*vacha*), *Curcuma zedoaria* (*sati*), *Stephania hernandifolia* (*páthá*), *Pinus deodara*, cardamoms, seeds of *Argyreia speciosa (vridhya dàraka)* each two tolás, rub together with the juice or decoction of chebulic myrobalans and make into ten-grain pills. They are given in hydrocele and elephantiasis of the scrotum. The remark that, when a disease has a long list of drugs for curing it, one may take it for an incurable one, is well exemplified in this medicine for elephantiasis of the scrotum.

MICA OR TALC.

Sans. अभ्र *Abhra.*

FOUR varieties of talc are described by Sanskrit writers, namely, white, red, yellow and black. Of these the white variety is used as a substitute for glass in making lanterns etc, and the black variety called *vajrábhra* is used in medicine. It is of a black colour, hard and heavy, and generally known by the name of *krishnábhra* or *sheábhra*.

Talc is purified in the following manner. It is first heated and washed in milk. The plates are then separated and soaked in the juice of *Amaranthus polygamus* (*tandulia*) and *kánjika* for eight days. Talc thus purified is reduced to powder by being

---

वृद्धदारकम्। एतानि समभागानि संचूर्ण्य वटिकां कुरु। हरीतकीरसं दत्वा पञ्चगुञ्जामितां शुभाम्। एकैकां खादयेन्नित्यं शीतलञ्च जलं पिवेत्। श्लीपदं कफवातोत्थं रक्तमांसाश्रितञ्च यत्। मेदोगतं धातुगतं हन्त्यवश्यं न संशयः। अर्व्वुदं गण्डमालाञ्च अन्त्रवृद्धिं चिरन्तनीम्। वातवृद्धिं पित्तवृद्धिं श्लेष्मवृद्धिं निहन्ति च। अग्निवृद्धिं करोत्येष बलवर्णकरः परः। श्रीमद्गहननाथेन निर्म्मितो विश्वसम्पदे। नित्यानन्द रसो नाम यथोक्तः श्लीपदे गदे॥

रसेन्द्रसारसंग्रहः।

rubbed with paddy within a thick piece of cloth, when the powdered talc passes through the pores of the cloth in fine particles and is collected for use. Talc, thus reduced to powder, is called *dhányábhraka.* It is prepared for medicinal use by being mixed with cow's urine and exposed to a high degree of heat within a closed crucible, repeatedly for a hundred times. Sometimes the process is said to be repeated a thousand times. When this is the case, the preparation is called *sahasra putita abhra* and sold at high price (eight rupees per tolá). It is considered to be of superior efficacy. Prepared talc is a powder of brick-dust colour and a saline, earthy taste. Chemically it consists of silicate of magnesia with iron in excess. It is considered tonic and aphrodisiac and is used in combination with iron in anæmia, jaundice, chronic diarrhoea and dysentery, chronic fever, enlarged spleen, urinary diseases, impotence etc. Its efficacy is said to be increased by combination with iron. Dose, grains six to twelve.

Jvaràsani rasa.[1] Take of mercury, sulphur, rock salt, aconite and copper, one part each, prepared iron and talc, five parts each, rub together with the juice of *Vitex Negundo* leaves, then add one part of black pepper and make into two-grain pills. They are administered with the juice of betle leaves in chronic fever and enlarged spleen.

Agnikumára rasa.[2] Take of mercury, sulphur, borax, iron,

---

1 ज्वराशनि रसः। रसं गन्धं सैन्धवञ्च विषं ताम्रं समं समम्। सर्व्वं चूर्णसमं लौहं तद्वत् शुद्धमभ्रकम्। लौहे च लौहदण्डेन निर्गुण्डीस्वरसेन च। मर्द्दयेद् यत्नतः पश्चात् मरिचं सुनतुल्यकम्। नागवल्लीदलेनैव दातव्यं रक्तिसम्मितम्। सर्व्वज्वरहरः श्रेष्ठः ज्वरान् हन्ति सुदारुणान्। कासं श्वासं महाघोरं विषमाख्यं ज्वरं वमिम्। धातुस्थं प्रबलं दाहं ज्वरदोषं चिरोद्भवम्। यकृद्गुल्मोदरं प्लीह श्वयथुञ्च विनाशयेत्॥ भैषज्यरत्नावली।

2 अग्निकुमार रसः। रसं गन्धं विषं व्योषं टङ्कणं लौहभस्मकम्। अजमोदाऽहिफेणञ्च सर्व्वतुल्यं मृताभ्रकम्। चित्रकत्वक्कषायेण मर्द्दयेद्याममात्रकम्। मरिचाभां वटीं खादेदजीर्णे ग्रहणीं तथा। नाशयेन्नात्र सन्देहो गुह्यमेतच्चिकित्सितम्॥ भैषज्यरत्नावली।

aconite, ginger, long pepper, black pepper, *ajowan* and opium each one part, prepared talc ten parts, rub together for three hours with the decoction of *Plumbago rosea* (*rakta chitraka*) and make into pills of the size of black peppers. This preparation is used in chronic diarrhoea and indigestion.

Sulachanámritábhra.[1] Take of prepared talc eight tolás, rub it with eight tolás each of the fresh juice or decoction of the following drugs, namely, pulp of *Ziziphus Jujuba* (*kola*), *Chavica officinarum* (*chaviká*), root of *Andropogon muricatus* (*usira*), *pomegranate* fruit, lemon juice, emblic myrobalan and *Oxlais corniculata* (*amlaloniká*), and make into pills about six grains each. This medicine is used in loss of appetite, disinclination for food, dyspepsia, vomiting, urinary diseases, anasarca and debility. It is tonic, alterative and aphrodisiac. The preparation called *Kandarpa kumárábhra* is very similar to the above in composition. In disorders of the urine the following called *Harisankara rasa*[2] in used. Soak some prepared talc in the juice of emblic myrobalans seven times in the course of a week and make into two-grain pills.

Arjunábhra.[3] In heart disease talc is used with the juice of the *arjuna* bark which last is considered a specific for this complaint. *Arjunbhra* is prepared by soaking some prepared talc in the juice of the bark of *Terminalia Arjuna*, seven times, and dividing

---

1 सुलोचनामृताभ्रम्। पलं सुजीर्णं गगणन्तु वज्रकं तेजोवती कोल सुशीरदाड़िमम्। धात्र्यम्ललोनीरुचकं पृथक्रसैः पलोन्मितैर्मर्द्दितमेव सेवितम्। अरोचकं वातकफत्रिदोषजं पित्तोद्भवं गन्धससुद्भवं नृणाम्। कासं स्वराघात सुरोग्यहं रुजं श्वासं बलासं यकृत्भगन्दरम्। प्लीहाग्निमान्द्यं श्वयथुं समीरणं मेहं भ्रमं कुष्ठमसृग्दरक्रमीन्। शूलाम्लपित्तं क्षयरोगसुद्गतं स रक्तपित्तं वमिदाहमश्मरीम्। निहन्ति चार्शांसि सुलोचनामृतं बलप्रदं वृष्यमिदं रसायनम्। रसेन्द्रसारसंग्रहः।

2 हरिशङ्कर रसः। मृताभ्रं मामलकजैः सप्ताहं भावयेत् रजः। हरिशङ्करः सञ्ज्ञः स्यात् भुक्तः सर्वप्रमेहजित्। रसेन्द्रसारसंग्रहः।

3 अर्ज्जुनाभ्रं। सप्तधा पुटितैः सिद्धं वज्राभ्रमर्ज्जुनत्वचः। सत्त्वैर्विमर्द्दितं सप्तदिनं खल्ले विशोषितम्। छायाशुष्कात्वटीकार्य्या नाम्नेदमर्ज्जुना-

the mass into two-grain pills. In phthisis and chronic bronchitis the following called *Sringárábhra*[1] is used. Take of prepared talc sixteen tolás, camphor, cardamoms, nutmegs, mace, cloves, root of *Pavonia odorata* (*bàlá*), *Pothos officinalis* (*gajapippuli*), leaves called *tejpatra*, *jatamansi* root, leaves of *Pinus Webbiana* (*tálisapatra*), cinnamon, flowers of *Mesua ferrea* (*nágakesara*), root of *Aplotaxis auriculata* (*kushtha*), flowers of *Woodfordia Flori bunda* (*dhátaki*) and purified sulphur, each one tolá, mercury half a tolá. Powder the ingredients, mix and make into four-grain pills with water. One pill at a time is to be chewed with betle leaves and ginger, and a little water is to be taken afterwards. The pills may be taken three or four times daily. The diet should consist of *ghee*, milk and broth.

Mohàlakshmi bilásarasa.[2] This preparation is used as an alterative tonic and aphrodisiac in general debility, impotence etc. To prepare it, take of talc eight tolás, mercury four tolás, sulphur four tolás, tin two tolás, silver one tolá, orpiment one tolá, copper half a tolá, gold half a tola, camphor, nutmegs and mace, each four tolás, seeds of *Argyreia speciosa* (*bridhadáraka*) and of *datura*, two tolás each. Mix together, rub with the juice of betle leaves and

---

भ्रकम्। हृद्रोगं सर्व्वशूलार्शो हृल्लासच्छर्द्यरोचकान्। अतिसारं मन्दमग्निं रक्तपित्तं क्षतक्षयम्। शोथोदराम्लपित्तं विषमज्वरमेव च। हन्त्यन्यानपिरोगांश्च बल्यं वृष्यं रसायनम्। अनुपानं पिबेच्चात्र हृद्रोगे च कफात्मके।

रसेन्द्रसारसंग्रहः।

1 शृङ्गाराभ्रम्। शुद्धं कृष्णाभ्रचूर्णं द्विपलपरिमितं शाणमानं यदन्यत्। कर्पूरं जातीकोषं सजलमिभकनातेजपत्रं लवङ्गम्। मांसीतालीशचोचेगजकुसुमगदं धातकीचेति तुल्यं। एलाजातीफलाख्यं स्थितितलविभिनाशुद्धगन्धाश्मकोलं। कोलार्द्धं पारदस्य प्रतिपदविहितं पिष्टमेकत्रमिश्रं। पानीयेनैव कार्य्यः परिणतचनकस्विन्नतुल्यास्तवट्यः। प्रातः खाद्यास्ततस्तु तदनु खलु कियत् शृङ्गवेरं सपर्णं। पानीयं पीतमन्तर्भुवमपहरति क्षिप्रमेतान् विकारान्। कोष्ठेदुष्टाग्निजातान् ज्वरमुदररुजां राजयक्ष्मक्षयञ्च। कासं श्वासं सशोथं नयनपरिभवं मेहमेदोविकारान्।

सारकौमुदी।

2 महालक्ष्मीविलासः। पलं कृष्णाभ्रचूर्णस्य तदर्द्धं गन्धपारदं। वङ्गभस्म तदर्द्धञ्च तदर्द्धं तारकस्य च। तत् समं हरितालञ्च तदर्द्धं ताम्रभस्मकं। रसतुल्यं कर्पूरञ्च

make into pills of about six grains each. Another preparation of composition similar to the above is called *Manmathábhra rasa.* It is, as its name implies, intended for the votaries of Cupid.

Galitakushthári rasa.[1] Take of mercury, sulphur, prepared copper and iron, bdellium, plumbago root, *silájatu*, nux vomica, and the three myrobalans, each one part, prepared talc and the seeds of *Pongamia glabra* (*karanja*), four parts each, rub together with honey and *ghee*, and preserve in an earthen pot smeared with *ghee.* Dose about a drachm. It is given in leprosy with ulceration of the toes and fingers. The diet should consist of fine rice, milk, sugar and honey. The patient must live apart from his wife.

ALUM.

Sans. स्फटिकारि *Sphatikári.*

Alum is prepared from alum shale in the Punjab and Behar It is not mentioned by Susruta, in his list of metallics, but later writers give its synonyms and uses. It is described as an astringent, and as useful in leucorrhœa, strangury, vomiting, ulcers, white leprosy, eye diseases etc. It enters into the composition of several applications to the eye in combination with *rusot*, opium etc, for which see *Berberis Asiatica.* It is seldom used internally.

जातीकोषफलं तथा । वृद्धदारकवीजञ्च वीजं स्वर्णफलस्य च । प्रत्येकान् कार्षिकान् भागान् मृतस्वर्णञ्च शाणकम् । नागवल्लीरसैः पिष्ट्वा त्रिगुञ्जाफलमानतः । वटीकार्य्यानुपानञ्च व्याधिं वीक्ष्य प्रयोजयेत् । निहन्ति सन्निपातोत्थान् गदान् घोरान् सुदारुणान् । प्रोक्तः प्रयोगराजोयं अगस्त्येन महात्मना । महालक्ष्मीविलासोयं वासुदेवो जगद्गुरुः । अस्य प्रसादाद् भगवान् लक्ष्म नारीषु वल्लभः ।

रसेन्द्रसारसंग्रहः ।

1 गलितकुष्ठारि रसः ! रसोवलिस्ताम्रमयः पुरोऽग्निशिलाजतु स्याद्विषतिन्दुकञ्च । वराच तुल्यं गगणं करञ्जवीजं पृथक् भागचतुष्टयञ्च । संमर्द्य सर्वं मधुनाज्यतेन घृतस्थपात्रे निहितं प्रयत्नात् । कर्षं भजेत् प्रत्यहमस्य पथ्यं शाल्योदनं दुग्ध मधुत्रयञ्च । विशीर्णकर्णाङ्गुलिनासिकोऽपि भवेदनेन स्मरतुल्यमूर्त्तिः । दारा परित्याग इह प्रदिष्टो जलौदनं तत्र निवद्धमूले ॥ भाव प्रकाशः ।

BORAX

Sans. टङ्कण, *Tankana. Vern. Sohágá.*

BORAX was known to the ancient Hindus from a very remote period, and is mentioned by Susruta. It is brought from Thibet across the Himalaya, and from Nepal, and is used in medicine as well as in the arts. It is purified for medicinal use by being steeped for a night in *kánjika,* and dried in the sun. Borax is said to be useful in loss of appetite, painful dyspepsia, cough, asthma, skin diseases and diarrhœa. It is also used for procuring abortion and promoting uterine contractions. Borax enters into the composition of numerous formulæ for dyspepsia, such as the *Amritakalpa rasa, Tankanádi vati* etc.

Amirtakalpa rasa.[1] Take of mercury, sulphur and aconite, one part each, borax three parts, soak them for three days in the juice of *Wedelia calendulacea* (*bhringarája*) and make into two-grain pills. This medicine is said to be useful in loss of appetite, indigestion and dyspepsia. *Tankanádi vati* contains the above ingredients with the addition of ginger and black pepper, all in equal parts.

Chandrámrita rasa.[2] Take of the three myrobalans, ginger, long pepper and black pepper, *Chavica officinarum* (*chaviká*), coriander, cumin seeds and rock salt, each one tolá, and rub them together with goat's milk. Then add mercury, sulphur and iron, each two tolás, borax eight tolás and black pepper four tolás, all in fine powder, mix and make into pills or boluses about eighteen grains each. They are administered with goat's milk in chronic bronchitis and various sorts of cough with copious expectoration. Along with

---

1 अमृतकल्परसः। पारदं गन्धकञ्चैव समानौ कज्जलीकृतौ। तयोरर्द्धं विषं शुद्धं तत् समं टङ्कणं भवेत्। भृङ्गराज द्रवैर्भाव्यं त्रिदिनं यत्नतः पुनः। गुञ्जाप्रमाणा वटिका कर्त्तव्या भिषजांवरैः। वटीद्वयं हरेच्छूलं अग्निमान्द्यं सुनिश्चितं। अजीर्णं जरयत्याशु धातुपुष्टिं करोति च। नाना व्याधि हराचेयं वटी गुरुवचो यथा। अनुपानविशेषेण सम्यग् गुणकरी भवेत्॥ रसेन्द्रसारसंग्रहः।

2 चन्द्रामृतरसः। त्रिफला त्रिकटु चव्यं धान्यं जीरकं सैन्धवम्। प्रत्येकं तोलकं ग्राह्यं छागीदुग्धेन पेषयेत्। रसगन्धक लौहानि प्रत्येकं कार्षिकानि च। टङ्कणस्य

these pills a decoction made of *gulancha*, *Adhatoda vasica* (*vásaka*), *Clerodendron Siphonanthus* (*brahmayashti*), *Cyperus rotundus* (*mustaka*), and *Solanum Jacquinii* (*kantakári*) should be administered.

Borax enters into the composition of several prescriptions for diarrhœa, along with opium, such as the *Grahanikapáta rasa* and *Nripavallava rasa*, for which see Opium.

A mixture of equal parts of borax, long pepper and *baberung* seeds is given for five days, at the menstrual periods for the purpose of preventing conception.[1] It is also used for procuring abortion and inducing labour pains. Borax rubbed into a paste with the root of *Vallaris dichotoma* (*bhadravalli*) is applied to diseased nails.

LIME.

Sans. शङ्खभस्म, *Sankha bhasma.* चूर्ण, *Churna.*

Several sorts of lime are used in Hindu medicine. Thus we have lime from limestone called *churna*. Then we have lime from calcined cowries, conch-shells, bivalve-shells and snail-shells, called respectively, *Kapardaka bhasma*, *Sankha bhasma*, *Sukti bhasma*, and *Sambuka bhasma*. These shells are purified by being soaked in lemon juice, and are prepared for use by being calcined within covered crucibles. Lime is used internally in dyspepsia, enlarged spleen and other enlargements in the abdomen, and externally as a caustic. Lime enters into the composition of a great many prescriptions for different sorts of dyspepsia. The following are a few examples.

पलंदत्वा मरिचस्य पलार्द्धकं। नवगुञ्जा प्रमाणेन वटिकां कारयेद् भिषक्। एकैकां वटिकां खादेत् रक्तोत्पल जलप्लुताम्। नीलोत्पल रसैर्व्वापि कुलत्थस्य रसेन वा। छागीक्षीरेण मण्डेन केशराजरसेन वा। निहन्ति विविधं कासं यक्ष्माणमपि दारुणम्। वासा गुडूचिका भार्गीमुस्तकं कण्टकारिका। समभागं कृतं क्वाथं प्रत्यहं भक्षयेदनु॥ रसेन्द्रसारसंग्रहः।

1 पिप्पली विडङ्ग टङ्कण समचूर्णं या पिबेत् पयसा। ऋतु समये नहि तस्याः गर्भः सञ्जायते क्वापि॥ भावः प्रकाशः।

Amrita vati.[1] Take of calcined cowries five parts, aconite two parts, black pepper nine parts, and make into two-grain pills. They are used in loss of appetite and indigestion.

Agnikumára rasa.[2] Take of borax, mercury and sulphur, each one tolá, aconite, calcined cowries and conch-shells, each three tolás, black pepper eight tolás, rub them together for twelve hours with lime juice and make into twelve-grain pills. This medicine is said to increase the appetite and cure indigestion. Calcined conch-shell in half a drachm doses is recommended to be taken with lime juice in enlarged spleen.[3]

Lime is used in various combinations as a caustic for different diseases. Thus a mixture of conch-shell lime, impure carbonate of soda (*sarjiká*) and the ashes of *Raphanus sativus* (*mulaka*), is applied to tumours and enlarged glands.[4] A mixture of lime, carbonate of soda, sulphate of copper and borax is applied as a caustic to tumours and warts. Lime enters into the composition of depilatories. Thus take of conch-shell lime three tolás, orpiment and the ashes of *Butea frondosa* (*palása*), one tolá each, and rub them together with the juice of plantain stalks or of *Calotropis gigantea* (*arka*). This paste is applied seven times to the part from which the hair is to be removed.[5]

---

1 अमृतवटी । अमृतवराटक मरिचैर्द्विपञ्चनवभागिकैः क्रमशः । वटिका-गुञ्जमानाकफपित्ताग्निमान्द्यहारिणी । भैषज्यरत्नावली ।

2 अग्निकुमारोरसः । रसेन्द्रगन्धौ सहटङ्कणेन समं विषं योज्य मिह-त्रिभागम् । कपर्द्दशङ्खाविह नेत्रभागौ मरिच मात्राष्टगुणं प्रदेयम् । सुपक्व-जम्बीररसेनघृष्टः सिद्धो भवेदग्नि कुमारएषः । विसूचिकाजीर्णसमीरणार्त्तौ दद्यात् द्विवल्लं ग्रहणी गदे च । भैषज्यरत्नावली ।

3 रसेन जम्बीरफलस्य शङ्खनाभिरजः पीतमवश्यमेव । शाणप्रमाणं शमये-दशेषं प्लीहामयं कूर्म्मसमानमाशु । भावप्रकाशः ।

4 सर्जिकामूलकक्षारः शङ्खचूर्णसमन्वितः । प्रलेपोविहितस्तीक्ष्णोहन्ति ग्रन्थ्यर्बुदादिकान् । चक्रदत्तः ।

5 तालकं शाणयुग्मं स्यात् षट्शाणं शङ्खचूर्णकम् । द्विशाणिकं पलाशस्य क्षारं दत्त्वा प्रमर्दयेत् । कदलीदण्डतोयेन रविपत्ररसेन वा । अस्यापि सप्तभिर्लेपै-र्लोम्नां शातनमुत्तमम् । शार्ङ्गधरः ।

CHLORIDE OF SODIUM.

Sans. लवण, *Lavana.*

SUSRUTA describes the following varieties of salts, VIZ., 1 *Sáindhava*, 2 *Sámudra*, 3 *Vit* or *Vid*, 4 *Sauvarchala*, 5 *Romaka*, 6 *Audbhida*, 7 *Gutiká*, 8 *Pánsuja*, also called *Ushasuta*. The first five in the above list generally pass by the name of *pancha lavana* or the five salts, and are often used in combination. The other varieties are rarely used in medicine.

सैन्धव *Saindhava* literally means produced in Sinde, or the country along the Indus. The term is applied to rock salt which is regarded as the best of salts. Three varieties of rock salt are recognized, VIZ., white, red and crystalline. The pure white crystalline salt is preferred for medicinal use. For alimentary purposes also, rock salt is considered superior to the other varieties. It is regarded as digestive, appetizing, sweet and agreeable, and is much used in dyspepsia and other abdominal diseases.

सामुद्र *Sámudra* literally means produced from the sea. The term is applied to sun-dried sea-salt, manufactured in the Madras Presidency. It is called *karkach* in the vernacular. Orthodox natives, who consider common salt as impure from the circumstance of its having undergone the process of boiling, and who take only rock salt, substitute *karkach* for rock salt, if the latter is not available. Sun-dried sea-salt is described as somewhat bitter and laxative. In other respects its properties are said to resemble those of rock salt.

विट्लवण. *Vit lavana* occurs in dark red shining granules somewhat resembling coarsely powdered lac in appearance. It has a mild, saline and somewhat nauseous taste. Dr. Fleming says "that the following process for making this salt was communicated by a native druggist to Mr. Turnbull at Mirzapore and was actually performed in his presence. Fifty six pounds of sambar salt are mixed with twenty ounces of dried *aonlás* (*emblic myrobalans.*) One fourth of these materials is put into a round earthen pot with a narrow mouth, which is put in a fire-place made of clay. The fire-place has a hole at the bottom for introducing the firewood. After the fire has been lighted about an hour, and the materials, in the pot, appear to be heated, the rest of the materials is added by degrees. The whole is then exposed to a strong red heat for about six hours. The fire is then allowed to die away, and the pot to cool; which upon being broken is found to contain about forty-eight pounds of *calanemuc* or *bitlaban*."*

Vit lavana, besides possessing the properties of salts in general, is said to be carminative and stomachic, and to be useful in enlarged spleen, dyspepsia, indigestion, bowel complaints, etc.

सौवर्चल *Sauvarchala* called *sonchal* or *kálánimak* in Hindustani is said to be aromatic, agreeable and digestive, and useful in the same sort of cases as *vitlavana.* It is described in the Report on Punjab Products as "a dark colored salt said to be made by dissolving common salt in a solution of "*sajimáti*" (crude soda) and evaporating it; this salt contains chloride of sodium, sulphate of soda, caustic soda and a little sulphate of sodium, but no carbonate of soda." *Sonchal* salt is not available in the drug shops of Calcutta. Some Bengali physicians give this name to a crystalline form of rock salt, but up-country physicians always translate *sauvarchala* as *sonchal* or *kálánimak.* The latter interpretation appears also to obtain in the Punjab where a specimen of *sonchal* salt from Ram Sing, a noted druggist, is said in the Report on Punjab Products, " to be a salt of the same kind as *kálánimak.*"

रोमक *Romaka,* also called **शाकम्बरी** *Sákambari,* is the salt produced from the Sambar Lake near Ajmere. The name *romaka* is said to be derived from a river called Rumá. It is obtained by the evaporation of salt water in the shape of clear rhomboidal crystals. It has a pungent taste, and is considered laxative and diuretic, in addition to possessing the other properties of salts. It is said to be the best and purest of evaporated salts.

औद्भिद *Audbhid,* that is, produced of itself from the earth, is the name applied to a salt produced as an efflorescence on *reh* lands. The salt is called *reha* or *kalar* in the vernacular. It consists principally of sulphate of soda with a little chloride of sodium, and is described as alkaline, bitter, pungent and nauseating. It is said to be so abundant in some parts of the Punjab as to render

* Asiatic Researches Vol. XI. Page 192.

the soil quite barren. Some physicians or rather writers substitute this article for *sambar* salt in the composition of *pancha lavana* or the five salts.

गुटिका *Gutiká.* This salt, mentioned by Susruta and some later writers, cannot be identified at present. In the treatise called *Dravyaguna* by Chakra Datta, his commentator Siva Dass says that the name *gutiká* is derived from the circumstance of the salt assuming a hard, granular or nodular shape from boiling. So that it is a sort of boiled salt. Susruta describes it as stomachic digestive and laxative.

पांशुज *Pánsuja* or *Ushasuta* literally means, salt manufactured from saline earth. *Pángá* or common salt, manufactured from earth impregnated with salt water, would come under this head.

Rock salt with warm water. is used as an emetic.[1] The different varieties of salt enter into the composition of a great many medicines for dyspepsia, indigestion, enlarged spleen and other tumours in the abdomen. The following are a few illustrations.

Nárikelakshára. [2] Take a cocoa-nut fruit full of water, make a hole in it and fill the cocoa-nut with rock salt, that is, dissolve the salt in its water. Then close the opening, cover the nut with a ayer of clay and roast it in a pit of fire. The salt thus roasted is esteemed as a valuable medicine in the form of dyspepsia which is attended with pain, two or three hours after meals. It is given with the addition of long pepper. Dose about a quarter tolá.

Bháskara lavana. [3] Take of *karkach* salt sixteen tolás, *sonchal* salt ten tolàs, black salt, rock salt, coriander, long pepper, long

---

1 वमनं त्वलसे पूर्व्वं लवणेनोष्णवारिणा चक्रदत्तः।

2 नारिकेलक्षारः। नारिकेलं स तोयञ्च लवणेन प्रपूरितम्। विपक्वमग्निना सम्यक् परिणामजशूलनुत्। वातिकं पैत्तिकञ्चैव श्लैष्मिकं सान्निपातिकम्।
चक्रदत्तः।

3 भास्करलवणचूर्णं। सामुद्रलवणं कार्य्यमष्टकर्षमितं बुधैः। पञ्चसौवर्च्चलं प्राह्यं विड़सैन्धवधान्यकम्। पिप्पलीपिप्पलीमूलं कृष्णजीरकपत्रकम्। नागकेशरं तालीशमम्लवेतसकं तथा। द्विकर्षमात्राण्येतानि प्रत्येकं कारयेद् बुधः। मरिचं जीरकं विश्वमेकैकं कर्षमात्रकम्। दाड़िमं स्यात्त्वचश्चैव त्वगेलाचार्द्धकार्षिके।

pepper root, leaves called *tejpatra,* seeds of *Nigella sativa* (*krishnajiraka*), leaves of *Pinus Webbiana* (*talisa patra*), flowers of *Mesua ferrea* (*nágakesara*), fruits of *Calamus fasciculatus* (*amlavetasa*), four tolás each, black pepper, cumin seeds and ginger, two tolás each, pomegranate seeds eight tolás, cinnamon and cardamoms one tolá each, powder, mix and soak seven times in lemon juice. Dose about a drachm with whey or wine, in enlarged spleen and other tumours in the abdomen, dyspepsia, loss of appetite, constipation etc. Rock salt is applied to opacities on the cornea, either singly or in combination with other drugs, as in the following. Take of the seeds of *Acacia Lebbek* (*sirisa*), long pepper, black pepper and rock salt in equal parts, rub them together with water, and make into pellets or pencils. These are rubbed on opacities of the cornea.

CARBONATE OF POTASH.

Sans. यवक्षार, *Yavakshára.*

THIS article, as well as the next one called *sarjikákshára*, is mentioned by Susruta, and has been used in medicine from a very remote period. *Yavakshára* is prepared by reducing to ashes the green spikes of the barley *(Hordeum hexastichum)*, dissolving the ashes in water, straining the solution through thick cloth, and evaporating it over the fire. The resulting salt is a clear amorphous powder with a saline and partly acid taste. Chemically it is carbonate of potash with some impurities. *Yavakshára* is described as stomachic, laxative and diuretic. It is used in urinary diseases, dyspepsia, enlarged spleen and other enlargements of the abdominal viscera. A decoction of chebulic myrobalan and *rohitaka* bark is given with the addition of carbonate of potash and long pepper in enlarged spleen and liver, and in tumours in the abdomen called

---

बीजपूररसेनैव भावितं सप्तवारकम्। एतच्चूर्णीकृतं सर्वं लवणं भास्कराभिधम्।
शाणप्रमाणं देयन्तु मस्तुतक्रसुरासवैः। वातश्लेष्मभवं गुल्मं प्लीहानमुदरं क्षयम्।
मन्दाग्निं नाशयेदेतद्दीपनं पाचनं परम्। सर्वलोकहितार्थाय भास्करेणोदितं
पुरा। शार्ङ्गधरः।

gulma.[1] In strangury or painful micturition, carbonate of potash with sugar is considered a very efficacious remedy.[2] It enters into the composition of numerous saline medicines.

CARBONATE OF SODA.

Sans. सर्जिकाक्षार *Sarjikákshára. Vern. Sájji.*

Sájji or barilla is produced from several species of salt-worts growing in brackish soil in the Punjab and North-West Provinces. The process of manufacturing *sájji* is described in full detail in the "Report on Punjab Products". The plants are cut down during the cold months, dried and burnt in a pit of a hemispherical shape, about six feet in circumference and three feet deep. At the bottom of this pit, one or more inverted *ghards* or earthen vessels having small holes pierced in their upper portion are buried. The holes are kept closed at the commencement of the operations. Into the pit is thrown a small quantity of the plants and burnt, fresh plants being gradually added to keep up a constant fire, and this is continued till the pit fills up. During this process a liquid matter exudes from the plants. As soon as this is observed the orifices in the *ghards* are opened and the liquid runs down into them below the fire. After all the liquid has run down, the ashes are stirred up with a stick and covered over with earth. The alkali found in the earthen vessels is *sájji* of the first quality, called *sájji lotá* because it is found in the *lotá* or pot. The residuary mass in the pit is crude dirty potash.

Sarjikákshára or *sájji*, as used in medicine, occurs in porous granular masses of a greyish white colour, and with a strong alkaline taste of soda. Chemically, it consists of carbonate of soda with certain impurities, such as organic matter, sulphate of soda,

---

1 पथ्यारोहितकं क्वाथं यवक्षारकणायुतम् । पिबेत् प्रातर्यकृत्प्लीहगुल्मोदरनिवृत्तये । शार्ङ्गधरः ।

2 यवक्षारस्य चूर्णन्तु संयोज्य सितया सह । भक्षयेन्नियतं तस्य प्रशमेन्मूत्रनिग्रहः । भावप्रकाशः ।

potash etc. The properties of *sarjiká* are said to be like but somewhat inferior to those of *yavakáshara.* It is chiefly used in combination with other medicines of its class in the treatment of acidity, dyspepsia, and enlargements of the abdominal viscera. Externally it is used as a caustic.

Sáji, or barilla, should not be confounded with *sájimati* or fuller's earth. The latter is earth impregnated with soda and not a barilla. *Sájimáti* occurs in great abundance on the surface of the soil in many parts of India, and is chiefly used in washing cloth. The following is an example of a saline medicine containing *sarjiká.*

Sarjikádya churna. [1] Take of *sarjikákshára* and *yavakshára,* rock, *sonchal, vit, sámbar* and *karkach* salts in equal parts, powder, soak in lemon juice or the juice of pomegranate fruits and dry in the sun. Dose about twenty grains. This medicine is said to promote the appetite, to remove local swellings or tumours in the abdomen and to cure dyspepsia with severe pain after meals.

A paste made of equal parts of *yavakshára* and *sarjikákshára* with water is applied to abscesses, for the purpose of opening them.

NITRATE OF POTASH.

NITRE was unknown to the ancient Hindus. There is no recognized name for it in Sanskrit. The Bhávaprakása mentions *Suvarchiká* as a variety of *sarjiká* or barilla, and gives *sorá* as its vernacular equivalent. But *suvarchiká,* according to standard lexicons, is a synonym of *sarjiká* and not a separate article. Some recent Sanskrit formulæ for the preparation of mineral acids containg nitre, mention this salt under the name of *Soraka.* This word

1 स्वर्जिकाद्यचूर्णम् । स्वर्जिका च यवक्षारः सिन्धुसौवर्च्चलं विड्म् । सामुद्रिकं रोमकञ्च कोलमात्राणि कारयेत् । एकीकृत्याखिलं चूर्णं भावयेन्मातुलुङ्गजैः । रसैर्वा दाड़िमैर्वापि शोषयेदातपेन वा । तच्चूर्णं नाशयेद्गुल्मं ग्रहणीमामजां रुजम् । अग्निञ्च कुरुते दीप्तं रुचिकृत् कफनाशनम् ।
शार्ङ्गधरः ।

however is not met with in any Sanskrit dictionary and is evidently Sanskritized from the vernacular *sorá*, a term of foreign origin. The manufacture of nitre was therefore most probably introduced into India after the adoption of gunpowder as an implement of warfare. It is necessary to observe here that many writers have erroneously translated nitre into the Sanskrit term *yavakshára.* This last however is not a nitrate but an impure carbonate of potash obtained by reducing to ashes the spikes of the barley.

Chloride of ammonium is not mentioned by Susruta and the older writers. In recent Sanskrit works it is called *narasára*, a term apparently derived from the vernacular *nausadar* of Persian oirgin. Another salt mentioned in recent Sanskrit compilations is the impure sulphate of soda called *Khárinoon* in the vernacular. It is called *Kshári lavana* in Sanskrit, and is used in combination with other saline medicines.

ALKALINE ASHES.

Sans, क्षार, *Kshára.*

The ashes of a number of plants containing more or less potash are employed both externally and internally. A list of these plants used in the preparation of caustic pastes, has been already given in the Introduction (see page 21). It remains now to notice the preparations of alkaline ashes for internal use. A solution of the ashes of these plants or of such of them as are available, is prepared by mixing them with six parts of water and straining the fluid through cloth for twenty-one times, that is, the strained fluid is poured over the ashes twenty-one times in succession, and made to percolate through them. Lastly the fluid is allowed to stand and the clear solution drained off. This alkaline solution is given in doses of one to three drachms in dyspepsia, ascites, enlargements of the abdominal viscera, calculous affections, etc. It is regarded as laxative, diuretic and antacid.

Váisvánarakshára.[1] Take of the mixed ashes of *Euphorbia*

---

[1] वैश्वानरक्षारः । स्नुह्यर्कचित्रकैरण्डवरुणं च पुनर्नवम् । तिलापामार्ग-

neriifolia (*snuhi*), *Calotropis gigantea* (*arka*), *Plumbago Zeylanica* (*chitraka*), *Ricinus communis* (*eranda*), *Cratæva Roxburghii* (*varuna*), *Boerhaavia diffusa* (*punarnavá*), *Sesamum Indicum* (*tila*), *Achyranthes aspera* (*apámárga*), *Musa sapientum* (*kádali*), *Butea frondosa* (*palása*), and of the shells of tamarinds, two seers in all, boil in sixteen seers of water till reduced to one-fourth. Allow the solution to stand, and drain the clear liquid. To the clear solution add two seers of rock salt, boil again till the fluid is evaporated, dry and powder. To this powder add the following carminatives, namely, *ajowan*, cumin seeds, *káldjirá*, ginger, long pepper, black pepper and assafœtida, each four tolas, and mix. This combination is given in doses of one to two scruples, with cold water in dyspepsia, anasarca etc.

Abhayá-lavana.[1] This is a preparation similar to *Vaisránara-kshára* above described. It is much used in enlarged spleen of long standing, and often with success. To prepare this two seers of mixed alkaline ashes are boiled in sixty-four seers of water till it is reduced to one-fourth. One seer of chebulic myrobalans, two seers of rock salt, and sixteen seers of cow's urine are then added, and the mixture boiled till it is reduced to a thick syrupy consistence. Lastly are added cumin seeds, ginger, black pepper, long pepper,

---

कदली पलाशं तिन्तिड़ीं तथा । गृहीत्वा ज्वालयेदेतत् प्रस्थं भस्माखिलं यथा । जलाढ़के विपक्तव्यं यावत् पादावशेषितम् । सुप्रसन्नं विनिस्राव्य लवणं प्रस्थसंयुतम् । पक्वं निर्धूमकठिनं सूक्ष्मचूर्णीकृतं पुनः । यवानी जीरकव्योषस्थूलजीरकहिङ्गुभिः । शीतोदकेन तच्चूर्णं पिबेत् प्रातर्हि मात्रया । तस्मिन् जीर्णेऽन्नमश्नीयाद् यूषैर्जाङ्गलजैः रसैः । ईषदम्लैः स लवणैः सुखोष्णैर्वह्निदीपनैः । एतेनाग्निर्विवर्द्धेत बलमारोग्यमेव च । तत्रानुपानं शस्तं हि तक्रं वा भोजनेहितम् । मन्दाग्न्यर्शोविकारेषु वातश्लेष्मामयेषु च । सर्वाङ्गशोथरोगेषु शूलगुल्मोदरेषु च । अश्मर्य्यां शर्करायाञ्च विषमूत्रानिलरोगिषु । भावप्रकाशः ।

1 अभयालवणम् । पारिभद्रपलाशार्कस्नुह्यपामार्गचित्रकम् । कर्णाग्निमन्थवरुणं खदिरं बृहतीद्वयम् । पूतिकास्फोतकुटजकोषातक्यः पुनर्नवा । समूलपत्रशाखाश्च क्षोदयित्वा उदूखले । तिलनालेन दीप्ताग्नि सुदग्धं भस्मशीतलम् । क्षारं प्रस्थं

assafœtida, *ajowan*, root of *Aplotaxis auriculata*, (*kushtha*), and *Curcuma Zedoaria* (*sati*), each four tolás, and the whole intimately mixed. This medicine is given in doses of half to one tolá once daily in enlarged spleen, liver disease, ascites etc. If the bowels are not sufficiently moved it is given in larger doses.

DIAMOND.

Sans. हीरक, *Hiraka.*

Of the precious stones enumerated in page 14, diamond, pearls and coral only are much used in medicine. The rest are rarely used or not used at all. Diamond is purified by being enclosed within a lemon and boiled in the juice of the leaves of *Agati grandiflora* (*vaka*). It is reduced to powder in the following manner. A piece of the root of a cotton plant is beaten to a paste with the juice of some betle leaves. Both these vegetables should not be less than three years old. The diamond is enclosed within this paste and roasted in a pit of fire. The process is repeated seven times, when the stone is easily reduced to a fine powder. Another process consists in roasting the diamond enclosed in a paste made of horn-shavings, for three times in succession. Diamond thus prepared is said to be a powerful alterative tonic that improves nutrition, increases the strength and firmness of the body and removes all sorts of diseases. Dose about one grain.

Diamond enters into the composition of several alterative and tonic medicines, such as the *Trailakya chintámani rasa*, *Ratnagiri-rasa*, *Sarvánga sundara rasa*, etc. These medicines are similar in

---

गृहीत्वा च न्यसेत् पात्रे नवे दृढे। जलद्रोणे विपक्तव्यं यावत् पादावशेषितं। पूर्ववत्क्षारकल्केन साधयेद्विविचक्षणः। प्रस्थमेकञ्च लवणं तदर्द्धञ्च हरीतकीम्। गोमूत्रस्याढ़कं दत्वा चारशत् साधयेत् शनैः। किञ्चिद्वारिणि सान्द्रे च सम्यक् सिद्धेऽवतारिते। अजाजीत्र्यूषणं हिङ्गुयमानी पुष्करं शठी। एतैरर्द्धपलैर्भागैश्चूर्णीकृत्य प्रदापयेत्। लवणञ्चाभयानाम भक्षयेच्च यथाबलम्। व्याधीन वेच्य मतिमाननुपानं यथाबलम्। यकृत्प्लीहोदरानाह गुल्माष्ठीलाग्निमान्द्यजित्। यावत् कोष्ठगता रोगान् निहन्त्याशुनसंशयः। प्रतितुन्यर्त्ति हृद्रोगशर्कराश्मरिनाशनम्॥

भैषज्यरत्नावली।

composition. They all contain diamond, pearls, gold, iron, talc, mercury, etc, in varying proportions and are used in similar cases.

Trailakya chintámani rasa[1] is thus prepared. Take of diamond, gold and pearls, each one part, iron, talc and *Rasa sindura* or red preparation of mercury, four parts each, rub together with the juice of *Aloe Indica* and make into two-grain pills. This medicine is used as an alterative tonic with suitable adjuncts in various diseases.

PEARLS AND CORAL.

Sans. मुक्ता *Muktá, Pearls.* प्रवाल *Pravàla, Coral.*

THESE gems have been used in medicine from a very ancient period and are mentioned by Susruta. Pearls are purified by being boiled in the juice of the leaves of *Sesbania aculeata* (*jayanti*), or of the flowers of *Agati grandiflora* (*vaka*). Coral is purified by being boiled in a decoction of the three myrobalans. Both are prepared for medicinal use by being calcined in covered crucibles and then reduced to powder. The properties of both these articles are said to be alike and they are generally used in combination. They are said to be useful in urinary diseases, consumption etc, and to increase the strength, nutrition, and energy of weak persons. The following are examples of prescriptions containing pearls and coral.

Pittántaka rasa.[2] Take of nutmegs, mace, *jatámánsi* root, root

---

1 त्रैलोक्यचिन्तामणिरसः। हीरं सुवर्णं मुक्ताञ्च तारं एषां समं तीक्ष्णरजश्चतुर्णम्। समं मृताभ्रं रससिन्दूरञ्च निष्पेष्यतीक्ष्णास्य तथा प्रवारा। खल्ले द्रवेणैव कुमारिकाया गुञ्जाप्रमाणाथ वटी प्रकार्य्या। अद्यादिमं योगशतैरवाप्यमिव प्रणाशाय मुनिप्रणीतम्। रसेन्द्रसारसंग्रहः।

2 पित्तान्तकरसः। जातीकोषफलं मांसी कुष्टं तालीशपत्रकं। माक्षिकाभ्रत लौहञ्च भस्म दिव्यं समांशकं। सर्व्वतुल्यं मृतं तारं सम्यक्निष्पेष्य वारिणा। द्विगुञ्जाभावटीकार्य्या पित्तरोगविनाशिनी। कोष्ठाश्रितञ्च यत्पित्तं शाखाश्रितमथापि वा। मूत्रञ्चैवाम्लपित्तञ्च पाण्डुरोगं हलीमकम्। दुर्नामश्चाग्निवान्तीश्च क्षिप्रमेव विनाशयेत्। रसः पित्तान्तकोह्येष काशीराजेन भाषितः। तारशब्देनात्र शुद्धमौक्तिकं गृह्यते बुधैः। रसेन्द्रसारसंग्रहः।

of *Aplotaxis auriculata* (*kushtha*), leaves of *Pinus Webbiana* (*tálisa patra* , aconite, iron pyrites, iron, talc and realgar, one part each, prepared pearls equal in quantity to all the above ingredients. Beat them together into a paste with the aid of water and make into four-grain pills. This medicine is said to be useful in diseases supposed to be caused by deranged bile, such as dyspepsia, jaundice, biliousness, vomiting of bile, etc.

Vasanta Kusumákara rasa.[1] Take of prepared gold and camphor, each two parts, of prepared tin, lead and iron, three parts each, prepared talc, pearls and coral, four parts each. Rub these ingredients together in a mortar and soak the powder seven times successively in each of the following fluids, namely milk, sugar-cane juice, juice of *Adhatoda Vasica* (*vàsaka*), decoction of lac and of *Pavonia odorata* (*bálá*), juice of the flowers and root-stock of the plantain tree, of the root-stock of *Nelumbium speciosum* (*padma*) and of the flowers of *Aganosma caryophyllata* (*málatipuspa*). Lastly soak in an infusion of musk prepared by macerating one part of musk in eight parts of warm water for twelve hours. Divide this mass into four-grain pills. They are given with sugar, honey and *ghee* in urinary diseases, impotence, gleet, diabetes, consumption and general debility. This medicine is regarded as a valuable alterative tonic in chronic gonorrhœa and spermatorrhœa and is much prescribed in these complaints in combination with an extract called *Kusávalehá* (see Sugar cane).

---

1 वसन्तकुसुमाकरः। पृथग् द्वौ हाटकं चन्द्रं त्रयो वङ्गाहिकान्तकम्। चत्वारि शुद्धमभ्रञ्च प्रवालं मौक्तिकं तथा। भावना गव्यदुग्धेन भावनेक्षुरसेन च। वासा लाक्षारसोदीच्यरम्भाकन्दप्रसूनकैः। शतपत्ररसेनैव मालत्याः कुसुमोदकैः। पश्चान्मृगमदैर्भाव्यं सुगन्धिरससम्भवे। गुञ्जाद्वयमिदं सेव्यं सितामध्वाज्यसंयुतम्। मेहघ्नं कान्तिदञ्चैव कामदं पुष्टिदं तथा। पलीपलितघ्नञ्चैव स्मृतिभ्रंशविनाशनम्। तुष्टिदं बल्यमायुष्यं पुत्रप्रसवकारकम्। प्रमेहान् विंशतिञ्चैव क्षयमेकादश तथा। तथा सोमरुजं हन्यात् साध्यासाध्यमथापि च। कुसुमाकरनामायं वसन्तपदपूर्ब्बकः। भैषज्यरत्नावली।

SILAJATU.

Silájatu literally means stone and lac. The term is applied to certain bituminous substances said to exude from rocks during the hot weather. It is said to be produced in the Vindhya and other mountains where iron abounds. It is a dark sticky unctuous substance resembling bdellium in appearance. It has a bitter taste and a strong smell resembling stale cow's urine. Over platinum foil it burns with a little inflammable smoke and leaves a large quantity of ashes consisting chiefly of lime, magnesia, silica, and iron in a mixed state of proto and peroxide.*

Silájatu is prepared for medicinal use by being washed with cold water and then rubbed into an emulsion with its bulk of hot water or milk in an iron pot. This emulsion is exposed to the sun, when a black cream-like substance collects on its surface and; this is removed. The process is continued as long as any cream rises. If the mixture becomes too thick, hot water is added from time to time as required, but too much water should not be added at once, for then the cream will not rise to the surface. The *silájatu* thus collected is dried in the sun and preserved for use. The dregs at the bottom are thrown away. The extract of *silájatu* thus obtained is purified by being soaked in a decoction of the following plants, namely. *Shorea robusta*, (*sála*), *Buchanania latifolia* (*piála*), *Terminalia tomentosa* (*asana*) and *Acacia catechu* (*khadira*). *Silájatu* is regarded as a powerful alterative tonic and is considered specially useful in urinary diseases, diabetes, gravel, anæmia, consumption, cough, and skin diseases. The extract of *silájatu* is given in doses of six to twelve grains. In strangury or painful micturition it is given with honey or with the decoction of *Tribulus terrestris* (*gokshura*).[1] In urinary complaints it is given in combination with preparations of lead or tin. As an alterative tonic, it is used in combination with iron, as in the following called *Yogarája*.

---

* The *silajit* or alum earth of Nepal is a different article from the *silájatu* of the Sanskrit Materia Medica. The former is an article of Yunáni not Hindu Medicine.

1 पेयं मूत्रविबन्धोत्थे शिलाजतु समाक्षिकम् । चक्रदत्तः ।

Yogarája. [1] Take of *silájatu,* prepared iron, iron pyrites and silver, each five parts, of the three myrobalans, ginger, black pepper and long pepper, plumbago root and *báberung* seeds, each one part, sugar eight parts. Powder, mix and make into a confection with honey. Dose about half a tolá. This medicine is considered a valuable alterative tonic, and is used in anæmia, jaundice, consumption, chronic fever, skin diseases, urinary diseases, piles, etc.

RED OCHRE.

Sans. गैरिक *Gairika. Vern. Gerumáti.*

Two sorts of *gairiká* or ochre are mentioned by Sanskrit writers, namely, red and yellow. The red variety, called also *Raktapáshána* is used in medicine. It is a silicate of alumina coloured with oxide of iron It is purified by being soaked in milk seven times, and is described as sweetish, astringent, cooling, and usefnl in ulcers, burns, boils etc. It is rarely used internally except as an ingredient of some of the complex prescriptions containing a large number of mineral drugs, such as the preparation called *Jvarakunjara párindra rasa,* which contains nearly all the mineral substances.

Besides *gairika* several other varieties of earth are described and occassionally used in medicine. A sweet scented earth brought from Surat and called *Saurástra mrittiká* is regarded as astringent and useful in hemorrhages. It enters into the composition of several medicines for relieving bleeding from internal organs.

---

1 योगराजः। त्रिफलायास्त्रयोभागास्त्रयस्त्रिकटुकस्य च। भागश्चित्रकमूलस्य विडङ्गानां तथैव च। पञ्चाश्मजतुनो भागास्तथा रूप्यमलस्य च। माक्षिकस्य विशुद्धस्य लौहस्य रजसस्तथा। अष्टौ भागाः सितायाश्च तत्सर्व्वं सूक्ष्मचूर्णितम्। माक्षिकेणाप्लुतं स्थाप्यमायसे भाजने शुभे। उडुम्बरसमां मात्रां ततः खादेत् यथाग्निना। दिने दिने प्रयोगेन जीर्णे भोज्यं यथेप्सितम्। वर्जयित्वा कुलत्थांश्च काकमाची कपोतकान्। योगराज इति ख्यातो योगोऽयममृतोपमः। रसायनमिदं श्रेष्ठं सर्व्वरोगहरं परम्। पाण्डुरोगं विषं कासं यक्ष्माणं विषमज्वरम्। कुष्ठान्यजरकं मेहं श्वासं हिक्कामरोचकम्। विशेषाद्धन्त्यपस्मारं कामलां गुदजानि च। चक्रदत्तः।

SANSKRIT MATERIA MEDICA.

PART II.

VEGETABLE MATERIA MEDICA

NAT. ORDER. RANUNCULACEÆ.

ACONITUM FEROX.

Sans. विष, *Visha.* वत्सनाभ, *Vatsanábha.*

Vern. Mithábish, Sringibish, Dagrá.

THE poisonous root called *bish* or *sringibish* is derived chiefly from *Aconitum ferox* and *Aconitum Napellus*, which are indigenous to the temperate and sub-alpine Himalaya. Other equally poisonous species of aconite are met with in these regions, and their roots collected for use. In the Introduction (page 7) it has been stated that of the nine virulent poisons mentioned by Sanskrit writers, the majority probably consist of species of aconite. The characters of these poisons are described in the Bhabaprakasa, as follows.

Vatsanábha. This root resembles in appearance the navel of children, hence it is called *Vatsanábha.* Its leaves are like those of *Vitex Negundo.* It is said that no plant can grow near it.

Háridra. This root resembles turmeric in appearance, hence it is so called.

Saktu. This poisonous tuber, when broken, is found to contain a white starch-like substance.

Pradipana. This variety is said to be red and shining in appearance, and to cause a severe burning sensation when taken internally.

Saurúshtrika is the variety of poisonous root produced in the country called Surat.

Sringi is a variety of aconite which if tied to the horn of a cow, is said to tinge her milk red.

Kálakuta. This poison is said to be the gum of a plant resembling the *Ficus religiosa* in appearance. It is a native of Malwa and the Concans.

Haláhala. The bunches of fruits of this plant resemble those of grapes. Its leaves are like those of the palm tree. It is found in the Himalaya, in the sea coast to the south, the Concan and in the mountain called Kishkindhya to the north of Mysore.

Brahmaputra. This poison is of a tawny colour and causes purging. It grows on the Malayáchala, that is, the Western Ghats on the Malabar Coast.

From the above description it would seem that of these nine poisons, the first six are probably species of aconite. Of these the variety called *Vatsanábha* has been used in medicine from a very remote period.

Aconite is purified by being cut in small slices and steeped in cow's urine for three days, before being used. It is regarded as heating and stimulant, and useful in diseases supposed to be caused by deranged phlegm and air. It is used in a great variety of affections, but is specially recommended in fever, cephalalgia, affections of the throat, dyspepsia and rheumatism. In recent or acute fevers the following is a favourite medicine.

Mrityunjaya rasa.[1] Take of purified aconite, sulphur, black pepper, long pepper and borax, each one part, cinnabar two parts; powder and beat them into a mass with water and make into two-grain pills. These pills are given with suitable adjuncts in fever supposed to be caused by deranged air, as also in those caused by the derangement of all the humours, that is, in ordinary remittent fever and in that of typhoid type. A composition very similar to the above is recommended by Sarangadhara under the name

---

1 मृत्युञ्जयरसः। विषस्यैकं तथा भागं मरिचं पिप्पलीकणा। गन्धटङ्कं तथा भागं द्विभागं हिङ्गुलं भवेत्। जलेन वटिका कार्य्या गुञ्जामात्रा प्रमाणतः। मधुना लेहनं कार्य्यं सर्व्वज्वरनिवृत्तये। रसरत्नाकरः।

of *A'nanda bhairava rasa.* If there is much constipation along with the fever, croton seeds are added to the above ingredients, as in the preparation called *Jvara murári rasa.*[1]

In fever complicated with cerebral symptoms aconite is used in combination with mercury and *datura*, as in the following called *Panchavaktra rasa.*[2] Take of purified mercury, sulphur, aconite, black pepper and borax, rub them together with the juice of *datura* leaves for twelve hours, and make into four-grain pills. Along with these pills a decoction of the root of *Calotropis gigantea* (*arka*) with the addition of long pepper, black pepper and ginger is recommended to be taken.

In chronic fever with strong shivering fits, copious perspiration, or much heat of body, aconite is used in combination with salts and aromatics, as in the follwing called *Saubhágya vatiká.*[3] Take of aconite, borax, cumin seeds, the five salts, *viz.* rock, sea, *sonchal*, *vit* and *sambar* salts, the three myrobalans, ginger, long pepper and black pepper, prepared talc, mercury and sulphur, in equal parts. First rub the mercury and sulphur together, then mix them with the other ingredients, soak the mixture seven times successively in the juice of the following leaves, namely, of *Vitex*

---

1 ज्वरमुरारिः । हिङ्गुलञ्च विषं व्योषं टङ्कणं नागराभया । जयपाल-समायुक्तं सद्योज्वरनिवारणम् । सर्व्वचूर्णसमं जयपालचूर्णं सर्व्वं पिष्ट्वा कलायप्रमाणा वटिका कार्य्या आर्द्रकस्वरसेन पिबेत् ।। भैषज्यरत्नावली ।

2 पञ्चवक्त्ररसः । शुद्धसूतम्विषं गन्धं मरिचं टङ्कणाङ्कणा । मर्द्दयेद्धूर्त्तजै-द्रावैर्दिनमेकञ्च शोषयेत् । पञ्चवक्त्रोरसोनामद्विगुञ्जःसन्निपातहा । अर्कमूल-कषायन्तुसत्र्यूषणमनुपाययेत् । शार्ङ्गधरः ।

3 सौभाग्यवटिका । सौभाग्यामृतः जीर पञ्चलवण व्योषा भयाच्चामला । निश्चन्द्राभ्रक शुद्धगन्धक रसानेकीकृतान् भावयेत् । निर्गुण्डीयुग भृङ्गराजक वृषा-पामार्गपत्रोल्लसत् । प्रत्येकस्वरसेन सिद्धवटिका हन्तित्रिदोषोदयम् । येषां शीतमतीव दाहमखिलं स्वेदप्रगाढ़ीकृतम् । निद्रां घोरतरां समस्तकरणव्यामो-हमूढं मनः । स्थूलं श्वासविकासकाससहितं मूर्च्छाद्धचित्रङ्ज्वरम् । तेषां वै परिहृत्य जीवितमसौ रक्षाति मृत्योर्मुखात् । भैषज्यरत्नावली ।

Negundo (*nirgundi*) *Nyctanthes Arbor-tristis* (*sephálikā*), *Eclipta prostrata* (*kesarája*), *Adhatoda Vasica* (*vásaka*) and *Achyranthes aspera* (*apámárga*), and make into four-grain pills.

Aconite is much used in dyspepsia with loss of appetite, in a variety of combinations. The following called *Rámavána rasa* [1] is an illustration. Take of mercury, aconite, cloves, and sulphur, each one part, black pepper, two parts, nutmeg, half a part, rub them together with tamarind juice and make into two-grain pills. These pills are given with the addition of powdered black pepper. Another preparation called *Hutásana rasa* is similar in composition to the above, and is recommended by several writers.

In diseases supposed to be caused by deranged phlegm, such as catarrh, sore throat, cough, asthma, discharges from the ears and nose etc, aconite is used in combination with other heating medicines. The following called *Kapha ketu rasa*[2] is a well known medicine for these diseases. Take of aconite, borax, long pepper, and conch-shell lime, equal parts; powder, mix and soak the mixture three times successively in fresh ginger juice. Dose, two grains, to be given with ginger juice. A preparation similar to the above and called *Bhairava rasa,* is used in hoarseness and loss of voice.

In cephalalgia and hemicrania it is recommended to be given in the following form. Take of aconite one part, liquorice root and the pulse of *Phaseolus Roxburghii* (*másha*), each two parts; powder and make into one-grain pills.

In boils and other skin diseases aconite is used in the form of liniment and ointment. The following is an illustration.

---

1 रामबाणरसः। पारदामृत लवङ्गगन्धकं भागयुग्म मरिचेन मिश्रितम्। तत्रजातिफलमर्द्धभागिकं तिन्तिड़ीफलरसेनमर्द्दितम्। वह्निमान्द्यदशवक्त्रना-शनो रामबाण इतिविश्रुतोरसः। रसेन्द्रचिन्तामणी।

2 कफकेतूरसः। टङ्कणं मागधीशङ्खं वत्सनाभं समंसमम्। आर्द्रकस्वरसे-नापि भावयेद्दिवसत्रयम्। गुञ्जामात्रं प्रदातव्यं आर्द्रकस्वरसेन वै। पीनसंश्वास कासञ्च गलरोगं गलग्रहम्। कर्णरोगं नेत्ररोगं दन्तरोगञ्च दारुणम्। एतान् रोगान्निहन्त्याशु कफकेतूरसोत्तमः। रसेन्द्रसारसंग्रहः।

Visha taila.[1] Take of sesamum oil four seers, aconite root eight tolas, seeds of *Pongamia glabra* (*karanja*), turmeric, wood of *Berberis Asiatica* (*dáruharidrá*), root of *Calotropis gigantea* (*arka*), of *Nerium odorum* (*karavira*), flowers of *Tabernaemontana coronaria* (*tagara*), *Acorus calamus* (*vacha*), *Aplotaxis auriculata* (*kushtha*) *Vallaris dichotoma* (*ásphotá*), red sandal wood, flowers of *Aganosma caryophyllata* (*málati*), bark of *Alstonia Scholaris*, (*saptaparna*), madder and leaves of *Vitex Negundo* (*nirgundi*), each four tolás, cow's urine sixteen seers. The solid ingredients should be beaten into a paste with water, and then boiled with the oil and cow's urine till the watery portion is evaporated. This oil is said to be useful in boils, prurigo, psoriasis, leucoderma and other skin diseases.

ACONITUM HETEROPHYLLUM

Sans. आतैच, *A'taicha*, अतिविष, *A'tivisha*. *Vern. A'tis.*

THE tuberous roots of this plant are considered tonic, astringent and stomachic, and are used in fever, diarrhœa, irritability of stomach and cough. *Atis* is also regarded as an antidote to poisons.

In fever with diarrhoea the following compound decoction[2] is much used in practice. Take of *átis*, ginger, *kurchi* bark, tubers of *Cyperus rotundus* (*mustaka*), and root of *Tinospora cordifolia* (*gulancha*), equal parts, in all two tolás, water thirty-two tolás. Boil till the water is reduced to one-fourth or eight tolás. This

---

1 विषतैलम् । नक्तमालं हरिद्रे द्वे अर्कस्तगरमेवच । करवीरं वचाकुष्ठमास्फोतारक्तचन्दनम् ॥ मालतीसप्तपर्णञ्च मञ्जिष्ठासिन्धुवारिका । एषामर्द्धपलान् भागान् विषस्यापिपलन्तथा । चतुर्गुणे गवां मूत्रे तैलप्रस्थं विपाचयेत् । श्वित्रविस्फोट किटिम कीटलूता विचर्चिकाः । कण्डूकच्छु विकाराश्च ये व्रणाविषदूषिताः । विषतैलमिदं नाम्ना सर्व्वव्रणविशोधनम् । चक्रदत्तः ।

2 नागरं कूटजोमुस्तममृतातिविषातया । एभिःकृतं पिवेत्क्वाथं ज्वरातीसारनाशनम् । शार्ङ्गधरः ।

quantity is given in two or three divided doses during the course of the day. Chakradatta recommends the following called *Hriverádi*[1] in similar cases. Take of *átis*, dried *bela*, root of *Pavonia odorata* (*bálá*) and *Cyperus rotundus* (*mustaka*), ginger and coriander, equal parts, in all two tolás and prepare a decoction in the usual way.

In the fever, diarrhœa, cough, and irritability of stomach of infants, *átis* is used alone or in the following combination. Take of *átis*, tubers of *Cyperus rotundus* (*mustaka*) and the horny excrescence of *Rhus succedanea* (*karkatasringi*), equal parts, powder and mix. This compound powder is given in suitable doses with the addition of honey. Sometimes long pepper is added to the above ingredients, when the powder is called *Bála-cháturbhadraka*,[2] from its being composed of four ingredients.

NIGELLA SATIVA.

Sans. कृष्णजीरक, *Krishnajiraka. Vern. Kálájirá, Beng. Mugrela, Hind.*

THE seeds of *Nigella sativa* are regarded as aromatic, carminative stomachic and digestive, and are used in indigestion, loss of appetite, fever, diarrhoea puerperal diseases etc. They are also said to increase the secretion of milk, and are therefore given to recently delivered females in combination with a few other medicines. Nigella seeds are scattered between layers of woolen clothes, shawls etc., to preserve them from insects. This use of the seeds appears to be common all over India.

In intermittent fever nigella seeds slightly roasted are recommended to be given in two drachm doses with the addition of an equal quantity of treacle.[3]

---

1 ह्रीवेरादिः । ह्रीवेरातिविषामुस्तबिल्वधान्यकनागरैः । पिबेत्पिच्छाविबन्धघ्नं शूलदोषामपाचनम् । सरक्तं हन्त्यतीसारं सज्वरं वाथ विज्वरम् ।
चक्रदत्तः ।

2 बालचातुर्भद्रिका । घनकृष्णारुणाशृङ्गीचूर्णं क्षौद्रेण संयुतम् । शिशोर्ज्वरातिसारघ्नं कासश्वासवमीहरम् । चक्रदत्तः ।

3 कालाजाजी तु सगुडा विषमज्वरनाशिनी । भावप्रकाशः ।

In loss of appetite and distaste for food a confection made of *Nigella* seeds, cumin seeds, black pepper, raisins, tamarind pulp, pomegranate juice and *sonchal* salt, with treacle and honey is said to be very useful.[1]

Chakradatta recommends the administration of nigella seeds with the addition of long pepper, *sonchal* salt and wine in the after pains of puerperal women.[2] In puerperal diseases, such as fever, loss of appetite and disordered secretions, after delivery, the following called *Pancha jiraka páka*[3] is used. Take of nigella seeds, cumin seeds, aniseeds, *ajowan*, seeds of *Carum sativum* (*ajamodá*) *Anethum Sowa* (*sulpha*) and *Trigonella Fœnum-græcum* (*methi*), coriander, ginger, long pepper, long pepper root, plumbago root, *habushá* (an aromatic substance) dried pulp of the fruit *Ziziphus Jujuba* (*vadari phala*), root of *Aplotaxis auriculata* (*kushtha*) and *kamala* powder, each one tolá, treacle one hundred tolás, milk one seer, clarified butter four tolas. Boil them together and prepare a confection. Dose about a drachm every morning.

NAT. ORDER. MENISPERMACEÆ.

STEPHANIA HERNANDIFOLIA.

Syn. Cissampelos hexandra. Rox.

Sans. अम्बष्ठा, *Ambashthá.* पाठा, *Páthá. Vern. A'kanádi, Nemuka.*

In the Pharmacopœia of India it is stated that the *Cissampelos hernandifolia*, Wall. is identical with Pareira Brava, and is

---

1 कारव्यजाजीमरिचं द्राक्षावृक्षाम्लदाडिमम् । सौवर्चलं गुडं क्षौद्रं सर्व्वारोचकनाशनम् । चक्रदत्तः ।

2 उपकुञ्चिकां पिप्पलीञ्च मदिरां लाभतः पिबेत् । सौवर्चलेन संयुक्तां योनिशूलनिवारणीम् । चक्रदत्तः ।

3 पञ्चजीरक पाकः । जीरकं स्थूलजीरञ्च शतपुष्पाद्वयं तथा । यवानी चाजमोदा च धान्यकं मेथिकापि च । शुण्ठी कृष्णाकणामूलं चित्रकं हबुषापि च । बदरीफल चूर्णञ्च कुष्ठं कम्पिल्लकं तथा । एतानि पलमात्राणि गुडं पलशतं मतम् । क्षीरप्रस्थद्वयं दद्यात्सर्पिषः कुडवं तथा । पञ्चजीरकपाको-

common throughout India. Other authorities say, that the true Pareira Brava is derived from *Chondodendron tomentosum.* The plant used by Kavirajas in Bengal under the name of *páthá* is identical with that figured by Roxburgh as *Cissampelos hexandra.* The root of this plant is regarded as light, bitter, astringent and useful in fever, diarrhœa, urinary diseases, dyspepsia etc.

In fever with diarrhœa, the following compound decoction[1] is recommended by Chakradatta. Take of *páthá* root, *indrajava* seeds, chiretta, tubers of *Cyperus rotundus* (*mustaka*), *Hedyotis biflora* (*parpati*), *gulancha*, and ginger, equal parts, in all two tolas, water thirty-two tolas; and boil till reduced to one-fourth. In diarrhœa caused by indigestion and attended with pain and slimy or bilious stools, the following decoction is used. Take of *páthá* root, *indrajava* seeds, chebulic myrobalan and ginger, each half a tola, water thirty-two tolas. Boil down to one-fourth.

In internal or deep seated inflammation, Chakradatta recommends the root of this plant to be taken with honey and water in which rice has been macerated.[2]

In urine depositing salts or a white flocculent substance, a decoction of *páthá* and aloes-wood is used.[3]

In painful micturition the following decoction[4] is considered useful. Take of *páthá* root, *Hedysarum lagopodioides* (*prisniparni*),

---

ऽयं प्रसूतानां प्रशान्तये । युज्यते सूतिकारोगे योनिरोगे ज्वरेऽक्षये । कासे श्वासे पाण्डुरोगे कार्श्ये वातामयेषु च । भावप्रकाशः ।

1 पाठेन्द्रयवभूनिम्ब मुस्तपर्पटकामृताः । जयन्त्याममतीसारं सज्वरं समहौषधाः । चक्रदत्तः ।

2 शमयति पाठामूलं क्षौद्रयुतं तण्डुलाम्भसा पीतम् । अन्तर्भूतं विद्रधिमुद्धतमाश्वेव मनुजस्य । अपक्के त्वेतदुद्दिष्टं पक्के तु व्रणवत् क्रिया । चक्रदत्तः ।

3 पारिजातजयानिम्बवह्निगायत्रिणां पृथक् । पाठायाः सागुरोः पीतद्रयस्य शारदस्य च । जले क्षुमद्यसिकताशनैर्लवणपिष्टकान् । सान्द्रमेहान् क्रमात् घ्नन्ति अष्टौ क्वाथाः सशाल्मिकाः । चक्रदत्तः ।

4 वृहतीधावनीपाठायष्टीमधुकलिङ्गकाः । पाचनीयो वृहत्यादिः कृच्छ्रदोषत्रयापहः । चक्रदत्तः ।

root of *Solanum Indicum (vrihati)*, liquorice root and *indrajava* seeds, equal parts, in all two tolás. Boil down to one-fourth.

TINOSPORA CORDIFOLIA.

Sans. गुडूची, *Guḍuchi.* अमृता, *Amritá.*

Vern. Gulancha, Beng. Gurach, Hind.

THE stem, leaves, roots and watery extract of this plant are all used in Hindu Medicine. The entire plant is regarded as a valuable alterative and tonic. It is used in general debility, fever, jaundice, skin diseases, rheumatism, urinary diseases, irritability of stomach, etc.

The fresh juice of the plant is taken with milk as a general tonic. In fevers it is used in a great variety of forms. Thus a cold infusion of *gulancha* is given with honey in bilious fever. A decoction[1] of *gulancha* or its fresh juice is given with the addition of long pepper and honey in chronic fever with cough. A compound decoction is thus prepared. Take of *gulancha, Hedyotis biflora* (*parparta*), *Cyperus rotundus* (*mustaka*), chiretta and ginger, each one drachm, water, half a seer. Boil down to one-fourth. It is said to be useful in fevers caused by deranged air and bile. Practically it is found very useful in chronic fevers, which have resisted other antiperiodics, and which are apt to recur after apparent recovery. In chronic fever with loss of appetite, the following confection is recommended by many writers.

Dhátrimodaka.[2] Take of chebulic and emblic myrobalans, ginger and long pepper, one part each, watery extract of *gulancha*, four parts, water sixteen parts. Boil till reduced to one-fourth, and prepare a confection with eight parts of sugar. When of proper

---

1 पिप्पलीमधुसंमिश्रं गुडूची स्वरसं पिबेत् । जीर्णज्वर कफ प्लीह कासारोचकनाशनम् । गुडूची पर्पटं मुस्तं किरातं विश्वभेषजम् । वात पित्तज्वरे देयं पञ्चभद्रमिदं शुभम् । भावप्रकाशः ।

2 धात्रीमोदकः । धात्रीं पथ्यां कणां शुण्ठीं तुल्यांश्च चूर्णयेद् दृढम् ।

consistence divide the mass into boluses of about a drachm each. One of these is taken every morning, in chronic fever with enlarged spleen, cough, loss of appetite, etc.

Gulancha enters into the composition of a large number of prescriptions for chronic skin diseases. The juice of the plant or its decoction is given alone, or with the addition of *guggulu* or bdellium.[1] Numerous compound decoctions with the addition of various other drugs such as *nim*, turmeric, catechu, etc. are used in these diseases, as well as in gout and rheumatism.[2] Several oils, for external application are prepared with *gulancha* and are much used in skin diseases, rheumatic affections and nervous complaints.

Guḍuchyádi taila.[3] Take of fresh *gulancha*, eight seers, water, sixty-four seers, boil till reduced to one-fourth and strain. To the strained decoction, add prepared sesamum oil, four seers, and *gulancha* beaten to a paste with water, one seer, boil together till the water is evaporated. This oil is a favourite application in eruptive skin diseases from impure blood. The *Vrihat guḍuchyádi taila* is prepared by the addition of a number of other medicines in the form of paste, to the decoction of *gulancha* and the oil. Another compound oil called *Váta guḍuchyádi taila* is thus prepared. Take of *gulancha*, twelve seers, and a half water sixty-four seers. Boil till reduced to one fourth. Take of the fresh juice of *Adhatoda Vasica* (*vásaka*) and of *datura* leaves, each four seers, prepared mustard oil, four seers, aromatics in the form of paste one seer. Boil together the decoction of *gulancha* with the vegetable juices, oil and paste, in the usual

---

चतुःसमाक्ततास्तेया शर्कराच पलं तथा । मधुना मोदकं कुर्य्यात् जीर्णज्वरहरं परं । मन्दाग्निदीपनं चैव सन्नोदाह विनाशनम् । प्लीहज्वरे तथाकासे श्वासे च रक्तपित्तके । दापयेत् मोदकं वैद्यः धात्रीनाममिदं महत् । सारकौमुदी ।

1 वत्सादन्युद्भवः क्वाथः पीतो गुग्गुलुसंयुतः ।

2 गुडूच्याः स्वरसं कल्कं चूर्णं वा क्वाथमेव वा । प्रभूत कालमासेव्य मुच्यते वातशोणितात् । चक्रदत्तः ।

3 गुडूचीक्वाथकल्काभ्यां तैलं वा वातरक्तनुत् । चक्रदत्तः ।

manner. This oil is recommended by Charaka in eruptive skin diseases with troublesome itching, as also in diseases of nervous origin.

NAT. ORDER. BERBERIDEÆ.

BERBERIS ASIATICA AND OTHER SPECIES.

Sans. दारुहरिद्रा, *Dáruharidrá.* दार्व्वीं, *Dárvi.*

Vern. Dáruhaldi. Hind.

THE wood, root-bark and extract of Indian Barberry have been used in Hindu Medicine from a very remote period. Its properties are said to be analogous to those of turmeric. The extract, called *Rasánjana** in Sanskrit and *Rasot* in the vernacular, is directed to be prepared by boiling together equal parts of a decoction of Indian barberry and milk, till reduced to the consistence of an extract.† The extract thus prepared, is said to be particularly useful in affections of the eyes. Indian barberry and its extract *rasot* are regarded as alterative and deobstruent, and are used in skin diseases, menorrhagia, diarrhœa, jaundice and above all, in affections of the eyes.

Rasánjanádi churna,[1] or compound powder of *rasot.* Take of *rasot, átis,* the bark and seeds of *Holarrhena antidysenterica,* flowers of *Woodfordia floribunda* (*dhátaki*) and ginger, in equal parts. Powder and mix. Dose, about a drachm, with rice water

* Galena or the sulphide of lead ore is sometimes called *rasánjana* in Sanskrit, and some physicians in Bengal use the lead ore for *rasánjana,* whenever this term occurs in a prescription. In the Upper Provinces however, *rasànjana* is invariably translated *rasot* in the vernacular. This, no doubt, is the correct practice. The mistake on the part of the Bengali physicians, probably occurred from their not being acquainted with *rasot,* which is the produce of plants indigenous to the Himalayan range.

† दार्व्वीक्वाथ समंक्षीरं पादपक्वा यथाघनम् । तदारसाञ्जनाख्यन्तु नेत्रयोः परमं हितम् ।

1 रसाञ्जनादि चूर्णः। रसाञ्जनं सातिविषं कुटजस्य फलं त्वचम् । धातकी-शृङ्गवेरञ्च प्रपिबेत्तण्डुलाम्बुना ॥ क्षौद्रेणयुक्तं तुदतिरक्तातिसारशूलनम् । मन्दं दीपयतेचाग्निं शूलञ्चापिनिवर्त्तयेत् । चक्रदत्तः ।

(*tandulámbu*) and honey. This powder is said to be useful in bilious diarrhœa.

Dárvyádi kvátha,[1] or compound decoction of Indian barberry. Take of the root bark of Indian barberry, *rasot*, chiretta, *Adhatoda Vasica* (*vásaka*), *Cyperus rotundus* (*mustaka*), *bela* fruit and marking nuts, equal parts, and prepare a decoction in the usual way. This is administered with honey in menorrhagia and copious discharges from the womb. Another combination said to be very useful in menorrhagia is as follows. Take of *rasot* and the root of *Amaranthus spinosus* (*tanduliya*) equal parts, beat into a paste with water, and administer with honey and water in which rice has been steeped.

Sárangadhara recommends a simple decoction of Indian barberry to be given with the addition of honey in jaundice. In painful micturition from bilious or acrid urine, a decoction of Indian barberry[2] and emblic myrobalan is given with honey. A decoction[3] of the root bark is used as a wash for unhealthy ulcers, and is said to improve their appearance and promote cicatrization. In the intertrigo of infants, *rasot* is recommended to be applied externally and administered internally.[4] *Rasot* mixed with honey, is said to be an useful application to aphthous sores.

The principal use of *rasot* however is in eye-diseases, in which it is employed in a great variety of forms. The following are a few illustrations. Take of *rasot*, chebulic myrobalan, rock salt and red ochre, equal parts, rub them together into a paste with water,

---

1 दार्व्व्यादिक्काथः । दार्व्वी रसाञ्जन वृषाब्द किरात विल्व भल्लातकैः रचितोमधुनाकषायः । पीतो जयत्यतिबलं प्रदरं सशूलं पीतासितारुण विलोहित नील शुक्लम् ॥ चक्रदत्तः ।

2 दार्व्वीं तथै वामलकीरसेन समाक्षिकां पैत्तिक मूत्रकृच्छ्रे । चक्रदत्तः ।

3 त्रिफला खदिरो दार्व्वी न्यग्रोधादिबलाकुशाः । निम्ब कोलकपत्राणि कषायः शोधने हितः । चक्रदत्तः ।

4 रसाञ्जनं विशेषेण पानालेपनयोर्हितम् ॥ गुदभ्रंशेगुदं स्नेहैरभ्यज्याशु प्रवेशयेत् । चक्रदत्तः ।

and apply round the orbit in inflammatory affections of the eyes.[1] *Rasot* mixed with honey may also be used in the same way. An emulsion of *rasot* made with milk is recommended to be poured into the eyes, or used as a collyrium for relieving pain, burning and lachrymation.[2]

NAT. ORDER. NYMPHÆACEÆ.

NELUMBIUM SPECIOSUM.

NYMPHÆA LOTUS ETC.

THESE beautiful aquatic plants had attracted the attention of the ancient Hindus from a very remote period, and obtained a place in their religious ceremonies and mythological fables; hence they are described in great detail by Sanskrit writers. The flowers of *Nelumbium speciosum*, called *Padma* or *Kamala*, are sacred to Lakshmi, the goddess of wealth and prosperity. The white variety of this plant is called *Pundaríka*, the red, *Kokanada* and the blue, *Indivara*. The entire plant including root, stem and flower is called *Padmini*. The torus or receptacle for the seed is, called *Karnikára*, and the honey formed in the flowers, *Makaranda*. The filaments round the base of the receptacle, pass by the name of *Kinjalka* and the leaf-stalk by that of *Mrinála*. The species of *Nymphæa* described, are as follows :—

Nymphæa Lotus. Kumuda, Sans. Sáluka. Beng. Koi. Hind.
Nymphæa stellata. Nilotpala, Sans. Nilsaphalá, Beng.
Nymphæa rubra. Raktotpala, Sans. Raktakambal, Beng.

The root-stocks of these water plants contain a sort of starch, and are eaten by the poorer classes. During the famine of 1866 in Orissa, they were much sought after by the starving people.

---

1 हरीतकीसैन्धवञ्च गैरिकञ्च रसाञ्जनम्। बिडालकोऽजलेपिष्टः सर्वनेत्रामयापहः॥
शार्ङ्गधरः।

2 दार्व्वीरसाञ्जनं वापि स्तन्ययुक्तं प्रपूरणम्॥ निहन्ति शीघ्रं दाहाश्रुवेदनाः स्यन्दसम्भवाः।
चक्रदत्तः।

The seeds of *Nelumbium speciosum* are eaten raw. The small seeds of *Nymphæa Lotus,* called *bheta,* are fried in heated sand and used as a light easily digestible food. The seeds of *Euryale ferox* called *makhánna* is Sanskrit, are also used in the same manner, and are regarded as light; invigorating food suited for sick people.

The filaments of these plants are used medicinally. They are considered astringent and cooling, and useful in burning of the body, bleeding piles and menorrhagia. In bleeding piles the filaments of the lotus are given with honey and fresh butter or with sugar.[1] In menorrhagia the filaments of *Nymphæa stellata* are given with the addition of *sonchal* salt, nigella seeds, liquorice powder, curdled milk and honey.[2] A compound decoction is thus prepared.

Utpaládi sritam.[3] Take of the filaments of *Nymphæa Lotus, N. stellata* and *N. rubra,* of the white váriety of *Nelumbium speciosum* and liquorice root, equal parts, in all, two tolás, and prepare a decoction in the usual way. This decoction is said to be useful in thirst, burning of the body, fainting, vomiting, hemorrhage from the internal organs, and bleeding from the womb during gestation.

A cooling application[4] for external use is prepared as follows. Take of the filaments and leaf-stalks of *Nelumbium speciosum, Nymphæa stellata,* and *Nymphæa Lotus* and of red sandal wood, equal parts, and rub them together into a thin paste with cold water. This is applied to the forehead in cephalalgia. A paste made of emblic

---

1 सपद्मकेशरं क्षौद्रं नवनीतं नवं लिहन्। सिताकेशर संयुक्तं रक्तार्शसि- सुखीभवेत्। भावप्रकाशः।

2 दध्ना सौवर्चलाजाजीमधुकं नीलमुत्पलम्। पिबेत् क्षौद्रयुतं नारीवाता- सृग्दरपीड़िता। चक्रदत्तः।

3 गुर्विण्या गर्भतोरक्तं स्रवेद्यदि मुहुर्मुहुः। तन्निरोधाय सा दुग्धमुत्पलादि सृतं पिबेत्। भावप्रकाशः।

4 मृणालबिसशालूकचन्दनोत्पलकेशरैः। स्निग्धशीतैः शिरोदिह्यात्तद्दा- मलकोत्पलैः। चक्रदत्तः।

myrobalans and the filaments of the lotus is also used for the same purpose. Similar compositions are recommended for external inflammations, erysipelas etc.

The large leaves of *Nelumbium speciosum* are used as cool bed-sheets, in high fever with much heat and burning of the skin.[1]

NAT. ORDER. PAPAVERACEÆ.

PAPAVER SOMNIFERUM.

Sans. अहिफेन, *Ahiphena. Vern. A'phim.*

Opium appears to have been brought into India by the Mussulmans, as its Sanskrit name is evidently derived from the Arabic *Afyun*, and as it is not mentioned by the older Sanskrit writers.

The capsules of the poppy are called *Khákhas*, and the seeds, *Khasatila*, in Sanskrit. The seeds yield a bland oil, which is used for culinary purposes and in lamps. The seeds themselves are innocuous and used as food. They are boiled, mixed with a little oil and salt, and taken as a curry with rice, or they are made into balls and formed with tamarind, into an acid curry. Poppy seeds are sprinkled over some sorts of native sweetmeats.

Sanskrit writers describe poppy seeds as demulcent and nutritive, and useful in cough and asthma. The capsules of the poppy are regarded as light, astringent, and narcotic. They promote talkativeness and destroy or diminish the sexual power. The properties of opium are said to be analogous to those of the capsules. Opium is used as an astringent and narcotic in bowel complaints, cough, external inflammations, urinary diseases, fractures, skin diseases etc.

In diarrhœa and cholera the following, called *A'marákshasi*,[2] is used. Take of opium, nutmeg, cloves, cinnabar and camphor,

---

1 चन्दनाम्बुकणास्यन्दितालवृन्तोपवीजितः। सुप्याद्दाहार्दितोऽम्भोजकदलीदलसंस्तरे ।
चक्रदत्तः ।

2 आमराक्षसी । जातीफलं लवङ्गं स्यादहिफेनं समोषितम् । कर्पूरं समभागञ्च वटीं कुर्यात् द्विरक्तिकाम् । अजस्योदकसुस्थान्तु अनुपानं प्रशस्यते ।

equal parts. Beat them into a mass with water, and make into four-grain pills.

In chronic diarrhœa and dysentery, the following called *Grahani kapáta rasa*,[1] is recommended. Take of nutmeg, borax, prepared talc and *datura* seeds, each one part, opium two parts, and make into two-grain pills with the juice of *Pæderia fœtida* (*prasárani*). In diarrhœa with anasarca the following, called *Dugdhavati*, is much used by the Kavirajas.

Dugdhavati.[2] Take of opium and aconite, twenty-four grains each, prepared iron ten grains, prepared talc twelve grains. Beat them into a mass with milk and make into four-grain pills. One pill is to be given every morning with milk. The diet is restricted to milk alone, water and salt being prohibited. In fever with diarrhœa, opium is used in combination with arsenic, as for example in the following preparation.

Sambhunátha rasa.[3] Take of orpiment, realgar, cinnabar, white arsenic, borax, aconite and alum each, one part, mercury,

---

असाध्येत्वामरोगे तु एषएवमहौषधम्। आमरात्तसीनामायं रसः परमदुर्लभः।

रसेन्द्रसारसंग्रहः।

1 ग्रहणीकपाटरसः। जातीफलं टङ्कणमभ्रकञ्च धूस्तूरबीजं समभागचूर्णम्। भागद्वयंस्यादहिफेणकस्य गन्धालिकापत्ररसेनमर्द्यम्। चणप्रमाणां वटिकां प्रकार्य्य यत्नाद्विदध्यात् ग्रहणीगदेषु। सामेषु शूलेषु सरक्तकेषु पक्केष्वपक्केषु गुदामयेषु। पथ्यं सदध्योदनमत्रदेयं रसोत्तमोयं ग्रहणीकपाटः।

रसेन्द्रसारसंग्रहः।

2 दुग्धवटी। अमृतं स्वर्णगुञ्जं स्यात् अहिफेणं तथैव च। पञ्चरक्तिक लौहञ्च षष्ठिरक्तिकमभ्रकम्। दुग्धे गुञ्जाद्वयमिता वटीकार्य्याभिषग्विदा। दुग्धानुपानं दुग्धंञ्च भोजनं सर्व्वथा हितम्। शोथं नानाविधं हन्ति ग्रहणी विषमज्वरम्। मन्दाग्निं पाण्डुरोगञ्च नाम्ना दुग्धवटी परा। वर्जयेत् लवनं वारि व्याधिनिःशेषतावधि।

भैषज्यरत्नावली।

3 शम्भुनाथ रसः। तालकं टङ्कणं रक्तं फटिकारी च मनःशिला। गोदन्तं वत्सनाभञ्च सर्व्वतुल्यञ्च भागिकम्। सर्वतुल्यं रसं गन्धं तत्समं फणिफेणकम्। शक्राशन रसैर्भाव्यं निर्गुण्ड्याश्च रसेन च। कनकस्य पत्ररसै र्निम्ब-

sulphur and opium, each seven parts. Soak them for seven days in each of the following fluids, namely, juice of the leaves of *Cannabis sativa, Vitex Negundo, datura* and *nim*. Make into two-grain pills. These are given with ginger juice in diarrhœa with high fever.

Akarádi churna.[1] Take of pellitory root, ginger, seeds called (*kakkola*), saffron, long pepper, nutmeg, cloves and red sandal wood, each two tolás, opium eight tolás. Rub them together and pass the powder through a cloth. Then add sugar, equal in quantity to all the above ingredients. Dose grains six to twelve, with honey. This medicine is used as an aphrodisiac.

Opium enters into the composition of some external applications in the form of paste, along with other medicines. A poultice made of poppy seeds with milk is prescribed by Sárangadhara in porrigo of the scalp.[2]

The Amritaságar recommends the following preparation of opium in diabetes. Take of camphor and musk, each one part, opium and mace, each four parts. Make into two-grain pills. They are administered with the juice of betel leaves.

पत्ररसैः पुनः । पृथगेषां रसैः सप्त भावयेत् कुशलोभिषक् । वटीं रक्तिद्वयं कुर्य्यात् शृङ्गवेरानुपानतः । सर्वरूपं सान्निपातम अतिसारञ्च नाशयेत् । ग्रहणी मामदोषञ्च ज्वरं सर्व्वं विनाशयेत् । उद्वेगे मस्तके तैलं पथ्यञ्च दधिभक्तकम् । शीतोपचारं कर्त्तव्यं क्रमेण गुणवर्द्धते । शम्भुनाथ इति ख्यातो महादेवेन भाषितः । भैषज्यतन्त्रः ।

1 अकरादिचूर्णः । अकराकरभः शुण्ठीकक्कोलं कुङ्कुमं कणा । जातीफलं लवङ्गञ्च चन्दनञ्चेतिकार्षिकान् । चूर्णानिमांस्ततः कुर्य्यादहिफेणं पलोन्मितम् । सर्वमेकीकृतं चूर्णं सूक्ष्मं तद्वस्त्रगालितम् । सितासर्व्वसमादेयामाषैकं मधुनालिहेत् । शुक्रस्तम्भकरं चूर्णं पुंसामानन्दकारकम् । नारीणां प्रीतिजननं सेवेतनिशिकामुकः । शार्ङ्गधरः ।

2 दुग्धेन खाखसंबीजं प्रलेपाद्दारुणं जयेत् । शार्ङ्गधरः।

NAT. ORDER. CRUCIFERÆ.

SINAPIS.

Sans. सिद्धार्थ, *Siddhártha.* राजिका, *Rájiká.*

Vern. Sarishá, Rái Sarishá, Beng.

Two varieties of mustard are mentioned by Sanskrit writers, namely, *siddhártha* or white mustard, (*Sinapis glauca* of Roxburgh, *Brassica campestris, L.*) and *rájiká* or dark brown variety, (*Sinapis ramosa* of Roxburgh, *Brassica juncea, Hooker, fil, et Thomson*). The latter is more pungent and preferred for external application as a rubefacient. Mustard oil is largely used by the natives for culinary purposes as well as for anointing the body before bathing. Mustard oil anointment is said to keep the body cool, and the skin soft, to promote the growth of hair and to remove prurigo, lice and scurf. The leaves of the mustard plant are used as a pot-herb, and considered pungent and stomachic.

Mustard enters into the composition of emetic mixtures, of which the following is an example. Take of mustard seeds, *Acorus Calamus* root (*vacha*), bark of *Symplocos racemosa* (*lodhra*), and rock salt, equal parts. Powder and mix.[1]

Mustard forms an ingredient of several prescriptions for loss of appetite, indigestion, etc. Thus take of mustard seeds, cumin seeds, fried assafœtida, ginger and rock salt, equal parts. Powder and mix. Dose, grains twenty-two with butter-milk.

Mustard is used externally, alone, or in combination with other medicines in a great variety of diseases, and notably in parotitis, sciatica, paraplegia, gout, inflammatory swellings, urticaria etc. Sárangadhara recommends the following application[2] in urticaria. Take of mustard seed, turmeric, *pátchuk* root, sesamum and the seeds of *Cassia Tora* (*chakramardaka*), equal

---

1 सिद्धार्थक वचालोध्र सैन्धवैश्च प्रलेपनम् । वमनञ्च निहन्त्याशु पिडकां यौवनोद्भवाम् । चक्रदत्तः ।

2 सिद्धार्थरजनीकुष्ठप्रपुन्नाडतिलैः सह । कटुतैलेन संमिश्रमुद्वर्त्तनं विलेपनम् । शार्ङ्गधरः ।

parts, and rub them together into a paste with mustard oil. In gout, sciatica, etc, simple mustard plasters are used.[1] In inflammatory affections, the following poultice is prescribed by Sáran-gadhara. Take of the root of *Boerhaavia diffusa* (*punarnavá*), wood of *Berberis Asiatica* (*dáruharidrá*), root of *Moringa pterygosperma* (*sobhánjana*), ginger and mustard seeds, equal parts, and rub them into a paste with fermented rice water.[2]

LEPIDIUM SATIVUM. The seeds of *Lepidium Sativum*, called *Chandra sura* in Sanskrit, and *Hálim* in Hindi, are described as tonic and alterative, and useful in hiccup, diarrhœa, and skin diseases from disordered blood. It is said to be a very efficaceous remedy in hiccup, for which the Bhávaprakása gives the following formula. *Hálim* seeds are macerated in eight times their weight of water; when the seeds are softened they are rubbed in the water, and the emulsion strained through cloth. This emulsion is recommended to be given frequently in doses of about an ounce for the relief of obstinate hiccup.[3]

NAT. ORDER. CAPPARIDACEÆ.

CRATÆVA RELIGIOSA.

Syn. Capparis trifoliata. Rox.

Sans. वरुण, *Varuna.* अश्मरिघ्न, *Asmarighna.*

Vern. Barun, Beng. Hind.

THE bark of the stem and root of this plant constitutes the principal medicine of the Hindu Pharmacopœia, for calculous affections. It is said to promote the appetite, increase the secretion of the bile, act as a laxative and remove disorders of the urinary organs.

---

1 गौरसर्षपकल्केन प्रदेहोवा रुजापहः । भावप्रकाशः ।

2 पुनर्नवांदारुशुण्ठीं सिद्धार्थं शिग्रुमेवच। पिष्टाचैवारनालेन प्रलेपः सर्व्वशोथहा । शार्ङ्गधरः ।

3 चन्द्रशूर रसः। चन्द्रसूरस्य बीजानि क्षिपेदष्टगुणे जले। यदा स्युर्मृदूनि मृदीयास्ततोवाससि गालयेत् ॥ हिक्कातिवेगविकलस्तज्जलं पलमात्रया। पिबेत् पिबेत् पुनश्चापि हिक्कावश्यं प्रशाम्यति ॥ भावप्रकाशः ।

In calculous affections it is used in a great variety of forms. Thus a simple decoction of the bark may be given with the addition of treacle.[1] A compound decoction is prepared along with equal parts of *Tribulus terrestris* (*gokshura*) and ginger, and is administered with the addition of *yavakshára* and honey.[2] A compound powder called *Varunádya churna*[3] is prepared as follows. A solution of the ashes of *varuna* is made as directed under the head of alkaline water (*Kshárodaka*). This solution is boiled with the addition of *varuna* bark in powder and *yavakshára* (impure carbonate of potash), till the water is entirely evaporated. The resulting powder is given in ascites, calculus, enlargements of the abdominal viscera, and affections of the bladder and uterus. A confection called *Varunádya guda* is prepared by adding to the fluid extract of the bark, treacle and a number of diuretic and aromatic substances.

Varunádya ghrita.[4] Take of coarsely powdered *varuna* bark twelve seers and a half, water sixty-four seers, boil together till reduced to one-fourth and strain. To the strained decoction, add four seers of clarified butter, and two tolás each of the following substances in the form of a paste, namely, *varuna* bark, unripe

---

1 वरुणत्वक्कषायन्तु पीतञ्च गुडसंयुतम् । अश्मरीं पातयत्याशु वस्तिशूल-निवारणम् । चक्रदत्तः ।

2 वरुणस्य त्वचं श्रेष्ठां शुण्ठीगोक्षुरसंयुताम् । यवक्षारगुडं दत्त्वा क्वाथयित्वा पिबेद्धिताम् । चक्रदत्तः ।

3 वरुणकभस्मपरिस्रुत सलिलं तच्चूर्णं यावशूकयुतम् । क्वथनीयं तत्तावद्याव-च्चूर्णत्वमायाति । तद्गुडयुक्तं हन्यात् तदुदरमश्मरीं घोराम् । प्लीहानं गुल्मज्वरं श्रोण्यां कुक्षौरुजां तीव्राम् । भावप्रकाशः ।

4 वरुणाद्यं घृतम् । वरुणस्य तुलां क्षुण्णां जलद्रोणे विपाचयेत् । पादशेषं परिस्राव्य घृतप्रस्थं विपाचयेत् । वरुणं कदली विल्वं तृणजं पञ्चमूलकम् । अमृताचाश्मजं देयं वीजञ्च त्रपुषोद्भवम् । शतपर्व्वतिलक्षारं पलाशक्षारमेव च । यूथिकायाश्च मूलानि कार्षिकाणि समावपेत् । अस्य मात्रां पिबेज्जन्तुर्देशका-लाद्यपेक्षया । जीर्णे तस्मिन् पिबेत् पूर्व्वं गुडं जीर्णन्तु मस्तुना । अश्मरीं शर्कराञ्चैव मूत्रकृच्छ्रञ्च नाशयेत् । भावप्रकाशः ।

plantains, *bela* fruit, the five roots called *trinaja pancha mulaka* (see Sugar cane), *gulancha*, leaves of *Coleus aromaticus* (*asmabheda*), cucumber seeds, *Acorus Calamus* root, bamboo-manna, the ashes of *Sesamum Indicum* (*tila*), and of *Butea frondosa* (*palása*) and the root of *Jasminum auriculatum* (*juthiká*). Boil them together and prepare a *ghrita* in the usual way. It may be given in doses of one to two tolás, according to the constitution of the patient. After this medicine is digested, butter-milk and treacle should be taken.

Varunádya taila.[1] This is an oil prepared with *varuna* bark, for injection into the bladder. Take of *varuna* bark and of the entire plant of *Tribulus terrestris* (*gokshura*). two seers each, water sixty-four seers, boil together till reduced to one-fourth and strain. Boil this strained decoction with four seers of prepared sesamum oil and half a seer each, of the above mentioned drugs in the form of paste. This oil is recommended to be injected into the bladder, for the relief of painful micturition, calculus and gravel.

In scrofulous enlargement of the glands under the lower jaw, a decoction[2] of *varuna* bark is prescribed by several writers. It is said to cure even old standing cases. In internal or deep seated suppurative inflammation, a decoction of *varuna* and *Boerhaavia diffusa* (*punarnavá*) is given internally.[3]

NAT. ORDER. MORINGACEÆ.

MORINGA PTERYGOSPERMA.

Sans. शोभाञ्जन, *Sobhánjana.* शिग्रु, *Sigru.*

THIS plant is cultivated all over the country for the sake of it's leaves, flowers, and seed vessels which are used by the natives

---

1 वरुणाद्यं तैलम् । त्वक्पत्रमूलपुष्पस्य वरुणात्त्रिकण्टकात् । कषायेण पचेत्तैलं वस्तिना स्थापनेन च । शर्कराश्मरीमूत्रघ्नं मूत्रकृच्छ्रनिवारणम् ।

चक्रदत्तः ।

2 काञ्चनारत्वचः क्वाथः शुण्ठीचूर्णेन नाशयेत् । गण्डमालां तथा क्वाथः क्षौद्रेण वरुणत्वचः । शार्ङ्गधरः ।

3 पुनर्नवावरुणयोः क्वाथोन्तर्विद्रधिञ्जयेत् । शार्ङ्गधरः ।

in their curries. The root is described as acrid, pungent, stimulant and diuretic. Applied externally it acts as a rubefacient. The seeds are described as acrid and pungent and are used externally as a stimulant. They are called *Sveta maricha* that is white pepper. The Bhávaprakása describes two varieties of *sobhánjana*, namely, white and red. The root of the white variety is said to be a stronger rubefacient, while that of the red, is preferred for internal use, for promoting the appetite and acting on the excretions.

In ascites and enlarged spleen, a decoction[1] of the root-bark of *Moringa pterygosperma* and the leaves of *Rumex vesicarius* (*amlaloniká*) is given with the addition of long pepper, black pepper and rock salt in powder. In enlarged spleen and liver, a decoction of the root-bark is recommended to be given with the addition of plumbago root, rock salt and long pepper, or of the ashes of *Butea frondosa* (*palása*), or of *yavakshára* (impure carbonate of potash).[2]

In internal and deep seated inflammation and abscess (*vidradhi*) a decoction of the root-bark is recommended to be given with the addition of assafœtida and rock salt.[3] The expressed juice of the root-bark is also given in these cases, with the addition of honey or rock salt.[4] The root-bark is used externally in the shape of plaster, and the inflamed part is fomented with its decoction.[5]

---

1 पीतः प्लीहोदरं हन्यात्पिप्पलीमरिचान्वितः। अम्लवेतससंयुक्तः शिग्रुक्वाथः ससैन्धवः। चक्रदत्तः।

2 शोभाञ्जनकनिर्यूहं सैन्धवाग्निकणान्वितम्। पलाशक्षारयुक्तं वा यवक्षारं प्रयोजयेत्। चक्रदत्तः।

3 शोभाञ्जनक निर्यूहो हिङ्गुसैन्धवसंयुतः। अचिरं विद्रधिं हन्ति प्रातः-प्रातर्निषेवितः। चक्रदत्तः।

4 शिग्रुमूलं जले धौतं दरपिष्टं प्रगालयेत्। तद्रसं मधुना पीत्वा हन्त्यन्तर्विद्रधिं नरः। चक्रदत्तः।

5 स्वेदोपनाहाः कर्त्तव्याः शिग्रुमूलसमन्विताः। चक्रदत्तः।

In calculous affections the decoction of the root-bark is given internally.[1]

The seeds of *Moringa pterygosperma* enter into the composition of some stimulant applications. The following is an illustration. Take of the seeds of *Moringa pterygosperma*, rock salt, mustard seeds and *putchuk* root, equal parts, and reduce them to a paste with goat's urine. When dried this is used as a snuff for rousing comatose or drowsy persons.[2] The fresh juice of the root bark is recommended to be poured into the ears, for the relief of otalgia. The gum of the tree mixed with sesamum oil, is also used for the same purpose.[3]

NAT. ORDER. GUTTIFERÆ.

MESUA FERREA.

Sans. नागकेशर, *Nágakesara. Vern. Nágkesar, Beng. Hind.*

The dried flowers of *Mesua ferrea* are much used as a fragrant adjunct to decoctions and oils. They are regarded as astringent and stomachic and useful in thirst, irritability of the stomach, excessive perspiration etc. A paste of the flowers with the addition of butter and sugar is recommended by most of the later writers, to be taken in bleeding piles.[4] The powdered flowers mixed with old clarified butter, that has been washed a hundred times in water, are said to be an effectual application in burning of the feet.[5]

---

1 क्वाथश्च शिग्रुमूलोत्थः कदुष्णोऽश्मरीघातनः । चक्रदत्तः ।

2 सैन्धवं श्वेतमरिचं सर्षपाः कुष्ठमेव च । वस्तमूत्रेण संपिष्टं तन्द्रालस्यं निद्रारणम् । भावप्रकाशः ।

3 शोभाञ्जनकनिर्यासस्तिलतैलेन संयुतः । व्यक्तोष्णः पूरणः कर्णे कर्णशूलोपशान्तये । चक्रदत्तः ।

4 नवनीततिलैः कल्कीजेतारक्तार्शसां स्रुतः । नवनीतसितानागकेशरश्चापि तद्विधः । शार्ङ्गधरः ।

5 नागकेशरचूर्णं वा शतधौतेन सर्पिषा । पिष्ट्वा लेपो विधातव्यो दाहे हर्षे च पादयोः । चक्रदत्तः ।

NAT. ORDER. DIPTEROCARPEÆ.

SHOREA ROBUSTA.

Sans. शाल, *Sála,* अश्वकर्ण, *Asvakarna.*

THE resin of *Shorea robusta,* called *Rála* in Sanskrit and *Dhuná* or *rál,* in the vernacular, is regarded as astringent and detergent and is used in dysentery, and for fumigations, plasters, etc. The resin thrown over the fire, gives out thick volumes of fragrant smoke, and is much used for fumigating rooms occupied by the sick. It is also a common practice with natives to burn some *rál* in their rooms every evening, about the time that *chirags* or lamps are lighted, as also during the worship of idols.

In the dysentery of children *rál* is recommended to be given in doses of about twenty grains, with an equal quantity of sugar or treacle.[1]

Rál enters into the composition of some plasters and ointments. The following is an illustration. Take of *rál,* rock salt, treacle, wax, honey, bdellium, red ochre and clarified butter, in equal parts, boil them together and prepare an ointment.[2]

NAT. ORDER. MALVACEAE.

SIDA CORDIFOLIA.

Sans. बला, *Balá.* वाट्यालक, *Bátyálaka.*

Vern. *Berela, Beng.* *Khareti, Hind.*

FOUR varietes of *balá* are mentioned by Sanskrit writers, namely, *Bátyálaka,* (*Sida cordifolia*). *Mahábalá,* (*Sida rhomboidea.*)* *Atibalá,* (*Sida rhombifolia*). *Nágabalá,* (*Sida alba*). The roots of all these species, are regarded as cooling, astringent, tonic and useful

---

* This is only a variety of *Sida rhombifolia, L.*

1 श्वेतोवा यदि वा रक्तःसुपक्वो पक्वणीगदः गुड़ेनाधिकसर्जेन भक्षितेनाशु-नश्यति । भावप्रकाशः ।

2 सिन्धुसम्भवगुड़मधुमञ्जिषाच्चगैरिकं सघृतम् । सिक्थकमेतत्पक्वं पादस्फुट-नापहं सिद्धम् । चक्रदत्तः ।

in nervous diseases, urinary diseases and disorders of the blood and bile. In intermittent fever, a decoction of the root of *Sida cordifolia* and ginger is given.[1] It is said to be useful in fevers with cold shivering fits, followed by strong heat of body. The powder of the root-bark is given with milk and sugar, for the relief of frequent micturition and leucorrhœa.[2]

In diseases of the nervous system, such as insanity, paralysis, facial palsy, etc. the root of *Sida cordifolia* is used alone or in combination with other medicines, as in the following, called *Másha balâdi kvátha*.[3] Take of the pulse of *Phaseolus Roxburghii* (*másha*), root-bark of *Sida cordifolia* (*balá*), root of castor oil plant and of *Mucuna pruriens* (*átmaguptá*), *Hygrophila polysperma* (*katrina*), *Vanda Roxburghii* (*rásná*), and *Withania somnifera* (*asvagandhá*), equal parts, in all two tolas, and prepare a decoction in the usual way. It is administered with the addition of assafœtida and rock salt, in hemiplegia, stiff neck, facial paralysis, and noise in the ears with headache. An oil for external application in these diseases, called *Balátaila*[4] is thus prepared. Take of the root of *Sida cordifolia*, four seers, water, thirty-two seers and boil down to eight seers. To this decoction, add eight seers of milk, four seers of prepared sesamum oil, and one seer of the root of *Sida cordifolia* in the form of paste, and prepare an oil in the usual way.

---

1 महाबलामूल महौषधाभ्यां क्वाथो निहन्याद्विषमज्वरं हि । शीतं सकम्पं परिदाहयुक्तं विनाशयेत् द्वित्रिदिनप्रयोगात् । भावप्रकाशः ।

2 प्रदरं हन्ति बलाया मूलं दुग्धेन मधुयुतं पीतम् । चक्रदत्तः ।

3 माषबलादिः । माषबलाशूकशिम्बीकत्तृणरास्नाश्वगन्धोरुबूकाणाम् । क्वाथो नस्यनिपीतो रामठलवणान्वितः कोष्णः । अपहरति पक्षवातं मन्यास्तम्भं सकर्णनादरुजम् । दुर्जयमर्दितवातं सप्ताहाज्जयति चावश्यम् । चक्रदत्तः ।

4 बलातैलम् । बलानिःक्वाथकल्काभ्यां तैलपक्वं पयोन्वितम् । सर्व्ववातविकारघ्नमेवं शैरीयपाचितम् । चक्रदत्तः ।

BOMBAX MALABARICUM.

Sans. शाल्मली, *Sàlmali*, मोचा, *Mochá.*

Vern. Simul, Rakta Simul. Beng.

"THIS is one of the largest of our Indian trees, often about one hundred feet high and the trunk thick and ramous in proportion. Flowering time the end of winter, when the tree is totally destitute of leaves. The great numbers of very large bright red flowers with which it is then covered make it remarkably conspicuous at a very great distance." The thick stems are used for making large boats called *kondas*, from their being made by hollowing out the trunks. Some of these boats are large enough to carry a freight of a thousand maunds. The smaller floats are in very common use in Eastern Bengal, for crossing over rice fields during the rainy season. In fact during the rains these little floats, constitute the only mode of conveyance from village to village in low alluvial tracts. The thick beds and pillows of the natives are stuffed with the Cotton attached to the interior of the seed vessels of this plant, while the thin quilts and stuffed clothing for winter, are made with *kárpása* (cotton of *Gossypium herbaceum*).

The gum of this tree, called *mocharasa* is used in medicine.* It is considered astringent, tonic and alterative, and is used in diarrhœa, dysentery and menorrhagia. *Mocharasa* with sugar in equal parts, is given in doses of twenty to forty grains, in the diarrhœa of children. In the dysentery of children, the following is used. Take of *mocharasa*, flowers of *Woodfordia floribunda* (*dhátaki*),

---

* In the Pharmacopœia of India it is stated. "To this tree (*Bombax Malabaricum*), which is common in some parts of India, two drugs which hold a prominent place in the Native Materia Medica, have been usually but erroneously referred. 1. An astringent gummy exudation, *Mucherus* (Hind). .... Its botanical source is unknown. 2, Dried roots well known as *Safed Musli* (Hind)." The Sanskrit term *Mocharasa* of which the Hindi *Mucherus* is a corruption, means the juice or exudation of the *Mocha* tree, and *Mocha* is one of the sanskrit names of *Bombax Malabaricum*. Hence there can be no error in attributing the origin of *Mucherus* to *Bombax Malabaricum*. *Safed Musli* is the *Tàlamuli* of Sanskrit Materia Medica, the *Hypoxis orchioides* of Botanists.

root of *Mimosa pudica* (*lajjálu*), and the filaments of the lotus, equal parts, in all one tolá, powdered rice one tolá, water eleven tolás, and boil together to the consistence of a gruel (*yavágu*).[1] In the dysentery of adults a decoction of *bela* fruit in goat's milk, is givenwith the addition of powdered *mocharasa* and *indrajava* seeds.[2]

HIBISCUS MOSCHATUS. *Sans.* लताकस्तुरिका *Latákasturiká*, *Vern.* *Latàkasturi Beng.* The scented seeds of this plant are much used in perfuming medicinal oils. They also enter into the composition of some compound prescriptions, being regarded as cooling, tonic and carminative.

PAVONIA ODORATA. *Sans.* बाला *Bálá*, ह्रीबेर *Hrivera*. *Vern.* *Sugandha bálá*, *Hind.* The fragrant roots of this plant are considered aromatic, cooling and stomachic and are much used in combination with other medicines of the sort in fever, inflammation, hemorrhage from internal organs etc. *Bálá* enters into the composition of a well-known fever drink called *shadanga pániya*, (see *Andropogon muricatum*).

NAT. ORDER STERCULIACEÆ.

PTEROSPERMUM SUBERIFOLIUM. *Sans.* मुचुकुन्द, *Muchukunda*. The flower of this tree, rubbed into a paste with *kánjika* is an ancient and well known application for hemicrania. It is mentioned by many writers and is used even at the present day, as a domestic remedy.[3]

---

1 मोचरसः समङ्गा च धातकीपद्मकेशरम् । पिष्टैरेतैर्यवागूः स्याद्रक्तातीसारनाशिनी । भावप्रकाशः ।

2 बिल्वं छागपयः सिद्धं सितामोचरसान्वितम् । कलिङ्गचूर्णसंयुक्तं रक्तातिसारनाशनम् । चक्रदत्तः ।

3 शिरोऽर्त्तिं वातजां हन्यात्पुष्पं वा मुचुकुन्दजम् । शार्ङ्गधरः ।

NAT. ORDER GERANIACEÆ.

OXALIS CORNICULATA.

Sans. अम्ललोणिका, *Amlaloniká.* चाङ्गेरी, *Chángerí.*

Vern. A'mrulsák, Beng.

THE leaves of *Oxalis corniculata* are used as a pot-herb. They are considered cooling, refrigerant, appetizing and stomachic. The fresh juice of the leaves is given to relieve intoxication from *datura*, and is said to be useful in dysentery and prolapsus of the rectum, for which it is recommended by most writers. Chakradatta gives the following formula for preparing a *ghrita* with this medicine.

Chángeri ghrita.[1] Take of clarified butter, four seers, the fresh juice of *Oxalis corniculata*, four seers, curdled milk called *dadhi*, sixteen seers and the leaves of *Oxalis corniculata* reduced to a paste, one seer. Boil them together in the usual way and prepare a *ghrita*. This preparation is said to be useful in diarrhœa, dysentery, prolapsus of the rectum, tympanites, piles and difficult micturition. The Bhávaprakása gives the following process for preparing a compound *ghrita*.[2] Take of the fresh juice of *Oxalis corniculata*, decoction of jujube fruits and ginger, alkaline water (see Alkalies), and curdled milk, each four seers, clarified butter four seers, and prepare a *ghrita* in the usual way. It is recommended for use in prolapse of the rectum.

AVERRHOA CARAMBOLA. *Sans.* कर्म्मरङ्ग, *Karmaranga. Vern. Kámrángá, Beng.* and *Hind.* The five-angled fruits of this plant contain an acid watery pulp, and are eaten raw as well as in curries. They enter into the composition of some cooling medicines for fever and other diseases.

---

1 चाङ्गेरीघृतम्। चाङ्गेरीस्वरसे सर्पिः कल्कैरेतैर्विपाचितम्। चतुर्गुणे च दध्ना च तद्घृतं कफवातनुत्। अर्शांसि ग्रहणीदोषं मूत्रकृच्छ्रं प्रवाहिकाम्। गुदभ्रंशार्त्तिमानाहं घृतमेतद्व्यपोहति। चक्रदत्तः।

2 चाङ्गेरी कोल दध्यम्ल क्षार नागर संयुतम्। घृतं विपक्वं पातव्यं गुदभ्रंशगदापहम्। भावप्रकाशः।

NAT. ORDER ZYGOPHYLLACEÆ.

TRIBULUS TERRESTRIS.

Sans. गोक्षुरी, *Gokshuri.* इक्षुगन्धा, *Ikshugandhá.*

Vern. Gokhuru, Beng. Hind.

THIS plant is also called *Sthala sringátaka* and *Trikantaka*, from the resemblance of its fruits to those of *Trapa bispinosa* and from their being armed with three spines. The entire plant but more particularly the fruits are used in medicine. They are regarded as cooling, diuretic, tonic and aphrodisiac and are used in painful micturition, calculous affections, urinary disorders and impotence. The fruits constitute an ingredient of *Dasamula* (see *Desmodium gangeticum*).

A decoction of the fruits is given with the addition of *yavakshára* (impure carbonate of potash), in painful micturition.[1] A decoction of the entire plant is given with *silájatu* (a bituminous substance) and honey, in the same affection. Equal parts of *gokhuru* and sesamum seeds, taken with goat's milk and honey, is said to cure impotence arising from bad practices.[2]

Gokshurádya valeha[3] or electuary of *gokshuri* is prepared as follows. Take of the entire plant of *Tribulus terrestris*, twelve

---

1 क्वाथं गोक्षुरबीजस्य यवक्षारयुतं पिबेत्। मूत्रकृच्छ्रं सकृज्जञ्च पीतं शीघ्रं निवारयेत्। चक्रदत्तः।

2 समतिलगोक्षुरचूर्णं छागीक्षीरेण साधितं समधु। भुक्तं क्षपयति षाण्ड्यं यज्जनितं कुप्रयोगेण। भावप्रकाशः।

3 गोक्षुरकाद्यवलेहः। गोकण्टकं सदलमूलफलं गृहीत्वा, संकुट्टितं पलशतं क्वथितं तु तोये। पादस्थितेन सलिलेन पलानि दत्त्वा पञ्चाशतन्तु विपचेदथ शर्करायाः। तस्मिन् घनत्वमुपगच्छति चूर्णितानि दद्यात् पलद्वयमितानि सुभाजनानि। शुण्ठीकणामरिचनागदलत्वगेलाजातीयकोषककुभत्वगुषीफलानि। वांशोपलाष्टकमिह प्रणिधाय नित्यम् लेह्यं तु शुद्धमश्नतं पलसम्मितन्तु। हन्त्याशु मूत्रपरिदाह विबन्ध शुक्रकृच्छ्राश्मरी रुधिरमेहमधुप्रमेहान्। भावप्रकाशः।

seers and a half, water, sixty-four seers and boil till reduced to one-fourth. To the strained decoction, add six seers and a quarter of sugar and again boil till reduced to the proper consistence for an electuary; then add the following substances in fine powder, namely, ginger, long pepper, black pepper, cinnamon, cardamoms, flowers of *Mesua ferrea* (*nágakesara*), leaves called *tejapatra*, nutmeg, bark of *Terminalia Arjuna*, and cucumber seeds, each sixteen tolás, bamboo-manna half a seer, and prepare an electuary. It is given in doses of two tolás, in painful micturition, suppression of urine, bloody urine, calculous affections etc.

NAT. ORDER RUTACEÆ.

CITRUS.

The different species of *Citrus* described by Sanskrit writers are as follows.

जम्बीर, *Jambira. Vern. Gorápebu, Beng. Citrus acida. Roxb. Var.* 3

लिम्पाक, *Limpáka. Vern. Pátinebu, Beng.* *do.* *do.* *1*

निम्बूक, *Nimbuka. Vern. Kágujinebu, Beng.* *do.* *do.* 2

बीजपूर, *Vijapura. Vern. Tabánebu, Beng.* *do.* *do.* 7

मधुकर्कटिका, *Madhukarkaṭiká, Vern. Miṭhánebu, Beng. do.* *do.* 9

मातुलुङ्ग, *Matulunga. Vern. Chholonga nebu, Beng. Citrus medica.*

करुणा, *Karuná, Sans. and Beng. Citrus medica, variety of.*

नागरङ्ग, *Nágaranga. Vern. Kamlánebu, Beng. C. Aurantium.*

The variety of *Citrus acida*,* called *Jambira*, yields the lemon juice used in medicine. *Limpáka* or *páti nebu* is much used as a sauce by the natives. The fruits are cut vertically into two pieces, and the fresh juice, squeezed out with the fingers, is sprinkled on soup, *dál*, curry etc. to which it imparts a pleasant acid taste and agreeable flavour. A pickle of *páti nebu*, in its own juice, and salt is a popular and effectual medicine for indiges-

* *Citrus acida* is itself a variety of the *Citrus medica* of Linnæus to which species *C. Limonum*, *C. Limetta* and *C. Lumia* are also reduced.

tion brought on by excess in eating, or by undigestible articles of diet. The fruits are first rubbed over a stone, or their rind scraped a little so as to thin it. They are then steeped in juice obtained from other fruits of the sort, and exposed to the sun for a few days with the addition of common salt. When crisp and of a brown colour, they are preserved in porcelain vessels or glass jars. This preparation is called *Járak nebu* (that is digestive lemon) in the vernacular.

The variety of *Citrus acida* called *káguji nebu* has larger fruits than that of *páti nebu*, and is also used as sauce like the latter, but its flavour and the fragrance of the essential oil in its rind is not so delicious.

Citrus Aurantium, or the sweet orange, comes from the valleys of the Khasia Hills and of the eastern Himalaya. It is called *kamlá nebu* in Bengali. The variety grown in the plains has an acid taste and is called *nárengá* in the vernacular.

The Sanskrit term *karuná nimbu* is variously translated by different authorities. Wilson in his Sanskrit dictionary calls it *Citrus decumana*. In the Hortus Bengalensis it is translated into *Citrus medica*, while Drury and other Madras authorities make the variety *Citrus Limonum*. The Sabdakalpadruma does not give any synonym or vernacular term for it, so that it is difficult to say, what form it really meant. In the vernacular the term *karuná* is applied to a variety of *Citrus medica*.

Citrus decumana has I believe no Sanskrit name. In the vernacular it is called *Bátávi nebu*, from its having been originally brought from Batavia. It is now much cultivated in gardens and is one of the common edible fruits of the country. Some varieties of the fruit have a pleasant taste and aroma, with little or no acidity.

Madhukarkatiká. This variety of *Citrus medica* is probably the one described by Roxburgh as *Miṭhá nebu*, that is sweet lemon. The variety of *Citrus* which has very large oblong fruits, almost equal in size to the shaddock, and the thick spongy rind of which constitutes the largest portion of the fruit, was shewn to me by a gardener in Malda, under the name of *madhukarkati.* The pulp of this variety is very limited in quantity, of a bland sweetish taste and without any aroma or acidity.

Lemon juice is considered cooling, refrigerant stomachic and useful in indigestion, dyspepsia, vomiting of meals, thirst, burning of the body, intoxication from spiritious drinks or narcotics, etc. Fresh lemon juice is recommended to be taken in the evening, for the relief of dyspepsia with vomiting of meals.[1] It enters into the composition of several carminative medicines for dyspepsia, such as the *Hingváshṭaka* (see Assafœtida), *Kravyádi churna* etc.

In rheumatic affections such as pleurodynia, sciatica, lumbago, pain in the hip joints etc., Sárangadhara recommends the administration of lemon juice with the addition of *yavakshára* (impure carbonate of potash) and honey.[2]

Rasáyanámrita lauha.[3] Take of long pepper, black pepper, ginger, the three myrobalans, *báberung* seeds, cumin and nigella seeds, *ajowan* and the seeds of *Cnidium diffusum* (*vanajamáni*), *chiretta*, *trivrit*, root of *Baliospermum montanum (danti)*, *nim* bark, and rock salt, each two tolás, prepared iron sixteen tolás, sugar two seers, decoction of the three myrobalans four seers, and lemon juice two seers. Boil all these ingredients together till the watery portion is evaporated, lastly add clarified butter, half a seer and

---

1 जम्बीरस्वरसः पीतः साय हन्त्यन्नपित्तकम्। चक्रदत्तः।

2 बीजपूररसः पानान्मधुक्षारयुतोजयेत्। पार्श्वहृद्वस्तिशूलानि कोष्ठवायुञ्च दारुणम्। शार्ङ्गधरः।

3 रसायनामृतलौहः। त्रिकटु त्रिफला मुस्तं विडङ्गं जीरकद्वयम्। यमानीद्वयं भूनिम्बं त्रिवृद्दन्तीच निम्बुकम्। सर्वेषां कार्षिकं भागं सैन्धवं कर्षमर्द्धकम्। खण्डस्य षोड़शपलं प्रस्थञ्च त्रिफलाजलम्। जम्बीराणां रसं दद्यात् पलषोड़शकं तथा। पाच्यं सर्व्वं प्रयत्नेन लौहं दत्वा पलद्वयम्। सिद्धे पाके पुनर्दद्यात् घृतं पलचतुष्टयम्। सर्वरोगेषु संयोज्यं महामृतरसायनम्। गुल्मं पञ्चविधं हन्ति यकृत्प्लीहोदराणि च। कामलां पाण्डुरोगञ्च शोथं जीर्णज्वरन्तथा। रोगान् सर्व्वान् निहन्त्याशु भास्करस्तिमिरं यथा। भैषज्यरत्नावली।

prepare a confection. Dose one to two tolás, in enlargements of the abdominal viscera, anæmia, jaundice, anasarca and chronic fever.

In fever complicated with pain in the head, throat and chest, the following mixture is directed to be used as a snuff for promoting discharge of phlegm. Take of lemon juice, ginger juice, rock salt, black salt, and *sonchal* salt, equal parts, and mix. The mixture should be warmed a little before use.

The root of the variety of *Citrus acida*, called *limpáka* constitutes one of the principal ingredients in the composition of a medicine called *Yakridari lauha*, described under Iron.

ÆGLE MARMELOS.

Sans. विल्व, *vilva. Vern. Bela, Beng. Hind.*

THE *Ægle Marmelos* is held in great veneration by the Hindus. It is sacred to Siva whose worship cannot be accomplished without its leaves. Hence this tree is always met with near temples dedicated to Siva. It is incumbent on all Hindus to cultivate and cherish this tree, and it is sacrilegious to up-root or cut it down. The Hindu who expires under a *bela* tree, expects to obtain immediate salvation, notwithstanding that he may have committed innumerable sins.

The *Ægle Marmelos* is used in medicine in a variety of ways. The unripe or half ripe fruit is regarded as astringent, digestive and stomachic and as useful in restraining discharges from the alimentary canal. The ripe fruit is described as sweet, aromatic, cooling and laxative. It is not easily digested and has a tendency to cause flatulence. The dried pulp of the fruit, called *Vilva peshiká* in Sanskrit, is regarded as astringent and a specific for dysentery. The root-bark is considered useful in diseases supposed to be caused by deranged air. It constitutes an ingredient of *dasamul* or the ten roots, (see *Desmodium gangeticum.*) The fresh juice of the leaves is given with honey as a domestic laxative and febrifuge.

17

The dried pulp of the fruit is given with treacle, in recent dysentery with griping, pain in the loins and costiveness.[1] A compound powder[2] is prepared with equal parts of dried *bela*, tubers of *Cyperus rotundus* (*mustaka*), flowers of *Woodfordia floribunda* (*dhátaki*), root of *Stephania hernandifolia* (*páṭhá*) ginger and *mocharasa*. It is given in doses of twenty-two to forty-four grains with buttermilk and treacle. In the dysentery of children, a decoction and an electuary of the following drugs is used, namely dried *bela*, fruits of *Pothos officinalis* (*gajapippuli*), root of *Pavonia odorata* (*bálá*), flowers of *Woodfordia floribunda* (*dhátaki*), and bark of *Symplocos racemosa* (*lodhra*), in equal parts.[3]

A decoction of the root of *Ægle Marmelos*,[4] is given with sugar and fried rice, for checking diarrhœa and gastric irritability in infants.

The fresh juice of the leaves is given, with the addition of black pepper, in anasarca with costiveness and jaundice.[5] In external inflammations, the juice of the leaves is given internally, to remove the supposed derangement of the humours.

Vilva taila is thus prepared.[6] Take of dried *bela* fruits, twelve seers and a half and boil in sixty-four seers of water, till reduced

---

1 गुडेन खादयेद्बिल्वं रक्तातिसारनाशनम् । आमशूलविबन्धघ्नं कुक्षिरोगविनाशनम् । चक्रदत्तः ।

2 बिल्वाब्द धातकी पाठा शुण्ठी मोचरसाः समाः । पीता रुन्धन्त्यतीसारं गुड़तक्रेण दुर्ज्जयम् । चक्रदत्तः ।

3 बिल्वञ्च पुष्पाणिच धातकीनां जलं सलोध्रं गजपिप्पलीच। क्वाथावलेहौ मधुनाविमिश्रौ बालेषु योज्यावतिसारितेषु । चक्रदत्तः ।

4 बिल्वमूलकषायेण लाजाश्चैवसशर्कराः । आलोड्य पाययेद्बालं छर्द्दतीसारनाशनम् । चक्रदत्तः ।

5 बिल्वपत्ररसं पूतं सोषणं श्वयथौत्रिजे । विट् सङ्गेचैवदुर्नाम्नि विदध्यात्कामलास्वपि । चक्रदत्तः ।

6 बिल्वतैलम् । शतं संपक्वबिल्वस्य जलद्रोणे विपाचयेत्। तेनपादावशेषेण तैलप्रस्थं विपाचयेत् । रास्ना पुनर्नवाकुष्ठं नागरं बिल्वमेव च । धातकीदेव-

to one-fourth. To the strained decoction, add four seers of prepared sesamum oil and six tolás each of the following substances, in the form of paste, namely, *Vanda Roxburghii* (*rásná*). *Boerhaavia diffusa* (*punarnavá*), *Aplotaxis auriculata* (*kushṭa*), ginger, dried *bela*, flowers of *Woodfordia floribunda* (*dhátaki*), wood of *Pinus deodara* (*devadáru*), bark of *Symplocos racemosa* (*lodhra*), tubers of *Cyperus rotundus* (*mustaka*), *Acorus Calamus* (*vachá*), and gum of *Bombax Malabaricum* (*sálmaliveshṭa*), and prepare an oil in the usual way. This oil is used externally in chronic bowel complaints.

FERONIA ELEPHANTUM.

Sans. कपित्थ *Kapittha. Vern. Kathbel, Beng. Kaith, Hind.*

THE wood apple tree is met with throughout India and is cultivated for the sake of the fruits, the pulp of which is edible. A *chátni*, made of the ripe pulp with the addition of oil, salt, tamarind and spices, is esteemed by many. The unripe fruit is described as astringent and is used in combination with *bela* and other medicines in diarrhœa and dysentery. The ripe fruit is said to be useful in hiccup and affections of the throat. The leaves are aromatic and carminative.

Kapitthásh̤ṭaka churna.[1] Take of the pulp of unripe wood apples eight parts, sugar six parts, pomegranate juice, tamarind

---

दारुध्रलोध्रं मुस्तं वचा तथा । शाल्मलीवेष्टकञ्चैव पृथक्कर्षत्रयं पचेत् । अस्य तैलस्य सिद्धस्य शृणु वीर्य्यमतः परम् । दुर्णामग्रहणीरोग मतीसारं सवेदनम् । कामला पाण्डुरोगघ्नं क्रिमिदोषविनाशनम् । वह्निसन्दीपनं वल्यं मेदमांस विवर्द्धनम् । अपचीं गण्डमालाञ्च ज्वरं जीर्णं व्यपोहति । अश्विभ्यां निर्म्मितं पूर्व्वं विल्वतैलमिदं महत् ॥ तैलावलीसंग्रहोक्तं ।

1 कपित्थाष्टकचूर्णम् । अष्टौ भागाः कपित्थस्य षड्भागाः शर्करामताः । दाड़िमं तिन्तिड़ीकञ्च श्रीफलं धातकीतथा । अजमोदाच पिप्पल्यः प्रत्येकं स्युस्त्रिभागिकाः । मरिचं जीरकं धान्यं ग्रन्थिकं वालकन्तथा । सौवर्चलं

pulp, *bela* fruit, flowers of *Woodfordia floribunda (dhátaki)*, *ájmad*, and long pepper, each three parts, black pepper, cumin seeds, coriander, long pepper root, root of *Pavonia odorata* (*bálá*), *sonchal* salt, *ájowan*, cardamoms, cinnamon, *tejapatra*, flowers of *Mesua ferrea* (*nágakesara*), ginger and plumbago root, each one part, powder the ingredients finely and mix. Dose, about one drachm. This preparation is used in chronic diarrhœa and dysentery with loss of appetite and in affections of the throat.

XANTHOXYLUM HOSTILE. *Sans.* तुम्बुरु, *Tumburu. Vern. Nepáli dhaniá, Tumri, Hind.* The aromatic and pungent fruits of this plant, resemble coriander in appearance and are used as aromatic adjuncts, in compound prescriptions and in perfuming medicinal oils.

NAT. ORDER BURSERACEÆ.

BALSAMODENDRON MUKUL.

Syn. Balsamodendron Agallocha.

Sans. गुग्गुलु, *Guggulu. Vern. Guggul. Beng. Hind.*

Guggulu or Indian bdellium is obtained by making incisions in the tree, through which the gum resin exudes. According to Sanskrit writers, new or recently exuded *guggulu* is moist, viscid, fragrant and of a golden colour. It burns in the fire, melts in the sun and forms a milky emulsion with hot water. Old *guggulu* is dry and without flavour or colour; it should not be used in medicine.

Guggulu is said to be demulcent, aperient, alterative and a purifier of the blood. It is used in rheumatism, nervous diseases, scrofulous affections, urinary disorders, and skin diseases. In rheumatism it is used in a great variety of forms. The following called *Yogarája guggulu* is a favourite preparation.

यमानीञ्च चातुर्जातं सचित्रकम्। नागरञ्चैकभागाः स्युः प्रत्येकं सूक्ष्मचूर्णिताः। कपित्थाष्टकसंज्ञं स्यात् चूर्णमेतद्गदामयान्। अतीसारं क्षयञ्चैव ग्रहणीञ्च व्यपोहति। शार्ङ्गधरः।

Yogarája guggulu.[1] Take of plumbago root, long pepper root *ájowan*, seeds of *Nigella sativa* (*kálájirá*), *báberang* seeds, seeds of *Carum Roxburghianum* (*ajamodá*), cumin seeds, *Pinus Deodara* (*devadáru*), *Chavica officinarum* (*chavya*), cardamoms, rock salt, root of *Aplotaxis auriculata* (*kushṭha*), root of *Vanda Roxburghii* (*rásná*), fruits of *Tribulus terrestris* (*gokshura*), coriander, the three myrobalans, tubers of *Cyperus rotundus* (*mustaka*), long pepper, black pepper, ginger, cinnamon, root of *Andropogon muricatus* (*usira*), *yavakshára* (impure carbonate of potash), leaves of *Pinus Webbiana* (*tálisapatra*) and the leaves called *tejapatra*, one part each, in fine powder, bdellium in quantity, equal to all the above ingredients. Rub them together with clarified butter and preserve the preparation in an earthen pot smeared with clarified butter. Dose from a half to one tolá. It is given in rheumatic affections and other diseases supposed to be caused by deranged air, in unhealthy ulcerations, affections of the joints etc. Another preparation called *Trayodasánga guggulu* is similar in composition to the above. It is made with thirteen aromatic adjuncts, hence its name, and is recommended for use in rheumatism affecting the loins and the sacrum. In rheumatism affecting the joints and bones the following preparation called *A'dityapáka guggulu*[2] is used. Take

---

1 योगराजगुग्गुलुः । चित्रकं पिप्पलीमूलं यमानीं कारवीन्तथा । विडङ्गान्यजमोदाश्च जीरकं सुरदारुच ॥ चव्यैलासैन्धवं कुष्ठं रास्नागोक्षुरधान्यकम् । त्रिफलामुस्तकं व्योषं त्वगुशीरं यवाग्रजम् । तालीशपत्रं पत्रञ्च सूक्ष्मचूर्णानि कारयेत् । यावन्त्येतानि चूर्णानि तावन्मात्रन्तु गुग्गुलुम् । संमर्द्य सर्पिषा गाढं स्निग्धे भाण्डे निधापयेत् । ततोमात्रां प्रयुञ्जीत यथेष्टाहारवानपि । योगराजइतिख्यातोयोगोऽयममृतोपमः । आमवाताद्यवातादीन् क्रमिदुष्टव्रणानपि । प्लीहागुल्मोदरानाहदुर्नामानि विनाशयेत् । अग्निञ्च कुरुते दीप्तं तेजोवृद्धिं बलन्तथा वातरोगान् जयत्येष सन्धिमज्जगतानपि ।

चक्रदत्तः ।

2 आदित्यपाक गुग्गुलु वटकः । पृथक् पलांशा त्रिफला पिप्पलीचेति-चूर्णितम् । दशमूलाम्बुना भाव्यं त्वगेलार्द्धपलान्वितम् । दत्त्वा पलानि पञ्चैव

of the three myrobalans and long pepper each eight tolás, cinnamon and cardamoms four tolás each; powder the ingredients finely and soak for seven days in a decoction of the ten drugs, called *dasamula* (see *Desmodium gangeticum*). Then add forty tolás of *guggulu* and beat together into a uniform mass. Dose, half to one tolá.

Vatári rasa [1] This preparation is used in paralysis and nervous diseases. To prepare, it take of mercury one part, sulphur two parts, the three myrobalans, three parts in all, plumbago root four parts and pure *guggulu* five parts. Rub them together with castor oil for twelve hours, then add to the mass the compound powder, called *Hingvastaka* (see Assafœtida), in weight equal to all the above ingredients, and again rub together for twelve hours. Dose, about half a drachm.

Kaisara guggulu.[2] Take of pure bdellium, *gulancha* and the three myrobalans, each two seers, water ninety-six seers. First boil the *gulancha* and the myrobalans in the water till the latter is reduced to one-half, and strain the decoction ; to the strained fluid add the bdellium and boil in an iron vessel till the whole is reduced to the consistence of treacle. Now add to it the following

---

गुग्गुलोर्वटकीकृतः। एष मांसरसाभ्यासाद्वातरोगान् विशेषतः। हन्ति सन्ध्य-स्थिमज्जस्थान् वृक्षमिन्द्राशनिर्यथा। भाव्यद्रव्यसमं क्वाथ्यं क्वाथोऽष्टांशस्तुतेन च। आर्द्रं यावद्दिनं भाव्यं सप्ताहं भावनाविधिः। चक्रदत्तः।

1 वातारिरसः। रसो गन्धो वरा वह्नि गुग्गुलुः क्रमवर्द्धितः। त्रिभागा त्रिफला योज्या चतुर्भागस्तुचित्रकः। गुग्गुलुः पञ्च भागः स्यादेरण्डतैलेन मर्द्दितः। क्षिप्त्वा तत्रोदितं चूर्णं तेन तैलेन मर्द्दयेत्। गुटिकां कर्षमात्रान्तु भक्षयेत् प्रातरेवहि। वातारिसंज्ञकोह्येष रसो नियतसेवितः। मासेन महतो रोगान् हरेत् सुरतवर्जिनः। भावप्रकाशः।

2 कैशर गुग्गुलुः। त्रिफलायास्त्रयः प्रस्थाः प्रस्थैकाचामृता भवेत्। सङ्कुट्य-लौहपात्रेण सार्द्धद्रोणाम्बुना पचेत्। जलमर्द्धभृतं ज्ञात्वा गृह्णीयाद्वस्त्रगा-लितम्। ततः क्वाथे क्षिपेच्छुद्धं गुग्गुलुं प्रस्थसम्मितम्। पुनर्दद्यमयःपात्रे दार्व्या संघर्षयेन्मुहुः। सान्द्रीभूतं ततो ज्ञात्वा गुडपाकसमाकृतिम्। चूर्णीकृत्य तत-स्तत्र द्रव्याणीमानि प्रक्षिपेत्। त्रिफला द्विपला ज्ञेया गुडूचीपलिका मता। षडक्षं

substances in fine powder, namely, the three myrobalans, each sixteen tolás, *gulancha* eight tolás, ginger, long pepper and black pepper, each six tolás, *báberang* seeds four tolás, root of *Baliospermum montanum* (*danti*) and *Ipomœa Turpethum* (*trivrit*), each two tolás, and beat them together into a uniform mass. Dose from a quarter to one tolá, to be taken with a decoction of madder, tepid milk or water. This medicine is said to be useful in various skin diseases from deranged or vitiated blood. It is said to act as an alterative tonic and to improve the nutrition of the body.

Sadanga guggulu.[1] In affections of the eyes with pain, swelling and inflammation, (rheumatic ophthalmia?) bdellium is recommended to be given with a decoction of the three myrobalans, root of *Momordica dioica* (*patala*), *nim* bark, and the leaves of *Adhatoda vasica* (*vásaka*). A similar preparation is recommended for secondary syphilitic ulcerations. In unhealthy ulcerations, the following, called *Amrita guggulu*[2] is recommended. Take of *gulancha*, root of *Momordica dioica* (*patala*), the three myrobalans, long pepper, black pepper, ginger, and *baberung* seeds in equal parts, *guggulu*, in quantity equal to all the above ingredients and beat them together into a mass. Dose about a drachm every morning.

OLIBANUM. The gum of the *Salai* tree of India (*Boswellia*

त्र्यूषणं प्रोक्तं विडङ्गानां पलार्द्धकम् । दन्तीकर्षमिता कार्य्या त्रिवृत्कर्षमिता तथा । ततः पिण्डीकृतं सर्व्वं घृतपात्रे विनिक्षिपेत् । गुटिकां शाणमात्रेण युञ्ज्याद्दोषत्वपेक्षया । अनुपानं भिषग्दद्यात्कोष्णं नीरं पयोऽथवा । मञ्जिष्ठादिशृतं वापि युक्तियुक्तं ततः परम् । जयेत्सर्वाणि कुष्ठानि वातरक्तं त्रिदोषजम् । सर्व्वव्रणानि गुल्मांश्च प्रमेहपिडकांस्तथा । शार्ङ्गधरः ।

1 षडङ्गगुग्गुलुः । विभीतक शिवा धात्री पटोलारिष्ट वासकैः । क्वथो गुग्गुलुना पेयः शोथशूलाक्षिपाकहा । पिल्लञ्च सव्रणं शुक्रं रागादींश्चापि नाशयेत् । एतैश्चापि घृतं पक्वं रोगांस्तांश्च व्यपोहति । चक्रदत्तः ।

2 अमृतागुग्गुलुः । अमृता पटोलमूल त्रिफला त्रिकटु कृमिघ्नानाम् । समभागानां चूर्णं सर्व्वसमो गुग्गुलोर्भागः । प्रतिवासरमेकैकां खादेदक्षप्रमाणाम् । जेतुं व्रणानुवातास्रगुल्मोदरश्वयथुरोगादीन् । चक्रदत्तः ।

thurifera), is called *Kunduru* in Sanskrit. It is used as an incense and as a local application to buboes.[1]

MYRRH is called *Vola* in Sanskrit and is described as an article to be had in the *beniah's* shop, thereby implying it to be an imported drug. It is said to be useful in fever, epilepsy and uterine affections, but is not much used in practice.

NAT. ORDER MELIACEÆ.

AZADIRACHTA INDICA.

Sans. निम्ब, *Nimba. Vern. Nim, Beng. Hind.*

THIS useful tree is indigenous to India and is cultivated all over the country for the sake of its bark, leaves and fruits. These have been used in Hindu medicine from a very remote period. The bark is regarded as bitter, tonic, astringent and useful in fever, thirst, nausea, vomiting and skin diseases. The bitter leaves are used as a pot-herb being made into soup or curry with other vegetables. The slightly aromatic and bitter taste which they impart to the curries thus prepared, is much relished by some. The leaves are moreover an old and popular remedy for skin diseases. The fruits are described as purgative and emollient and useful in intestinal worms, urinary diseases, piles etc. The oil obtained from the seeds is used in skin diseases, and ulcers.

The bark is used in fever in combination with other medicines for this disease as for example, in the following compound decoction called *Amritáshṭaka*.[2] Take of *nim* bark, *gulancha*, root of *Picrorrhiza Kurroa* (*katuki*), tubers of *Cyperus rotundus* (*mustaka*), seeds of *Holarrhena antidysenterica* (*indrayava*), leaves of

---

1 अजाक्षीरेण गोधूमकल्कं कुन्दुरुकस्य वा। प्रलेपनं सुखोष्णं स्याद्व्रध्न-शूलहरः परः। चक्रदत्तः।

2 अमृताष्टकः। अमृतारिष्ट कटुका मुस्तेन्द्रयव नागरैः। पटोलचन्दनाभ्याञ्च पिप्पलीचूर्णयुक्तं शृतम्। अमृताष्टकमेतच्च पित्तश्लेष्मज्वरापहम्। छर्द्यरोचकहृल्लास दाह तृष्णा निवारणम्। शार्ङ्गधरः।

Momordica dioica (*paṭala*), ginger and red sandal wood, each quarter of a tolá, water half a seer, boil till reduced to one-fourth. This decoction is given with the addition of honey and long pepper in fever supposed to be caused by deranged phlegm and bile and attended with vomiting, nausea, thirst and lassitude.

The fresh juice of the leaves is given with salt in intestinal worms, and with honey in jaundice and skin diseases. The juice of *nim* leaves and of emblic myrobalans, quarter of a tolá each, are recommended to be given with the addition of clarified butter in prurigo, boils and urticaria.[1] *Nim* enters into the composition of several compound preparations used in skin diseases, such as the *Pancha tikta ghrita*, *Pancha nimba guḍiká*, *Pancha kasháya*, etc.

Pancha tikta ghrita.[2] Take of *nim* bark, leaves of *Momordica dioica* (*patala*), *Solanum Jacquinii* (*kantakári*), *gulancha*, and bark of *Adhatoda vasica* (*vásaka*), each eighty tolás, and boil them in sixty-four seers of water till it is reduced to one-fourth. To the strained decoction, add four seers of clarified butter and a seer of the three myrobalans in the form of a paste, and prepare a *ghrita* in the usual way. This preparation is given in doses of three to six drachms in chronic skin diseases.

As an external application to ulcers and skin diseases, *nim* leaves are used in a variety of forms such as poultice, wash, ointment and liniment.[3] A poultice made of equal parts of *nim* leaves

---

1 निम्बस्य पत्राणि सदा घृतेन धात्रीविमिश्राण्यथ योपयुञ्ज्यात् । विस्फोटकोठक्षत शीतपित्तं कण्डूस्रपित्तं सहसा च जह्यात् । चक्रदत्तः ।

2 पञ्चतिक्तकं घृतम् । निम्बं पटोलं व्याघ्रीञ्च गुडूचीं वासकं तथा । कुर्य्याद्दशपलान् भागानेकैकस्य सुकुट्टितान् । जलद्रोणे विपक्तव्यं यावत्पादावशेषितम् । घृतप्रस्थं पचेत्तेन त्रिफलागर्भसंयुतम् । पञ्चतिक्तमिदं ख्यातं सर्पिः कुष्ठविनाशनम् । चक्रदत्तः ।

3 निम्बार्जुनाश्वत्थकदम्बशाल जम्बूवटोडुम्बर वेतसेषु । प्रक्षालनालेप घृतानि कुर्य्याच्चूर्णानि पित्तास्रभवोपदंशे । चक्रदत्तः ।

and sesamum seeds is recommended by Chakradatta for unhealthy ulcerations.[1]

The following preparation of *nim* oil is prescribed by several writers for application to suppurating scrofulous glands with numerous openings. Take of the oil of *nim* seeds, four seers; orpiment, realgar, marking nut, cardamoms, aloes wood, sandal wood, leaves of *Jasminum grandiflorum* (*játipatra*), and of *Limnanthenum cristatum* (*tagarapáduká*), each eight tolás, in the form of a paste, and water sixteen seers. Boil them together and prepare an oil in the usual way.[2]

NAT. ORDER AMPELIDEÆ.

VITIS VINIFERA, *Linn.*

Sans. द्राक्षा, *Drákshá.* मृद्वीका, *Mridviká*

Vern. A'ngurphal, Kismis, Manakká, Beng. Hind.

GRAPES have been known in India from a very remote period and are mentioned by Susruta and Charaka. The dried fruits called raisins, are used in medicine. They are described as demulcent, laxative, sweet, cooling, agreeable and useful in thirst, heat of body, cough, hoarseness and consumption.

Raisins enter into the composition of numerous demulcent and expectorant medicines. The following is an illustration. Take of raisins, emblic myrobalans, dates, long pepper and black pepper, equal parts, rub them together with honey and clarified butter and administer as a linctus.[3]

Drákshá arishṭa. This is a medicinal wine prepared as follows. Take of raisins six seers and a quarter, water one hundred and

---

1 निम्बपत्रं तिलैः कल्को मधुना व्रणशोधनः । चक्रदत्तः ।

2 मनःशिलालभल्लातसूक्ष्मैलागुरुचन्दनैः । जातीपल्लवकल्कैश्च निम्बतैलं विपाचयेत् । वल्मीकं नाशयेत्तद्धि बहुच्छिद्रं बहुस्रवम् । भावप्रकाशः ।

3 द्राक्षामलकखर्जूरं पिप्पलीमरिचान्वितम् । पित्तकासापहं ह्येतत् लिह्यान्माक्षिकसर्पिषा । शार्ङ्गधरः ।

twenty-eight seers, boil them together till reduced to one-fourth, and strain. To the strained decoction add twenty-five seers of treacle and eight tolás each of the following substances in fine powder, namely, cinnamon, cardamoms, *tejpatra*, flowers of *Mesua ferrea* (*nágakesara*), fruit of *Aglaia Roxburghiana* (*priyangu*), black pepper, long pepper and *báberang* seeds, and set aside for fermentation. This liquor is considered invigorating and nourishing and is used in consumption, cough, difficult breathing and hoarseness.[1]

NAT. ORDER SAPINDACEÆ.

CARDIOSPERMUM HALICACABUM, *Linn.*

Sans. ज्यौतिष्मती, *Jyautishmati.*

Vern. Latáphaṭkari, Nayáphaṭki, Beng.

THE root of this climbing plant is described as emetic, laxative, stomachic and rubefacient, and is used in combination with other remedies in rheumatism, nervous diseases, piles etc. The fried leaves of *Cardiospermum Halicacabum* are said to bring on the secretion of the menses.[2] Another prescription for amenorrhœa is as follows. Take of *yautishmati* leaves, *sarjiká*, (impure carbonate of potash) *Acorus Calamus* root (*vachá*) and the root-bark of *Terminalia tomentosa* (*asana*) in equal parts and reduce to a paste with milk. This medicine, should be taken in doses of about a drachm for three days.[3]

---

1 द्राक्षारिष्टः। द्राक्षा तुलार्द्धं द्विद्रोणे जलस्य विपचेत् सुधीः। पादशेषे कषाये च पूते शीते विनिःक्षिपेत्। गुडस्य द्वितुलां तत्र त्वगेला पत्र केशरम्। प्रियङ्गु मरिचं कृष्णां विडङ्गं चेति चूर्णयेत्। पृथक् पलोन्मितैर्भागैस्ततो भाण्डे निधापयेत्। समन्ततोऽवघट्टयित्वा पिबेज्जातरसन्ततः। उरःक्षतं क्षयं हन्ति कासश्वास गलामयान्। द्राक्षारिष्टाह्वयः प्रोक्तो बलकृन्मलशोधनः। शार्ङ्गधरः।

2 सक्षाराङ्क्तिकं जवापुष्पं भृष्टं ज्यौतिष्मतीदलम्। दूर्व्वापिष्टञ्च संप्राश्य वनिता त्वार्त्तवं लभेत्॥ चक्रः।

3 पीतं ज्योतिष्मतीपत्रं सर्ज्जिका वचासनम्। त्र्यहं शीतेन पयसा पिष्टं कुसुमं जनयेत् ध्रुवम्। भावप्रकाशः।

NAT. ORDER ANACARDIACEÆ.

RHUS SUCCEDANEA, *Linn.*

Sans. कर्कटशृङ्गी, *Karkatasringi.*

Vern. Kákrásringi, Beng. Kakarsing, Hind.

THE horn-like excrescences caused by insects on the branches of *Rhus Succedanea* are called *karkatasringi.* They "are large, hollow, thin-walled, generally cylindrical, tapering to either extremity." They are considered tonic, expectorant and useful in cough, phthisis, asthma, fever, want of appetite and irritability of stomach. Dose, about twenty grains. This medicine is much used in cough, in combination with other drugs for the disease. The following is an example.[1] Take of *karkatasringi,* root of *Clerodendron Siphonanthus* (*brahmayashti*), raisins, ginger, long pepper and *Curcuma Zedoaria* (*sati*), equal parts, powder and mix. Dose, about thirty grains with treacle or honey, in dry cough. In catarrhal fever with difficult breathing a powder composed of equal parts of *karkatasringi,* bark of *Myrica sapida* (*katphala*), and long pepper is recommended to be given in doses of about a drachm, with honey.[2] The following called *Sringyádi churna* is much esteemed as a cough linctus for children. Take of *karkatasringi, átis,* and long pepper, equal parts; powder and make into a linctus with honey.[3]

MANGIFERA INDICA, *Linn.*

Sans. आम्र, *A'mra. Vern. A'm. Beng. Hind.*

THE Mango is well known as the most delicious of Indian fruits. The ripe fruit is somewhat laxative and useful to persons

---

1 भार्गी द्राक्षा शटी शृङ्गी पिप्पली विश्वभेषजैः । गुड़तैलयुतो लेहो हितो मारुतकासिनाम् । चक्रदत्तः ।

2 मधुना कृष्णा कट्फल कर्कटशृङ्गी भवं चूर्णम् । श्वासामय मह्योघे लीढ्वा लोकः सुखी भवति । भावप्रकाशः ।

3 शृङ्ग्यादिचूर्णम् । शृङ्गीप्रतिविषां कृष्णां चूर्णितां मधुना लिहेत् । शिशुःकासज्वरच्छर्दिशान्त्यै वा केवलां विषाम् । शार्ङ्गधरः ।

of constipated habits. The bark and kernel are regarded as astringent and useful in hæmorrhages, diarrhœa and other discharges.

In diarrhœa, a decoction of the kernel is given alone or in combination with *bela* and ginger.[1] In bleeding from the nose the juice of the kernel is recommended to be snuffed. In bleeding from internal organs, a cold infusion of the barks of *Mangifera Indica*, *Eugenia Jambolana*, and *Terminalia Arjuna* is prescribed.[2] This infusion is also used in diarrhœa. The Bhávaprakása recommends a confection made of the juice of the ripe mango sugar and aromatics, for use as a restorative tonic.

SEMECARPUS ANACARDIUM, *Linn.*

Sans. भल्लातक, *Bhallátaka.* अरुष्कर, *Arushkara.*

Vern. Bhelá. Beng. Hind.

THE acrid juice of marking nuts is a powerful vesicant and is often employed by the natives for producing fictitious marks of bruises. These can be distinguished from actual bruises caused by blows with a stick or other weapon, by their deep bluish-black colour and from their presenting small vesicles or minute blisters on their surface.

The practice of causing blisters by the application of the juice of marking nuts among the Hindus appears to have been at one time very common, for in our ancient medical works a section or paragraph is generally devoted to the treatment of ulcerations thus produced.

The ripe fruits are regarded as acrid, heating, stimulant, digestive, nervine and escharotic, and are used in dyspepsia, piles

---

1 योज्यश्छर्द्यतिसारेषु बिल्वाम्रास्थिभवस्तथा । शार्ङ्गधरः ।

2 आम्रजम्बू च ककुभं चूर्णीकृत्य जलेक्षिपेत् । हिमं तस्य पिबेत्प्रातः सक्षौद्रं रक्तपित्तजित् । शार्ङ्गधरः ।

skin diseases, nervous debility, etc. They are prepared for internal use by being boiled with cow-dung and afterwards washed with cold water. Equal parts of marking nuts, chebulic myrobalans and sesamum seeds, are made into a confection with treacle and administered in doses of forty to sixty grains.[1]

Amrita Bhallátaki.[2] Take of ripe marking nuts divided into halves, eight seers, boil them in thirty-two seers of water till the latter is reduced to one-fourth and strain. Again boil the nuts in sixteen seers of milk with the addition of four seers of clarified butter, till reduced to a thick consistence. Then add sugar two seers and set aside for seven days, when the prepartion will be ready for use. It is described as a powerful restorative tonic, which increases the appetite, promotes nutrition and strength, prolongs-life and so forth. It is used in hæmorrhoids and other diseases of the rectum. Dose, about one to two scruples. Another confection of marking nuts, made with the addition of a number of aromatic substances, is recommended for use in skin diseases and leprosy.

Marking nuts enter into the composition of some caustic applications for warts and piles. They form an ingredient of a liniment for rheumatic affections called *Saindhavádyataila*, for which see Ginger.

---

1 तिलभल्लातकं पथ्या गुडश्चेति समांशिकम्। दुर्नामकासश्वासघ्नं प्लीहपाण्डुज्वरापहम्। चक्रदत्तः।

2 अमृतभल्लातकी। सुपक्वभल्लातफलानि सम्यक् द्विधाविदार्य्याढ़कसम्मितानि। विपाच्यतोयेन चतुर्गुणेन चतुर्थशेषे व्यपनीयतानि। पुनः पचेत् क्षीरचतुर्गुणेन घृतांशयुक्तेन घनं यथा स्यात्। सितो पलाषोडशभिः पलैस्तु विमिश्र्य संस्थाप्यदिनानि सप्त। ततः प्रयोज्याग्निबलेन मात्रां जयेद्गुदोत्थानखिलान् विकारान्। कचान् सुनीलान् घनकुञ्चिताग्रान् सुपर्णदृष्टिं सुकुमारताञ्च। जवं हयानाञ्च मातङ्गजं बलं स्वरं मयूरस्य हुताशदीप्तिम्। स्त्रीवल्लभत्वं लभते प्रजाञ्च नीरोगमव्दद्विशतानि चायुः। चक्रदत्तः।

NAT. ORDER LEGUMINOSÆ.

SARACA INDICA, *Linn.*

Syn. Jonesia Asoca, Roxb.

Sans. अशोक, *Asoka. Vern. Asok, Hind. Beng.*

DR. ROXBURGH says, "when this tree is in full blossom I do not think, the whole vegetable kingdom affords a more beautiful object." It is famed in Hindu mythology from the circumstance of Sita the wife of Rámchandra, having been confined by Rávana in a grove of *asoka* trees. The bark is much used by native physicians in uterine affections and especially in menorrhagia. A decoction[1] of the bark in milk, is prepared by boiling eight tolás of the bark in eight tolás of milk and thirty-two tolás of water till the latter is evaporated. This quantity is given in two or three divided doses during the course of the day, in menorrhagia. A *ghrita* called *Asoka ghrita* is prepared with a decoction of the bark and clarified butter with the addition of a number of aromatic substances in the form of a paste.

GLYCYRRHIZA GLABRA, *Linn.*

Sans. यष्टिमधु, *Yashṭi madhu,* मधुक, *Madhuka.*

Vern. Jashṭi madhu, Beng. Mulhaṭṭi. Hind.

LIQUORICE root, though not indigenous to India, has been used in Hindu Medicine from a very remote period, and is mentioned by Susruta. It is described as sweet, demulcent, cooling and useful in inflammatory affections, cough, hoarseness, thirst etc. It is much used for flavouring medicinal decoctions, oils and *ghritas.* It enters into the composition of numerous external cooling applications along with red sandal wood, madder, *Andropogon muricatus*

---

1 अशोकवल्कलक्वाथशृतं दुग्धं सुशीतलम्। यथाबलं पिबेत्प्रातस्तीव्रा-
सृग्दरनाशनम्। चक्रदत्तः।

etc. I have not met with any notice in Sanskrit works, of the watery extract of liquorice, sold in the bazars in the shape of black pencils, and called *Rubas sus* in Hindustani.

TRIGONELLA FŒNUM-GRÆCUM, *Linn.*

Sans. मेथि, *Methi. Vern. Methi, Hind. Beng.*

THE *Trigonella Fœnum-græcum* is extensively cultivated in many parts of India. Its seeds are used as a condiment and its aromatic leaves, as a pot-herb. Fenugreek seeds are considered carminative, tonic and aphrodisiac. Several confections made with this article are described under the names of *Methi modaka, Svalpa methi modaka* etc., and are recommended for use in dyspepsia with loss of appetite, in the diarrhœa of puerperal women and in rheumatism. All these preparations consist of a number of aromatic substances, one part each, and fenugreek seed equal in quantity to all the other ingredients. The following is an illustration.

Methi modaka.[1] Take of the three myrobalans, ginger, long pepper and black pepper, tubers of *Cyperus rotundus* (*mustaka*), nigella and cumin seeds, coriander, bark of *Myrica sapida* (*katphala*), *pátchak* root, *Rhus succedanea* (*karkatasringi*), *ajowan*, rock salt, black salt, leaves of *Pinus Webbiana* (*tálisa*), flowers of *Mesua ferrea* (*nágakesara*), *tejpatra*, cinnamon, cardamom, nutmegs, mace, cloves, sandal wood and camphor one part each; fenugreek seed, in quantity equal to all the above ingredients; powder them all and prepare a confection with old treacle. Dose, one to two drachms to be taken in the morning with clarified butter and honey.

---

1 मेथिमोदकः। त्रिकटुत्रिफलामुस्तजीरकद्वयधान्यकम्। कट्फलं पौष्करं शृङ्गी यमानी सैन्धवं विडम्। तालीशकेशरं पत्रं त्वगेला च फलं तथा। जातीकोषं लवङ्गञ्च सुराकर्पूरचन्दनम्। यावन्त्येतानि चूर्णानि तावदेव तु मेथिका। संचूर्ण्य मोदकः कार्य्यः पुरातनगुडेन च। घृतेन मधुना किञ्चित् खादेदग्निबलं प्रति। अग्निञ्च कुरुते दीप्तं सामे मेदे महौषधम्। भैषज्यरत्नावली।

ALHAGI MAURORUM, *Tournef.*

Sans. दुरालभा, *Duralabhá*, यवास, *Yavása. Vern. Yavása Hind.*

THIS plant is described as laxative, diuretic and expectorant. The thorny flower-stalks or branches are supplied by druggists as the parts used in medicine. An extract obtained by evaporating a decoction of the plant is called *yásasarkará* or the sugar obtained from *yavása*. It has a sweetish bitter taste, and is used as a demulcent in the cough of children. There is no mention in Sanskrit of any saccharine oxudation or manna obtained from this plant.

The fresh juice of the plant is used as a diuretic in suppression of urine. The following compound decoction[1] is recommended by Sárangadhara in constipation with suppression of urine. Take of *Alhagi Maurorum*, chebulic myrobalans, pulp of *Cassia Fistula* (*áragbadha*), fruits of *Tribulus terrestris* (*gokshura*), and root of *Coleus aromaticus* (*páshanbhid*), prepare a deoction in the usual way, and administer it with honey. The following electuary is recommended by several writers for the cough of children. Take of the extract of *yavása*, raisins, chebulic myrobalans and long pepper in equal parts, powder and mix with honey and clarified butter.[2]

DESMODIUM GANGETICUM, *DC.*

Syn. Hedysarum Gangeticum. (*Roxb.*)

Sans. शालपर्णी, *Sálaparni. Vern. Sálpáni, Beng. Sarivan, Hind.*

THIS little shrub is regarded as febrifuge and anti-catarrhal. It forms an ingredient of the compound decoction called *dasamula kvatha* a combination, much used in a great variety of diseases. *Dasamula* is made up of *Desmodium Gangeticum* (*sálaparni*), *Uraria lagopodioides* (*prisniparni*), *Solanum Jacquinii* (*kantakári*), *Solanum Indicum* (*vrihati*), *Tribulus terrestris* (*gokshura*), *Ægle Marmelos* (*vilva*), *Calosanthes Indica* (*syonáka*), *Gmelina arborea* (*gambhári*), *Stereospermum suaveolens* (*pátalá*) and *Premna spinosa* (*ganikáriká*).

1 हरीतकी दुरालभा आरग्वधक गोक्षुरैः। पाषाणभेदसहितैः क्वाथमाक्षिक संयुतः। विबन्धं मूत्रकृच्छ्रञ्च सद्योहन्ति सरुजं हितः शार्ङ्गधरः।

2 द्राक्षा यासाभया कृष्णा चूर्णं क्षौद्र सर्पिषा। लीढं श्वासं निहन्त्याशु कासञ्च तमकं तथा। चक्रदत्तः।

The first five in the above list, are collectively called *hrasvapancha mula* or the five minor plants, and the last five are called *vrihat pàncha mula* or the five major plants. A decoction of the *hrasva pancha mula* is used in catarrhal fever, cough and other diseases supposed to be caused by deranged phlegm. The *vrihat pancha-mula* is used in fever and other diseases supposed to be caused by deranged air. The ten drugs together are used in remittent fever, puerperal fever, inflammatory affections within the chest, affections of the brain and many other diseases supposed to be caused by derangement of all the humours.[1] Another combination called *Ashṭádasánga páchana* consists of the ten drugs above mentioned, with the addition of the eight following, namely, *chiretá*, *devadáru*, ginger, tubers of *Cyperus rotundus* (*mustaka*), root of *Picrorrhiza Kurroa* (*katuki*), *indrajava* seeds, coriander, and fruits of *Pothos officinalis.* A decoction of these eighteen drugs is used in fevers of a severe type with drowsiness, delirium, picking of bed clothes, insensibility, and difficult breathing. A preparation of aconite and arsenic is generally given along with it.[2]

Dasamula taila. This is an oil prepared with a decoction of the ten drugs above mentioned, and is much used as a cooling application in headache and other diseases. To prepare it take of the ten drugs, in all twelve seers and a half, water sixty four seers. Boil down to sixteen seers and strain. To the strained decoction add four seers of lemon juice, four seers of prepared sesamum oil and a seer of the usual aromatics and colouring agents in the form of a paste and boil them together.

---

1 दशमूलम्। बिल्वश्योनाक गाम्भारी पाटला गणिकारिकाः। दीपनं कफवातघ्नं पञ्चमूलमिदं महत्। शालपर्णी पृश्निपर्णी बृहतीद्वय गोक्षुरम्। वातपित्तहरं वृष्यं कनीयः पञ्चमूलकम्। उभयं दशमूलन्तु सन्निपातज्वरापहम्। कासे श्वासे च तन्द्रायां पार्श्वशूले च शस्यते। पिप्पलीचूर्णसंयुक्तं कण्ठहृद्ग्रहनाशनम्। चक्रदत्तः।

2 पित्तश्लेष्महरोऽष्टादशाङ्गः। भूनिम्ब दारु दशमूल महौषधाब्द तिक्तेन्द्रबीज धनिकेभकणाकषायः। तन्द्राप्रलाप कसनारुचि दाहमोह श्वासादियुक्तमखिलं ज्वरमाशु हन्ति। चक्रदत्तः।

URARIA LAGOPODIOIDES, *Dc. Edgew. Syn. Doodia lagopodioides Roxb. Sans.* पृश्निपर्णी, *Prisniparni. Vern. Chákuliá, Beng. Pitvan, Hind.* This plant is an ingredient of the *dasamula* above described, and is thus much used in native medicine. It is considered alterative, tonic and anti-catarrhal, but is seldom used alone.

CLITOREA TERNATEA, *Linn.*

Sans. अपराजिता, *Aparájitá,* विष्णुक्रान्ता, *Vishnukrántá.*
Vern. Aparájitá, Beng. Aprájit, Hind.

THE root of *Clitorea ternatea* is regarded as laxative and diuretic, and is generally used in combination with other medicines of the sort in ascites, fever, etc. The following is an example of a prescription containing *aparájitá* root. Take of the roots of *aparájitá, Pladera decussata (sankhini), Baliospermum montanum (danti)* and *Indigofera tinctoria (nilini)*, in equal parts, rub them together into an emulsion with water and administer with cow's urine. This preparation is given in ascites and enlargements of the abdominal viscera.[1]

MUCUNA PRURIENS, *DC.*

Sans आत्मगुप्ता, *A'tmaguptá.* कपिकच्छु, *Kapikachchhu.* वानरी, *Vánari.*
Vern. A'lkusi, Beng. Kiwach, Hind.

THE English names Cowage or Cowitch are derived from the Hindi *Kiwach*. The plant is indigenous to India and has been used in Hindu medicine from a very ancient period. Susruta describes the seeds as a powerful aphrodisiac, and gives the following formula for their use. Take of the seeds of *Mucuna pruriens* and the fruits *Tribulus terrestris (gokshura)* equal parts and administer in doses of about a drachm with sugar and tepid milk.[2] The Bháva-

---

1 गवाक्षी शङ्खिनी दन्ती नीलिनीकल्कसंयुतम्। सर्व्वोदरविनाशाय गोमूत्रं पातुमाचरेत् ॥ चक्रः ।

2 स्वयं गुप्तेक्षुरकयोर्बीज चूर्णं सशर्करम् । धारोष्णेन नरः पीत्वा पयसा न क्षयं व्रजेत् । सुश्रुतः ।

prakása recommends the following preparation called *Vánari vati*. Take of the seeds of *Mucuna pruriens* thirty-two tolás, boil them in four seers of cow's milk till the latter becomes thick. The seeds should now be decorticated and pounded, then fried in clarified butter and made into a confection with double their weight of sugar. The mass should then be divided into balls which should be steeped in honey. Dose, about a tolá. This preparation is said to be the best of aphrodisiacs.[1]

The root of *Mucuna pruriens* is considered tonic and useful in diseases of the nervous system, such as facial paralysis, hemiplegia etc. It is generally used in combination with other medicines of its class, as for example in the compound decoction called *Máshbaládi*, for which see Assafœtida.

BUTEA FRONDOSA, *Roxb.*

Sans. पलाश, *Palása.* किंशुक, *Kinsuka. Vern. Dhák. Hind.*

Dr. Hooker states "that when in full flower the *Dhák* tree is a gorgeous sight; the masses of flowers resembling sheets of flame, their bright orange red petals contrasting brilliantly against the jet black velvety calyx." These beautiful flowers were used as ear-ornaments by the ancient Hindu women and much admired by the poets. The seeds of *Butea frondosa* are said to be laxative and anthelmintic and are used, both alone and in combination with other medicines, for expelling intestinal worms. Thus the fresh juice of the seeds, or the seeds beaten to a paste are given with honey.[2] Sárangadhara gives the following recipe for worms.

---

1 वानरीवटिका। बीजानि कपिकच्छ्वाः कुडव मितानि स्वेदयेच्छनकैः। प्रस्थे गोभवदुग्धे तावत् यावद्भवेत् गाढ़म्। त्वग्रहितानि च कृत्वा सूक्ष्मं संपेषयेत्तानि। पिष्टिका या लघुवटिकाः कृत्वा गव्ये पचेदाज्ये। द्विगुणित शर्करयाक्ता वटिकाः सम्यक्कया लेप्याः॥ वटिका माक्षिक मध्ये मज्जनयोग्ये विरलाः स्थाप्याः॥ पञ्चटङ्क मितास्तासु प्रातः सायञ्च भक्षयेत्। अनेन शीघ्रद्रावी यो यश्च स्यात्पतितध्वजः। सोऽपि प्राप्नोति सुरते सामर्थ्यमति वाजिवत्। मानेन सदृशं किञ्चिद्द्रव्यं वाजिकरं परम्। भावप्रकाशः।

2 पलाशबीजस्वरसं पिबेद्वा क्षौद्रसंयुतम्। पिबेत्तद्बीजकल्कं वा तक्रेण क्रिमिनाशनम्। भावप्रकाशः।

Take of the seeds of *Butea frondosa*, root of *Ipomœa Turpethum* (*trivrit*), seeds of *Hyoscyamus niger* (*párasika yamáni*), *kamalá* powder, *báberang* seeds and treacle, equal parts, beat them together into a paste with water and administer with butter-milk.[1]

The gum of *Butea frondosa*, now used as a substitute for kino, was employed by the ancient Hindus, externally only, as for example in the following. Take of red sandal wood one part, rock salt two parts, chebulic myrobalans three parts, and the gum of *Butea frondosa* four parts, powder and mix. This powder is recommended to be applied to pterygium and opacities on the cornea.[2]

The alkaline ashes of this plant are used in the preparation of caustic pastes, and diuretic medicines, along with others of their class.

PHASEOLUS ROXBURGHII, W. & A. ETC.

The following varieties of leguminous pulses are mentioned by Sanskrit writers.

मुद्ग, *Mudga.* *Phaseolus Mungo, Linn. Vern: Mug, B.*

माष, *Másha.* *Phaseolus Roxburghii, W. & A. Vern. Urid, H.*

मुद्गपर्णी, *Mudgaparni. P. trilobus, Ait. Vern. Mugáni, B.*

मकुष्ठ, *Makushṭha. P. aconitifolius, Jacq. Vern. Mot, H.*

कुलत्थ, *Kulattha. Dolichos uniflorus, Lamark. Vern. Kulthi, H.B.*

राजमाष, *Rájamásha. Vigna Sinensis, Linn. Vern. Barbati, B.*

शिम्बि, *Simbi.* A common name for several species of *Dolichos.*

चणक, *Chanaka. Cicer arietinum, Linn. Vern. But, Beng. Chená, H.*

मसुर, *Masura. Vicia Lens, Benth. Vern. Masur, H. B.*

सतिला, *Satilá. Pisum sativum, Linn. Vern. Matar. H. B.*

---

1 त्रिवृत्पलाशबीजानि पारसीकयमानिका । कम्पिल्लकं विडङ्गञ्च गुडश्च समभागिकः । तक्रेण कल्क एतेषां पीतः क्रिमिगणापहः । शार्ङ्गधरः ।

2 चन्दनं सैन्धवं पथ्या पलाशतरुशोणितम् । क्रमवृद्धमिदं चूर्णं शुक्रार्म्मादिविलेखनम् । चक्रदत्तः ।

आढ़की, *A'ḍhaki. Cajanus Indicus, Sprengel. Arar, B. Tor, H.*

त्रिपुटी, *Triputi. Lathyrus sativus, Linn. Khesári, H. B.*

माषपर्णी, *Máshaparni. Glycine labialis, Linn. Vern. Másháni, H.B.*

Some of these pulses have several varieties. For example seven sorts of *mudga* are mentioned, namely, *krishna* or black, *mahá* or large, *gaura* or pale red, *harita* or green, *pita* or yellow, *sveta* or white and *rakta* or red.

Mudga, ordinarily known as *moong ká dál*, and especially its green variety, is considered most wholesome and suited to sick persons. A soup made of this pulse is often the first article of diet prescribed after recovery from acute illness. The following varieties are also considered wholesome and suited for use by convalescent persons, namely, *masura, chanaka, kulattha* and *makushṭha*. *Vicia Lens* or lentils, which take rank first among the pulses as containing the largest proportion of flesh-forming matter, are regarded by the Hindus as highly nutritive, and useful in bowel complaints. A poultice made of this pulse is an effectual domestic medicine for checking secretion of milk and reducing distension of the mammary glands. *Cicer arietinum* is perhaps the most favourite pulse with the natives, and is used as an article of diet in a great variety of ways. It is taken raw, or cooked in its green as well as ripe state. Gram is made into *dál*, is roasted and ground into meal and is prepared in many other ways.

The acid liquid exuded from the hairs of the stem and leaves of *Cicer arietinum* is called *chanakámla* in Sanskrit. It is collected by spreading a cloth over the plants during the night and rinsing the fluid absorbed by it. *Chanakámla* is described as acid, refrigerent, saltish, and useful in dyspepsia, indigestion and costiveness. It enters into the composition of some medicines for dyspepsia along with other vegetable acids.

Dolichos uniflorus is used medicinally chiefly as an external application in the shape of poultices and pastes. Its soup is said to be useful in gravel and urinary disorders.

The *Phaseolus Roxburghii* or *másha* is much used in medicine both internally and externally in paralysis, rheumatism and affections of the nervous system. It enters into the composition of several decoctions used in these diseases. The following is an illustration. Take of the pulse of *Phaseolus Roxburghii*. root of castor oil plant, of *Mucuna pruriens* (*átmaguptá*) and *Sida cordifolia* (*balá*), half a tolá each, and prepare a decoction in the usual way. This decoction is given with the addition of rock salt and assafœtida.[1] Several oils for external application in the above mentioned diseases have the pulse of *Phaseolus Roxburghii* for their basis or principal ingredient, as for example the following.

Svalpa másha taila.[2] Take of the pulse of *Phaseolus Roxburghii* eight seers, water sixty-four seers, boil down to sixteen seers, and strain. Boil the strained decoction with four seers of sesamum oil, and one of rock salt till the water is evaporated. This oil is said to be useful in rheumatism, contracted knee joint, stiff shoulder joint, etc.

ABRUS PRECATORIUS, *Linn.*

Sans. गुञ्जा, *Gunjá.*

Vern. Kuch, Beng. Chirmiti, Hind.

"THIS plant is remarkable for its small egg-shaped seeds, which are of a brilliant scarlet colour with a black scar indicating the place where they were attached to the pods." Sanskrit writers mention two varieties, namely, white and red seeded. The properties of both are said to be identical. The seeds are described as poisonous, and are used internally in affections of the nervous system and externally in skin diseases, ulcers, affections of the hair, etc. The root of the plant is described as emetic and useful in poisoning. The seeds constitute the *ratti* weight used by Hindu jewellers and druggists. Ninety-six *rattis* make one tolá or rupee.

---

1 माषात्मगुप्तैरण्डवाट्यालकशृतं पिबेत्। हिङ्गुसैन्धवसंयुक्तं पक्षाघातनिवारणम्। चक्रदत्तः।

2 स्वल्पमाषतैलम्। तैलं सङ्कुचितेऽभ्यङ्गो माषसैन्धवसाधितम्। बाहुशीर्षगते नस्यं पानञ्चोत्तरभक्तिकम्। क्वाथोऽत्र माषनिष्क्वाथः सैन्धवं कल्कमेव च। चक्रदत्तः।

Gunjá bhadra rasa.[1] Take of the seeds of *Abrus precatorius* six parts, mercury three parts, sulphur twelve parts, *nim* seeds, *Cannabis sativa* leaves and croton seeds, each one part. Rub them together and soak for one day in each of the following fluids, namely, lemon juice, juice of the leaves of *Cannabis sativa*, of datura leaves and of the leaves of *Solanum nigrum (kákamáchi)*. This medicine is given in doses of about eight grains, with rock salt and assafœtida, in paraplegia. The seeds of *Abrus precatorius* reduced to a paste are recommended to be applied locally in sciatica, stiffness of the shoulder joint, paralysis and other nervous diseases.[2]

In white leprosy, a paste composed of *gunjá* seed and plumbago root is applied as a stimulant dressing. In alopecia a paste of *gunjá* seed is recommended to be rubbed on the bare scalp.[3]

Gunjádya tailam.[4] Take of prepared sesamum oil four seers, juice of the leaves of *Wedelia calendulacea* (*bhringarája*) sixteen seers, seeds of *Abrus precatorius* reduced to a paste, one seer, and boil them together in the usual way. This oil is used as a local application in scurf of the scalp, prurigo and other skin diseases.

---

1 गुञ्जाभद्ररसः। निष्कत्रयं शुद्धसूतं निष्कद्वादश गन्धकम्। गुञ्जाबीजञ्च षन्निष्कं निम्बबीजं जयातथा। प्रत्येकं निष्कमानन्तु निष्कं जैपालबीजकं। जयाजम्बीर धुस्तूरकाकमाची द्रवैर्दिनम्। भावयित्वा वटीं कृत्वा दद्याद्गुञ्जाचतुष्टयम्। गुञ्जाभद्ररसो नाम हिङ्गु सैन्धव संयुतः। शमयत्युल्बणं दुःखपक्षस्तम्भं सुदारुणम्। रसेन्द्रः सारसंग्रहः।

2 तत्प्रदेशे दद्यात्सुपिष्टं गुञ्जा फलैःकृतम्। तेनाश्वशाखजा पीडा विपची स्तम्भशीतया। अन्यापि वातजापीडा प्रशमं याति वेगतः। शार्ङ्गधरः।

3 गुञ्जाफलाग्निचूर्णाभ्यां लेपितं श्वेतकुष्ठनुत्। शार्ङ्गधरः।

गुञ्जाफलैस्सिरं लिम्पेत् केशभूमिं समन्ततः। हस्तीदन्तमसीं कृत्वा मुख्यञ्चैव रसाञ्जनम्। लोमान्यनेन जायन्ते म्लषां पाणितलेष्वपि। चक्रदत्तः।

4 गुञ्जादि तैलम्। गुञ्जाफलैः शृतं तैलं भृङ्गराजरसेन च। कण्डुदारुण हृत् कुष्ठकपालव्याधिनाशनम्। भावप्रकाशः।

PONGAMIA GLABRA, *Vent.*

Sans. करञ्ज, *Karanja.* नक्तमाल, *Nactamála.*

Vern. Darkaranja, Beng. Kiramál, Hind.

THIS tree appears to be common in, and well known all over India. The seeds are much used as an external application in skin diseases. The expressed oil of the seeds is used in these diseases as well as in rheumatism. A poultice of the leaves is applied to ulcers infested with worms. The seeds of *Pongamia glabra*, *Cassia Tora* (*chakramarda*), and the root of *Aplotaxis auriculata* (*kushṭha*), are rubbed into a paste with cow's urine, and applied to eruptive skin diseases.[1]

Prithisára taila.[2] Take of the expressed oil of the seeds of *Pongamia glabra* one seer, *kánjika* eight tolás, roots of *Plumbago Zeylanica* (*chitraka*), *Nerium odorum* (*karavira*), *Vitex Negundo* (*nirgundi*), aconite, and the seeds of *Corchorus olitorius* (*náḍika*), eight tolás each, in the form of a paste made wlth *kánjika.* Mix them together and warm in the sun. This oil is said to be usoful in various sorts of skin diseases, ulcers etc.

Tiktádya ghrita.[3] Take of the leaves and fruits of *Pongamia glabra*, root of *Picrorrhiza Kurroa*, (*katuki*), wax, turmeric, liquorice root, leaves of *Trichosanthes dioica* (*patala*), *Aganosma caryophyllata* (*málati*) and *Azadirachta Indica* (*nim*), equal parts, in all one seer. Beat them into a paste and boil with four seers of clarified butter and sixteen seers of water in the usual manner. This preparation is used as an ointment in unhealthy ulcerations and wounds.

GUILANDINA BONDUCELLA, *Linn.* The properties of Bonduc nuts called पूतीकरञ्ज, *Putikaranja* in Sanskrit, and *Nátáka-*

---

1 करञ्जबीजैडगजः सकुष्ठो गोमूत्रपिष्टश्च वरः प्रदेहः । चक्रदत्तः।

2 पृथ्वीसारतैलम् । चित्रकस्याथनिर्गुण्ड्या हयमारस्य मूलतः । नाडीच-बीजाद्विषतः काञ्जिपिष्टं पलं पलम् । करञ्जतैलादष्टपलं काञ्जिकस्य पलं पुनः । मिश्रितं सूर्यसन्तप्तं तैलं कुष्ठव्रणास्रजित् । चक्रदत्तः ।

3 तिक्ताद्यं घृतम् । तिक्ता सिक्थ निशायष्टी नक्ताह्वफलपल्लवैः । पटोल मालती निम्बपत्रैश्च समं घृतं पचेत् । चक्रदत्तः ।

ranja in Bengali, are said to resemble those of the seeds of *Pongamia glabra*. Their antiperiodic virtues were not known to Sanskrit writers.

PTEROCARPUS SANTALINUS. *Linn.*

Sans. रक्तचन्दन, *Raktachandana.*

Vern. Raktachandan, Beng. Lálchandan, Hind.

THE *Pterocarpus Santalinus* is indigenous to the Indian Peninsula and is chiefly of importance from its yielding the red dye-wood known as red saunders, large quantities of which are annually exported from India. Sanskrit writers describe several varieties of sandal or *chandana*. Of these *srikhanda* or white, *pitachandana* or yellow, and *raktachandana* or red, sandal wood are best known. The first two varieties are founded on the difference in the shades of the colour of the wood of *Santalum album*. It has been a question however how the wood of *Pterocarpus santalinus*, which is nearly inodorous, came to be called by the name of *raktachandana* in Sanskrit and the vernaculars of India. I am inclined to think that the name is owing to the similarity in the uses to which the Hindus put both these articles. Both sandal wood and red sandal wood are rubbed on a piece of stone with water, and the emulsions are used for painting the body after bathing and in religious services.

Red sandal wood is described as an astringent tonic. It enters into the composition of numerous prescriptions of an astringent character and of cooling external applications for inflammation, headache, etc.,[1] but is seldom used alone. It is also much used as a coloring agent in the preparation of medicated oils.

The *Pterocarpus marsupium* or Indian kino tree is translated into "*peet sál*," Beng. by Roxburgh. The Sanskrit term *Pitasála* is however a synonym of *Asana* (*Terminalia tomentosa*). I have not found any notice of the Indian kino tree in Sanskrit works. It was probably unknown to the ancients.

---

[1] तिलाः पयः सिता क्षौद्रं तैलं मधुक चन्दनम् । लेपेन शोधयन् दाह रक्तं निर्व्वापयेद्व्रणान् । चक्रदत्तः ।

CASSIA FISTULA, *Linn.*

Sans. आरग्वध, *A'ragbadha.* सुवर्णक, *Suvarnaka.*

Vern. A'multás, Hind. Sondháli, Beng.

Cassia fistula is indigenous to India and is an old medicine of the Hindu Materia Medica. "The tree is uncommonly beautiful when in flower, few surpassing it in the elegance of its numerous long pendulous racemes of large bright yellow flowers, intermixed with the young lively green foliage." Hence I believe its Sanskrit name of *Rájataru* or the king of trees. The pulp of the fruit is used as a mild cathartic. The root is also described as laxative, and useful in fever, heart diseases, retained excretions, biliousness, etc.

Aragbadhádi.[1] The compound decoction which passes by this name is a very commonly used purgative in native practice. To prepare it, take of the pulp of *Cassia fistula, Picrorrhiza Kurroa* (*katuki*), chebulic myrobalans, long pepper root and the tubers of *Cyperus rotundus (mustaka)*, about sixty-four grains each, water thirty-two tolás, and boil down to eight tolás. Half of this quantity, or in strong constitutions the whole of it, is given for a dose. The root of *Cassia fistula* enters into the composition of numerous compound prescriptions.

CASSIA SOPHORA, *Linn. Sans.* कासमर्द, *Kásamarda. Vern. Kálkásundá, Beng. Kásundá, Hind.*

CASSIA TORA, *Linn. Sans.* चक्रमर्द, *Chakramarda. Vern. Chákundia, Beng. Chakaund, Hind.*

CASSIA ALATA, *Linn. Sans.* दद्रुघ्न, *Dadrughna. Vern. Dádmardan. Beng. and Hind.*

THE leaves and seeds of these three plants are used in skin diseases, and enter into the composition of numerous prescriptions for them. *Kásamarda* signifies destroyer of cough. It is described as expectorant and useful in cough and hoarseness, but it does not appear to be much used in these diseases.

---

1 आरग्वधादि। आरग्वध कणामूल मुस्त तिक्ताभयाकृतः। क्वाथः शमयति क्षिप्रं ज्वरं वातकफोत्तरम्। शार्ङ्गधरः।

The seeds of *Cassia Sophora, Raphanus sativus* (*mulaka*) and sulphur, in equal parts, are rubbed into a paste with water and applied to patches of pityriasis and psoriasis.[1] The seeds of *Cassia Tora* are steeped in the milky juice of *Euphorbia neriifolia*, and afterwards rubbed into a paste with cow's urine for application to keloid tumours.[2] Equal parts of the seeds of *Cassia Tora* and *Pongamia glabra* (*karanja*) with a fourth part of the root of *Tinospora cordifolia* (*gulancha*) are rubbed together into a paste and applied in ringworm.[3] *Dadrughna* or *Dádamardana* signifies curer of ringworm. Its leaves are used in this disease.

BAUHINIA VARIEGATA, *Linn.*

Sans. काञ्चनार, *Kánchanára.* कोविदार, *Kovidára.*

Vern. Kachnár, Hind. Rakta Kánchan, Beng.

Two species of *Bauhinia*, namely purple and white flowered (*Bauhinia variegata* and *acuminata*), are noticed in the Bhávaprakása under the names of *Kovidára* and *Kánchanára* and the properties of both are said to be identical. The bark of *Bauhinia variegata* is described as alterative, tonic, astringent and useful in scrofula, skin diseases and ulcers.

Chakradatta recommends the bark of the red variety to be rubbed into an emulsion with rice water and administered, with the addition of ginger, in scrofulous enlargement of the glands of the neck.[4] Sárangadhara gives the following preparation for the same affection.

---

1 कासमर्द्दकबीजानि मूलकानां तथैवच । गन्धपाषाणमिश्राणि सिध्मानां परमौषधम् । चक्रदत्तः ।

2 चक्राह्वयं स्नुहीक्षीरभावितं मूत्रसंयुतम् । दविनघ्नं हि किश्चित्तु लेपनात् किटिमापहम् । चक्रदत्तः ।

3 चक्रमर्द्दकबीजानि करञ्जसमांशकम् । स्तोकं सुदर्शनामूलं दद्रुकुष्ठविनाशनम् । चक्रदत्तः ।

4 पिष्टा ज्येष्ठाम्बुनापेयाः काञ्चनारत्वचः शुभाः । विश्वभेषजसंयुक्ता गण्डमालापहाः पराः । चक्रदत्तः ।

Kánchanára guggulu.[1] Take of the bark of *Bauhinia variegata*, eighty tolás, the three myrobalans sixty tolás, ginger, black pepper, long pepper and the bark of *Cratæva religiosa* (*varuna*), eight tolás each, cardamoms, cinnamon, and *tejpatra* leaves, each two tolás, powder them all and rub together with *guggulu*, equal in weight to all the other ingredients. Dose, half a tolá to be taken every morning with a decoction of *Sphæranthus mollis* (*mundi*) or of catechu. This medicine is said to be useful in scrofulous enlargement of glands, tumours, ulcers, skin diseases, etc.

TAMARINDUS INDICA, *Linn.*

Sans. तिन्तिड़ी, *Tintidi.* अम्लिका, *Amliká.*

Vern. *Tentul, Beng.* *Imli, Hind.*

THE tamarind tree is met with throughout India, and has been known from a very remote period. "From the Hindus it would seem that the fruit became known to the Arabians who called it *Tamare-hindi* :" from which last the word tamarind is derived. Tamarinds form an important ingredient in native cookery. The unripe fruit is very acid and possesses a peculiar aroma for which it is much relished when cooked with curry. The ripe fruit is regarded as refrigerant, digestive, carminative and laxative, and useful in diseases supposed to be caused by deranged bile, such as burning of the body, costiveness, intoxication from spirituous liquors or *datura*, etc. The shells of the ripe fruit are burnt, and their ashes used in medicine as an alkaline substance, along with other medicines of the sort, as for example in the preparation called *Abhayá-lavana*, (see Alkaline ashes). The pulp of the ripe fruit, as well as

---

1 काञ्चनारगुग्गुलु। काञ्चनारत्वचोग्राह्यं पलानां दशकं बुधैः। त्रिफला षट्पला ग्राह्या त्रिकटु स्यात्पलत्रयम्। पलैको वरुणः कार्य्य एलात्वक्पत्रकन्तथा। एकैकं कर्षमात्रं स्यात्सर्वाण्येकत्र चूर्णयेत्। यावच्चूर्णमिदं सर्वं तावन्मात्रस्तु गुग्गुलुः। सङ्कुट्य सर्वमेकत्र पिण्डं कृत्वा च धारयेत्। गुटिकाः शाणिकाः कृत्वा प्रातर्ग्राह्या यथोचितम्। गण्डमालां जयत्युग्रामपचीमर्वुदानि च। ग्रन्थिव्रणानि गुल्मांश्च कुष्ठानि च भगन्दरम्। प्रदेयश्चानुपानार्थं क्वाथो मुण्डितिकाभवः। क्वाथः खदिरसारस्य पथ्याक्वाथोऽथवोष्णकम्। शार्ङ्गधरः।

a poultice of the leaves, is recommended to be applied to inflammatory swellings.

Amliká pána.[1] Macerate some tamarind pulp in water; strain, and add black pepper, sugar, cloves, camphor and cardamoms to taste. This preparation is prescribed as an agreeeable cooling draught in loss of appetite and disinclination for food. In intoxication from spirituous liquors the following mixture is recommended by Chakradatta. Take of dates, raisins, tamarind pulp, pomegranate seeds, fruits of *Grewia Asiatica* (*parushaka*) and ripe emblic myrobalans, each one tolá, pound them together, and make an emulsion with thirty-two tolás of water. Dose, about two ounces.[2]

ACACIA CATECHU, *Linn.*

Sans. खदिर, *Khadira. Vern. Kat, Hind. Khaer, Beng.*

Khadira or catechu is obtained by boiling the wood of *Acacia catechu* in water and inspissating the decoction. The Bhávaprakása mentions two varieties of catechu, namely, *khadira* or the ordinary dark brown catechu, and *kadara* or pale catechu. This last is known as *pápri khaer*, or catechu having a laminated structure. Fluckiger and Hanbury thus describe the preparation of pale catechu in Northern India. "Instead of evaporating the decoction to the condition of an extract, the inspissation is stopped at a certain point and the liquor allowed to cool, "coagulate," and crystallize over twigs and leaves thrown into the pots for the purpose."[3] Pale catechu is a porous, opaque, earthy looking substance with a laminated texture, light and easily broken.

The chief use of catechu in India, is as an ingredient of the packet of betle leaf chewed by the natives. For this purpose it is sometimes aromatized in various ways. The packets of betle

---

1 अम्लिकापानम्। अम्लिकायाःफलंपक्वं मर्द्दितं वारिणादृढं। शर्करा मरिचोन्मिश्रं लवङ्गेन्दु सुवासितं। अम्लिकाफल सम्भूतं पानकं वातनाशनम्। पित्तश्लेष्मकरं किञ्चित् सुरुच्यं वह्नि दीपकं। भावप्रकाशः।

2 मन्थः खर्जूर मृद्वीका वृक्षाम्लाम्लीकदाडिमैः। परूषकैः सामलकैर्युक्तो मद्य विकारनुत्। चक्रदत्तः।

3 Pharmacographia, page 250.

leaf sold in all the Indian bazars under the name of *golábi khili*, are prepared with catechu dissolved in rose water. Again, catechu is softened with the addition of water, and mixed with powdered spices, such as cardamoms, nutmeg, cloves, etc., the mixture is enclosed within the fragrant floral leaves of *Pandanus odoratissimus* (*ketaki*), and dried. The leaves adhere to the catechu, which is cut into small pieces suitable for use with the betle leaf.

Catechu is described as astringent, cooling, digestive, and useful in hoarseness, diseases of the mouth and gums, cough and skin diseases. In diarrhœa it is sometimes used in combination with other medicines of its class, as for example in a prescription in the Bhaisajya Ratnávali, called *Grahani kapáta rasa*, which contains catechu along with a large number of other drugs, but it is not regarded as an important medicine for this disease.

In hoarseness, catechu rubbed with oil, is recommended to be kept in the mouth.[1] In diseases of the mouth and gums the following called *Svalpakhadira vatiká* is a favourite medicine. To prepare it, take of catechu twelve seers and a half, water sixty-four seers, boil down to eight seers, then add nutmeg, camphor, betle-nuts and *kakkola*, each half a seer in fine powder, and prepare a mass fit for being made into balls or boluses. They are directed to be kept in the mouth, in affections of the teeth, gums, palate and tongue.[2]

In skin diseases, catechu is much used in a variety of forms both externally and internally. A decoction of catechu is used as a wash for inflamed parts and ulcers.[3] Water in which catechu is dissolved is recommended to be used as a drink, wash and bath. The following decoction called *khadiráshṭaka* is prescribed by several writers for internal use in boils, prurigo, measles and other

---

1 तैलाक्तं स्वरभेदेवा खदिरं धारये मुखे । चक्रदत्तः ।

2 स्वल्पखदिरवटिका । खदिरस्य तुलां सम्यग् जलद्रोणे विपाचयेत्। शेषेऽष्ट भागे तत्रैव प्रतिवापं प्रदापयेत्। जातीकर्पूरपूगानि कक्कोलकफलानि च। इत्येषा गुड़िका कार्य्या मुखसौभाग्यवर्द्धिनी । दन्तौष्ठमुखरोगेषु जिह्वातालुगदेषु च। चक्रदत्तः ।

3 खदिरोकषाय व्रणशोधने हितः। चक्रदत्तः।

skin diseases.[1] Take of catechu, the three myrobalans, *nim* bark, leaves of *Trichosanthes dioica* (*patala*), *gulancha* and *Justicia Adhatoda* (*vásaka*), equal parts, and prepare a decoction in the usual way Sárangadhara describes a fermented liquor called *khadirárishṭa* for use in skin diseases. It is prepared with catechu and the wood of *Pinus Deodara*, and some other ingredients in smaller proportions.[2]

ACACIA ARABICA, *Willd.* *Sans.* वब्बुल, *Vabbula. Vern. Bábul, Beng. Hind.* The tender leaves beaten into a pulp, are given in diarrhœa as an astringent. A decoction of the bark is used as an astringent gargle and wash. I have not met with any notice of gum acacia in Sanskrit works.

NAT. ORDER COMBRETACEÆ.

TERMINALIA CHEBULA, *Retz.*

Sans. हरीतकी, *Haritaki.* अभया, *Abhayá.* पथ्या, *Pathyá.*

Vern. Har. Hind. Haritaki, Beng.

THE chebulic myrobalan was highly extolled by the ancient Hindus as a powerful alterative and tonic. It has received the names of *Pránadá*, or life-giver, *Sudhá* or nectar, *Bhishakpriya* or physician's favourite and so forth. So highly esteemed was this plant by the ancient Hindus, that a mythological origin has been attributed to it. It is said that when Indra was drinking nectar in heaven, a drop of the fluid fell on the earth and produced the *haritaki* plant. Seven varieties of *haritaki* are described by Sanskrit writers, the distinctions being founded upon the shape, colour and marks on the outer covering of the fruits. At the present day, however, two varieties only are recognised, namely, the large ripe fruit called *haritaki*, and the unripe dried fruit called *jangi*

---

1 प्रलेपोद्वर्त्तन स्नान पान भोजनकर्म्मसु । शीलितं खादिरं वारि सर्व्वत्वगदोषनाशनम् ।
चक्रदत्तः ।

2 खदिराष्टकः। खदिर त्रिफलारिष्ट पटोलाम्रृत वासकैः। काथोऽष्टकाङ्गो जयति रोमान्तिकमसूरिकाः । कुष्ठविसर्प स्फोट कण्ड्वादीनपि पानतः ।
चक्रदत्तः ।

haritaki in the vernacular. A good *haritaki* fit for medicinal use should be fresh, smooth, dense, heavy and rounded in shape. Thrown into water it should sink in it. *Haritaki* fruits weighing four tolás and upwards, are also considered fit for use, although they may not possess some of the above-mentioned properties. The seeds are rejected and their coats only are used in medicine. Those fruits which have small seeds and abundant cortex are preferred.

Chebulic myrobalans are described as laxative, stomachic, tonic and alterative. They are used in fevers, cough, asthma, urinary diseases, piles, intestinal worms, chronic diarrhœa, costiveness, flatulence, vomiting, hiccup, heart diseases, enlarged spleen and liver, ascites, skin diseases, etc. In combination with emblic and belleric myrobalans, and under the name of *triphalá* or the three myrobalans, they are extensively used as adjuncts to other medicines in almost all diseases.

Two or three chebulic myrobalans, rubbed into a paste and taken with a little rock salt, act as a mild laxative. The following compound decoction called *Pathyádi kvátha* is also much used as a purgative. Take of chebulic myrobalans, pulp of *Cassia fistula* (*áragbadha*), root of *Picrorrhiza Kurroa* (*katuki*), root of *Ipomœa Turpethum* (*trivrit*) and emblic myrobalans, equal parts, in all two tolás, and prepare a decoction in the usual way. Dose, two to four ounces. Bengali practitioners now a days often add senna and rhubarb to the above preparation, but these last were not known to the ancient writers, and are not mentioned in their works.[1]

As an alterative tonic for promoting strength, preventing the effects of age and prolonging life, chebulic myrobalan is used in a peculiar way. One fruit is taken every morning with salt in the rainy season, with sugar in autumn, with ginger in the first half of the cold season, with long pepper in the second half, with honey in spring, and with treacle in the two hot months. These adjuncts are supposed to agree best with the humours that are liable to be

1 पथ्यादिक्वाथः । पथ्यारग्वधतिक्ता त्रिवृदामलकैः शृतपेयं । पाचनसारक युक्तं नवजीर्णज्वरे माने ।

deranged in the different seasons. This old device for prolonging life is still believed in, and acted upon, by some superstitious elderly native gentlemen.[1]

Numerous preparations of *haritaki* for special diseases are described in books, such as the *Amrita haritaki* for dyspepsia, *Danti haritaki* for enlargements in the abdomen called *gulma*, *Bhrigu haritaki* in cough, *Agasti haritaki* in consumption, *Dasa muli haritaki* in anasarca, etc.

Amrita haritaki[2] is thus prepared. One hundred large sized chebulic myrobalans are boiled in butter-milk, and their seeds are taken out. Four tolás each of long pepper, black pepper, ginger, cinnamon, plumbago root, root of *Piper Chaba* (*chaviká*), the five salts, *ájowan*, and the seeds of *Seseli Indicum*, (*vanayamáni*), *yavakshára*, *sarjikákshára*, borax, assafœtida and cloves, are reduced to powder, and soaked for three days respectively in a decoction of tamarind and in lemon juice. This mixture is introduced within the seedless myrobalans, which are then exposed to the sun and dried. One of these prepared myrobalans is directed to be taken every morning for the relief of various sorts of dyspepsia and indigestion. *Danti haritaki* will be described under *Baliospermum montanum*. The other preparations of chebulic myrobalan are not much in vogue at present.

TERMINALIA BELLERICA, *Roxb.*

Sans. विभितकी, *Vibhitaki. Vern. Baherá, Hind. Beng.*

BELLERIC myrobalans are described as astringent and laxative and useful in cough, hoarseness, eye diseases, etc. As a constituent

---

1 गुड़ेन मधुना शुण्ठ्या कृष्णया लवणेन वा। द्वे द्वे खादन् सदा पथ्ये जीवेद्वर्षशतं सुखी। सिन्धूत्थशर्करा शुण्ठीकणामधुगुडैः क्रमात्। वर्षादिष्वभया सेव्या रसायनगुणैषिणा। चक्रदत्तः।

2 हरीतक्याः शतं स्थाप्यं तक्रे स्विन्नञ्च कारयेत्। यत्नाद्बीजं समुद्धृत्य षड्रूषणं पञ्चपटु। यमानीद्वयमेव च। त्रिक्षारं हिङ्गु दिव्यञ्च कर्षद्वयमितं पृथक्। सूक्ष्मचूर्णीकृतं सर्व्वं चुक्राम्लेनापि भावयेत्। निम्बाकस्वरसेनापि भावयेच्च दिनत्रयम्। खादयेदभयामेकां सर्व्वाजीर्णविनाशिनीम्। भैषज्यरत्नावली।

of *triphalá* or the three myrobalans, they are used in almost al diseases. The kernel of the fruits is said to be narcotic and astringent, and is used as an external application to inflamed parts.[1]

In hoarseness, belleric myrobalans, rock salt and long pepper, rubbed into a paste with butter-milk, are recommended to be used as a linctus.[2] Another prescription for sore throat and hoarseness is as follows. Belleric myrobalans are fried in clarified butter; they are then covered with a paste of wheat-flour and slightly roasted on a fire. The cortical portion of the fruits thus prepared, is recommended to be kept in the mouth for the relief of sore throat, cough and catarrh.[3]

TERMINALIA ARJUNA, *Bedd.*

Sans. अर्जुन, *Arjuna.* ककुभ, *Kukubha.*

Vern. Arjuna, Beng. Kahu, Hind.

THE bark of this timber tree is considered tonic, astringent and cooling, and is used in heart diseases, contusions, fractures, ulcers, etc. In diseases of the heart it is used in a variety of ways. Thus a decoction of the bark with milk is given as a nourishment. The powdered bark is given with milk, treacle or water.[4] A *ghrita* is prepared with the decoction and paste of the bark for internal use.[5]

---

1 विभीतफलमज्जस्तु लेपोदाहार्त्तिनाशनः । शार्ङ्गधरः ।

2 कलितरुफलं सिन्धु कणाचूर्णं तक्रेण लीढमपहरति। स्वरभेदं गोपयसापीतं वामलकचूर्णञ्च । चक्रदत्तः ।

3 विभीतकफलं किञ्चिद्घृतेनाभ्यज्य लेपयेत् । गोधूमपिष्टैरङ्गारैर्विपचेत्पुट-पाकवत् । ततः पक्वं समुद्धृत्य त्वचन्तस्य मुखेक्षिपेत् । कासश्वास प्रतिश्याय स्वर भङ्गाञ्जयेत्ततः । शार्ङ्गधरः ।

4 अर्जुनस्य त्वचासिद्धं क्षीरं योज्यं हृदामये । सितयापञ्चमूल्यावा घृतेवा मधुकेन वा । घृतेन दुग्धेन गुडाम्भसावा पिबन्तिचूर्णं ककुभ त्वचोये । हृद्रोग-जीर्णज्वर रक्तपित्तं हत्वा भवेयुश्चिरजीविनस्ते । चक्रदत्तः ।

5 अर्जुनघृतम् । पार्थस्य कल्क स्वरसेन सिद्धं शस्तं घृतं सर्व्वं हृदामयेषु । चक्रदत्तः ।

In fractures and contusions with extensive ecchymosis, powdered *arjuna* bark is recommended to be taken internally with milk.[1] A decoction of the bark is used as a wash in ulcers and chancres.

NAT. ORDER MYRTACEÆ.

EUGENIA JAMBOLANA, *Lam.*

Syn. Syzygium Jambolanum, W. & A.

Sans. जम्बु, *Jambu. Vern. Kálajám, Beng. Jámun, Hind.*

THIS tree, which yields an abundant crop of sub-acid edible fruits during the months of July and August, is common all over the country. In some places the fruits attain the size of a pigeon's egg and are of superior quality. A vinegar prepared from the juice of the ripe fruit, is an agreable stomachic and carminative. It is also used as a diuretic in scanty or suppressed urine. A sort of spirituous liquor called *Jámbava* is described in recent Sanskrit works as prepared by distillation from the juice of the ripe fruits. The bark is astringent, and is used, alone or in combination with other medicines of its class, in the preparation of astringent decoctions, gargles and washes. The fresh juice of the bark is given with goat's milk in the diarrhœa of children.[2] The expressed juice of the leaves is used alone or in combination with other astringents in dysentery with bloody discharge, as for example in the following prescription. Take of the fresh juice of the leaves of *jambu*, mango and emblic myrobalan about a drachm each, and administer with goat's milk and honey.[3]

CARYOPHYLLUS AROMATICUS, *Linn. Sans.* लवङ्ग, *Lavanga.* Cloves, as might be expected, are much used in Hindu

---

1 भग्नः पिबेत्त्वक्पयसार्जुनस्य गोधूमचूर्णं सघृतेनवाथ । चक्रदत्तः ।

2 बिल्वपक्वाम्बुमोचाब्द शिङ्घमाजं पयःशिशोः । समांसरक्तां पञ्चणीं पीतं ह्रण्यात् त्रिरात्रतः । तद्वदजाक्षीरसमो जम्बुत्वगुद्भवोरसः । चक्रदत्तः ।

3 जम्ब्वाम्रामलकीनान्तु पल्लवानथ कुट्टयेत् । संगृह्य स्वरसं तेषामजाक्षीरेण योजयेत् । तं पीवेन्मधुनायुक्तं रक्तातिसारनाशनम् । भावप्रकाशः ।

Medicine, as an aromatic adjunct. They are regarded as light, cooling, stomachic, digestive and useful in thirst, vomiting, flatulence, colic, etc. An infusion of cloves is given to appease thirst.[1] The following pill, called *Chatuḥsama vati*, is commonly used in indigestion. Take of cloves, ginger, *ájowan* and rock salt, equal parts, and make into eight-grain pills.

NAT. ORDER LYTHRACEÆ.

WOODFORDIA FLORIBUNDA, *Salisb.*

Syn. Grislea tomentosa, Roxb.

Sans. धातकी, *Dhátaki.* अग्निज्वाल, *Agnijvála.*

Vern. Dháiphul, Beng. Dhái, Hind.

The Sanskrit synonyms of this beautiful flowering shrub well describe some of its prominent characters. It is called *Támrapushpi* or red flowered, on account of its bright red permanent calyx, and *Guchchhapushpi* or having clusters of blossoms, on account of its numerous small flowers, which give it a gaudy appearance. From the circumstance of its being common in mountainous tracts, it has got the name of *Párvati* or hill-born.

The dried flowers of *Woodfordia floribunda* are regarded as stimulant and astringent and are much used, in combination with other astringent medicines, in bowel complaints and hæmorrhages. Two drachms of the dried flowers are given with curdled milk in dysentery, and with honey in menorrhagia.[2] In the dysentery of children, the following combination is recommended to be given in the form of powder or decoction with the addition of honey. Take of the flowers of *Woodfordia floribunda*, *bel* fruits, bark of *Symplocos racemosa* (*lodhra*), root of *Pavonia odorata* (*bálá*), and the fruits of *Pothos officinalis* (*gajapipul*), in equal parts, two tolás in all, and prepare a decoction in the usual way.[3]

---

1 पिपासायामनुत्क्लेशे लवङ्गस्याम्बु शस्यते । चक्रः ।

2 धातक्याश्चाक्षमात्रं वा आमलक्यामधुद्रवम् । पाण्डुप्रदरशान्त्यर्थं पिबेत्तण्डुलवारिणा । चक्रदत्तः ।

3 धातकीबिल्वलोध्राणि बालकं गजपिप्पली । एभिः कृतं शृतं शीतं शिशुभ्यः क्षौद्रसंयुतम् । प्रदद्याद्वलेहं वा सर्वातीसारशान्तये । शार्ङ्गधरः ।

The powdered flower is sprinkled over ulcers for diminishing their discharge and promoting granulation.[1]

NAT. ORDER HAMAMELIDEÆ.

LIQUIDAMBAR ORIENTALE, *Miller. Sans.* सिह्लक, *Silhaka. Vern. Siláras, Hind.* Liquid storax is described in Sanskrit works as a product of Turkey. It is considered useful in affections of the throat, copious perspiration and skin diseases, but is chiefly used in perfuming medicinal oils.

NAT. ORDER, GRANATEÆ.

PUNICA GRANATUM, *Linn.*

Sans. दाडिम, *Dáḍima. Vern. A'nár, Hind.*

The pomegranate is indigenous to North Western India. The best fruits, having sweet juice and very small seeds come from Cabul. The fresh juice of the fruits is much used as an ingredient of cooling and refrigerent mixtures and of some medicines for dyspepsia. The rind of the fruit is used as an astringent in diarrhœa. In the Pharmacographia it is stated that the use of the root-bark as an anthelmintic by the Hindus attracted the notice of Buchanan at Calcutta about the year 1805. This physician pointed out the efficacy of the root-bark which was further shown by Fleming and others. I have not been able to find any notice of pomegranate root-bark in Sanskrit works.

Dáḍimáshṭaka.[2] Take of pomegranate rind one seer, bamboo-manna two tolás, cardamom, cinnamon, *tejapátra,* and flowers of *Mesua ferrea* (*nágakesara*), each four tolás, *ájowan,* coriander, cumin seeds, long pepper root, long pepper, black pepper and ginger, each eight tolás, sugar one seer. Powder the ingredients and mix. Dose, about one drachm in chronic bowel complaints.

---

1 धातकीचूर्णसोप्तैर्व्वा तथा रोहन्ति ते व्रणाः । चक्रदत्तः ।

2 दाडिमाष्टकः। कर्षोन्मिता तुगाक्षीरी चातुर्जातं द्विकार्षिकम् । यमानी धान्यकाजाजी ग्रन्थिव्योषं पलांशिकम् । पलानि दाडिमादष्टौ सितायाश्चैकतः कृतः । गुणैः कपित्थाष्टकवच्चूर्णोऽयं दाडिमाष्टकः । चक्रदत्तः ।

NAT. ORDER CUCURBITACEÆ.

BENINCASA CERIFERA, *Savi.*

Syn. Cucurbita Pepo, Roxb.

Sans. कुष्माण्ड, *Kushmánda. Vern. Kumrá, Beng. Pethá, Hind.*

The large fruit or gourd of *Benincasa cerifera* is eaten by the natives in their curries, and is extensively cultivated all over India. It is considered tonic, nutritive and diuretic, and a specific for hæmoptysis and other hæmorrrhages from internal organs. It would appear that the older Sanskrit writers were not acquainted with its peculiar action on the circulatory system by which it rapidly puts a check to hæmorrhage from the lungs. The Rája Nirghantu, the oldest work on therapeutics, gives a long account of its virtues, but does not allude to its use in phthisis or hæmoptysis. Neither does Susruta mention it in his chapters on the treatment of hæmorrhage and phthisis, though the plant is alluded to by him elsewhere. The more recent compilations, such as Chakradatta Sangraha, Sárangadhara etc. give numerous preparations of the article and detail its uses.

Khanda kushmándaka,[1] or confection of squash. In preparing this medicine, old ripe gourds are selected. Those not at least a year old, are not approved. They are longitudinally divided into two halves and the pulp scraped out in thin flakes by an iron comb or scratcher. The watery juice that oozes out abundantly during

[1] खण्डकुष्माण्डकः। कुष्माण्डकात् पलशतं सुस्विन्नं निष्कुलीकृतम्। पचेत्तप्ते घृतप्रस्थे शनैस्ताम्रमये दृढे। यदा मधुनिभः पाकस्तदा खण्डशतं न्यसेत्। पिप्पली शृङ्गवेराभ्यां द्वे पले जीरकस्य च। त्वगेलापत्रमरिच धान्यकानां पलार्द्धकम्। न्यसेच्चूर्णीकृतं तत्र दर्व्या संघट्टयेन्मुहुः। तत्पक्वं स्थापयेद्भाण्डे दत्वा क्षौद्रं घृतार्द्धकम्। तद्यथाग्निबलं खादेद्रक्तपित्ती क्षतक्षयी। कासश्वास तमश्छर्दि तृष्णाज्वरनिपीड़ितः। वृष्यं पुनर्नवकरं बलवर्णप्रसाधनम्। उरः सन्धान करणं बृंहणं स्वरबोधनम्। अश्विभ्यां निर्म्मितं सिद्धं कुष्माण्डकरसायनम्। खण्डामलकमानानुसारात् कुष्माण्डकद्रवात्। पात्रं पाकाय दातव्यं यावान्वा तत्र रसो भवेत्। अत्रापि शुद्धया पाको निस्त्वचं निष्कुलीकृतम्।

चक्रदत्तः।

this process is preserved, the seeds being rejected. The pulp is boiled in the above mentioned juice, till softened. It is then tied up tightly in a cloth, and the fluid portion allowed to strain through it. The softened and drained pulp is dried in the sun and the watery portion preserved for future use. Fifty tolás of the prepared pulp are fried in sixteen tolás of clarified butter, and again boiled in the juice of the fruit, till reduced to the consistence of honey. To this are added fifty tolás of refined sugar, and the whole is heated over a gentle fire, till the mass assumes such a consistence as to adhere to the ladle. The pot is now removed from the fire, and the following substances, namely, long pepper and ginger, each two tolás, cumin seeds, cardamoms, cinnamon, leaves called *tejapatra*, black pepper and coriander, each half a tolá in fine powder, are aded to the syrup and stirred briskly with a ladle, till the mass is cool. Eight tolás of honey are now added to the confection which is preserved in a new earthen pot. The dose of this medicine is from one to two tolás, according to the age and strength of the patient. It is useful in hæmoptysis, phthisis, marasmus, cough, asthma, ulceration of the lungs, hoarseness, etc.

Vásá kushmánḍa khanḍa.[1] Take of the root of *Justicia Adhatoda* (*vásaka*), one seer, water eight seers; boil together till reduced to one-fourth and strain. Then take of the pulp of *Benincasa cerifera*, prepared as above described, fifty tolás; fry it in thirty-two tolás of clarified butter, and boil in the decoction of *vásaka* till the whole is reduced to the consistence of honey. Add to it sugar, one hundred tolás, and apply heat till the mass thickens to the proper consistence. Remove from the fire, add the following substances in fine powder, namely, tubers of *Cyperus rotundus*, (*mustaka*), dried emblic myrobalan, bamboo manna, root of *Clerodendron Siphonanthus* (*brahmayasti*), a fragrant substance called

---

1 वासाखण्डकुष्माण्डकः। पञ्चाशत्पलं स्विन्नं कुष्माण्डात्प्रस्थमाज्यतः।
पाच्यं पलशतं खण्डं वासाक्वाथाढ़के पचेत्। मुस्ताधात्री शुभाभार्गी त्रिसुग-
न्धैश्च कार्षिकैः। ऐलेय विश्वधन्याकमरिचैश्च पलांशिकैः। पिप्पलीकुडवञ्चैव मधु-
मानीं प्रदापयेत्। कासं श्वासं क्षयं हिक्कां रक्तपित्तं हलीमकम्। हृद्रोगम-
म्लपित्तञ्च पीनसञ्च व्यपोहति। चक्रदत्तः।

elabáluka, cinnamon, cardamom, *tejapatra*, each quarter of a tolá, ginger, coriander, and black pepper each one tolá, long pepper, four tolás, stir well till the confection cools, and lastly add eight tolás of honey. This preparation is used in cough, asthma, phthisis, hæmoptysis, heart disease, and catarrh.

In insanity, epilepsy and other nervous diseases, the fresh juice of the squash is given either with sugar or as an adjunct to other medicines for these diseases. A *ghrita* for use in these diseases is also prepared as follows.

Kushmáṇḍaka ghrita.[1] Take of the juice of *Benincasa cerifera* eighteen seers, clarified butter, one seer, liquorice root beaten into a paste with water, quarter of a seer. Boil them together and prepare a *ghrita* in the usual way. Dose, one to two tolás.

TRICHOSANTHES DIOICA, *Roxb.*

Sans. पटोल, *Paṭola. Vern. Palwal, Hind.*

THE *Trichosanthes dioica* is extensively cultivated as an article of food in Bengal. The unripe fruits are much used by the natives as a culinary vegetable and are considered very wholesome and especially suited for the convalescent. In fact they constitute one of the most palatable vegetables grown in this country. The tender tops are also used as a pot-herb and are regarded as tonic and vermifuge.

The leaves, fresh juice of the fruits and the root are all used medicinally. The leaves are described as a good, light and agreeable bitter tonic. The fresh juice of the unripe fruit is often used as a cooling and laxative adjunct to some alterative medicines such as the preparation called *Rasa sindura*, etc. The bulbous root is called *Ramyaka* in Sanskrit and is classified amongst purgatives by Susruta.

In bilious fever, a decoction of *paṭola* leaves and coriander, in equal parts, is given as a febrifuge and laxative.[2] The leaves

---

1 कुष्माण्डकघृतम् । कुष्माण्डकरसे सर्पिरष्टादशगुणे पचेत् । यष्ट्याह्वकल्कं तत्पानमपस्मारविनाशनम् । चक्रदत्तः ।

2 दीपनं कफविच्छेदि वातपित्तानुलोमनम् ज्वरघ्नं पाचनं भेदि शृतं धान्यपटोलयोः । चक्रदत्तः ।

enter into the composition of several compound decoctions for fever. The following called *Paṭoládi kváṭha* is an illustration. Take of *paṭola* leaves, red sandal wood, root of *Sanseviera Zeylanica* (*murvá*), *Picrorrhiza Kurroa* (*katuki*), *Stephania hernandifolia* (*páṭhá*) and *gulancha*, each one drachm, water half a seer, boil together till reduced to one-fourth.[1]

Paṭola enters into the composition of several compound decoctions for boils and other skin diseases for which it is considered a very efficacious remedy. The following is an illustration. Take of *paṭola* leaves, *gulancha*, *mustaka*, *chiretá*, *nim* bark, catechu, root-bark of *Justicia Adhatoda* (*vásaka*), and *Oldenlandia herbacea* (*parpaṭa*), equal parts, in all two tolás, and prepare a decoction in the usual way. This decoction is regarded as a valuable alterative, tonic and febrifuge.[2]

The root is used in combination with *Ipomœa Turpethum* and other adjuncts as a drastic purgative in jaundice, anasarca and ascites. The following called *Paṭoládya churna* is an illustration. Take of the root of *Trichosanthes dioica* (*paṭola*), turmeric, *báberang* seeds, *kamalá* powder, and the three myrobalans, two tolás each, cinnamon, and the root of the indigo plant, three tolás each, *Ipomœa Turpethum* (*trivrit*) four tolás ; powder the ingredients finely and mix. Dose, about one drachm with cow's urine. After the use of this medicine, light food only (such as gruel) should be taken.[3]

---

1 पटोलं चन्दनं मूर्वा तिक्ता पाठामृता गणः। पित्तश्लेष्मारुचिच्छर्दि ज्वर-कण्डूविषापहः। चक्रदत्तः।

2 पटोलामृतभूनिम्ब वासकारिष्टपर्पटैः। खदिराब्दयुतैः क्वाथो विस्फोटार्त्तिज्वरापहः। चक्रदत्तः।

3 पटोलाद्यं चूर्णम्। पटोलमूलं रजनी विडङ्गं त्रिफलात्वचम्। कम्पिल्लकं नीलिनीञ्च त्रिवृताञ्चेति चूर्णयेत्। षडाद्यान् कार्षिकानन्त्यांस्त्रीन्द्वित्रिचतुर्गुणान्। कृत्वा चूर्णं ततो मुष्टिं गवां मूत्रेण ना पिबेत्। विरिक्तो जाङ्गलरसैर्भुञ्जीत मृदुभोजनम्। मण्डं पेयाञ्च पीत्वा च सव्योषं षडहं पयः। शृतं पिबेत्तु तच्चूर्णं पिबेदेवं पुनः पुनः। हन्ति सर्वोदराण्येतच्चूर्णं जातोदकान्यपि। कामलां पाण्डुरोगञ्च श्वयथुञ्चापकर्षति। चक्रदत्तः।

The fresh juice of the leaves of *Trichosanthes dioica* is recommended by several writers, to be applied to the bald patches of alopecia.[1]

CUCUMIS MELO, *Linn.*

Syn. Cucumis utilissimus, Roxb.

Sans. कर्कटी, *Karkaṭi. Vern. Kánkur, Beng. Kákri, Hind.*

The seeds of this useful species of *Cucumis* are described as cooling, edible, nutritive and diuretic, and are used in painful micturition and suppression of urine. Two drachms of the seeds rubbed into a pulp with water, are given alone or in combination with salt and *kánjika*.[2]

The seeds of *Cucumis sativa*, (*Sans.* त्रपुष, *Trapusha. Vern. Khirá, Hind.*) and of *Benincasa cerifera* (*Sans. Kushmánḍa.*) are also used as diuretics like those of *Cucumis utilissimus*.[3]

COCCINIA INDICA, *W. & A. Syn. Momordica monodelpha, Roxb. Sans.* बिम्ब, *Vimba, Vern. Telákuchá, Beng.* The expressed juice of the thick tap-root of this plant is used by the leading native Kavirájas of Calcutta, as an adjunct to the metallic preparations prescribed by them in diabetes. I have not found this use of the plant noticed in any written work, but I know several patients who have taken the juice of the root along with *Vangesvara or Somanátha rasa* and who were benefitted by the use of these remedies. I am inclined to think that the juice of the root of this plant probably acts beneficially in some way. It is very desirable that its therapeutic action should be tested. The expressed juice is directed to be taken in doses of one tola along with a pill, every morning.

---

1 रसस्तिक्तपटोलस्य पत्राणां तद्विलेपनात्। इन्द्रलुप्तापहो लेपो मधुनाक्तस्तवी-रसः। भावप्रकाशः।

2 कल्कमेर्व्वारुबीजानामक्षमात्रं ससैन्धवम्। धान्याम्लयुक्तं पीत्वैव मूत्राघातादिमुच्यते। चक्रदत्तः।

3 कुष्माण्डस्य तुबीजानि बीजानि त्रपुषस्य च। वस्तौ सन्धारयेत् तेन प्रयात्यश्मूत्र निग्रहः। भावप्रकाशः।

CITRULLUS COLOCYNTHIS, *Schrad.*

Syn. Cucumis Colocynthis, Linn.

Sans. इन्द्रवारुणी, *Indravárunì. Vern. Indráyan. Hind.*

INDIAN colocynth is common on the lower slopes of the Western Himalaya and also on the plains of the drier parts of India. It is procurable in the bazars of the North-West Provinces under the name of *indráyan*. The pulp of the fruit is described as bitter, acrid, cathartic, and useful in biliousness, constipation, fever and worms. The root of the plant is considered cathartic and useful in jaundice, ascites, enlargements of the abdominal viscera, urinary diseases, rheumatism, etc.

Jvaraghni guṭiká.[1] Take of mercury one part ; sulphur, colocynth pulp, cardamoms, long pepper, chebulic myrobalan, and pellitory root, each four parts. Rub these ingredients with the juice of *indravárunì* root and make into pills weighing about twenty grains each. These pills are administered with the fresh juice of *gulancha* in recent fever. They move the bowels and reduce the fever.

An oil prepared from the seeds of Indian colocynth, is used for blackening grey hairs. A poultice of the root is said to be useful in inflammation of the breasts.[2]

NAT. ORDER UMBELLIFERÆ.

The following aromatic fruits belonging to this natural order, are noticed by Sanskrit writers and are used in medicine or as condiments by the natives.

यमानि, *Yamáni. Ptychotis A'jowan,* DC. Vern. A'jowan Hind.*

वनयमानि, *Vanayamáni. Seseli Indicum, W. & A. Vern. Banjoán, B.*

---

1 ज्वरघ्नीगुटिका। भागैकः स्याद्रसाच्छुद्धाद्वैलीयः पिप्पलीशिवा। अकारकरभोगन्धः कटुतैलेन शोधितः। फलानिचेन्द्रवारुण्याश्चतुर्भागमितान्यमी। एकत्रमर्दयेच्चूर्णमिन्द्रवारुणिकारसैः। कार्षोन्मितांवटीङ्कृत्वा दद्यात्सद्यज्वरेभिषक्। छिन्नारसानुपानेनज्वरघ्नीगुटिकामता। शार्ङ्गधरः।

2 इन्द्रवारुणिकाबीजतैलेनाभ्यङ्गमाचरेत्। प्रत्यहन्तेन काकाग्निसन्निभाकुन्तलाश्चलम्। शार्ङ्गधरः।

* Now included in the genus *Carum* by Hooker and Bentham.

अजमोदा, *Ajamodá. Carum Roxburghianum, Benth. Vern. A'jmad, Hind. Rándhuni, Beng.*

जीरक, *Jiraka. Cuminum Cyminum, Linn. Vern. Jirá, Beng.*

सुषवि, *Sushavi. Carum Carui, Linn. Vern. Shiá jirá, Hind.*

मधुरिका, *Madhuriká. Fœniculum vulgare, Gœrtn. Mauri, Beng. Sonf, Hind.*

मिश्रेया, *Misreyá. Anethum Sowa,* Roxb. Vern. Sulphá, B. Sowá, H.*

धन्याक, *Dhanyáka. Coriandrum sativum, Linn. Vern. Dhaniá, H.*

PTYCHOTIS AJOWAN. The seeds of *Ptychotis Ajowan* have an aromatic smell and warm pungent taste. They are used for culinary purposes, as spices along with betel nuts and *pan* leaves, and as a carminative medicine. A tea spoonful of *ájowan* with a little rock salt, is a common domestic remedy for indigestion from irregular diet. The following compound powder is used in cases of colic or pain in the bowels. Take of *ájowan*, rock salt, *sonchal* salt, *yavakshára*, assafœtida, and chebulic myrobalan, equal parts ; powder the ingredients and mix. Dose, grains ten to twenty, to be taken with wine.[1] *A'jowan*, taken daily with treacle, is said to cure urticaria within a week.[2] *A'jowan*, as well as the seeds of *Seseli Indicum* (*vanajamáni*), are much used as aromatic adjuncts in compound prescriptions.

CARUM ROXBURGHIANUM. The seeds of *Carum Roxburghianum* (*ajamodá*) are an essential ingredient of native cookery, They are said to be useful in hiccup, vomiting and pain in the region of the bladder. They enter into the composition of several carminative and stimulant preparations, such as the *Ajamodádi churna* (see *Argyreia speciosa*), etc.

CUMINUM CYMINUM. Cumin seeds form an ingredient of some curry powders and pickles used by the natives. They are regarded as stomachic, carminative, astringent and useful

---

1 यमानी हिङ्गु सिन्धूत्थ क्षार सौवर्च्चलाभयाः। सुरामण्डेन पातव्या शूलगुल्म निवारणाः। चक्रदत्तः।

2 सगुड़ं दीप्यकं यस्तु खादेत् पथ्याशभुङ्नरः। तस्य नश्यति सप्ताहादुदर्द्दः सर्व्वदेहजः। चक्रदत्तः।

* *Anethum* is reduced by Drs. Hooker and Bentham to *Peucedanum.*

in dyspepsia, diarrhœa, etc. A confection of cumin seeds is prepared as follows:

Jirakádi modaka. Take of the three myrobalans, tubers of *Cyperus rotundus* (*mustaka*), watery extract of *gulancha*, prepared talc, flowers of *Mesua ferrea* (*nágakesara*), leaves called *tejapatra*, cinnamon, cardamoms, cloves, coriander, ginger, long pepper, *Oldenlandia herbacea* (*parpati*), root of *Andropogon muricatum* (*usira*), *Pavonia odorata* (*bálá*), and *Plumbago Zeylanica* (*chitraka*), each one part, cumin seed, nineteen parts or equal in weight to all the other ingredients; powder them all and mix. Add two parts of sugar to one of the powder and make into a confection with honey and clarified butter. Dose, one drachm. This medicine is prescribed in chronic diarrhœa and dyspepsia with loss of appetite.

Jirakádya taila.[1] Take of powdered cumin seeds, eight tolás, minium or red lead, four tolás, prepared mustard oil three seers, water twelve seers, boil them together in the usual way for the preparation of medicinal oils. This oil is used in eczema.

A poultice made of cumin seeds, with the addition of honey, salt and clarified butter, is recommended to be applied to scorpion bites.[2]

FŒNICULUM VULGARE. Fennel seeds are largely used as a condiment. In medicine they are chiefly used as an aromatic adjunct to other articles. Distilled fennel water is prepared and sold in India, under the name of *A'rak bádian,* and is used as a domestic carminative.

CARUM CARUI. The fruits called *shiá jirá* in the vernacular, do not appear to differ from European caraway. The plant grows wild largely in the "high alpine region of Lahul in the Western Himalaya," but is rare in the plains. The fruits contain a volatile oil and are used as a carminative like cumin seeds.

---

1 जीरकाद्यं तैलम् । जीरकस्य पलं पिष्टं सिन्दुरार्द्धपलं तथा । कटुतैलं पचेद्भाभ्यां सर्व्वपामाहरं परम् । भावप्रकाशः ।

2 जीरकस्य कृतः कल्को घृतसैन्धव संयुतः। सुखोष्णो मधुमालेपो वृश्चिकस्य विषं हरेत् । भावप्रकाशः ।

CORIANDRUM SATIVUM. Coriander is largely used by the natives as a condiment and along with betel nuts and *pán* leaves. It is described as carminative, refrigerent, diuretic, tonic and aphrodisiac. A cold infusion of coriander is given with sugar for the relief of internal heat and thirst.[1] A decoction of coriander and ginger is given in dyspepsia and indigestion. Coriander enters into the composition of numerous cooling and carminative medicines. The fresh leaves of the plant are pungent and aromatic. They are used for preparing a sauce or *cháṭni*, in the same way as the leaves of spearmint *(pudiná)*.[2]

FERULA ASSAFŒTIDA, *Linn.*

Sans. हिङ्गु, *Hingu. Vern. Hing, Beng. Hind.*

SANSKRIT writers describe assafœtida as an exudation from the root of the assafœtida plant which is indigenous to Persia, Khorasan and Multan.* Assafœtida is regarded as a stimulant and carminative and is much used in dyspepsia, flatulence, colic, and diseases of the nervous system. It is fried before being used internally. Raw or unfried assafœtida is said to cause vomiting.

Hingvashṭaka churna.[3] Take of fried assafœtida, ginger, long pepper, black pepper, *ájowan*, cumin seeds, nigella seeds and rock salt, equal parts ; reduce them to powder and mix. Dose, ten to twenty grains, to be taken with the first morsel of rice and clarified butter taken at breakfast. Thus administered, it is said to increase the appetite and digestive powers and to cure flatulence. Some writers recommend the above powder to be made into pills with lemon juice.

---

1 प्रातः सशर्करः पेयोहिमोधन्याकसम्भवः। अन्तर्दाहं तथातृष्णां जयेत्स्रोतोविशोधनः। भावप्रकाशः।

2 धान्यनागर सिद्धन्तु तोयं दद्याद्विचक्षणः। आमाजीर्णे दीपनं प्रशमनं वस्तिशोधनम्। चक्रदत्तः।

3 हिङ्ग्वष्टकं चूर्णम्। त्रिकटुक मजमोदा सैन्धवं जीरके द्वे समधरण धृतानामष्टमो हिङ्गुभागः। प्रथम कवलभुक्तं सर्पिषा चूर्णमेतज्जनयति जठराग्निं वातरोगांश्च हन्यात्। भैषज्य रत्नावली।

* Not now found at Multan. G. K.

In the flatulence of infants a powder composed of assafœtida, rock salt, cardamoms, ginger, and the root of *Clerodendron Siphonanthus* (*bhárgi*), in equal parts, is prescribed by several writers.[1] In flatulent colic with costiveness, a suppository made of assafœtida, rock salt and honey, and smeared over with clarified butter, is introduced into the rectum.[2]

In hemiplegia, stiff-neck, facial palsy, sciatica and other diseases of the nervous system, fried assafœtida is given along with a compound decoction called *Máshabaládi*, (see *Phaseolus Roxburghii*). A bit of warm assafœtida, placed in the cavity of a carious tooth, is said to relieve pain.[3]

HYDROCOTYLE ASIATICA, *Linn. Sans.* मण्डूकपर्णि, *Manḍukaparni. Vern. Thalkuri, Beng. Bráhmamanḍuki, Hind.* The properties of this plant are said to resemble those of *Bráhmi* (*Herpestes Monniera*), both being regarded as alterative, tonic, and useful in diseases of the skin, nervous system and blood. The fresh juice of the leaves is given with milk and liquorice powder, as an alterative tonic.[4]

NAT. ORDER RUBIACEÆ.

OLDENLANDIA HERBACEA, *DC.*

Syn. Oldenlandia biflora, Roxb.

Sans. पर्पट, *Parpaṭa. Vern. Khetpáprá. Beng.*

THE *Oldenlandia herbacea* is a "small, weak, straggling delicate plant, appearing in the rainy season" in fields and low ground

---

1 घृतेन सिन्धुविश्वैला हिङ्गुभार्गीरजोऽलिहन्। आनाहं वातिकं शूलं जयेत्तोयेन वा शिशुः। चक्रदत्तः।

2 हिङ्गुमाक्षिकसिन्धूत्थैः पक्त्वा वर्त्तिं सुनिर्मिताम्। घृताभ्यक्तां गुदे दद्यादुदावर्त्तविनाशिनीम्। चक्रदत्तः।

3 हिङ्गु सोष्णन्तु मतिमान् क्रिमिदन्तेषु दापयेत्। चक्रदत्तः।

4 मण्डूकपर्ण्याः स्वरसः प्रयोज्यः क्षीरेण यष्टीमधुकस्य चूर्णम्। रसो गुडूच्यास्तु समूलपुष्प्याः कल्कः प्रयोज्यः खलु शङ्खपुष्प्याः। आयुःप्रदान्यामयनाशनानि मेध्या विशेषेण तु शङ्खपुष्पी। चक्रदत्तः।

on the banks of water courses. The entire plant is used in medicine, and is regarded as a valuable bitter tonic and febrifuge. It enters into the composition of numerous prescriptions for fever, diarrhœa, skin diseases, etc. A simple decoction of the plant is used in bilious fever, with irritability of the stomach or delirium.[1] *Parpaṭa* enters into the composition of numerous febrifuge and tonic decoctions. The following is an example.

Panchabhadra.[2] Take of *parpaṭa*, tubers of *Cyperus rotundus* (*mustaka*), *gulancha*, *chireta* and ginger, equal parts, in all two tolás, and prepare a decoction in the usual way. This preparation is much used in fever supposed to be caused by deranged air and bile, that is, remittent fever with gastric irritability, nervousness, etc.

RANDIA DUMETORUM, *Linn.*

Sans. मदन, *Madana. Vern. Mayin, Hind.*

THE *Randia dumetorum* is a small thorny tree common in waste places. The fruit when ripe, looks like a small apple, and has a peculiar sweetish, sickly smell. It is described by Sanskrit writers, as the best or safest of emetics. In fact the ancient Hindus depended chiefly upon this drug for causing emesis. One ripe fruit is generally administered for this purpose. It is also used in combination with other medicines, as for example in the following prescription.

Pancha kasháya.[3] Take of *Justicia Adhatoda* (*vásaka*), *Acorus Calamus* (*vachá*), nim bark, leaves of *Trichosanthes dioica* (*paṭola*), and bark of *Aglaia Roxburghiana* (*priyangu*), equal parts, half

---

1 एकः पर्पटकः श्रेष्ठः पित्तज्वरविनाशनः। किंपुनर्यदि युज्येत चन्दनोशीरवालकैः। दर्पणः।

2 पर्पटाब्दामृताविश्वकिरातैः साधितं जलम्। पञ्चभद्रमिदं ज्ञेयं वातपित्तज्वरापहम्। शार्ङ्गधरः।

3 पञ्चकषायः। आटरूषं वचानिम्बं पटोलं फलिनीत्वचम्। क्काथयित्वा-पिबेत्तोयं माक्षिकन्मदनान्वितम्। क्काथ्यद्रव्यस्य कुडवं श्रपयित्वा जलाढके। चतुर्भागावशिष्टन्तु वमनेष्ववचारयेत्। चक्रदत्तः।

a seer in all, water eight seers; boil them together till reduced to one-fourth. This decoction is given with the addition of the pulp of *Randia dumetorum* for causing emesis.

RUBIA CORDIFOLIA, *Linn.*

Syn. Rubia Manjisṭa, Roxb.

Sans. मंजिष्ठा, *Manjishṭhá, Vern. Manjiṭ, Beng. Hind.*

Indian madder, well known as a red dye, is used in medicine chiefly as a colouring agent. All medicated oils are first prepared for use by being boiled with madder. It is regarded as astringent and useful in external inflammations, ulcers and skin diseases. Madder and liquorice root, rubbed into a paste with *kánjika,* is applied over fractures, to reduce inflammation and swelling. Madder rubbed with honey, is recommended by several writers to be applied to brown spots on the face (*pityriasis versicolor*).[1]

Manjishṭhádya ghrita,[2] is prepared with clarified butter and a paste composed of equal parts of madder, red sandal wood, and the root of *Sanseviera Zeylanica* (*murvá*), and applied to ulcers from burns.

PÆDERIA FŒTIDA, *Linn.*

Sans. प्रसारणी, *Prasárani.*

Vern. Gandhabháduli, Beng. Gandháli, Hind.

The *Pæderia fœtida* is a long climbing plant, twining up and over trees. All parts of the plant give off a most offensive odour when bruised. The leaves, boiled and made into soup, are considered wholesome and suitable for the sick and convalescent. The entire plant including stem, leaves and root, is much used both internally and externally in rheumatic affections for which it is regarded as a specific.

Prasárani leha, or electuary of *Pæderia fœtida.* Take of the leaves, root and stem of *Pæderia fœtida,* two seers, water, thirty-

---

1 आलेपनार्थं मञ्जिष्ठा मधुकं चाम्लपेषितम् । चक्रदत्तः ।

2 मञ्जिष्ठाद्यं घृतम्। मञ्जिष्ठां चन्दनं मूर्वां पिष्ट्वा सर्पिर्विपाचयेत् । सर्व्वेषा मग्निदग्धानामेतद्रोपणमिष्यते । चक्रदत्तः ।

wo seers, boil till reduced to one-fourth. To the strained decoction add, two seers of treacle, and again boil till reduced to the consistence of a thick syrup. Lastly add powdered ginger, long pepper, black pepper, plumbago root and the root of *Piper Chaba* (*chaviká*), equal parts, in all half a seer. Dose, about one tolá in acute rheumatism.[1]

Several oils or liniments for external application are prepared with this plant. The following, called *Kubja prasárani taila*,[2] is argely used by native physicians. Take of the entire plant of *Pæderia fœtida* eight hundred tolás, boil in sixty-four seers of water till reduced to sixteen seers, and strain. To the strained decoction, add sesamum oil, sixteen seers, milk, thirty-two seers, whey and fermented paddy water (*kánjika*), each sixteen seers, and the following substances, namely, root of *Pæderia fœtida*, plumbago root, long pepper root, liquorice, rock salt, *Acorus Calamus* root, dill seeds, bark of *Cedrus Deodara*, root of *Vanda Roxburghii* (*rásná*), *Scindapsus officinalis* (*gajapippali*), *jaṭámánsi* root and marking nuts, each two tolás in the form of a paste. First boil the oil with the decoction of *Pæderia fœtida* till the water is nearly evaporated, then boil the oil successively with the addition of milk, whey and *kánjika*, adding the aromatic paste during the last process of boiling. This oil is used externally in rheumatism with contraction and stiffness of the joints. After the application of the oil, the affected parts should be fomented with dry heat.

---

1 प्रसारणीलेहः। प्रसारण्याढके क्वाथे प्रस्थो गुड़रसोमतः। पक्वः पञ्चोषणरजः युक्तः स्यादामवातहा। भावप्रकाशः।

2 कुब्जप्रसारणी तैलम्। प्रसारणीशतं क्षुण्णं पचेत्तोयार्म्मणे शुभे। पादशिष्टे-समं तैलं दधिदद्यात्सकाञ्जिकम्। द्विगुणञ्च पयोदत्त्वा कल्कान् द्विपलिकांस्तथा। चित्रकं पिप्पलीमूलं मधुकं सैन्धवं वचाम्। शतपुष्पां देवदारु रास्नां वारणपिप्पलीम्। प्रसारण्याश्च मूलानि मांसी भल्लातकानि च। पचेन्मृद्वग्निना तैलं वातश्लेष्मामयान् जयेत्। अशीतिं नरनारीणां वातरोगानपोहति। कुब्जं स्तिमितपङ्गुत्वं गृध्रसीखञ्जकार्द्दितम्। हनुपृष्ठशिरोग्रीवास्तम्भं चापि नियच्छति। चक्रदत्तः।

NAT. ORDER VALERIANACEÆ.

NARDOSTACHYS JATAMANSI, *DC.*

Syn. Valeriana Jatamansi, Jones.

Sans. जटामांसि, *Jaṭámánsi. Vern. Jaṭámánsi, Beng. Báluchar, Hind.*

THE *Nardostachys Jatamansi* is a native of the mountains of Northern India and has been used in Hindu medicine from a very ancient period. The fragrant root is considered a nervine tonic, and is much used as an aromatic adjunct in the preparation of medicinal oils and *ghritas*. It does not appear however to have been used internally except as an ingredient of complex prescriptions. In the Pharmacopœia of India it is stated that *jaṭámánsi* enters into the composition of a nostrum highly recommended in the treatment of epilepsy by Susruta. I do not find in Susruta's work any prescription for epilepsy, containing *jaṭámánsi*, except the following, in which however it can hardly be said to be an active ingredient. Take of the pulse of *Phaseolus Roxburghii* (*kulattha*), barley, jujube fruit, seeds of *Crotolaria juncea* (*sana*), bdellium, *jaṭámánsi* root, the ten drugs collectively called *dasamula* (see *Desmodium gangeticum*), and chebulic myrobalan, equal parts; and prepare a decoction in the usual way. This decoction is recommended to be administered with the addition of clarified butter and goat's urine.[1]

NAT. ORDER COMPOSITÆ.

SAUSSUREA AURICULATA, *Bth. et Hf.*

Syn. Aplotaxis auriculata, DC.

Sans. कुष्ठ, *Kushṭha. Vern. Kur, Páchak. Hind. Beng.*

THE *Aplotaxis auriculata* is a native of the mountains around Cashmere, and has been used in Hindu medicine from an early age. Its root is described as aromatic, stimulant and useful in cough, asthma, fever, dyspepsia and skin diseases. It enters also into the composition of some pastiles for fumigation.

---

1 कुलत्थ यवकोलानि शणबीजं पलङ्कषाम् । जटिलां पञ्चमूल्यौ द्वे पथ्या श्चोत्क्वाथ्य यत्नतः । बस्तमूत्रयुतं सर्पिः पिवेत्सदातिके हितम् । सुश्रुतः ।

Agnimukha churna.[1] Take of assafœtida, one part, *Acorus Calamus* (*vachá*) two parts, long pepper, three parts, ginger, four parts, *ajowan* five parts, chebulic myrobalan, six parts, plumbago root, seven parts, and the root of *Aplotaxis auriculata*, eight parts. Powder the ingredients, mix and pass the powder through a cloth. Dose, twenty to forty grains with whey or wine in dyspepsia with loss of appetite.

A liniment composed of the root of *Aplotaxis auriculata*, *kánjika* and castor oil is recommended by several writers to be applied to the o rehead in cephalalgia.[2] The fried root, mixed with mustard oil, is applied to the scalp in porrigo. Equal parts of the powdered root and of rock salt, mixed with mustard oil and fermented paddy water (*kánjika*), are rubbed on joints affected with chronic disease.[3]

WEDELIA CALENDULACEA, *Less.*

Syn. Verbesina calendulacea, Roxb.

Sans. भृङ्गराज, *Bhringarája.* केशराज, *Kesarája.*

Vern. Kesarája, Beng. Bhánrá, Hind.

THERE is some confusion between the Sanskrit and vernacular names of *Wedelia calendulacea*, and *Eclipta prostrata*. Both these plants are called *kesaráj* or *kesuriá* in Bengali, and the two Sanskrit names of *bhringarája* and *kesarája* are used as synonyms. The Hindustani term *bhángrá*, derived from the Sanskrit *bhringarája* is however generally applied to *Wedelia calendulacea*, and this is the plant used in medicine at present. The leaves, which have a slight camphoraceous taste, are considered tonic, alterative,

---

1 अग्निमुखं चूर्णम्। हिङ्गुभागोभवेदेकोवचा च द्विगुणाभवेत्। पिप्पली त्रिगुणाचैव शृङ्गवेरं चतुर्गुणम्। यमानिका पञ्चगुणा षड्गुणा च हरीतकी। चित्रकं सप्तगुणितं कुष्ठञ्चाष्टगुणं भवेत्। एतद्वातहरं चूर्णं पीतमात्रं प्रसन्नया। चूर्णमग्निमुखं नाम न क्वचित्प्रतिहन्यते। चक्रदत्तः।

2 कुष्ठमेरण्डतैलेन लेपात्काञ्जिकपेषितम्। शिरोर्त्तिं वातजां हन्यात्पुष्पं वा मुचुकुन्दजम्। शार्ङ्गधरः।

3 कुष्ठसैन्धवयोः कल्कश्चुक्रतैलसमन्वितः। सुखोष्णो मर्द्दने योज्यः खल्लीशूलनिवारणः। भावप्रकाशः।

and useful in cough, cephalalgia, skin diseases and alopecia. The juice of the leaves is much used as a snuff in cephalalgia, and in soaking various sorts of powders for the preparation of pills.[1] "In tattooing the natives after puncturing the skin, rub the juicy green leaves of *Eclipta prostrata* over the part ; which gives the desired indelible colour, namely a deep bluish black." The leaves of both these plants are used in various ways for the purpose of dyeing grey hair and for promoting the growth of hair.

Játiphaládya churna.[2] Take of nutmeg, *baberang* seeds, plumbago root, flowers of *Tabernœmontana coronaria* (*tagara*), sesamum seeds, leaves of *Pinus Webbiana* (*tálisa*), red sandal wood, ginger, cloves, cumin seeds, camphor, chebulic and emblic myrobalans, black pepper, long pepper, bamboo-manna, cinnamon, cardamom, *tejapatra*, and the flowers of *Mesua ferrea* (*nágakesara*), each two tolás, powdered leaves of *Wedelia calendulacea*, fifty six tolás, sugar, in quantity equal to all the above ingredients. Powder and mix. Dose, about a drachm. This preparation is said to be useful in phthisis, cough and catarrh.

Shaḍbindu taila.[3] Take of sesamum oil, four seers, goat's, milk four seers, juice of *bhringarája* leaves, sixteen seers and prepare an oil with a paste composed of the following substances, namely, root of castor oil plant, and of *Tabernœmontana coronaria* (*tagara*), dill seeds, *Cœlogyne ovalis* (*jivanti*), *Vanda Roxburghii* (*rásná*), rock salt, *Wedelia calendulacea* (*bhringarája*), *baberang* seeds

---

1 भृङ्गराजरसः च्छागीक्षीर तुल्योऽर्कतापितः। सूर्य्यावर्त्तं निहन्त्याशु नस्येनैव प्रयोगराट्। भावप्रकाशः।

2 जातीफलाद्यं चूर्णम्। जातीफलं विड़ङ्गानि चित्रकं तगरंतिलाः। तालीसं चन्दनं शुण्ठी लवङ्गमुपकुञ्चिका। कर्पूरश्चाभया धात्री मरिचं पिप्पली तुगा। एषा स्वक्समा भागश्चातुर्जातक संयुताः। पलानि सप्त भृङ्गायाः सिता सर्व्वसमा मता। चूर्णमेतत् क्षयं कासं श्वासञ्च ग्रहणीगदम्। अरोचकं प्रतिश्यायं तथाचानल मन्दताम्। एतान् रोगान् निहन्त्येव दृष्ट मिन्द्राशनिर्य्यथा। भावप्रकाशः।

3 षड्बिन्दुतैलम्। एड़ण्डमूलं तगरं शताह्वा जीवन्ति रास्ना सहसैन्धवञ्च। भृङ्गं विडङ्गं मधुयष्टिकाच विश्वौषधं कृष्णतिलस्य तैलम्। आजंपयस्तैलविमि

liquorice root, and ginger, in all one seer. Six drops of this oil, drawn in through the nostrils, are said to relieve headache and other affections of the head.

Bhringarája taila.[1] Take of sesamum oil four seers, juice of *bhringarája* leaves, sixteen seers, iron rust, the three myrobalans and the root of *Ichnocarpus frutescens* (*syámalatá*), reduced to a paste, in all one seer, and prepare an oil in the usual way. This oil is said to remove scurf from the head, turn grey hairs black, and cure alopecia.

The fresh juice of the leaves of *Eclipta prostrata*, is rubbed on the shaven scalp for the purpose of promoting the growth of hair.

VERNONIA ANTHELMINTICA, *Willd.*

Syn. Serratula anthelmintica, Roxb.

Sans. सोमराजी, *Somaráji.* अवल्गुज, *Avalguja.* वाकुची, *Vákuchi.*
Vern. Hákuch, Somráj, Beng. Bákchi, Hind.

The seeds of *Vernonia anthelmintica* are of great repute in Sanskrit Materia Medica as a medicine for white leprosy (leucoderma), and other skin diseases. It is mentioned also as an anthelmintic, but is not much used as such, except in combination with a number of other medicines.

In chronic skin diseases the seeds are taken alone or in combination with other medicines. In the severer forms of skin diseases, such as psoriasis and lepra, the medicine is recommended to be continued daily for one year, when a complete cure is said to be effected. The following combination is used in these cases. Take of *vákuchi* seeds, and black sesamum, equal parts ; powder and mix. Dose, about a drachm to be taken in the morning, with

---

श्रितञ्च चतुर्गुणे भृङ्गरसे विपक्वम्। षड्बिन्दवो नासिकयाविधेयाः शीघ्रं निहन्तुः शिरसोविकारान्। च्युतांश्च केशांश्च पलितांश्च दन्तान् दृढमूलांश्च दृढीकरोति। सुपर्णदृष्टिप्रतिमञ्च चक्षुर्बाह्वोर्बलञ्चाभ्यधिकं ददाति। चक्रदत्तः।

1 भृङ्गराज तैलम्। भृङ्गराजरसेनैव लोहकिट्टफलत्रिकम्। सारिवाच पचेत्कल्कैस्तैलं दारुणनाशनम्। अकालपलितं कण्डूमिन्द्रलुप्तञ्च नाशयेत्।

शार्ङ्गधरः।

tepid water. The medicine should be taken after perspiration has been induced by exercise or exposure to the sun. The diet should consist of milk and rice. In leucoderma a decoction of emblic myrobalan and catechu is given with the addition of powdered *vákuchi* seeds.[1]

Externally it is used in skin diseases in a variety of forms such as paste, oil, etc. The following combination is said to be very useful in eruptions attended with itching. Take of *vákuchi* seeds, seeds of *Cassia Sophora* (*kásamarda*) and *Cassia Tora* (*chakramarda*), turmeric and common sea salt, equal parts; rub them together into a paste with whey and fermented paddy water (*kánjika*), and apply over the eruptions.[2] *Vákuchi* seeds four parts, and orpiment one part are rubbed into an emulsion with cow's urine, and applied to the patches of white leprosy or leucoderma.[3]

Somaráji taila. Take of *vákuchi* seeds, twelve seers and a half, water sixty four seers, and boil down to sixteen seers. Take of the seeds of *Cassia Tora* (*chakramarda*) twelve seers and a half, water sixty four seers and boil down to sixteen seers. Boil these two decoctions with sixteen seers of cow's urine, sixteen seers of mustard oil and the following substances in the form of a paste, namely root of *Plumbago rosea* (*raktachitráka*), of *Gloriosa superba* (*lánguli*), ginger, turmeric, *pátchak* root, seeds of *Pongamia glabra* (*karanja*), root *Clitoria ternatea* (*aparájitá*), of *Nerium odorum* (*karavira*) and of *Calotropis gigantea* (*arka*), bark of *Alstonia scholaris* (*saptaparni*), wood of *Acacia catechu* (*khadira*), of *symplocos*

---

1 अवल्गुजाद्बीजकर्षं पीत्वाकोष्णेन वारिणा। भोजनं सर्पिषा कार्य्यं सर्व्वकुष्ठप्रणाशनम्। तीव्रेण कुष्ठेन परीतदेहो यः सोमराजीं नियमेन खादेत्। संवत्सरं कृष्णतिलद्वितीयां स सोमराजीं वपुषातिशेते। घर्मसेवी कदुष्णेन वारिणा वागुजी पिवेत्। चक्रदत्तः।

2 अवल्गुजं कासमर्द्दं चक्रमर्द्दं निशायुतम्। माणिमन्थेन तुल्यांशं मस्तुकाञ्जिकपेषितम्। कच्छुं कण्डूं जयत्युग्रां सिद्ध एष प्रयोगराट्। चक्रदत्तः।

3 कुडवोऽवल्गुजबीजाद्धरितालचतुर्थभागसंमिश्रः। मूत्रेण गवां पिष्टः सवर्णकरणः परः श्वित्रे। चक्रदत्तः।

Racemasa (*ladhra*), black pepper, *nim* leaves, leaves of *Cassia Sophora* (*kásamarda*), juice of cow-dung, orpiment and realgar, each eight tolás. This oil is said to cure all sorts of skin diseases from vitiated blood, ringworm, prurigo, etc.[1]

ANACYCLUS PYRETHRUM, *DC.* Pellitory root was unknown to the ancient Hindus. In later compilations as Sárangadhara and the Bhávaprakása it is occasionally mentioned under the name of *Akarákarava*, and is used as an ingredient of compound prescriptions, as for example in the *Akarádi churna* described under opium.

ENHYDRA HELONCHA, *DC.* *Syn. Hingtsha repens, Roxb. Sans.* हिलमोचिका, *Hilamochiká. Vern. Hingchá, Beng. Harhuch, Hind.* The leaves of this water plant are eaten by the natives as a vegetable. Being somewhat bitter they are regarded as wholesome and invigorating. Medicinally they are described as laxative and useful in diseases of the skin and nervous system. The fresh juice of the leaves, in doses of about a tolá is, prescribed by some Kavirajas in Calcutta, as an adjunct to tonic metallic medicines given in neuralgia and other nervous diseases.

NAT. ORDER PLUMBAGINACEÆ.

PLUMBAGO ZEYLANICA, *Linn.*

Sans. चित्रक, *Chitraka. Vern. Chitá, Beng. Hind.*

THE root of *Plumbago Zeylanica* is said to increase the digestive power, to promote the appetite and to be useful in dyspepsia, piles, anasarca, diarrhœa, skin diseases, etc. It is much used as a stimulant adjunct to other preparations, in the form of a com-

1 बृहत्सोमराजी तैलम् । सोमराजी तुलाक्वाथे दद्रुघ्नस्य तथैव च । विपचेत्पलिकैर्भागैः कटुतैलाढकं भिषक् । चित्रकं लाङ्गली लोध्रं नागरं कुष्ठमेव च । हरिद्रा नक्तमालञ्च हरितालं मनःशिला । आस्फोता करवीरञ्च सप्तपर्णार्क गोमयं । खदिरं निम्बपत्रञ्च मरिचं कासमर्दकम् । गोमूत्रस्याढकं दत्वा शनैर्मृद्वग्निनापचेत् । हन्ति सर्व्वाणि कुष्ठानि कण्डु दुष्टव्रणानपि । किटिभं दद्रुजातञ्च गात्र वैवर्ण्य नाशनं । राढीयसारसंग्रहः ।

bination called *trimada* consisting of plumbago root, *báberang* seeds and the tubers of *Cyperus rotundus* (*mustaka*).

It enters into the composition of numerous medicines for dyspepsia. The following is an illustration. Take of plumbago root, rock salt, chebulic myrobalan, and long pepper, equal parts; powder and mix. Dose, about forty grains.[1] A favourite medicine for flatulence is an old prescription of Susruta called *Shaḍdharana yoga*. It is a powder composed of equal parts of the following substances, namely, plumbago root, *indrayava seeds*, root of *Stephania hernandifolia* (*páṭhá*), of *Picrorrhiza Kurroa* (*kaṭuki*), *átis*, and chebulic myrobalan. Dose, about a drachm.[2]

The root of *Plumbago Zeylanica* is said to exercise a beneficial effect on piles, in which disease it is given in various combinations. One mode of administering it, is as follows. An earthen jar or pot is lined in its interior with a paste of the root, and curdled milk (*dadhi*) or *kánjika* is prepared in this pot, and taken by persons affected with hæmorrhoids, and prurigo.

Plumbago root reduced to a paste is applied to abscesses with the object of opening them. It enters also into the composition of several preparations used as caustics. The following is an illustration. Take of plumbago root, root of *Baliospermum montanum* (*danti*), the milky juice of *Euphorbia neriifolia* (*snuhi*), and of *Calotropis procera* or *Hamiltonii* (*arka*), marking nut, sulphate of iron, treacle and rock salt, equal parts; mix them together and make into a paste.[3]

PLUMBAGO ROSEA, *Linn. Sans.* रक्तचित्रक, *Raktachitraka. Vern. Lálchitá, Beng.* The properties of the root of *Plumbago rosea* are said to be like those of *P. Zeylanica*. It has besides a specific

---

1 सिन्धूत्थपथ्यामगधोद्भववह्निचूर्णमुष्णाम्बुनापिबति यः खलुनष्टवह्निः । तस्या मिषेण सघृतेन वरं नवान्नं भस्मीभवत्यशितमात्रमिहक्षणेन । चक्रदत्तः ।

2 चित्रकेन्द्रयवाः पाठा कटुकातिविषाभयाः । महाव्याधिप्रशमनो योगः षड्धरणः स्मृतः ॥ चक्रदत्तः ।

3 दन्ती चित्रकमूलत्वक् सुधार्कपयसीगुड़ः । भल्लातकशकाशीशं सैन्धवं दारणे स्मृतः । शार्ङ्गधरः ।

action on the uterus.* The root of *Plumbago rosea* taken internally will expel the fœtus from the womb, whether dead or alive.[1] This root is a more powerful vesicant than that of *P. Zelanica*, and enters into the composition of caustic pastes, and stimulant and rubefacient applications.

NAT. ORDER MYRSINACEÆ.

EMBELIA RIBES, *Burm.*

Sans. विडङ्ग, *Vidanga. Vern. Báberang, Hind.*

SUSRUTA describes the seeds of *Embelia Ribes* as anthelmintic, alterative and tonic and recommends their use along with liquorice root for the purpose of strengthening the body and preventing the effects of age. Later writers regard *báberang* as carminative stomachic, anthelmintic and useful in intestinal worms, dyspepsia, and skin diseases.

For expelling intestinal worms, the powder of the seeds is given in drachm doses with honey, or with an infusion of the seeds. A compound powder and a *ghrita* are also prepared by the addition of various other drugs.[2]

---

* It is generally known that the scraped root of *Plumbago rosea* is introduced into the mouth of the womb, for the purpose of procuring abortion. The root is sometimes put to another use, a knowledge of which is likely to be of importance in a medico-legal point of view. Many years ago I had under my treatment a married female, who had accidental abortion and copious hæmorrhage after it. On the third day after the accident, she was brought to hospital, suffering from severe pain in the pelvic region, purulent discharge and high fever. On examination I found a piece of the *lálchitrá* root, with a little rag wrapped round it, projecting into the vagina from the cervix uteri. I was told that a midwife had introduced it into the womb with the object of checking hæmorrhage after the abortion. If this woman had been a widow and had died from the effects of the abortion, and if on examination of the dead body, the root of the *lálchitrá* had been found in the position mentioned above, the inevitable conclusion would have been, that it was introduced for the purpose of procuring abortion.

1 गरोमदनदहनमूलं चिरजमपि गर्भं मृतममृतं वा निपातयति ॥

चक्रदत्तः ।

2 विडङ्गं घृतपाचीयं विडङ्गेनावचूर्णितम् । पीतं कृमिहरं कृष्णं कृमिजांश्च गदाञ्जयेत् । लिह्याद्विडङ्गचूर्णं वा मधुना कृमिनाशनम् ॥

भावप्रकाशः ।

Báberang enters into the composition of several applications for ringworm and other skin diseases. The following is an example. Take of *báberang*, rock salt, chebulic myrobalan, *bakuchi*, mustard, turmeric and the seeds of *Pongamia glabra* (*karanja*), equal parts and make them into a thin paste with cow's urine.[1]

NAT. ORDER SAPOTACEÆ.

BASSIA LATIFOLIA, *Roxb.*

Sans. मधूक *Madhuka.* *Vern.* *Mauá*, *Beng.* *Hind.*

THE flowers of *Bassia latifolia* yield a distilled spirit which is described by Susruta as heating, astringent, tonic and appetizing. The flowers are regarded as cooling, tonic and nutritive. They enter into the composion of several mixtures of a cooling and demulcent character. The following is an example. Take of the flowers of *Bassia latifolia*, bark of *Gmelina arborea (gambhári)*, red sandal wood, root of *Andropogon muricatum* (*ushira*), coriander and raisins, equal parts, and prepare an infusion in the usual way. This infusion is given with the addition of sugar for the relief of thirst, burning of the body and giddiness.[2]

The seeds of *Bassia latifolia* yield by expression a thick concrete oil which is used in lamps, and by the poorer classes, for culinary purposes. This oil called *madhuka sára* in Sanskrit, is recommended to be applied to the head in cephalalgia.[3]

MIMUSOPS ELENGI, *Linn.*

Sans. बकुल, *Vakula.* *Vern.* *Maulsarau*, *Hind.*

THIS ornamental tree is generally reared in gardens for the sake of its fragrant flowers from which a distilled water is prepared. The ripe fruits are sweetish and edible. The unripe

---

1 विडङ्ग सैन्धव शिवा शशिरेखा सर्षप करञ्जरजनीभिः।गोजलपिष्टोलेपः कुष्ठहरोदिवसनाथसमः । चक्रदत्तः ।

2 मधूकपुष्पगम्भारी चन्दनोशीरधान्यकैः। द्राक्षायाश्च कृतः फाण्टः शीतः-शर्करयायुतः ॥ तृष्णापित्तहरः प्रोक्तोदाहमूर्च्छाभ्रमाञ्जयेत् । शार्ङ्गधरः ।

3 मधूकसारेणशिरः स्निग्धञ्चास्य विरेचयेत् ॥ चक्रदत्तः ।

fruits are astringent and are recommended to be chewed for the purpose of fixing loose teeth.[1] The bark is described as astringent. A decoction of the bark is used as a gargle in diseases of the gums and teeth.[2]

NAT. ORDER STYRACEÆ.

SYMPLOCOS RACEMOSA, *Roxb.*

Sans. लोध्र, *Lodhra.* तिल्लक, *Tillaka. Vern. Lodh, Beng. Hind.*

THE bark of this tree, used in dyeing red, is considered cooling, astringent and useful in bowel complaints, eye diseases, ulcers, etc. It enters into the composition of numerous prescriptions for bowel complaints, along with *bela*, and *kurchi* bark. A decoction of the wood is used as a gargle for giving firmness to spongy and bleeding gums.[3] In bleeding from the gums, a paste composed of *lodhra* bark, *rasot*, tubers of *Cyperus rotundus* (*mustaka*) and honey, is applied to the gums.[4] The Amritaságara recommends the following application for ophthalmia. Take of *lodhra* bark liquorice root, burnt alum and *rasot*, equal parts, and rub into a paste with water. This is applied round the eyes.

NAT. ORDER JASMINACEÆ.

NYCTANTHES ARBOR TRISTIS, *Linn.*

Sans. शेफालिका, *Sepháliká.* रजनीहासा, *Rajanihásá.*

Vern. Siuli, Beng. Harsingár, Hind.

THIS plant is cultivated in gardens for the sake of its flowers. These open at sunset, and before morning strew the ground thick-

---

1 चलदन्त स्थिरकरं कार्य्यं बकुलचर्व्वणम् । चक्रदत्तः ।

2 दन्तचालेतु गण्डूषोबकुलत्वक् कृतोहितः । चक्रदत्तः ।

3 भिन्नोदककषायेण तथैवामलकस्य वा । प्रक्षालयेत् मुखं नेत्रे स्वस्थपीतोदकेन वा । निलीकां मुखशोषञ्च पीड़कां व्यङ्गमेवच । रक्तपित्तकृतान् रोगान् सद्यएव विनाशयेत् ।। सुश्रुतः ।

4 शैशिरे हृतरक्ते च लोध्रमुस्तरसाञ्जनैः । सक्षौद्रैः शस्यते लेपोगण्डूषे क्षीरिणोहिताः ।। चक्रदत्तः ।

ly with their fallen corollas. Native women and children collect them and, separating the orange coloured tubes from the white petals, dry them in the sun and preserve them for dyeing their clothes a beautiful buff or orange colour.

The leaves are used in medicine. They are regarded as useful in fever and rheumatism. The fresh juice of the leaves is given with honey in chronic fever.[1] Some preparation of iron is also generally given along with it. A decoction of the leaves prepared over a gentle fire is recommended by several writers as a specific for obstinate sciatica.[2]

JASMINUM GRANDIFLORUM, *Linn.*

Sans. जाती, *Játi. Vern. Chámeli, Hind.*

The fragrant flowers of *Jasminum grandiflorum* are used for preparing a scented oil, which is considered cooling, and is much used by the richer natives for anointing their bodies before bathing. The leaves of this plant are used medicinally in skin diseases, ulcers in the mouth, otorrhœa, etc. and enter into the composition of numerous prescriptions for these diseases.

The fresh juice of the leaves is applied to soft corns between the toes.[3] In ulcerations or eruptions in the mucous membrane of the mouth, the leaves are recommended to be chewed.[4] An oil prepared with the juice of the leaves is poured into the ear in otorrhœa.[5]

JASMINUM SAMBAC, *Willd. Sans.* वार्षिकी, *Várshiki. Vern. Bel, Beng. Hind.* The properties of this plant are said to resemble those of *Jasminum grandiflorum.*

---

1 मधुना सर्वज्वरनुच्छेफालीदलजोरसः । चक्रदत्तः ।

2 शेफालिकादलैः क्वाथो मृद्वग्निपरिसाधितः। दुर्व्वारं गृध्रसीरोगं पीतमात्रं समुद्धरेत् । चक्रदत्तः ।

3 जातीपत्रञ्च संमर्द्य दद्यादलसके भिषक् ॥ चक्रदत्तः ।

4 मुखपाके शिरावेधः शिरः कायविरेचनम् । कार्य्यञ्च बहुधानित्यं जातीपत्रस्य चर्व्वणम् ॥ भावप्रकाशः ।

5 जातिपत्ररसे तैलं विपक्वं पूतिकर्णजित् ॥ चक्रदत्तः ।

NAT. ORDER APOCYNEÆ.

NERIUM ODORUM, *Solander.*

Sans. करवीर, *Karavira.* अश्वमारक, *Asvamáraka.*

Vern. Karabi, Beng. Kaner, Hind.

Two varieties of *Karavira* are described in the Bhávaprakása, namely, white and red flowered. The properties of both are identical, their roots being regarded as poisonous when taken internally and useful in skin diseases and inflammatory affections. The *Nerium odorum* has several synonyms in Sanskrit signifying horse-killer. It would seem from this, that the poisonous roots were used for destroying horses.

Karavirádya taila.[1] Take of sesamum oil four seers, decoction of the root of *Nerium odorum*, eight seers, cow's urine, eight seers, *Plumbago rosea* root and *báberang* seeds, each half a seer, in the form of a paste ; boil them together and prepare an oil in the usual way. This oil is used in eczema, impetigo and other skin diseases.

The root of *Nerium odorum* beaten into a paste with water is recommended to be applied to chancres and ulcers on the penis.[2] The fresh juice of the young leaves is poured into the eyes in ophthalmia with copious lachrymation.[3]

ALSTONIA SCHOLARIS, *R.Br.*

Sans. सप्तपर्ण, *Saptaparna.* विशालत्वक्, *Visálatvak.*

Vern. Chhátin, Beng. Chhátián, Hind.

The bark of *Alstonia scholaris* is very thick and spongy, hence the tree has recieved the names of *Visálatvak*, *Vrihattvak*,

---

1 करविराद्यं तैलम् । श्वेतकरवीररसो गोमूत्रं चित्रकं विडङ्गञ्च । कुष्ठेषु तैलयोगः सिद्धोऽयं सम्मतो भिषजाम् । चक्रदत्तः ।

2 करवीरस्य मूलेन परिपिष्टेन वारिणा । असाध्यापि व्रजत्यस्तं लिङ्गोत्था-रुक्प्रलेपनात् । शार्ङ्गधरः ।

3 करवीरतरुणकिशलयच्छेदोद्भव बहुलसलिलसंपूर्णम् । नयनयुगं भवति दृढं सहसैव तत्क्षणात् कुपितम् । चक्रदत्तः ।

etc. It is described as tonic, alterative and useful in fever and skin diseases. Susruta gives the following formula for use in catarrhal fever. Take of the bark of *Alstonia scholaris*, *gulancha*, *nim* bark and the bark of *Betula Bhojpattra*, equal parts, in all two tolás and prepare a decoction in the usual way.[1] It enters into the composition of several formulæ for skin diseases. The following is an illustration.

Amritáshṭaka páchana. Take of the bark of *Alstonia scholaris*, *gulancha*, leaves of *Justicia Adhatoda* (*vásaka*) and *Trichosanthes dioica* (*paṭola*), tubers of *Cyperus rotundus* (*mustaka*), *Calamus Rotang* (*vetra*), catechu and *nim* leaves, and prepare a decoction in the usual way.

HOLARRHENA ANTIDYSENTERICA, *R. Br.*

Sans. कुटज, *Kuṭaja*, कालिङ्ग, *Kálinga.*

Vern. Kurchi, *Beng. Kureyá*, *Kaureyá*, *Hind.*

The bark of *Holarrhena antidysenterica* constitutes the principal medicine for dysentery in the Hindu Pharmacopæia. Before the discovery of the efficacy of ipecacuana in this disease, many chronic cases which did not get well under European medical treatment, used to be cured by the Kavirajes, by their preparations of this bark. The seeds called *Indrayava* in Sanskrit and *Indrajav* in the vernacular, are also used in medicine, they being regarded as astringent, febrifuge and useful in fever, dysentery, diarrhœa, and intestinal worms.

The bark of *Holarrhena antidysenterica* is administered in a variety of ways. The expressed juice of the bark is given with honey.[2] A fluid extract of the bark is given with the addition of ginger and *átis*.[3] A compound decoction called *Kuṭajáshṭaka* is

---

1 सप्तच्छदं गुडूचीञ्च निम्बस्फूर्ज्जकमेव च। क्वाथयित्वा पिबेत्क्वाथं सक्षौद्रं कफजे ज्वरे। सुश्रुतः।

2 स्थूलवल्कलिकापत्ररसः पानाद्व्यपोहति। सर्वातिसारान्सक्षौद्रोनाककुट-जत्वपसोयथा। शार्ङ्गधरः।

3 कुटजत्वक्कृतः क्वाथो घनीभूतः सुशीतलः। लीढ़ितोऽतिविषायुक्तः सर्व्वातीसारनुद्भवेत्। चक्रदत्तः

thus prepared. Take of *kuṭaja* bark, *átis*, root of *Stephania hernandifolia (páṭhá)*, flowers of *Woodfordia floribunda (dhátaki)*, bark of *Symplocos racemosa (lodhra)*, root of *Pavonia odorata (bálá)*, rind of pomegranate fruit, and the tubers of *Cyperus rotundus (mustaka)*, quarter tolá each, water thirty two tolas; boil together till reduced to one-fourth.[1]

Kuṭajaleha[2] or confection of *kuṭaja* bark. Take of *kuṭaja* bark twelve seers and a half, water sixty-four seers; boil down to sixteen seers and strain. Boil the strained decoction till reduced to a thick consistence, then add *sonchal* salt, *yavakshára*, *vit* salt, rock salt, long pepper, flowers of *Woodfordia floribunda (dhátaki)*, *indrayava* seeds and cumin seeds, each sixteen tolas, in fine powder, and prepare a confection. Dose, about a drachm with honey in chronic and acute dysentery.

Paṭhádya churna.[3] Take of the root of *Stephania hernandifolia*, fruit of *Ægle Marmelos (vilva)*, plumbago root, long pepper, black pepper, ginger, bark of *Eugenia Jambolana*, rind of pomegranate fruit, flowers of *Woodfordia floribunda (dhátaki)*, root of *Picrorrhiza Kurroa (kaṭuki)*, *átis*, tubers of *Cyperus rotundus (mustaka)*, wood of *Berberis Asiatica (dárvi)*, *chiretá*, seeds of *Holarrhena antidysenterica (indrayava)*, one part each, *kuṭaja* bark, equal in weight

---

1 कुटजातिविषा पाठा धातकी लोध्र मुस्तकैः । ह्रीबेर दाडिमयुतैः श्रुतः क्वाथः समाक्षिकः । पेयो मोचरसेनैव कुटजाष्टकसंज्ञकः । अतीसारान् जयेद्दाह रक्तशूलामदुस्तरान् । शार्ङ्गधरः ।

कुटजलेहः । शतं कुटजमूलस्य क्षुस्रं तोयार्मणे पचेत् । क्वाथे पादावशेषेऽस्मिन् लेहं पूते पुनः पचेत् । सौवर्च्चल यवक्षार विड्सैन्धव पिप्पली । धातकीन्द्रयवाजाजी चूर्णं दत्त्वापलद्वयम् । लिह्याद्बदरमात्रं तत् शीतं क्षौद्रेणसंयुतम् । पक्वापक्वमतीसारं नानावर्णं सवेदनम् । दुर्व्वारं ग्रहणीरोगं जयेच्चैव प्रवाहिकाम् । चक्रदत्तः ।

3 पाठाद्यं चूर्णम्। पाठा विल्वानल व्योष जम्बू दाडिमधातकी। कटुकातिविषामुस्त दार्व्वी भूनिम्बवत्सकैः । सर्व्वैरेतैः समं चूर्णं कौटजं तण्डुलाम्बुना । सक्षौद्रञ्च पिबेच्छर्द्दिज्वरातिसारशूलवान् । हृद्दाहग्रहणीदोषारोचकानलसादजित् । चक्रदत्तः ।

to all the above ingredients ; powder them finely and mix. Dose, about one to two scruples to be taken with rice-water and honey. Another compound powder called *Gangádhara churna*, is of similar composition to the above, with a few additional substances.

Kuṭajárishṭa,[1] or fermented liquor of *kuṭaja*. Take of *kuṭaja* root-bark, twelve seers and a half, raisins, six seers and a quarter, flowers of *Bassia latifolia* (*madhuka*), and bark of *Gmelina arborea* (*gambhári*), eighty tolás each ; boil them together in two hundred and fifty-six seers of water, till reduced to sixty-four seers, and strain. Then add flowers of *Woodfordia floribunda* (*dhátaki*), two seers and a half, treacle twelve seers and a half, and let the mixture ferment for a month, after which it will be ready for use. Dose, one to three ounces.

An oil for external application called *Grahanimihira taila* is prepared with sesasum oil, decoction of *kuṭaja* bark and a number of astringent and aromatic substances in small quantities.

Pradarári lauha.[2] Take of *kuṭaja* bark, twelve seers and a half and prepare a fluid extract as in the preparation called *kuṭajaleha*, above described. Then add the following substances in fine powder, namely, gum of *Bombax Malabaricum* (*mocharasa*), Indian madder, root of *Stephania hernandifolia*, (*páṭhá*), *bela* fruit, tubers of *Cyperus rotundus* (*mustaka*), flowers of *Woodfordia floribunda* (*dhátaki*), *átis*, prepared talc and iron, each eight tolás, mix them

---

1 कुटजारिष्टः। तुलांकुटजमूलस्य मृद्वीकार्द्धतुलान्तथा। मधूकपुष्पकाश्मर्य्योर्भागान्दशपलोन्मितान्। चतुर्द्रोणेऽम्भसः पक्त्वा क्वाथयेद्द्रोणशेषिते। धातक्या विंशतिपलं गुडस्य च तुलां क्षिपेत्। मासमात्रं स्थितोभाण्डे कुटजारिष्टसंज्ञकः। ज्वरान्प्रशमयेत्सर्व्वान् कुर्य्यात्तीक्ष्णं धनञ्जयम्। शार्ङ्गधरः।

2 प्रदरारिलौहं। कुटजकस्य तुलां सम्यक् जलद्रोणे विपाचयेत्। अष्टभागावशिष्टन्तु कषायमवतारयेत्। वस्त्रपूते घनीभूते द्रव्याणीमानि दापयेत्। समङ्गाशाल्मलं पाठा विल्वं मुस्तञ्च धातकी। अतिविषा तथा व्योमकं लौहं प्रत्येकन्तु पलंपलं। कोलमात्रां प्रयुञ्जित कुशमूलं पयोऽनु। श्वेतं रक्तं तथानीलं पीतंप्रदरदुस्तरं। कुक्षिशूलं कटीशूलं देहशूलञ्च सर्व्वगं। प्रदरारिरयं लौहो हन्तिरोगान् सुदुस्तरान्। आयुःपुष्टिकरश्चैव बलवर्णाग्निवर्द्धनः। भैषज्यरत्नावली।

intimately and prepare a confection. Dose, about a drachm. This preparation is given in menorrhagia and other discharges from the uterus.

The seeds of *Holarrhena antidysenterica* enter into the composition of a good many prescriptions for fever, bowel complaints, piles, intestinal worms, etc. The following are a few illustrations Take of *indrayava* seeds and the tubers of *Cyperus rotundus* (*mustaka*), each four tolas, rub them into a paste with water and boil in one seer of water, till the latter is reduced to one-fourth. This boiled emulsion is given in doses of about a half to one ounce with honey.[1]

Laghu gangádhara churna.[2] Take of *indrayava* seeds, tubers of *Cyperus rotundus*, (*mustaka*), *bela* fruit, bark of *Symplocos racemosa* (*lodhra*), gum of *Bombax Malabaricum* (*mocharasa*), and flowers of *Woodfordia floribunda* (*dhátaki*) equal parts; powder and mix. Dose, about a drachm with butter-milk and treacle, in various sorts of bowel complaints.

ICHNOCARPUS FRUTESCENS. *Sans.* शारिवा, *Sárivá.* *Vern. Shyámalatá.* The properties of the roots of this plant are said to be identical with those of *Hemidesmus Indicus.* These two drugs are often used in combination under the designation of *Sárivádvaya*, (see next article).

NAT. ORDER ASCLEPIADEÆ.

HEMIDESMUS INDICUS, *R. Br.*

Sans. अनन्तमूल, *Anantamula,* शारिवा, *Sárivá.*
Vern. Anantamul, Beng. Hind.

In Sanskrit Medicine, *Hemidesmus Indicus* and *Ichnocarpus frutescens* are both called *sárivá* and are described under the name

---

1 मुस्तकेन्द्रयवैःसिद्धा प्रमथ्या द्विपलोन्मिता। सुशीता मधुसंयुक्ता रक्तातीसार-नाशिनी। शार्ङ्गधरः।

2 लघुगङ्गाधरचूर्णम्। मुस्तमिन्द्रयवं बिल्वं लोध्रं मोचरसन्तथा। धातकीं चूर्णयेत्तक्र गुडाभ्यां पाययेत् सुधीः। सर्वातीसारशमनं निरुणद्धि प्रवाहिकाम्। लघुगङ्गाधरं नामचूर्णं संग्राहकं परम्। शार्ङ्गधरः।

of *sárivádvaya* or the two *sárivás*. They are often used together. When however *sárivá* is used in the singular number it is the usual practice to interpret it as *syámalatá* (*Ichnocarpus frutescens*). The roots of these plants are said to be sweet, demulcent, alterative and useful in loss of appetite, disinclination for food, fever, skin diseases, syphilis and leucorrhœa. They are generally used in combination with a number of other medicines. The following are a few illustrations. Take of *anantamula*, root of *Pavonia odorata* (*bálá*), tubers of *Cyperus rotundus* (*mustaka*), ginger, and the root of *Picrorrhiza kurroa* (*kaṭuki*), equal parts, in all two tolás, and reduce them to a paste with water. This dose administered with warm water in the morning, is said to clear the bowels and relieve fever.[1]

A decoction of the roots of colocynth, *anantamula*, *sárivá* and *Hedyotis biflora* (*parparṭa*), prepared in the usual way, is administered with the addition of powdered long pepper and bdellium in chronic skin diseases, syphilis, elephantiasis, loss of sensation and hemiplegia.[2]

CALOTROPIS GIGANTEA AND PROCERA, *R. Br.*

Syn. Asclepias gigantea, Roxb.

Sans. अर्क, *Arka,* अलर्क, *Alarka.*

Vern. A'kanda, Beng. Mádár, Hind.

Calotropis procera and *C. gigantea*, both pass by the native native name of *mádár*. " *C. procera* the smaller of the two, prefers the drier climate of the Deccan, the Upper Provinces of Bengal, the Punjab and Scinde ; *C. gigantea*, lower Bengal, the

---

1 अनन्ता बालकं मुस्तं नागरं कटुरोहिणी । पिष्टा सुखाम्बुना कल्कं पाययेद्च सम्मितं । कल्कः स्वल्पेनकालेन हन्यात् सर्व्वज्वरामयं । विदध्यात् कोष्ठसंशुद्धिं दीपयेच्च हुताशनं । भैषज्यरत्नावली ।

2 इन्द्रवारुणिकानन्ता शारिवा पर्पटैः समैः । एभिः कृतं पिवेत् क्वाथं कणागुग्गुलूसंयुतम् । अष्टादशेष्वकुष्ठेषु वातरक्तार्दिते तथा । उपदंशेश्लीपदेच प्रसुप्ते पक्षघातके । शार्ङ्गधरः ।

Madras and Malayan Peninsulas, and Ceylon." Sanskrit writers mention two varieties founded upon the colour of the flowers, namely, white, called *alarka*, and red, called *arka*. The milky juice, flowers, root-bark and leaves are all used in medicine. The root-bark is said to promote the secretions and to be useful in skin diseases, enlargements of the abdominal viscera, intestinal worms, cough, ascites, anasarca, etc. The milky juice is regarded as a drastic purgative and caustic and is generally used as such in combination with the milky juice of *Euphorbia neriifolia*. The flowers are considered digestive, stomachic, tonic and useful in cough, asthma, catarrh and loss of appetite.

The leaves mixed with rock salt are roasted within closed vessels, so that the fumes may not escape. The ashes thus produced are given with whey in ascites and enlargements of the abdominal viscera.[1]

The following inhalation is prescribed for cough. Soak the powdered root-bark of *árka* in its own milky juice and dry. Bougies are prepared with this powder and their fumes inhaled.[2] The root-bark, reduced to a paste with sour congee, is applied to elephantiasis of the legs and scrotum.[3] The milky juices of *Calotropis gigantea* and *Euphorbia neriifolia* are made into tents with the powdered wood of *Berberis Asiatica*, for introduction into sinuses and fistula in ano.[4] The milky juice is applied to carious teeth for relief of pain.[5]

---

1 अर्कपत्रं सलवणमन्तर्धूमं दहेत्ततः। मस्तुनातत्पिबेत्क्षारं गुल्मप्लीहोदरापहम्। चक्रदत्तः।

2 मरिच श्वेतार्कक्षीरैर्वार्कीं त्वचमाशुभावितांशुष्काम्। कृत्वाविधिनाधूमं पिबतः कासाः शमं यान्ति। चक्रदत्तः।

3 निष्पिष्टमारनालेन लपिकामूलवल्कलम्। प्रलेपाच्छ्लीपदं हन्ति बद्धमूलमपिदृढम्। चक्रदत्तः।

4 स्नुह्यर्कदुग्ध दार्व्वीभिर्व्वर्त्तिं कृत्वा विचक्षणः। भगन्दरगतिं ज्ञात्वा पूरयेत्तां प्रयत्नतः। चक्रदत्तः।

5 सप्तच्छदार्कदुग्धाभ्यां पूरणं क्रिमिदन्तजित्। चक्रदत्तः।

Arka taila.[1] Take of prepared sesamum oil, four seers, juice of *arka* leaves, sixteen seers, and turmeric reduced to a paste, one seer; boil them together in the usual way. This oil is said to be useful in eczema, and other eruptive skin diseases. Sometimes orpiment is substituted for turmeric is this preparation.

NAT. ORDER LOGANIACEÆ.

STRYCHNOS NUX VOMICA, *Linn.*

Sans. कुपीलु, *Kupilu*, कुलक, *Kulaka*, विषमुष्टी, *Vishamushṭi.*

Vern. Kuchilá, Beng. Hind.

Nux vomica has been introduced into Hindu Medicine at a recent period. There is no generally recognized Sanskrit name for it. In some recent Sanskrit compilations it is mentioned under its vernacular name *kuchilá*, a term which is not to be found in standard Sanskrit dictionaries. Sárangadhara and other writers give some prescriptions containg a drug named *vishamushṭi*, which is generally interpretted to mean in these places, nux vomica seeds; but *vishamushṭi* according to the Bhávaprakása has an edible fruit and is called *Kareruá* in Hindi. In this work the Sanskrit term *kupilu* with its synonyms, *kulaka*, *vishatinduka*, *markaṭatinduka*, etc., is said to be the Sanskrit synonyms for *kuchilá*- and this translation is followed in some Hindi medical books, as for example in the treatise on the properties of drugs, compiled by Pundit Keshava Prasáda. Dvivedi of the Agra College. This interpretation however is not accepted in Bengal, for neither Wilson nor Sir Rájá Rádhákunta Deva has given *kuchilá* as the Vernacular for *kupilu*, nor does this term or any of its synonyms above mentioned, occur in any Sanskrit medical prescription. In our account of this drug we will according to the practice of ous kavirájas in Bengal interpret *vishamushṭi* as *kuchilá*.

The *Strychnos nux vomica* is indigenous to most parts of India. I found it to be common in the jungles about Manbhom. The

---

1 अर्कतैलम् । अर्कपत्ररसेपक्वं कटुतैलं निशायुतम्। मनःशिलायुतं वापि पामाकच्छ्वादिनाशनम् । चक्रदत्तः ।

ripe fruits of the size of apples, have a beautiful orange colour and contain a bitter gelatinous pulp, within which the flat and curiously umbilicated seeds are found imbedded.

Nux vomica seeds produce a sort of intoxication, for which they are habitually taken by some natives as an aphrodisiac. Those who do so gradually become so far accustomed to this poison that they often come to take one seed daily, which is cut into small pieces and chewed with a packet of betel leaf. Medicinally the seeds are used in dyspepsia and diseases of the nervous system.

Samiragaja kesari. Take of nux vomica, opium and black pepper equal parts, and make into two-grain pills. These are given with the juice of betel leaves in diseases of the nervous system.

Sulharanayoga.[1] Take of chebulic myrobalan, long pepper, black pepper, ginger, nux vomica, assafœtida, sulphur and rock salt, equal parts and make into four-grain pills. These are given with warm water in dyspepsia with pain after meals, and in diarrhœa. Sárangadhara gives the following prescription in which the term *vishamushṭi* is usually understood to mean nux vomica. Take of mercury, sulphur, aconite, ajowan, the three myrobalans, *sarjiká* (impure carbonate of soda), *yavakshára* (impure carbonate of potash), rock salt, plumbago root, cumin seeds, *sonchal* salt, sea-salt, *báberang*, black pepper, long pepper and ginger, equal parts, *vishamushṭi* (nux vomica seeds) equal in weight to all the above ingredients and make into pills of the size of black pepper corns with lemon juice. These pills are given to promote the appetite and increase the digestive power.[2]

---

1 शूलहरणयोगः। हरीतकी त्रिकटुकं कुचिलाहिङ्गु गन्धकं। सैन्धवञ्चसमं सर्व्वंवटीं कुर्य्यात् सुखावहाः। लघुकोलप्रमाणास्ता भक्षयेत्प्रातरेव च। एकैकावटिकाग्राह्या गुल्मशूलनिवारिणी। पक्तिशूलमतिसारे च साजीर्णमन्दपावके। योजयेदुष्णपयसा सुखमाप्नोति तत्क्षणात्। रसेन्द्रसारसंग्रहः।

2 शुद्धसूतं विषं गन्धमजमोदा फलत्रयम्। स्वर्जिक्षारं यवक्षारं वह्निसैन्धव-जीरकम्। सौवर्चलं बिडङ्गानि सामुद्रं त्र्यूषणंसमम्। विषमुष्टिः सर्वतुल्यं जम्बीराम्लेन मर्द्दयेत्। मरिचाभांवटींखादेद्वह्नि मान्द्यप्रशान्तये। शार्ङ्गधर।

STRYCHNOS POTATORUM, *Linn. fil.*

Sans. कतक, *Kataka,* अम्बुप्रसाद, *Ambuprasáda. Vern. Nirmali, B.*

The use of these seeds for the purpose of clearing muddy water is as old as Susruta, who mentions it in his chapter on water. Medicinally it is chiefly used as a local application in eye-diseases. The seeds are rubbed with honey and a little camphor, and the mixture applied to the eyes in lachrymation or copious watery discharge from them. Rubbed with water and rock salt they are applied to chemosis in the conjunctiva. They enter also into the composition of several complex preparations for ulcer of the cornea, etc.[1]

NAT. ORDER GENTIANACEÆ.

OPHELIA CHIRATA, *Grisebach.*

Syn. Gentiana Chirayita, Roxb.

Sans. किराततिक्त, *Kirátatikta,* भूनिम्ब, *Bhunimba.*
Vern. Chiretá, Beng. Hind.

The *Ophelia Chirata* is indigenous to the "mountainous regions of Northern India from Simla through Kumaon to the Morung district in South-Eastern Nepal." Its Sanskrit name *kirátatikta,* means "the bitter plant of the Kirátas, an outcast race of mountaineers in the north of India." It is also called *Anáryatikta* or the bitter plant of the Non-Aryans. The Bhavaprakása mentions a variety of *chiretá,* under the name of *Naipála,* that is, produced in Nepál, and describes it as a febrifuge.

Chiretá is regarded as tonic, febrifuge and laxative, and is used in fever, burning of the body, intestinal worms, skin diseases, etc. It is much used in fevers of all sorts in a variety of forms and in combination with other medicines of its class. The following are a few illustrations. Take of *chiretá, gulancha,* raisins, emblic myrobalan and zedoary root, equal parts and prepare a decoction

---

1 घृष्टः क्षौद्रेण संयुक्तः कतकः सैन्धवेन वा । सितयार्णवफेनो वा पृथगञ्जनमर्जुने । चक्रदत्तः ।

in the usual way.[1] A compound powder called *Sudarsana churna*, is prepared by taking equal parts of fifty-four different substances and of *chireta*, equal to one-half the weight of all the other ingredients, and mixing them together. It is largely prescribed by native physicians in chronic febrile diseases.

Kirátádi taila, or oil of *chiretá*.[2] Take of *chiretá* one seer, water sixteen seers, boil together till reduced to four seers and strain. Boil this decoction of *chiretá*, with four seers each of prepared mustard oil, *kánjika* and whey, and two tolás each of the following substances in the form of a paste, namely, root of *Sanseviera Zeylanica* (*murvá*), lac, turmeric, wood of *Berberis Asiatica* (*dáruharidrá*), madder, root of *Citrullus Colocynthis* (*indraváruni*), *páchak* root, root of *Pavonia odorata* (*bálá*), of *Vanda Roxburghii* (*rásná*), *Scindapsus officinalis* (*gajapippali*), long pepper, black pepper, ginger, root of *Stephania hernandifolia*, (*páṭhá*), *indrajava* seeds, *sonchal*, *vit*, and rock salts, root of *Justica Aḍhátoda* (*vásaka*), *Calotropis gigantea* (*arka*), *Ichnocarpus frutescens* (*shyámalatá*), *Cedrus Deodara* (*devadáru*) and the fruit of *Trichosanthes palmaṭa* (*mahákála*). The oil thus prepared is rubbed on the body in chronic fever with emaciation and anæmia.

CANSCORA DECUSSATA, *R. et Sch.*

Syn. Pladera decussata, Roxb.

Sans. शङ्खपुष्पी, *Sankhapushpi.*

Vern. Dánkuni, Beng. Sankháhuli, Hind.

THIS little plant is regarded as laxative, alterative and tonic and is much praised as a nervine. It is used in insanity, epilepsy

---

1 किरात तिक्तममृता द्राक्षा मामलकीं शठी। निष्क्वाथ्य शतकाथ्यं वातपित्तज्वरे पिबेत्। भैषज्यरत्नावली।

2 किरातादि तैलम्। मूर्वालाक्षा हरिद्रे द्वे मञ्जिष्ठा सेन्द्रवारुणी। पुष्करं ह्रीवेरं रास्ना कपिवल्ली कटुत्रयं। पाठा सेन्द्र यवञ्चैव श्यामालता संयुतं। वासकार्क श्यामादारु महाकाल फलं तथा। दधि मस्त्वारनालेन कैरातेनच संपचेत्। प्रस्थं प्रस्थं समादाय तैल प्रस्थे विपाचयेत्। क्षिप्र मुक्त ज्वरश्चैव

and nervous debility. The fresh juice of the plant, in doses of about an ounce, is given, with the addition of honey and *páchak* root, in all sorts of insanity.[1] A paste made of the entire plant, including roots and flowers, is recommended to be taken with milk as a nervine and alterative tonic.[2] The following compound powder is used in similar cases. Take of *gulancha, Achyranthes aspera* (*apámárga*), *báberang, páchak* root, root of *Asparagus racemosus* (*satamuli*), *Acorus Calamus* (*vachá*), chebulic myrobalan, and *Canscora decussata*, in equal parts; powder and mix. It is said that the use of this powder for three days will enable a student to learn by rote a thousand couplets of poetry.[3]

NAT. ORDER BIGNONIACEÆ.

CALOSANTHES INDICA, *Bl.*

Syn. Bignonia Indica, Linn.

Sans. श्योनाक, *Syonáka.* अरलु, *Aralu.*

Vern. Násoná, Beng. Arlu, Hind.

THIS is a small tree, growing over a large part of India. The root-bark is used in medicine. It is considered astringent, tonic, and useful in diarrhœa and dysentery. It is also an ingredient of *dasamula* (see *Desmodium gangeticum*), and is thus largely used in a great variety of diseases. The tender fruits are described as grateful, carminative and stomachic.

सन्ततं सततं तथा। धातुस्थं अस्थिमज्जस्थं सर्व्वं ज्वरं व्यपोहति। कामलां प्रहणीञ्चैव अतिसारं हलीमकं। प्लीहा पाण्डुश्वयथुञ्च नाशयेत् नात्रसंशयः। नास्ति तैल वरञ्चैव ज्वरदर्पं कुलान्तकं। भैषज्यरत्नावली।

1 ब्राह्मी कुष्माण्ड षट्ग्रन्थाशङ्खीनीस्वरसः पृथक्। मधु कुष्ट युतः पीतः सर्व्वोन्मादापहारकः। चक्रदत्तः।

2 रसोगुडूच्यास्तु समूलपुष्प्याः कल्कः प्रयोज्यः खलुशङ्खपुष्प्याः। आयुः प्रदान्यामयनाशनानि बलाग्निवर्णस्वरवर्द्धनानि। मेध्यानि चैतानि रसायनानि मेध्याविशेषेणतु शङ्खपुष्पी। चक्रदत्तः।

3 गुडूच्यपामार्ग विडङ्ग शङ्खिनी वचाभया कुष्ठशतावरीसमा। घृतेन लीढा प्रकरोति मानवं त्रिभिर्दिनैः श्लोकसहस्रधारिणम्। चक्रदत्तः।

The root-bark is enclosed within some leaves and a layer of clay and roasted. The juice expressed from this roasted bark is given in diarrhœa and dysentery with the addition of *mocharasa* (gum of *Bombax Malabarium*).[1]

In otorrhœa, Sárangadhara recommends the use of an oil prepared by boiling, over a gentle fire, sesamum oil with a paste made of the root-bark of *Calosanthes Indica.*[2]

STEREOSPERMUM SUAVEOLENS, *DC.*

Syn. Bignonia suaveolens, Roxb.

Sans. पाटला, *Páṭalá. Vern. Párul, Beng. Páḍ, Hind.*

THIS is a middle sized flowering tree, a native of Bengal. The flowers are large, of a dark crimson colour and exquisitely fragrant. Steeped in water they impart their fragrance to it. Rubbed up with honey they are given to check hiccup. The root-bark is an ingredient of *dasamula* (see *Desmodium gangeticum*), and is thus largely used in native medicine. It is regarded as cooling, diuretic and tonic, and is generally used in combination with other medicines. The ashes of this plant are used in the preparation of alkaline water and caustic pastes.

NAT. ORDER. CONVOLVULACEÆ.

IPOMŒA TURPETHUM, *R. Br.*

Syn. Convolvulus Turpethum, Roxb.

Sans. त्रिवृत्, *Trivrit.* त्रिपुटा, *Tripuṭá.*

Vern. Teori, Beng. Nisoth, Tarbud, Hind.

Two varieties of *trivrit* are described by most writers, namely, *sveta* or white and *krishna* or black. The white variety is pre-

---

1 अरलुत्वक्कृतस्यैव पुटपाकोऽग्निदीपनः। मधुमोचरसाभ्याञ्च युक्तः सर्व्वातिसारजित्। शार्ङ्गधरः।

2 तैलं श्योनाकमूलेन मन्दाग्नौ परिपाचितम्। हरेदाशु त्रिदोषोत्थं कर्णशूलं प्रपूरणम्। शार्ङ्गधरः।

ferred for medicinal use as a moderate or mild cathartic. The black variety is said to be a powerful drastic and to cause vomiting, faintness and giddiness. *Trivrit* has been used as a purgative from time immemorial and is still used as such by native practitioners, alone, as well as in various combinations. In fact this medicine is the ordinary cathartic in use amongst natives, just as jalap is among Europeans. The usual mode of administering it is as follows. About two scruples of the root are rubbed into a pulp with water and taken with the addition of rock salt and ginger or sugar and black pepper.

A compound powder called *Nárácha churna*,[1] is thus prepared. Take of *trivrit* root two tolás, long pepper two tolás, sugar eight tolás; powder and mix. About a scruple of the powder is recommended to be taken before meals in constipation with hard fæces.

Tumburádya churna.[2] Take of the fruits of *Xanthoxylum hostile* (*tumburu*), rock, *vit* and *sonchal* salts, *ajowan*, *páchak* root, *yavakshára*, chebulic myrobalan, assafœtida and *baberang* seeds, one part each, *trivrit* three parts; powder the ingredients and mix. Dose, about a drachm with warm water, in painful dyspepsia with costiveness and flatulence.

In anasarca supposed to be caused by deranged bile, a decoction of *trivrit*, *gulancha*, and the three myrobalans is recommended to be taken. Milk diet should be prescribed along with this medicine.[3]

---

1 नाराचचूर्णम्। खण्डपलं त्रिवृतासमसुपकुल्या कर्षचूर्णितं श्लक्ष्णम्। प्राग्भोजनेच समधु विडालपदकं लिहेत्प्राज्ञः। एतद्गाढपुरीषे पित्ते कफेच विनियोज्यम्। सुस्वादुर्नृपयोग्योऽयं चूर्णोनाराचकोनाम्ना। भावप्रकाशः।

2 तुम्बुर्वाद्यं चूर्णम्। तुम्बुरूणि त्रिलवणं यवानी पुष्कराह्वयम् यवक्षाराभयाहिङ्गु विडङ्गानि समानिच। त्रिवृत्त्रिभागिकाज्ञेया सूक्ष्म चूर्णानि कारयेत्। पिवेदुष्णेन तोयेन यवक्वाथेन वा पिवेत्। जयेत्सर्वाणि शूलानिगुल्मा ध्मानोदराणिच। शार्ङ्गधरः।

3 क्षीराशनः पित्तकृतेऽथशोथे त्रिवृद्गुडूची त्रिफलाकषायम्। चक्रदत्तः।

BATATAS PANICULATUS, *Choisy.*

Syn. Convolvulus paniculatus, Roxb.

Sans. विदारी, *Vidári,* भूमिकुष्माण्ड, *Bhumikushmánda.*

Vern. Bhui kumrá, Beng, Bilai kand, Hind.

THE large tuberous root of this handsome climber is considered tonic, alterative, aphrodisiac, demulcent and lactagogue. The powdered root-stock is given with wine, for the purpose of increasing the secretion of milk.[1] In the emaciation of children with debility and want of digestive power, the following diet is recommended. Take of *vidári,* wheat-flour and barley equal parts, and make into a confection with milk, clarified butter, sugar and honey.[2] Susruta gives several prescriptions for its use as an aphrodisiac. The simplest is as follows. Macerate the powder of the root in its own juice and administer with honey and clarified butter.[3] *Vidári* enters into the composition of several diuretic and demulcent mixtures. The following is an illustration.

Mutrakrichchhántaka rasa.[4] Take of *vidári*, fruits of *Tribulus terrestris,* (*gokshura*), liquorice root, and flowers of *Mesua ferrea* (*nágakesara*), equal parts and prepare a decoction with water. This decoction is given with the preparation of mercury called *rasasindura,* in scanty or acrid urine, to promote this secretion.

PHARBITIS NIL, *Choisy.* The seeds of this plant, called *káládáná* in the vernacular and now commonly used as a purgative

---

1 विदारीकन्दं सुरयापिबेद्वा स्तन्यवर्द्धनम् । चक्रदत्तः ।

2 यदा तु दुर्ब्बलो बालः खादन्नपि च वह्निमान् । विदारीकन्द गोधूमयवचूर्णं घृतप्लुतम् । खादयेत्तदनुक्षीरं शृतं समधुशर्करम् । भावप्रकाशः ।

3 चूर्णं विदार्य्याः सुकृतं स्वरसेनैव भावितम् । सर्पिःक्षौद्रयुतं लीढ्वा शतं गच्छेद्वराङ्गनाः । सुश्रुतः ।

4 मूत्रकृच्छ्रान्तकरसः । विदारीं गोक्षुरं यष्टी केशरञ्च समं पचेत् । तत्कषायं पिबेत् क्षौद्रं रसभस्मयुतं पुनः । मूत्रकृच्छ्रहरं ख्यातं सप्राह्नात् पित्तसम्भवम् । रसेन्द्र सारसंग्रहः ।

all over India, were unknown to the ancient Hindus. There is no name for them in Sanskrit.

ARGYREIA SPECIOSA, *Sweet.*

Syn. Lettsomia nervosa, Roxb.

Sans. **वृद्धदारक,** *Vriddhadáraka. Vern. Bijtarká, Beng.*

THE root of this plant is regarded as alterative, tonic and useful in rheumatic affections, and diseases of the nervous system. As an alterative and nervine tonic it is prescribed in the following manner. The powdered root is soaked, seven times during seven days, in the juice of the tubers of *Asparagus racemosus* (*satamuli*) and dried. The resulting powder is given in doses of a quarter to half a tolá, with clarified butter, for about a month. It is said to improve the intellect, strengthen the body and prevent the effects of age.[1] In synovitis the powdered root is given with milk.[2]

Ajamodádi churna.[3] Take of *ajowán*, *báberang*, rock salt, plumbago root, *Cedrus deodara*, long pepper root, long pepper, black pepper and dill seeds each two tolsá, chebulic myrobalan ten tolás, root of *Argyreia speciosa* twenty tolás, ginger twenty tolás ; powder and mix. Dose, about two drachms with treacle. This preparation is said to be useful in rheumatic affections and hemiplegia.

---

1 वृद्धदारकमूलानि श्लक्ष्णचूर्णानि कारयेत्। शतावर्य्या रसेनैव सप्तरात्राणि भावयेत्। अक्षमात्रन्तु तच्चूर्णं सर्पिषा सह भोजयेत्। मासमात्रोपयोगेन मतिमान् जायते नरः। मेधावी स्मृतिमांश्चैव वलिपलितवर्ज्जितः। चक्रदत्तः।

2 गुग्गुलुं क्रोष्टुशीर्षे तु गुडूचीत्रिफलाम्भसा। क्षीरेणैरण्डतैलं वा पिबेद्वा वृद्धदारकम्। भावप्रकाशः।

3 अजमोदाद्यं चूर्णम्। अजमोदाविड़ङ्गानि सैन्धवं देवदारु च। चित्रकं पिप्पलीमूलं शतपुष्पा च पिप्पली। मरिचञ्चेति कर्षांशं प्रत्येकं कारयेद्बुधः। कर्षास्तु पञ्च पथ्याया दश स्युर्वृद्धदारकात्। नागराच्च दशैव स्युः सर्वाण्येकत्र चूर्णयेत्। पिबेत्कोष्णजलेनैव चूर्णञ्च गुड़सम्मितम्। भक्षयेदथवा सम्यक् परं श्वयथुनाशनम्। आमवातरुजं हन्ति सन्धिपीड़ाञ्च गृध्रसीम्। कटिपृष्ठगुदस्थाञ्च जङ्घयोश्च रुजां जयेत्। तूनीं प्रतूनीं विश्वाचीं कफवातामयान् जयेत्। शार्ङ्गधरः।

NAT. ORDER SOLANACEÆ.

DATURA ALBA, *Rumph. and* FASTUOSA, *Linn.*

Sans. धूस्तूर, *Dhustura*, उन्मत्त, *Unmatta.*

Vern. Dhuturá, Hind. and Beng.

SANSKRIT writers do not make any distinction in the properties of the two varieties of *Datura*, and in practice both are indiscriminately used. Sometimes the white flowered variety is specified, as for example in a prescription for insanity, quoted below. *Dhaturá* leaves are used in smoking by debauched devotees and others accustomed to the use of *gánja*. The seeds are added to the preparations of *bháng* (leaves of *Cannabis sativa*) used by natives, for increasing their intoxicating powers. The use of the powdered seeds in sweet-meats, curry powder, etc., for the purpose of stupifying travellers and then robbing them, is well known.

The seeds, leaves and roots are all used in medicine. They are considered useful in insanity, fever with catarrhal and cerebral complications, diarrhœa, skin diseases, lice, etc.

Svalpajvaránkusa.[1] Take of mercury, sulphur, aconite, ginger, long pepper and black pepper, each one part, *dhaturá* seeds two parts; rub them together with lemon juice and make into four-grain pills. These pills are used in fever attended with catarrh or cough. Several other preparations of composition similar to the above, are in use under the names of *Nava jvaránkusa, Kálári, Jvaránkusa*, etc.

The root of *Datura alba* (*svetonmatta*) is boiled in milk and this milk is administered with the addition of clarified butter and treacle in insanity.[2] A metallic preparation called *Unmádankura rasa* and composed of the sulphides of mercury and copper together with a number of other substances and *dhaturá* seeds, is also used

---

[1] रसं गन्धं विषञ्चैव प्रत्येकं समभागिकम् । द्विभागं धुस्तुबीजञ्च त्रिकटु तदर्द्धभागिकम् । जम्बीराणां रसैर्मर्द्दयेद्वटीगुञ्जाद्वयमिता । कणाचूर्णं पिबेत् चानुपीत सश्लेष्मज्वरं जयेत् । रसेन्द्रसारसंग्रहः ।

[2] श्वेतोन्मत्तोत्तरदिङ्मूलसिद्धस्तु पायसः । गुडाज्यसंयुतो हन्ति सर्व्वोन्मादांस्तु दोषजान् । चक्रदत्तः ।

in this disease. The fresh juice of the leaves alone, or mixed with opium, is a common domestic application to inflamed parts.

In inflammation of the breasts, a paste composed of turmeric and *dhatura* fruits is recommended to be applied.[1] An oil prepared in the usual manner with the paste and juice of *dhaturá* leaves, is applied to the head for destroying lice.[2] An oil prepared by boiling *dhaturá* seeds, and sesamum oil, with an alkaline water made from the ashes of *Colocasia Indica (mánaka)*, is used in psoriasis.[3]

In the Bengal Dispensatory (page 469) it is stated that "we are indebted to the native practitioners of India for a method of using stramonium in spasmodic asthma, which is certainly found of great benefit in numerous cases. We allude to the practice of smoking the leaves or dried stems." The smoking of *dhatura* leaves is prescribed at present both by English and native practitioners in spasmodic asthma, but I have not met with any written prescription for it in Sanskrit or vernacular medical works, nor does the Taleef Shereef allude to the practice as known to the Mussulman hakims. It would seem therefore that this use of the drug is of recent origin.

SOLANUM XANTHOCARPUM, VAR. JACQUINIS, *Schrad.*

Syn. *Solanum Jacquinii, Linn.*

Sans. कण्टकारी, *Kanṭakári,* निदिग्धिका, *Nidigdhiká.*

Vern. *Kanṭakári, Beng. Kaṭeli, Kaṭai, Hind.*

THE root of *Solanum Jacquinii* is much esteemed as an expectorant and is used in cough, asthma, catarrhal fever and pain in the chest. It is an ingredient of *dasamula* (*see Desmodium gangeticum*), and is thus largely used in a great variety of diseases. The fruits are said to possess properties similar to those of the roots and are eaten as a vegetable.

---

1 निशाकणककफलाभ्यां लेपश्चापिस्तनार्त्तिहा । चक्रदत्तः ।

2 धत्तुरपत्रकल्केन तद्रसेनैव पाचितम्। तैलमभ्यङ्गमात्रेण युका नाशयति क्षणात् । भावप्रकाशः ।

3 उन्मत्तकस्य वीजेन माणकक्षारवारिणा । कटुतैलं विपक्तव्यं शीघ्रं हन्याद्विपादिकाम् । चक्रदत्तः ।

Kanṭakári is used in medicine in various forms, such as decoction, electuary, *ghrita*, etc. A decoction of the root is given with the addition of long pepper and honey, in cough and catarrh, and with rock salt and assafœtida in spasmodic cough.[1] Several compound decoctions made along with other expectorant and demulcent drugs are in use. The following is an example. Take of *kanṭakári*, root of *Justicia Adhatoda* (*vásaka*), pulse of *Dolichos uniflorus* (*kulattha*) and ginger, equal parts, in all two tolas; prepare a decoction in the usual way and administer, with the addition of *páchak* root, in cough with difficult breathing.[2]

Kanṭakáryavaleha[3] or electuary of *Solanum Jacquinii.* Take of *kanṭakári* root twelve seers and a half, water sixty-four seers, boil till reduced to one fourth and strain. Boil the strained decoction till reduced to the consistence of a fluid extract, and add to it the following substances in fine powder, namely, *gulancha*, *Piper Chaba* (*chavya*), plumbago root, tubers of *Cyperus rotundus* (*mustaka*), *Rhus succedanea*, (*karkaṭa sringi*), long pepper, black pepper, ginger, *Alhagi Maurorum* (*yásá*), *Clerodendron Siphonanthus* (*várgi*), *Vanda Roxburghii*, (*rásná*) and zedoary root, each eight tolas, sugar two seers and a half, sesamum oil and clarified butter each one seer, and boil together till reduced to the proper consistence. Lastly add honey one seer, bamboo-manna and long pepper in fine powder, each half a seer. This electuary is given in various sorts of cough.

---

1 कण्टकारीकृतः क्वाथः सकृष्णः सर्व्वकासहा । चक्रदत्तः ।

2 व्याघ्री कुलत्थ वासाभिर्नागरेण च साधितः । क्वाथः पौष्करचूर्णाढ्यः श्वासकासौ निवारयेत् । शार्ङ्गधरः ।

3 कण्टकार्य्यवलेहः । कण्टकारी तुलां नीरद्रोणे पक्त्वा कषायकम् । पादशेषं गृहीत्वा च तत्र चूर्णानि दापयेत् । पृथक्पलांशान्येतानि गुडूची चव्यचित्रकौ । मुस्तं कर्कटशृङ्गी च त्र्यूषणं धन्वयासकः । भार्गी रास्ना शटी चैव शर्करापलविंशतिः । प्रत्येकं च पलान्यष्टौ प्रदद्यात् घृततैलयोः । पक्त्वावलेहत्वमानीय शीते मधुपलाष्टकम् । चतुर्भागन्तु गाक्षीर्य्याः पिप्पली च चतुःपलम् । क्षिप्त्वा निदध्यात् सुदृढे मृन्मये भाजने शुभे । लेहोऽयं हन्ति हिक्कार्त्तिकासश्वासानशेषतः । भावप्रकाशः ।

Kanṭakári ghrita.[1] This is prepared in the usual proportions with the fresh juice of *kanṭakári*, clarified butter and the following substances in the form of a paste, namely, *Vanda Roxburghii* (*rásná*), *Sida cordifolia*, (*bálá*), ginger, long pepper, black pepper and the fruits of *Tribulus terrestris* (*gokshura*). It is used in the same cases as the electuary.

SOLANUM NIGRUM, *Linn. Sans.* काकमाची, *Kákamáchi, Vern. Kákmáchi, Beng. Makoy, Hind.* The berries of this plant are considered tonic, diuretic and useful in anasarca and heart disease. For the mode of administering them in heart disease, see *Hridayárnava rasa*, (page 66).

SOLANUM INDICUM, *Linn.*

Sans. बृहती, *Vrihati.* भण्टाकी, *Bhantáki.*

Vern. Byákura, Beng. Barhantá, Hind.

THE root of *Solanum Indicum* is an ingredient of *dasamula* (see *Desmodium gangeticum*) and is thus used in a great variety of diseases. It is regarded as expectorant and useful in cough and catarrhal affections. The following is an example of a compound decoction containing this drug. Take of *Solanum Indicum* (*vrihati*), *Solanum Jacquinii* (*kanṭakári*), *Sida cordifolia* (*bálá*), *Justicia Adhatoda* (*vásaka*) and raisins, equal parts and prepare a decoction in the usual way. This decoction is given in bronchitis with fever.[2]

WITHANIA SOMNIFERA, *Don.*

Syn. Physalis flexuosa, Roxb.

Sans. अश्वगन्धा, *Asvagandhá. Vern. Asvagandhá, Beng. Asgand, Hind.*

THE root of this plant is long, smooth, rounded, whitish brown externally and of a fine white colour internally. It is said that the

1 कण्टकारीघृतम् । घृतं रास्नाबलाव्योष श्वदंष्ट्राकल्कपाचितम् । कण्टकारीरसे सर्पिः पञ्चकासनिषूदनम् । चक्रदत्तः ।

2 बलाद्विबृहतीवासाद्राक्षाभिः क्वथितं जलम्। पित्तकासापहं पेयं शर्करामधुयोजितम् । चक्रदत्तः ।

root smells like a horse whence the Sanskrit name *asvangandhá*. The specimen in my possession however has scarcely any odour or taste. It is regarded as tonic, alterative and aphrodisiac and is used in consumption, emaciation of children, debility from old age, rheumatism, etc.

In consumption a decoction of *asvagandhá* root and long pepper is given with the addition of clarified butter and honey.[1] For improving the nutrition of weakly children, the root reduced to a paste, is recommended to be taken with milk and clarified butter for a fortnight.[2]

Asvagandhá ghrita.[3] Take of the decoction of *asvagandhá* root one part, milk ten parts, clarified butter one part; boil them together and prepare a *ghrita*. It is said to promote the nutrition and strength of children.

In rheumatism, a *ghrita* prepared with a decoction and paste of the root, is used internally and an oil prepared with a decoction of the root and a number of aromatic substances in the form of a paste, is used externally.

About half a drachm of *asvagandhá* root, taken with milk or clarified butter is said to act as an aphrodisiac and restorative to old men. *Asvagandhá* enters into the composition of several medicines intended for use as aphrodisiacs.[4]

HYOSCYAMUS NIGER, *Linn.* The seeds of *Hyoscyamus niger* are used in Hindu medicine under the name of *khorásáni yamáni*. They are considered stimulant or heating, narcotic,

---

1 कृष्णाद्राक्षासितालेहः क्षयहा क्षौद्रतैलवान्। मधुसर्पिर्युतो वाश्वगन्धाकृष्णासितोद्भवः। चक्रदत्तः।

2 पीताश्वगन्धापयसार्द्धमासं घृतेन तैलेन सुखाम्बुना वा। कृशस्य पुष्टिं वपुषो विधत्ते बालस्य शस्यस्य यथाम्बुवृष्टिः। चक्रदत्तः।

3 अश्वगन्धाघृतम्। पादकल्केऽश्वगन्धायाः क्षीरे दशगुणे पचेत्। घृतं पेयं कुमाराणां पुष्टिकृद्बलवर्द्धनम्। चक्रदत्तः।

4 अश्वगन्धादिचूर्णम्। अश्वगन्धा दशपला तस्मात्त्रो वृद्धदारकः। चूर्णीकृत्योभयं विद्वान् घृतभाण्डे निधापयेत्। कर्षकं पयसा पीत्वा नारीभिर्नैव तृप्यति। अगत्वा प्रमदां भूयाद्वलीपलितवर्जितः। शार्ङ्गधरः।

astringent and digestive, and are used in combination with other medicines of their class.

NICOTIANA TABACUM, *Linn.* According to Royle, the tobacco plant was introduced into India (A.D. 1605) towards the end of the reign of Jelaludeen Akbar. It is not described even in the latest Sanskrit medical works such as the Bhávaprakása or Rája Vallava. The Sabdakalpadruma mentions it under the name of ताम्रकूट *Támrakuṭa,* and quotes as authority for the use of the word, a passage from the Kulárnáva Tantra where it is stated to be one of eight intoxicating agents.

CAPSICUM FRUTESCENS, *Linn. and* MINIMUM, *Roxb.* have no Sanskrit name. Although they are now cultivated all over India and form an essential ingredient of all curry powders, they are not mentioned in any Sanskrit medical work and are evidently of recent introduction into this country.

NAT. ORDER SCROPHULARIACEÆ.

PICRORRHIZA KURROA, *Royle.*

Sans. कटुका, *Kaṭuká,* कटुरोहिणी, *Kaṭurohini. Vern. Kaṭki, H. B.*

THE root of *Picrorrhiza Kurroa* is described as bitter, acrid and stomachic and in larger doses a moderate cathartic. It is used in fever and dyspepsia and as an ingredient of various purgative medicines. About two drachms of the powdered root given with sugar and warm water, is said to act as a mild purgative.[1] In bilious fever the following decoction is highly recommended. Take of *kaṭuki* root, liquorice, raisins, and *nim* bark, half a tolá each, water thirty-two tolás; boil till reduced to one-fourth.[2] The following is an example of a powder containing *kaṭuki* root, used in dyspepsia. Take of *kaṭuki, Acorus Calamus* (*vachá*), chebulic myrobalans and plumbago root, equal parts ; powder and mix.

---

1 सशर्करासच्चमात्रां कटुकामुष्णवारिणा । पीत्वा ज्वरं जयेज्जन्तुः कफपित्तसमुद्भवम् । चक्रदत्तः ।

2 मृद्वीका मधुकं निम्बं कटुका रोहिणी समा । अवश्यायस्थितं पाक्यमेतद् पित्तज्वरापहम् । चक्रदत्तः ।

Dose, about a drachm with cow's urine in dyspepsia with severe pain.

HERPESTIS MONNIERA, *H. B. K.*

Syn. Gratiola Monniera, Roxb.

Sans. ब्राह्मी, *Brahmi*, मण्डूकी, *Manduki*, *Vern. Brahmi*, *Beng. Hind.*

The herb used by the native physicians of Calcutta under the name of *brahmi* is the *Herpestis Monniera.* Roxburgh however gives *brahmi* and one of its synonyms *somalatá* as the Sanskrit for *Ruta graveolens.* This descrepancy induced me to get specimens of the plant from different parties, but every where I got the *Herpestis Monniera* under the name of *brahmi.* This plant is considered a nervine tonic, useful in insanity, epilepsy and hoarseness. Half a tolá of the fresh juice of the leaves, with two scruples of *páchak* root and honey, is recommended to be given in insanity. The leaves fried in clarified butter are taken to relieve hoarseness.[1]

A powder composed of equal parts of *brahmi*, *Acorus Calamus* (*vachá*), chebulic myrobalan, root of *Justicia Adhatoda* (*vásaka*) and long pepper, is given with honey in the hoarseness of phthisis.[2] Several *ghritas* are prepared with the juice of *brahmi* leaves and various other substances in the form of paste. They are used in insanity, epilepsy and hoarseness. The following is an example.

Brahmi ghrita.[3] Take of old clarified butter four seers, fresh juice of *brahmi* four seers, *Acorus Calamus* (*vachá*), *páchak* root, and the root of *Canscora decussata* (*sankhapushpi*), equal parts, in all thirty-two tolás, in the form of a paste and boil them together till the watery portion is evaporated.

---

1 See note 1 page 202.

2 ब्राह्मीवचा भयावासा पिप्पली मधुसंयुता । अस्यप्रयोगात् सप्ताहात्किन्नरैः सह गीयते । भावप्रकाशः ।

3 ब्राह्मीघृतम् । ब्राह्मीरसे वचाकुष्ठ शङ्खपुष्पीभिरेव च । पुराणं मेध्यमुन्माद-ग्रहापस्मारनुद्घृतम् । चक्रदत्तः ।

NAT. ORDER ACANTHACEÆ.

JUSTICIA ADHATODA, *Roxb.*

Syn. Adhatoda Vasica, Nees.

Sans. वासक, *Vásaka,* अटरुष, *Aṭarusha. Vern. Bákas,* B. *Arushá, H.*

THIS is a bushy shrub common in most parts of India and used in making fences. The leaves and roots of this plant are considered expectorant and antispasmodic and are much used in a variety of forms in cough, consumption, catarrhal fever and asthma. This medicine was considered so serviceable in phthisis that it was said no man suffering from this disease need despair as long as the *vásaka* plant exists.

The fresh juice or decoction of the leaves in doses of one tolá, is given with the addition of honey and long pepper in cough. A decoction of *vásaka* root, chebulic myrobalan and raisins is used in the same cases. Another compound decoction much used in fever with cough, is as follows. Take of *vásaka* root, *gulancha,* and the root of *Solanum Jacquinii* (*kanṭakári*) in equal parts, two tolás in all and prepare a decoction in the usual way. This is given with the addition of honey.[1] A *ghrita* is prepared with clarified butter, a decoction of the plant and a paste of the root taken in the usual proportions and is used in phthisis.

Vásávaleha[2] or electuary of *vásaka.* Take of the juice of *vásaka* leaves four seers, white sugar one seer, long pepper sixteen tolás, clarified butter sixteen tolás, boil them together till reduced to the consistence of an extract. When cool add honey

---

1 कोश्लो वासकः क्वाथः पीतः क्षौद्रेण नाशयेत् । वासकः स्वरसः पेयो मधुना रक्तपित्तजित् । वासाद्राक्षाभया क्वाथः पीतः सक्षौद्रशर्करः । निहन्ति रक्तपित्तार्त्तिं श्वासकासञ्च दारुणम् । वासाक्षुद्रामृता क्वाथः क्षौद्रेण ज्वर-कासहा । शार्ङ्गधरः ।

2 वासावलेहः । वासकस्य रसप्रस्थं माणिकासितशर्करा । पिप्पल्यद्वि पलं तावत् सर्पिषस्य शनैः पचेत् । तस्मिन् लेहत्वमायाते शीते क्षौद्रपलाष्टकम् । दत्वावतारयेद्वैद्यो लीढ़ो लेहोऽयमुत्तमः । हन्त्येवराजयक्ष्माणं कासं च दारुणम् । पार्श्वशूलं च हृच्छूलं रक्तपित्तं ज्वरं तथा । भावप्रकाशः ।

one seer, and stir with a ladle till intimately mixed. Dose, one to two tolás in phthisis, cough with pain in the sides, hæmoptysis and asthma.

Vásáchandanádi taila.[1] Take of *vásaka* plant, twelve seers and a half, water sixty-four seers; boil till reduced to one-fourth. Take of lac eight seers, water sixty-four seers; boil down to sixteen seers. Take of red sandal wood, *gulancha*, root of *Clerodendron Siphonanthus (brahmayashti)*, the ten drugs called *dasamula* and *Solanum Jacquinii (nidigdhiká)*, each two seers and a half, water sixty-four seers; boil down to sixteen seers. To these decoctions, add of whey and prepared sesamum oil sixteen seers each and the following substances in the form of a paste, namely, red sandal wood, liquorice, wood of *Berberis Asiatica*, long pepper, black pepper, ginger, turmeric, *páchak* root, emblic myrobalans, *tejapatra* leaves, wood of *Cedrus Deodara*, cinnamon, and cardamom, seeds called *renuka*, pouch of civet cat, root of *Withania somnifera (asvagandhá)*, *Pæderia fœtida (prasárani)*, *Vanda Roxburghii (rásná)*, *saileya* (a sort of lichen), zedoary root, and the fruit of *Aglaia Roxburghiana (priangu)*, each eight tolás; and boil them together in the usual way. This oil is rubbed on the body in affections of the chest and especially in phthisis.

HYGROPHILA SPINOSA, *T. Anders. Syn. Asteracantha longifolia, Nees. Ruellia longifolia, Roxb. Sans.* कोकिलाक्ष, *Kokiláksha*, इक्षुगन्धा, *Ikshugandhá. Vern. Kuliákhará, Beng. Tálmakhána, Hind.*

---

1 बृहत्वासा चन्दनादितैलं। चन्दनं रेणुका पूति ह्यगन्धा प्रसारणी। त्रिसुगन्धकणामूलं नागकेशरमेवच। मेदे द्वे च त्रिकटुकं रास्ना मधुकशैलजं। शठी कुष्ठं देवदारु वनिता च बिभीतकं। एतेषां पलिकैर्भागैः पचेत्तैलाढ़कं भिषक्। वासायास्तुलां क्वाथ्यां जलद्रोणे विपाचयेत्। लाक्षारसाढ़कञ्चैव तथैव दधिमस्तुकं। चन्दनञ्चामृताभार्गीदशमूलं निदिग्धिका। एतेषां विंशतिपलं जलद्रोणे विपाचयेत्। पादशेषे स्थितेक्वाथे तैलं तेनैव साधयेत्। कासान् ज्वरान् रक्तपित्तं पाण्डुरोगंहलीमकं। कामलाञ्च क्षतक्षीणं राजयक्ष्माणमेवच। श्वासान् पञ्चविधं हन्ति बलवर्णाग्निपुष्टिकृत्। तैलं वासा चन्दनादि बृहदेतत् प्रकीर्त्तितं।

This little annual is met with in low places all over the country. The leaves are described as cooling and useful in jaundice and anasarca. They are used as a pot herb. The root is considered cooling, bitter, tonic and diuretic, and is used in rheumatism, urinary affections, and anasarca. The ashes of the plant are also used as a diuretic in dropsy.[1]

ANDROGRAPHIS PANICULATA, *Nees.* This bitter shrub is well-known in Bengal under the name of *kálmeg* and is the principal ingredient of a domestic medicine for infants called *A'lui.* There is some doubt regarding its Sanskrit name. A plant called *yavatiktá* with synonyms of *mohátiktá*, *sankhini*, etc., is said by some to mean this shrub but the term *mohátiktá* when occuring in Sanskrit prescriptions is usually interpreted as *Melia sempervirens, Sw.* and *yavatikta* has not been noted by me as having occurred in any prescription, so that I am inclined to think *Andrographis paniculata* was not used in Sanskrit medicine. The *álui* above referred to is made of the expressed juice of the leaves with the addition of powdered cardamoms, cloves, cinnamon etc., and is given to infants for the relief of griping, irregular stools and loss of appetite.

NAT. ORDER. SESAMEÆ.

SESAMUM INDICUM, *Linn.*

Sans. तिल, *Tila,* स्नेहफल, *Snehaphala. Vern. Til, Beng. and Hind.*

THIS plant is extensively cultivated in India for the sake of the seeds and their expressed oil, both of which articles are in great demand for various economic, religious and medicinal purposes. The word *taila,* the sanskrit for oil, is derived from *tila*; it would therefore seem, that sesamum oil, was one of the first, if not the first oil manufactured from oil-seeds by the ancient Hindus. The Bhávaprakása describes three varieties of *til* seeds, namely, black, white and red. Of these the black is regarded as the best, suited for medicinal use. It yields also

---

1 शोथनुत्कोकिलाक्षस्य भस्ममूत्रेण वाम्भसा । चक्रदत्तः ।

the largest quantity of oil. White *til* is of intermediate quality. *Til* of red or other colours is said to be inferior and unfit for medicinal use.

Sesamum seeds are used as an article of diet, being made into confectionary with sugar, or ground into meal. They form an essential article of certain religious ceremonies of the Hindus, and have therefore received the names of *homadhánya* or the sacrificial grain, *pitritarpana* or the grain that is offered as an oblation to deceased ancestors, etc. Sesamum oil forms the basis of most of the fragrant or scented oils used by the natives for inunction before bathing and of medicated oils prepared with various vegetable drugs. It is preferred for these purposes from the circumstance of its being little liable to turn rancid or thick, and from its possessing no strong taste or odour of its own.

Sesamum seeds are considered emollient, nourishing, tonic, diuretic, and lactagogue. They are said to be especially serviceable in piles, by regulating the bowels and removing constipation. Sesamum seeds ground to a paste with water are given with butter in bleeding piles.[1] Sweetmeats made of the seeds are also beneficial in this disease. A poultice made of the seeds is applied to ulcers.[2] Both the seeds and the oil are used as demulcents in dysentery and urinary diseases in combination with other medicines of their class.

NAT. ORDER. VERBENACEÆ.

VITEX NEGUNDO, *Linn.*

Sans. निर्गुण्डी, *Nirguṇḍi*, सिन्धुवार, *Sindhuvára.*

Vern. Nisinda, Beng. Nisindá, Sámbhalu, Hind.

SANSKRIT writers mention two varieties of *nirgundi.* That with pale blue flowers is called *sindhuvára* (*Vitex trifolia*) and that with blue flowers is called *nirgundi.* The properties of both are said to be identical, but the latter is generally used in

---

1 नवनीततिलैः कल्को जेता रक्तार्शसां स्मृतः । शार्ङ्गधरः।

2 कल्कः संरोपणः कार्य्यस्तिलानां मधुकान्वितः। चक्रदत्तः।

medicine. The root of *Vitex Negundo* is considered tonic, febrifuge and expectorant. The leaves are aromatic and regarded as tonic and vermifuge. Their juice is much used for soaking various metallic powders, before making the latter into pills.

A decoction of *nirgundi* leaves is given with the addition of long pepper in catarrhal fever with heaviness of head and dullness of hearing.[1] A pillow stuffed with the leaves of *nirgundi* is placed under the head for relief of headache. The juice of the leaves is said to remove fœtid discharges and worms from ulcers. An oil prepared with the juice of the leaves is applied to sinuses and scrofulous sores.[2]

GMELINA ARBOREA, *Linn.*

Sans. **गम्भारी**, *Ghambhári*, **श्रीपर्णी**, *Sriparni*, **काश्मरी**, *Kásmari.*
Vern. *Gámári*, *Beng.* *Gámbhár*, *Hind.*

THE root of this plant is described as bitter, tonic, stomachic, laxative, and useful in fever, indigestion, anasarca etc. It is an ingredient of *dasamula* (*see Desmodiun gangeticum*), and is thus much used in a variety of diseases. Bangasena says that *gambhári* root taken with liquorice, honey and sugar increases the secretion of milk. The fruits of *Gmelina arborea* are sweetish bitter and cooling; they enter into the composition of several cooling or refrigerent decoctions for fever and burning of the body. The following is an example. Take of the fruits of *Gmelina arborea*, *Grewia Asiatica* (*parushaka*), liquorice root, red sandal wood, and the root of *Andropogon muricatum* (*ushira*), equal parts, in all two tolás, water thirty-two tolás, and boil till reduced to one half. This decoction is used as a drink in bilious fever.[3]

---

1 सिन्धुवारदलक्वाथं कणाढ्यं कफजे ज्वरे । जङ्घयोश्च बले क्षीणे कर्णे च पिच्छिते पिबेत् ॥ भावप्रकाशः ।

2 निर्गुण्डितैलम् । समूलपत्रां निर्गुण्डीं पीड़यित्वा रसेन तु । तेन सिद्धं समं तैलं नाड़ीदुष्टव्रणापहम् । हितं पामापचीनान्तु पानाभ्यञ्जननावनैः । विविधेषु च स्फोटेषु तथा सर्व्वव्रणेषु च ॥ चक्रदत्तः ।

3 काश्मर्य्यशर्करायुक्तं पिबेत् तृष्णार्दितो नरः। श्रीपर्णीचन्दनोशीरसमधूकपरुषकम् । पानं पित्तज्वरं हन्यात् शारिवाद्य सशर्करम् । चक्रदत्तः ।

CLERODENDRON SIPHONANTHUS, *R. Br. Syn. Siphonanthus Indica,* *Lam. Sans.* ब्रह्मयष्टिका, *Brahmayashṭiká*, भार्गी, *Bhárgi. Vern. Bámanháṭi, Beng. Bhárangi, Hind.* The root of *Clerodendron Siphonanthus* is considered useful in asthma, cough and scrofulous affections. The root beaten to a pulp is given with ginger and warm water in asthma.[1] It enters into the composition of several compound decoctions for diseases of the lungs. A confection called *Bhárgiguḍa* is prepared with a decoction of this root and the ten drugs called *dasamula*, chebulic myrobalan, treacle and the usual aromatic substances. It is used in asthma. An oil, prepared with a decoction and paste of the root of *Clerodendron Siphonanthus* in the usual proportions, is recommended for external application in the marasmus of children.

PREMNA SERRATIFOLIA, *Linn. Syn. Premna spinosa, Roxb. Sans.* गनिकारिका, *Ganikáriká*, अग्निमन्थ, *Agnimantha. Vern. Ganiári, Beng. Arni, Hind.* The root of *Premna spinosa* is described as bitter, stomachic and useful in fever, anasarca, urticaria, etc. The leaves are bitter and carminative. A soup made of the leaves is occasionally used as a stomachic and carminative. The root forms an ingredient of *dasamula* (*see Desmodium gangeticum*), and is thus largely used in a variety of affections.

The root rubbed into a paste with water is recommended to be taken with clarified butter in urticaria and roseola, for a week.[2]

NAT. ORDER LABIATÆ.

OCIMUM SANCTUM, *Linn.*

Sans. तुलसी, *Tulasi*, पर्णास, *Parnása. Vern. Tulsi, Beng. Hind.*

SANSKRIT writers make two varieties of this plant (founded upon some difference in the colour of their leaves) namely, white and black. The *Ocimum sanctum* is held sacred to Vishnu of the

---

[1] हिक्काश्वासी पिबेद्भार्गीं सविश्वामुष्णवारिणा। नागरं वा सिता भार्गी सौवर्च्चलसमन्वितम् ॥ चक्रदत्तः।

[2] अग्निमन्थभवं मूलं पिष्टं पीतञ्च सर्पिषा। शीतपित्तोदर्द्दकोठान् सप्ताहाद्‌व्यपनाशयेत् ॥ चक्रदत्तः।

Hindu trinity, and is reared in every hindu house where it is daily watered and worshipped by all the members of the family. The beads or rosaries used by orthodox natives for counting the number of recitations of their deity's name, are made of the stems of this plant.

The leaves are regarded as anti-catarrhal or expectorant and are used in catarrh, cough and pain in the sides. The juice of the leaves is given with the addition of black pepper in catarrhal fever.[1] It is often used as an adjunct to metallic preparations, which are rubbed with it into a thin paste and then licked up. The leaves enter into the composition of some compound decoctions for cough and affections of the chest. The following is an example. Take of the leaves of *Ocimum sanctum*, *gulancha*, ginger, root of *Clerodendron Siphonanthus*, (*bhárgi*) and *Solanum Jacquinii (kanṭakári)*, equal parts and prepare a decoction in the usual way.[2] The dried leaves are used as snuff in ozæna. They also enter into the composition of some compound medicines used in this disease, as for example of an oil which is prepared with a paste of the leaves of *Ocimum sanctum*, roots of *Solanum Jacquinii* (*kanṭakári*), *Baliospermum montanum* (*danti*), *Acorus Calamus* (*vachá*), *Moringa pterygosperma* (*sigru*), long pepper, black pepper, and ginger.[3]

OCIMUM BASILICUM, *Linn. Syn. Ocimum pilosum, Willd. Sans.* बर्बर, *Varvara. Vern. Bábui tulsi. Beng.* The seeds of this plant, called *rehán* in the vernacular, are demulcent and nourishing. Steeped in water they swell into a mucilaginous jelly which is taken with the addition of sugar in dysentery, gonorrhœa and cough.

---

1 पीतोमरिचचूर्णेन तुलसीपत्रजोरसः। द्रोणपुष्पीरसोप्येवं निहन्तिविषमज्वरान् शार्ङ्गधरः।

2 अमृतानागरफञ्जीव्याघ्रीपर्णीभिः साधितः क्वाथः। पीतः सकणाचूर्णः कासश्वासौ जयत्याशु॥ चक्रदत्तः।

3 व्याघ्रीदन्तीवचाशिग्रुसुरसव्योषसैन्धवैः। पाचितं नावनं तैलं पूतिनासागदं जयेत्॥ चक्रदत्तः।

NAT. ORDER AMARANTACEÆ.

AMARANTHUS SPINOSUS. *Linn. Sans.* तण्डुलीय, *Tanduliya. Vern. Kantánatiá, Beng. Choláí, Hind.* This thorny weed is considered light, cooling and a promoter of the alvine and urinary discharges. Its root is said to be an efficaceous medicine for menorrhagia, in which disease it is given with *rasot* and honey.[1] It enters also into the composition of other medicines for this disease, as for example in the preparation called *Asoka ghrita.*

ACHYRANTHES ASPERA, *Linn.**

Sans. अपामार्ग, *Apámárga.* खरमञ्जरी, *Kharamanjari.*

Vern. A'páng, Beng. Latjirá, chirchirá, Hind.

THIS troublesome weed is chiefly valued on account of its ashes which contain a large quantity of potash. These are used in the preparation of alkaline medicines and caustic pastes, (see Alkaline ashes). The ashes mixed with orpiment are applied as a caustic to warts on the penis and other parts of the body.

Apámárga taila.[2] Take of sesamum oil four seers, the alkaline water prepared from the ashes of *Achyranthes aspera* sixteen seers, the ashes of the plant one seer, and boil them together in the usual way. This oil is poured into the meatus in cases of noise in the ears and deafness.

The weed itself is described as heating like fire, laxative and a promoter of secretions; it is used in combination with other medicines of its class in ascites and anasarca, (see *Cedrus Deodara*).

NAT. ORDER NYCTAGINACEÆ.

BOERHAAVIA DIFFUSA, *Linn.*

Sans. पुनर्नवा, *Punarnavá,* शोथघ्नी, *Sothaghni.*

Vern. Svetapunarnabá, Beng. Sánt, Hind.

BOTH the red and white varieties of this plant are noticed by Sanskrit writers but the white is preferred for use. Its root is

---

1 रसाञ्जनं तण्डुलकस्य मूलं क्षौद्रान्वितं तण्डुलतोयपीतम्। असृग्दरं सर्वभवं निहन्ति श्वासञ्च भार्गी सह नागरेण। भावप्रकाशः।

* The closely allied species *A. bidentata, Bl.* is probably used as frequently as this. G. K.

2 अपामार्गक्षारतैलम्। अपामार्गक्षारजले तत्क्षारकल्केन साधितं तिलजम्। अपहरति कर्णनादं वाधिर्य्यञ्चापि पूरणतः॥ चक्रदत्तः

regarded as laxative, diuretic and stomachic; it is used in jaundice, ascites, anasarca, scanty urine and internal inflammations. One of its Sanskrit synonyms, namely, *sothagni* means cure for dropsy. A decoction of *punarnavá* root is recommended to be given with the addition of powdered *chiretá* and ginger in anasarca.[1] A compound decoction much used in this disease is prepared as follows.

Punarnaváshṭaka.[2] Take of *Punarnavá* root, nim bark, leaves of *Trichosanthes dioica* (*paṭola*), ginger, *Picrorrhiza Kurroa* (*kaṭuki*), chebulic myrobalan, *gulancha*, and the wood of *Berberis Asiatica* (*dáruharidrá*), quarter of a tola each, water thirty-two tolas; boil together till reduced to one-fourth. This decoction is given in general anasarca with ascites, cough, jaundice, difficult breathing, etc. An oil, prepared with a decoction of the root and a number of the usual aromatics in the form of a paste, is rubbed on the body in general ansarca complicated with jaundice. It is called *Punarnavá taila.*[3]

The Bhávaprakása gives an electuary under the name of *Punarnavávaleha.* It is prepared with a decoction of the root of *Boerhaavia diffusa* and a number of other ingredients, and is used in strangury or scanty urine.

NAT. ORDER LAURACEÆ.

CINNAMOMUM CAMPHORA, *Nees et Ebermaier.*

Sans. कर्पूर, *Karpura,* चन्द्राह्व, *Chandráhba.*

Vern. Kápur, Hind. Karpur. Beng.

Two varieties of camphor are mentioned by Sanskrit writers, namely, *pakva* and *apakva,* that is prepared with the aid of heat

---

1 भूनिम्ब विश्वकल्कं जग्ध्वा पेयः पुनर्नवाक्वाथः। अपहरति नियतमाशु शोथं सर्व्वाङ्गजं न्टणाम् ॥

2 पुनर्नवाष्टकः। पुनर्नवानिम्बपटोलशुण्ठीतिक्तामृतादार्व्वभयाकषायः। सर्व्वाङ्गशोथोदर कासशूलश्वासान्वितं पाण्डुगदं निहन्ति ॥ चक्रदत्तः।

3 पुनर्नवातैलम्। पुनर्नवापलशतं जलद्रोणे विपाचयेत्। तेन पादावशेषेन तैलप्रस्थं विपाचयेत्। त्रिकटु त्रिफला शृङ्गी धन्याकं कट्फलं तथा। शठी दारुप्रियङ्गुश्च देवदारुहरेणुभिः। कुष्ठं पुनर्नवाघनं यमानी कारवी तथा। एला त्वचं पद्मकञ्च पत्रं नागरकेशरम्। एषाञ्च कार्षिकैः कल्कैः पेषयित्वा

and without it. The latter is considered superior to the former. It would seem from the above description that by the term *apakva karpura*, was probably meant the camphor obtained in Borneo from the trunk of *Dryobalanops aromatica*, (*Shorea Camphorifera*, *Roxb*). and by the term *pakva karpura*, the China camphor obtained by sublimation from the wood of *Cinnamomum Camphora*.

The *Rájanirghantu* describes an oil of camphor under the name of *karpura taila*. It is said to be useful in rheumatism and in giving firmness to loose teeth. This oil is not recognized or used by the native practitioners of the present day, but it most probably meant the camphor oil or liquid camphor obtained by making incisions on the Borneo camphor tree.

Camphor is regarded as carminative, stimulant and aphrodisiac; it is used in fever, diarrhœa, impotence, cough, eye-diseases, etc. It is also much used in the preparation of medicinal oils for imparting fragrance to them, singly as well as in combination with other aromatic substances. Camphor enters into the composition of numerous medicines for the diseases mentioned above. The following is an illustration.

Karpura rasa.[1] Take of cinnabar, opium, camphor, tubers of *Cyperus rotundus* (*mustaka*), *indrajava* seeds and nutmegs, equal parts; powder the ingredients, and make into four-grain pills with water. These pills are used in diarrhœa.

Camphor, rubbed with the milky juice of *Ficus Bengalensis*, is recommended to be applied to opacities on the cornea. It enters also into composition of several collyria.[2] A small tent made with

---

विनिक्षिपेत् । कामलापाण्डुरोगं च हलिमकमथापि वा । प्लीहानमुदरञ्चैव जीर्णज्वरव्यपोहति । तैलं पुनर्नवा नाममलव्याधिक्षयच्छति । सारकौमुदी ।

1 कर्पूररसः। हिङ्गुलमहिफेणञ्च मुस्तकेन्द्रयवं तथा । जातीफलञ्च कर्पूरं सर्वं संमर्द्य यत्नतः । जलेन वटिकाकार्य्या द्विगुञ्जापरिमाणतः । ज्वरातीसारिणे चैव तथातीसाररोगिणे । ग्रहणीषट्प्रकारे च रक्तातीसारलक्षणे । अत्र-केचित्टङ्कनमप्येकभागमिच्छन्ति । रसरत्नावली ।

2 वटक्षीरेणसंयुक्तं श्लक्ष्णं कर्पूरजं रजः । क्षिप्रमञ्जनतोहन्ति शुक्रञ्चापि घनोन्नतम् ॥ चक्रदत्तः ।

camphor is introduced into the urethra for the relief of irritability of the bladder and frequent micturition.[1]

CINNAMOMUM ZEYLANICUM, *Breyn.* Sans. गुड़त्वक्, *Guḍatvak.* Cinnamon is largely used as an aromatic adjunct in compound prescriptions. A combination of cinnamon, cardamoms and *tejapatra* leaves, passes by the name of *trijátaka*, these three aromatics being often used together.

CINNAMOMUM TAMALA, *Nees.* and other species, furnish the leaves called *tejapatra* in Sanskrit, and *tejpát* in the vernacular. They are an essential ingredient of Indian cookery. For remarks on their uses in medicine see *Cinnamomum Zeylanicum.*

NAT. ORDER MYRISTICEÆ.

MYRISTICA OFFICINALIS, *Linn.* Both nutmegs and mace enter into the composition of numerous medicines as aromatic adjuncts, but there is no peculiarity in their use that need special consideration here. An infusion of nutmegs is recommended by several writers as a serviceable drink in the thirst of cholera patients.[2]

NAT. ORDER SANTALEÆ.

SANTALUM ALBUM, *Linn.*

Sans. चन्दन, *Chandana,* श्रीखण्ड, *Srikhanḍa.*
Vern. Chandan, Beng. Saphed chandan, Hind.

SANSKRIT writers describe several varieties of *chandana* and some include the woods of *Pterocarpus Santalinus* (*raktachandana*) and *Cæsalpinia Sappan* (*pattanga*) under this common denomination. Excluding these last, two varieties of sandal wood are generally recognised, namely, *srikhanḍa* or white sandal wood

---

1 मेहनस्याययोनेर्वा सुखस्याभ्यन्तरे शनैः। घनसारयुतां वर्त्तिं धारयेन्मूत्रनिग्रहे। भावप्रकाशः।

2 पिपासायामनुत्क्लेशे लवङ्गस्याम्बु शस्यते। जातीफलस्य वा शीतं भृतं भद्रघनस्य वा। चक्रदत्तः।

and *pitachandana* or the yellow variety. These varieties are founded on the difference in the depth of colour in the heart-wood and not on any specific difference in the plants. The use of sandal wood in carving, and the elegant and fragrant articles made from it, are too well known to need description here. The Hindus use an emulsion of the wood in the worship of their idols and for painting or anointing their bodies after bathing. Rich natives sometimes use sandal wood for burning their dead relatives. Rich or poor, all add at least one piece of the wood to the funeral pile.

The essential oil of *chandan* (*chua chandana*) obtained by distillation from the heart-wood and roots, is of a pale yellow colour and has a peculiar fragrant smell best appreciated by rubbing a few drops of it on the hand. It is much used as a perfume by the Hindus both for themselves and for their idols. In Orissa it is a practice with the better classes to rub a little sandal oil in the spices which they take with their betle-leaf.

Sandal wood is described as bitter, cooling, astringent, and useful in biliousness, vomiting, fever, thirst and heat of body. An emulsion of the wood is used as a cooling application to the skin in erysipelas, prurigo and sudamina.[1] Two tolás of the watery emulsion of sandal wood, with the addition of sugar, honey and rice-water, is given to check gastric irritability and dysentery, and to relieve thirst and heat of body.[2]

NAT. ORDER EUPHORBIACEÆ.

PHYLLANTHUS EMBLICA, *Linn.*

Syn. Emblica officinalis, Gaertn.

Sans. आमलकी, *A'malaki,* धात्रि, *Dhátri.*

Vern A'mlaki, Beng. A'onlá, Hind.

Like chebulic myrobalan, emblic myrobalan is also extensively used in Hindu medicine, both alone and in combination

---

1 पित्तकृते विसर्पे लेपाविधेयाः बहवाः सुशीताः । प्रदेहाः परिषेकाश्च चन्दनैर्वा प्रशस्यते । चक्रदत्तः ।

2 पीतं मधुसितायुतं चन्दनं तण्डुलाम्बुना । रक्तातीसारजिद्रक्तपित्ततृड्दाहमेहनुत् ॥ भावप्रकाशः ।

with the two other myrobalans. The fresh fruits are glolular, six-striated, with a fleshy, acidulous pulp. A preserve of the ripe fruits made with sugar, is considered a wholesome article of diet and a preservative of health. The dried fruits are wrinkled, of a blackish grey colour, and have an acidulous, astringent taste.

The properties of emblic myrobaḷan are said to resemble those of the chebulic. The fresh juice is cooling, refrigerant, diuretic and laxative. The dried fruits are astringent and useful in hæmorrhages. It is said that the exudation from incisions made on the fruits while on the tree, is a very useful external application in recent inflammation of the eye. It is also used as a collyrium.[1]

The following preparation is used as a cooling and stomachic drink in irritability of the stomach. Take of emblic myrobalan, raisins, sugar and honey, eight tolas each, water half a seer; rub them together, strain through cloth and administer the strained fluid in suitable doses.[2]

About two drachms of emblic myrobalan is recommended to be given in the form of a paste, with the addition of honey for checking menorrhagia and discharge of blood from the uterus. The fresh juice of the ripe fruits is given with honey as a diuretic.[3] A paste of the fruits is applied over the pubic region in irritability of the bladder.[4]

Khanḍámalaki,[5] or confection of emblic myrobalan. Take of the pulp of an old gourd of *Benincasa cerifera, (kushmánḍa)* four

---

1 धात्रीफलनिर्य्यासोनवकोपं निहन्तिपूरणतः । तद्वत्सविद्धामलकरसः सर्व्वाक्षि रोगनुत् । चक्रदत्तः ।

2 पिष्ट्वाधात्रीफलं द्राक्षां शर्कराञ्चपलोन्मिताम् । दत्त्वा मधुपलञ्चात्र कुडवं सलिलस्य च। वाससागलितं पीतं हन्तिच्छर्दिं त्रिदोषजाम्। चक्रदत्तः ।।

3 धात्रीरसेन सक्षौद्रं सर्व्वमेहहरं परम् । चक्रदत्तः ।

4 आमलक्याश्च कल्केन वस्तिभागं प्रलेपयेत् । तेन शाम्यति क्षिप्रं नियमान्मूत्रनिग्रहः ।। भावप्रकाशः ।

5 खण्डामलकी । स्विन्नपीड़ितकुष्माण्डात्तुलार्द्धं भृष्टमाज्यतः । प्रस्थार्द्धे खण्डतुल्यन्तु पचेदामलकीरसात् । प्रस्थेस्विन्नकुष्माण्डरसप्रस्थे विघट्टयन् ।

hundred tolás, clarified butter two seers, sugar four hundred tolás, fresh emblic myrobalans four seers, juice of the gourd of *Benincasa cerifera*, four seers ; first dry the pulp of the gourd and fry it in the clarified butter. Express the juice of the emblic myrobalans and boil the fried pulp in the mixed juices of the emblic myrobalan and the pumpkin, with the addition of the sugar. When the syrup is thick enough, add the following aromatic substances, namely, long pepper, nigella seeds and ginger, each sixteen tolás, black pepper eight tolás, coriander, cinnamon, leaves called *tejapatra*, cardamoms, flowers of *Mesua ferrea (nágakesara)*, tubers of *Cyperus rotundus* (*mustaka*), and the leaves of *Pinus Webbiana* (*tálisa)*, each two tolás, (all in fine powder) and stir with a ladle till intimately mixed. Then add honey one seer and stir well till reduced to the consistence of a confection. This preparation is said to be useful in dyspepsia with pain and vomiting after meals, disinclination for food, pain in the precordial region, etc. It promotes the appetite and acts as a tonic.

Dhátri lauha.[1] Take of powdered emblic myrobalan, sixty-four tolás, prepared iron thirty-two tolás, liquorice powder sixteen tolás, mix them together and soak in the juice of *gulancha* for seven times successively. This preparation is given in doses of twenty to forty grains in anæmia, jaundice and dyspepsia.

दर्व्वीपाकं गते तस्मिंश्चूर्णीकृत्य विनिक्षिपेत्। द्वे द्वे पले कणाजाजीशुण्ठीनां मरिचस्य च। पलं तालीश धन्याक चातुर्जातक मुस्तकम्। कर्षप्रमाणं प्रत्येकं प्रस्थार्द्धं माक्षिकस्य च। पक्तिशूलं निहन्त्येतद्दोषत्रयभवञ्च यत्। छर्द्यम्लपित्तमूर्च्छाश्च श्वासकासावरोचकम्। हृच्छूलं रक्तपित्तञ्च पृष्ठशूलञ्च नाशयेत्। रसायनमिदं श्रेष्ठं खण्डामलकसंज्ञितम्। चक्रदत्तः।

1 धात्रीलौहम्। धात्रीचूर्णस्याष्टौ पलानि चत्वारि लौहचूर्णस्य। यष्टीमधुकरजश्च द्विपलं दद्यादुपले दृढम्। अमृताक्वाथेनैतच्चूर्णं भाव्यञ्च सप्ताहम्। चण्डातपेषु सुपक्वं भूयः पिष्ट्वा नवे घटे स्थाप्यम्। घृतमधुनासहयुक्तं भुक्तादौमध्यतोऽन्ते च। लीनपिबारान् खादेत्पथ्यं दोषानुबन्धेन। भक्तस्यादौ नाशयति व्याधीन् पित्तानिलोद्भवान्। मध्येऽन्नविष्टम्भं जयति नृणां विदह्यते नान्नम्। पानान्नकृतान् दोषान् भुक्त्यन्ते शीलितं जयति। एवं जीर्य्यति चान्ने शूलं नृणां सुकष्टमपि॥ चक्रदत्तः।

Dhátri arishṭa[1] or fermented liquor of emblic myrobalan. Take the fresh juice of two thousand emblic myrobalans, honey in quantity equal to one-eighth of the juice, powdered long pepper sixteen tolás, sugar six seers and a quarter; mix them together, boil for a while and leave the mixture to ferment in an earthen jar. This liquor is used in jaundice, dyspepsia, indigestion, cough, etc.

CROTON TIGLIUM, *Linn.*

Sans. जयपाल, *Jayapála.* कनकफल, *Kanakaphala*
Vern. Jaypál, Beng. Jamálgotá, Hind.

THE seeds of *Croton Tiglium* are considered heating, drastic, and useful in fever, constipation, intestinal worms, enlargements of the abdominal viscera, ascites, anasarca, etc. They are boiled in milk and their outer skin and embryo are removed before being used internally. Croton oil is not mentioned by any Sanskrit writer and was unknown to the ancient Hindus. Croton seeds enter into the composition of a great many medicines for the diseases mentioned above. The following are a few illustrations.

Ichchhávedivaṭiká.[2] Take of mercury, sulphur, borax and black pepper, one part each, ginger three parts, croton seeds nine parts; rub them together with water and make into two-grain pills. These are given in fever with constipation as also in ascites and anasarca.

Rukkesa rasa.[3] Take of chebulic myrobalan five parts, croton

---

1 धात्र्यरिष्टः। धात्रीफलसहस्रे द्वे पीड़यित्वा रसं भिषक्। क्षौद्राष्टभागं पिप्पल्याश्चूर्णार्द्धकुडवान्वितम्। शर्करार्द्धतुलोन्मिश्रं पक्वं स्निग्धघटे स्थितम्। प्रपिबेत्पाण्डुरोगार्त्तो जीर्णे हितमिताशनः। कामलापाण्डुहृद्रोगवातासृक्विषमज्वरान्। कासहिक्कारुचिश्वासानेषोऽरिष्टः प्रणाशयेत्।
चक्रदत्तः।

2 इच्छाभेदीरसः। शुद्धं पारदटङ्कणं समरिचं तुल्यांशगन्धा तथा विश्वा च त्रिगुणा ततो नवगुणं जैपालचूर्णं क्षिपेत्। गुञ्जैकप्रमितो रसो हिमजलैः संसेविते रेचयेद्यावन्नोष्णजलं पिबेदपि नरः पथ्यञ्च दध्योदनं। रसेन्द्रसारसंग्रहः

3 रुक्केशोरसः। अभयाचूर्णमादाय नूतनैर्जयपालजैः। पञ्चमांशेन मिलितैः स्नुहीदुग्धैर्विपाचितम्। गुडिकास्तस्य कर्त्तव्या वल्लाश्चणकप्रभाः। विष्टम्भे गुडिका देया चोदरे दारुणात्मके॥ रसेन्द्रसारसंग्रहः।

seeds one part, soak them in the milky juice of *Euphorbia neriifolia* (*snuhi*), and make into four-grain pills. These are given with a decoction of the root of *Ipomœa Turpethum* (*trivrit*), or *Baliospermum montanum* (*danti*), as a drastic purgative in obstinate constipation.

Mahánárácha rasa.[1] Take chebulic myrobalan, pulp of *Cassia Fistula*, emblic myrobalan, root of *Baliospermum montanum* (*danti*), *Picrorrhiza Kurroa* (*tiktá*), milky juice of *Euphorbia neriifolia* (*snuhi*), root of *Ipomœa Turpethum* (*trivrit*) and the tubers of *Cyperus rotundus* (*mustaka*), each one tolá; pound them to a coarse powder and boil in four seers of water till the latter is reduced to one-eighth. Then take a tola of husked croton seeds, tie them in a piece of thin cloth and boil them in the above mentioned decoction till the latter is reduced to the consistence of a fluid extract. To this extract add a powder composed of eight parts of purified croton seeds, three parts of ginger and two of black pepper, mercury and sulphur, in quantity sufficient to make a pill-mass; rub them together for twelve hours, and make into two-grain pills. These are given with cold water in tympanitis, colic, ascites, etc., as a drastic purgative. After the operation of this medicine, rice should be given with curdled milk and sugar.

BALIOSPERMUM MONTANUM, *Mull.*

Sans. दन्ती, *Danti. Vern. Danti, Hind. Beng.*

THE seeds of *Baliospermum montanum* are described as drastic. Like croton seeds they are boiled in milk before use. The root of the plant is considered cathartic. Both are much used in diseases where purgatives are indicated. The following are a few examples of prescriptions containing these medicines.

---

1 महानाराच रसः। अभयारग्वधो धात्री दन्ती तिक्ता स्नुही त्रिवृत्। मुस्ता-प्रत्येकमेतानि ग्राह्याणि पलमात्रया। तानि सङ्कुट्य सर्व्वाणि जलाढ़कयुगे पचेत्। तत्र तोयेऽष्टमं भागं कषायमवशेषयेत्। निस्त्वक्जैपालवीजानि नवानि पलमात्रया। तनुवस्त्रधृतान्येव तस्मिन् क्वाथे शनैः पचेत्। ज्वालयेदनलं मन्दं यावत् क्वाथो घनो भवेत्। ततः खल्वे क्षिपेद्भागानष्टौ जैपालवीजतः। भागान् त्रीन् नागरात् द्वौ च मरिचाद्द्वौ च पारदात्। गन्धकाद्द्वौ च तानीह यावद्यामं

Nárácha rasa.[1] Take of mercury, borax and black pepper, one part each, sulphur, ginger and long pepper two parts each, seeds of *Baliospermum montanum* nine parts; powder the ingredients and make into two-grain pills with water. These are given in constipation and tympanites.

Danti haritaki.[2] Take twenty-five large chebulic myrobalans and enclose them in a piece of cloth; then take of the roots of *Baliospermum montanum* and *Ipomœa Turpethum* (*trivrit*), each two hundred tolás, water sixty-four seers, boil them together till the water is reduced to eight seers. Strain the decoction, take out the chebulic myrobalans and fry them in thirty-two tolas of sesamum oil. To the strained decoction add two hundred tolás of old treacle; then boil till reduced to the proper consistence for a confection. Now add to the mass the following substances, namely powdered root of *Ipomœa Turpethum* (*trivrit*) thirty-two tolás, long pepper and ginger, each eight tolás, and stir them well; when cool add thirty-two tolás of honey, cinnamon, cardamom, leaves called *tejapatra*, and the flowers of *Mesua ferrea* (*nágakesara*) each

---

विमर्द्दयेत् । रसो नाराचनामायं भक्षितो रक्तिकामितः । जलेन शीतलेनैव रोगानेतान् विनाशयेत् । आध्मानं शूलमानाहं प्रत्याध्मानं तथैव च । उदावर्त्तं तथा गुल्ममुदराणि हरत्यसौ । वेगेशान्ते तु भुञ्जीत शर्करासहितं दधि । ततस्तत् सैन्धवेनापि ततो दध्योदनं समाक् । भावप्रकाशः ।

1 नाराचरसः । सूतटङ्कणकन्तुल्यं मरिचं समतुल्यकम् । गन्धकं पिप्पली शुण्ठी द्वौ द्वौ भागौ विचूर्णयेत् । सर्वतुल्यं क्षिपेद्दन्ती बीजन्निस्तुषितम्भवेत् । गुञ्जैकं रेचनं सिद्धन्नाराचोयं महारसः । आध्मानमलविष्टम्भमुदावर्त्तञ्च नाशयेत् । शार्ङ्गधरः ।

2 दन्तीहरीतकी । जलद्रोणे विपक्तव्या विंशतिः पञ्च चाभयाः । दन्त्याः पलानि तावन्ति चित्रकस्य तथैव च । तेनाष्टभागशेषेण पचेद्दन्तीसमं गुडम् । ताश्चाभया त्रिवृच्चूर्णात्तैलाच्चापि चतुःपलम् । पलमेकं कणाशुण्ठ्योः सिद्धे लेहे च शीतले । क्षौद्रं तैलसमं दद्याच्चातुर्जातपलन्तथा । ततो लेहपलं लीढ्वा जग्ध्वा चैकां हरीतकीम् । सुखं विरिच्यते स्निग्धो दोषप्रस्थमनामयः । प्लीहश्वयथुगुल्मार्शो हृत्पाण्डुग्रहणीगदाः । शाम्यन्त्युत्क्लेशविषमज्वरकुष्ठान्यरोचकाः । चक्रदत्तः ।

eight tolás, and prepare a confection. The chebulic myrobalans should be kept imbedded in the medicine. Two tolás of the confection and one of the chebulic myrobalans are to be taken every morning.

Gudáshṭaka.[1] Take of *danti*, *trivrit* and plumbago roots, black pepper, long pepper, ginger and long pepper root, equal parts in fine powder; treacle, equal in weight to all the other ingredients and mix. Dose, about a tola every morning in flatulence and retained secretions, anasarca, jaundice, etc.

RICINIS COMMUNIS, *Linn.*

Sans. एरण्ड, *Eranḍa.* रुवुक, *Ruvuka.*

Vern. Bherendá, Beng. Erenḍ. Hind.

THE root of *Ricinis Communis* and the oil obtained from the seeds have been used in medicine by the Hindus from a very remote period. They are mentioned by Susruta. Two varieties of the plant are described, namely red and white. Their properties are said to be identical. Castor oil is regarded as purgative and useful in costiveness, tympanitis, fever, inflammation, etc. It is much praised for its efficacy in chronic rheumatic affections in which it is used in various combinations. One of its synonyms is *vátári* or anti-rheumatic. The root of the plant is also said to be particularly useful in the local varieties of rheumatism such as lumbago, pleurodynia, and sciatica.

As a purgative, castor oil is recommended to be taken with cow's urine, or an infusion of ginger or a decoction of the combination called *dasamula* (see *Desmodium gangeticum*).[2]

---

1 गुड़ाष्टकम् । व्योषं दन्ती त्रिवृच्चित्रं कृष्णामूलं विचूर्णितम् । तच्चूर्णं गुड़सम्मिश्रं भक्षयेत् प्रातरुत्थितः । एतद्गुड़ाष्टकं नाम बलवर्णाग्निवर्द्धनम् । शोथोदावर्त्त शूलघ्नं प्लीहपाण्ड्वामयापहम् । सर्व्वचूर्णसमो गुड़ो देयः ।

भावप्रकाशः ।

2 दशमूलीकषायेण पिबेद्वा नागराम्भसा । कटिशूलेषु सर्व्वेषु तैलमेरण्डसम्भवम् ।

चक्रदत्तः ।

The seeds, freed from impurities and rubbed into a paste, are boiled in milk and water, and the decoction is given in lumbago and sciatica.[1] In pleurodynia, or pain in the sides, a decoction of the root is given with the addition of *yavakshára*, (impure carbonate of potash).[2] The root of *Ricinis communis* enters into the composition of various compound prescriptions for rheumatic affections and diseases of the nervous system.

In affections of the eyes, castor oil leaves and root are used in a variety of forms and several prescriptions containing them are given by most writers. A decoction of the bark, leaves and root of the plant, in goat's milk and water is recommended for use as a wash in recent ophthalmia.[3]

MALLOTUS PHILIPPENSIS, *Mull.*

Syn. Rottlera tinctoria, Roxb.

Sans. कम्पिल्ल, *Kampilla,* रेचनक, *Rechanaka.*

Vern. Kamilá, Beng. Kambilá, Kamalá, Hind.

ROXBURGH and Brandis give *Punnága* as the Sanskrit for this plant. As far as my information goes, *Punnága* is the Sanskrit for *Calophyllum inophyllum*, a large tree of the Coromandel Coast with beautiful white fragrant flowers and numerous stamens arranged in rows. *Kampilla* is the red mealy powder covering the capsules of *Mallotus Philippensis.* It is described as cathartic and anthelmintic and is chiefly used to expel intestinal worms. *Kampilla* powder given in doses of one tolá with treacle, is said to kill and expel all intestinal worms.[4] It enters into the composition of

---

1 विशोध्यैरण्डबीजानि पिष्ट्वा क्षीरे विपाचयेत्। तत्पायसं कटीशूले गृध्रस्यां परमौषधम्। भावप्रकाशः।

2 एरण्डमूलं द्विपलं जलेऽष्टगुणिते पचेत्। तत् क्वाथो यावशूकाढ्यः पार्श्वहृत्कफशूलहा। शार्ङ्गधरः।

3 एरण्डपल्लवे मूले त्वचि चाजं पयः शृतम्। कण्टकार्य्याश्च मूलेषु सुखोष्णं सेचने हितम्। चक्रदत्तः।

4 कम्पिल्लचूर्णकर्षार्द्धं गुडेन सह भक्षितम्। पातयेत् क्रिमीन् सर्व्वानुदरस्थान्नसंशयः। भावप्रकाशः।

numerous compound prescriptions for worms. The following is an illustration. Take of *kampilla*, *báberang* seeds, chebulic myrobalan *yavakshára* (impure carbonate of potash), and rock salt, equal parts; powder and mix. Dose, about a drachm, with butter-milk.[1]

EUPHORBIA NERIIFOLIA, *Linn.*

Syn. Euphorbia ligularia, Roxb.

Sans. स्नुहि, *Snuhi*, वज्री, *Vajri*, सेहुण्ड, *Sehunḍa*.

Vern. Mansásij, Beng. Sehund, Thohar, Hind.

THIS prickly shrub is sacred to Mansá the goddess of serpents. On the fifth day after full moon of the month of Sravana (July, August) it is planted in the court-yard of Hindu houses and worshipped as the representative of Mansá the goddess of serpents. *Euphorbia antiquorum*, called *tekáṭá sij* in Bengali on account of its triangular stem, is probably alluded to by some Sanskrit writers under the name of *vajri*, which is explained as a variety of *snuhi*. This plant is supposed to ward off lightening strokes and is generally kept in tubs or pots on the roofs or other exposed parts of native houses. Its popular medicinal uses are like those of *Euphorbia neriifolia*.

The milky juice of *Euphorbia neriifolia* is considered purgative and rubefacient. As a purgative it is generally used in combination with other medicines which are steeped in it. Chebulic myrobalan, long pepper, *trivrit* root, etc., are thus treated and administered as drastic purgatives, in ascites, anasarca and tympanitis.[2] It enters into the composition of several compound prescriptions of a drastic character as for example, the *Mahánárácha rasa* described under *Croton Tiglium*, and *Vindu ghrita* a preparation with clarified butter, of similar composition.

Turmeric powder mixed with the milky juice of *Euphorbia*

---

1 विड़ङ्गसैन्धवक्षारकाम्पिल्लकहरीतकीः । पिबेत्तक्रेण संपिष्टाः सर्व्वक्रिमिनिवृत्तये । चक्रदत्तः ।

2 त्रिवृद्धरीतकी श्यामाः स्नुहीक्षीरेण भावयेत् । वटिकामूत्रपीताश्चाः श्रेष्ठाश्चानाहभेदिकाः । चक्रदत्तः ।

neriifolia is recommended to be applied to piles.[1] Thread steeped in the above mentioned mixture is used in ligaturing external hæmorrhoids.[2] The powdered wood of *Berberis Asiatica* (*dáruharidrá*) is steeped in the milky juice of *snuhi* and of *Calotropis gigantea* (*arka*), and made into tents for introduction into the tracks of fistula in ano and other sinuses.[3]

NAT. ORDER MYRICEÆ.

MYRICA SAPIDA, *Wall.*

Sans. कट्फल, *Kaṭphala. Vern. Káephal, Hind.*

The bark of *Myrica sapida* (a Himalayan tree), is its most valuable product, and is largely exported to the plans. It is dark or browish grey, with deep vertical wrinkles, and is considered heating, stimulant and useful in diseases supposed to be caused by deranged phlegm, such as catarrhal fever, cough, and affections of the throat. It enters into the composition of numerous formulæ for these diseases. The following is an example.

Kaṭphaládi Churna.[4] Take of the bark of *Myrica sapida*, tubers of *Cyperus rotundus* (*mustaka*), root of *Picrorrhiza Kurroa* (*kaṭuki*), *Curcuma Zedoaria* (*saṭi*), *Rhus succedanea* (*karkarṭa sringi*), and the root of *Aplotaxis auriculata* (*kushṭa*), equal parts ; powder and mix. This powder is given in doses of about a drachm with the addition of ginger-juice and honey in affections of the throat, cough and asthma.

In catarrh with headache the powdered bark is occasionally used as a snuff.

---

1 स्नुक्क्षीरं रजनीयुक्तं लेपाद्दुर्नामनाशनम् । चक्रदत्तः ।

2 भावितं रजनीचूर्णैः स्नुहीक्षीरे पुनः पुनः । बन्धनात् सुदृढ़ं सूत्रं भिनत्त्यर्शो भगन्दरम् । चक्रदत्तः ।

3 स्नुह्यार्कदुग्ध दार्व्वीभिर्वर्त्तिं कृत्वा विचक्षणः । भगन्दरगतिं ज्ञात्वा पूरयेत्तां प्रयत्नतः । एषा सर्वशरीरस्थां नाड़ीं हन्यान्नसंशयः । चक्रदत्तः ।

4 कट्फलादिचूर्णम् । कट्फलं मुस्तकतिक्ता शटीशृङ्गी च पुष्करम् । चूर्णमेषाञ्च मधुना शृङ्गवेररसेन च लिह्येत् । ज्वरहरं कण्ठ्यं कासश्वासारुचीं-जयेत् । वायुच्छर्दिं तथाश्शूलं क्षयञ्चैव व्यपोहति । शार्ङ्गधरः ।

NAT. ORDER URTICEÆ.

FICUS RELIGIOSA, *Linn. Sans.* अश्वत्थ, *Asvattha. Vern. Pipal, Hind.*

FICUS BENGALENSIS, *Linn. Sans.* वट, *Vaṭa. Vern. Bar. Hind.*

FICUS GLOMERATA, *Willd. Sans.* उडुम्बर, *Uḍumbara. Vern. Jagnoḍumar, Beng. Gular, Hind.*

FICUS INFECTORIA, *Roxb. Sans.* पर्कटि, *Parkaṭi. Vern. Pákur, Beng. Pákri, Hind.*

THE root-barks of these four species of *Ficus* together with that of *Azadarachta Indica* pass by the name of *panchavalkala* or the five barks, and are used in combination. A decoction of these barks, called *pancha valkala kasháya* is much used as a gargle in salivation, as a wash for ulcers, and as an injection in leucorrhœa.[1] The powdered root-bark of *Ficus religiosa* rubbed with honey is applied to aphthous sores of children.[2] It is also sprinkled over unhealthy ulcers to improve their condition and promote granulation.[3]

The figs of *Ficus glomerata* are considered astringent, stomachic and carminative and are given in menorrhagia and hæmoptysis in doses of one tolá of the dried fruits with sugar and honey.[4] The fresh juice of the ripe fruit is given as an adjunct to a metallic medicine for diabetes and other urinary complaints, called *Vrihat vangesvara rasa*, (see Tin).

CANNABIS SATIVA, *Linn.* VAR. INDICA.

Sans. विजया, *Vijayá*, भङ्गा, *Bhangá*, गञ्जा, *Ganjá*, इन्द्रासन, *Indrásana. Vern. Siddhi, Bháng, Beng. Bháng. Hind.*

THE *Cannabis sativa* has been used from a very remote period both in medicine and as an intoxicating agent. A mythological

---

1 प्रदेहाः परिषेकाश्च शस्यन्ते पञ्चवल्कलैः । चक्रदत्तः ।

2 अश्वत्थत्वग्दलक्षौद्रैर्मुखपाके प्रलेपनम् । चक्रदत्तः ।

3 अन्तर्दग्धकुठारकोद्दहनजं लेपाश्चिहन्तिव्रणान्। अश्वत्थस्य विशुष्कवल्कलकृतं चूर्णं तथागुण्ठनात् । चक्रदत्तः ।

4 समाक्षिकः फल्गुफलोद्भवो वा पीतोरसः शोणितमाशुहन्ति। क्षौद्रयुक्तं

origin has been invented for it. It is said to have been produced in the shape of nectar while the gods were churning the ocean with the mountain called Mandára. It is the favourite drink of Indra the king of gods, and is called *vijayá*, because it gives success to its votaries. The gods through compassion on the human race sent it to this earth so that mankind by using it habitually may attain delight, loose all fear, and have their sexual desires excited.[1] On the last day of the Durga pooja, after the idols are thrown into water, it is customary for the Hindus to see their friends and relatives and embrace them. After this ceremony is over it is incumbent on the owner of the house to offer to his visitors a cup of *bháng* and sweet-meats for tiffin.

An intoxicating agent with such recommendations cannot but be popular and so we find it in general use amongst all classes especially in the North-West provinces and Behar. In Bengal it has latterly become the fashion to substitute brandy, but I well remember having seen in the days of my boyhood the free use of *bháng* among the better classes of people who would have shunned as a pariah any one of their society addicted to the use of the forbidden spirituous liquor. At the doors of many rich baboos, Hindustani durwans could be seen rubbing the *bháng* in a stone mortar with a long wooden pestle, and the paste so prepared was not solely intended for the use of the servants. I do not mean to say that all classes of Hindoos without exception are or were addicted to the use of *bháng*. Some castes among the up-country men and some classes of people amongst Bengalis are as a rule very temperate in their habits and do not use any narcotic at all; but the ordinary run of orthodox Hindus, accustomed to have their little excitements, use

---

फलरसं कोष्णोदुम्बरजं पिबेत् । असृग्दरविनाशाय सशर्करपयोन्नभुक् ।

चक्रदत्तः ।

1 जाता मन्दरमन्थनाज्जलनिधौ पीयूषरूपा पुरा त्रैलोक्यविजयप्रदेति विजया श्रीदेवराजप्रिया । लोकानां हितकाम्यया क्षितितले प्राप्ता नरैः कामदा सर्व्वातङ्कविनाशहर्षजननी यैः सेविता सर्वदा । राजवल्लभः ।

bháng for the purpose without incurring any opprobium such as would result from the use of spirituous liquors.

The three principal forms in which Indian hemp is met with in India are,—1, *Gánjá*, the dried flowering tops of the female plant, from which the resin has not been removed. 2, *Charas*, the resinous exudation from the leaves, stems and flowers. 3, *Bháng*, the larger leaves and seed vessels without the stalks.

Sir William O'Shaughnessy has so well described the preparations of Indian hemp in use amongst the natives, and his name is so intimately associated with the history of this drug, that I cannot do better than quote his account of them.

" *Sidhee*, *Subjee* and *Bháng* (synonymous) are used with water as a drink which is thus prepared :—About three tolás' weight (540 troy grains) are well washed with cold water, then rubbed to powder, mixed with black pepper, cucumber and melon seeds, sugar, half a pint of milk and an equal quantity of water. This is considered sufficient to intoxicate an habituated person. Half the quantity is enough for a novice. This composition is chiefly used by the Mahomedans of the better classes.

" Another recipe is as follows:—

The same quantity of *Siddhi* is washed and ground, mixed with black pepper, and a quart of cold water added. This is drank at one sitting. This is the favourite beverage of the Hindus who practice this vice, especially the Birjobassies and many of the Rajpootana soldiery.

" From either of these beverages intoxication will ensue in half an hour. Almost invariably the inebriation is of the most cheerful kind, causing the person to sing and dance, to eat food with great relish, and to seek aphrodisiac enjoyments. In persons of a quarrelsome disposition it occasions, as might be expected, an exasperation of their natural tendency. The intoxication lasts about three hours, when sleep supervenes. No nausea or sickness of stomach succeeds, nor are the bowels at all affected; next day there is slight giddiness and vascularity of the eyes, but no other symptom worth recording.

" *Gánja* is used for smoking alone: one rupee weight, (180 grains) and a little dried tobacco are rubbed together in the palm of the hand, with a few drops of water. This suffices for three persons. A little tobacco is placed in the pipe first, then a layor of the prepared *gánga*, then more tobacco and the fire above all. Four or five persons usually join in this debauch. The *hookáh* is passed round, and each person takes a single draught. Intoxication ensues almost instantly and from one draught to the unaccustomed; within half an hour, and after four or five inspirations to those more practised in the vice. The effects differ from those occasioned by the *siddhi*. Heaviness, laziness, and agreeable reveries ensue, but the person can be readily roused and is able to discharge routine occupations, such as pulling the pánkah, waiting at table, etc.

"The *Májoon* or hemp confection, is a compound of sugar, butter, flour, milk, and *siddhi* or *bháng*. The process has been repeatedly performed before us by Ameer, the proprietor of a celebrated place of resort for hemp devotees in Calcutta and who is considered the best artist in his profession. Four ounces of *siddhi* and an equal quantity of *ghee* are placed in an earthen or well-tinned vessel, a pint of water added, and the whole warmed over a charcoal fire. The mixture is constantly stirred until the water all boils away, which is known by the crackling noise of the melted butter on the sides of the vessel; The mixture is then removed from the fire, squeezed through cloth while hot, by which an oleaginous solution of the active principles and colouring matter of the hemp is obtained; and the leaves, fibres, etc., remaining on the cloth are thrown away. The green oily solution soon concretes into a buttery mass and is then well washed by the hand with soft water, so long as the water becomes coloured. The colouring matter and an extractive substance are thus removed and a very pale green mass, of the consistence of simple ointment, remains. The washings are thrown away; Ameer says that these are intoxicating, and produce constriction of the throat, great pain and very disagreeable and dangerous symptoms.

"The operator then takes two pounds of sugar, and adding a little water, places it in a pipkin over the fire. When the sugar dissolves and froths, two ounces of milk are added; a thick scum rises and is removed; more milk and a little water are added from time to time, and the boiling continued about an hour, the solution being carefully stirred until it becomes an adhesive clear syrup, ready to solidify on a cold surface ; four ounces of tyre (new milk dried before the sun) in fine powder are now stirred in, and lastly the prepared butter of hemp is introduced, brisk stirring being continued for a few minutes. A few drops of áttar of roses are then quickly sprinkled in, and the mixture poured from the pipkin on a flat cold dish or slab. The mass concretes immediately into a thick cake, which is divided into small lozenge-shaped pieces. A seer thus prepared sells for four rupees. One drachm by weight will intoxicate a beginner ; three drachms, one experienced in its use. The taste is sweet and the odour very agreeable. Ameer states that sometimes by special order of customers he introduces stramonium seeds, but never nux vomica ; that all classes of persons including the lower Portugese or Kala Feringhees and especially their females, consume the drug ; that it is most fascinating in its effects, producing extatic happiness, a persuasion of high rank, a sensation of flying, voracious appetite and intense aphrodisiac desire."*

The leaves of *Cannabis sativa* are purified by being boiled in milk before use. They are regarded as heating, digestive, astringent, and narcotic. The intoxication produced by *bháng* is said to be of a pleasant description and to promote talkativeness.

In sleeplessness, the powder of the fried leaves is given in suitable doses for inducing sleep and removing pain.[1]

Játiphaládya churna.[2] Take of nutmeg, cloves, cinnamon,

* Bengal Dispensatory, p. 582.

1 भृष्टन्तु विजयाचूर्णं मधुनामिश्रि भक्षयेत्। निद्रानाशेऽतिसारे च ग्रहणीयां पावकक्षये। दर्पणः।

2 जातीफलाद्यं चूर्णम्। जातीफललवङ्गैलापत्रैस्त्वग्नागकेशरैः। कर्पूरचन्दनतिलैस्त्वक्क्षीरीतगरामलैः। तालीशपिप्पलीपथ्या चित्रक स्थूलजीरकैः। शुण्ठीविडङ्गमरिचैः समभागानि चूर्णितैः। यावन्त्येतानि सर्वाणि कुर्याद्भङ्गा च तावती। सर्वचूर्णसमा देया शर्करा च भिषग्वरैः। कर्षमात्रं तथा खादेन्मधुना प्लावितं सुधीः। अस्य प्रभावाद्ग्रहणीकासश्वासारुचिक्षयान्। वातश्लेष्मप्रतिश्यायः प्रशमं यातिवेगतः। शार्ङ्गधरः।

cardamon, *tejapatra* leaves, flowers of *Mesua ferrea* (*nágakesara*), camphor, sandal wood, sesamum seeds, bamboo manna, flowers of *Tabernæmontana coronaria* (*tagara*), chebulic and emblic myrobalans, long pepper, black pepper, ginger, leaves of *Pinus Webbiana* (*tálisa*), plumbago root, cumin seeds and the seeds of *Embelia Ribes* (*viranga*), equal parts, purified *bháng* equal in weight to all the above ingredients, and sugar twice as much as the *bháng*. Powder and mix. Dose, about twenty to forty grains. This preparation is given in diarrhœa, indigestion and loss of appetite.

Jválánala rasa.[1] Take of *yavakshára*, and *sarjikákshára*, (impure carbonates of potash and soda) borax, mercury, sulphur, long pepper, black pepper, *Piper Chaba* (*chavya*) and ginger, equal parts, fried leaves of *Cannabis sativa* equal to all the above ingredients, root of *Moringa pterygosperma* half the weight of *bháng*; powder the ingredients, mix and soak the mixed powder for three days in each of the following fluids, namely a decoction or fresh juice of the leaves of *Cannabis Indica*, the roots of *Moringa pterygosperma*, and *Plumbago rosea*, and dry in the sun. Then roast the mass lightly and make into a pill mass with the juice of the leaves of *Wedelia calendulacea* (*bhringarája*). Dose, about half a drachm with honey. This medicine is given in indigestion and loss of appetite with nausea and vomiting.

Numerous confections of *bháng*, such as *Kámesvara modaka*, *Madana modaka*, *Bályasakrásana modaka*, etc., are described in books. These, as their names imply, are considered aphrodisiac and are used in chronic bowel complaints and nervous debility. Most of them are prepared with equal parts of a number of supposed tonic and aphrodisiac substances in small quantities and *bháng* equal in weight to all the other ingredients, together with

---

1 ज्वालानलोरसः। क्षारत्रयं सूतगन्धौ पञ्चकोलमिदं समम्। सर्वैस्तुल्या जया भृष्टा तदर्द्धा शिग्रुजा जटा। एतत्सर्वं जया शिग्रु वह्नीनां केवलैर्द्रवैः। भावयेत् त्रिदिनं घर्म्मे ततो लघुपुटे पचेत्। मार्कवस्य द्रवैर्द्दष्टो रसो ज्वालानलो भवेत्। निष्कोऽस्य मधुनालीढो ऽनुपानं गुड़नागरम्। हन्त्यजीर्णमतीसारं ग्रहणीमग्निमान्द्यम्। सशूलश्वासवमनमालस्य मरुचिं जयेत्। भावप्रकाशः।

sugar, honey and the usual aromatics. *Májoon*, the preparation of which has been already described, would I believe be a neater substitute for these complicated preparations. The following is an illustration.

Madana modaka.[1] Take of the three myrobalans, ginger, long pepper, black pepper, *Rhus succedanea* (*sringi*), *páchak* root, coriander, rock salt, zedoary root, leaves of *Pinus Webbiana* (*tálisa*), bark of *Myrica sapida* (*katphala*) flowers of *Mesua ferrea* (*nágakesara*), *ajowan*, seeds of *Seseli Indicum* (*vanuyamáni*), liquorice root, seeds of *Trigonella fœnum-græcum* (*methi*), cumin and nigella seeds equal parts ; hemp leaves with flowers and seeds fried in clarified butter, equal in weight to all the other ingredients ; sugar equal in weight to the hemp. Prepare a syrup with the sugar, then add the other substances in fine powder and make into a confection. Lastly add clarified butter, honey, powdered sesamum seeds, cardamoms, cinnamon, *tejapatra* leaves and camphor, each two tolás, and make into boluses of about eighty grains each. This confection is used in cough, chronic bowel complaints and impotence.

NAT. ORDER PIPERACEÆ.

PIPER NIGRUM, *Linn.*

Sans. मरिच, *Maricha,* उषण, *Ushana.*

Vern. Golmarich, Beng. Kálimarich, Hind.

THE use of black pepper as a condiment is too well known to require any notice here. Medicinally it is much used in combina-

---

1 मदनमोदकः। त्रैलोक्यविजयापत्रं सबीजं घृतभर्जितम्। त्रिकटु त्रिफला शृङ्गी कुष्ठं धान्यक सैन्धवम्। शठीतालीशपत्रञ्च कट्फलं नागकेशरम्। अजमोदा यमानी च यष्टीमधुकमेव च। मेथीजीरकयुग्मञ्च गृहीत्वा श्लक्ष्ण चूर्णितम्। यावन्त्येतानि चूर्णानि तावदेव तदौषधम्। तावदेवसिताद्देया यावदायाति बन्धनम्। घृतेन मधुनामिश्रं मोदकं परिकल्पयेत्। भर्जितं तिलचूर्णञ्च मोदको परिविन्यसेत्। त्रिसुगन्धसमायुक्तं कर्पूरेनाधिवासितम्। स्थापयेत् घृतभाण्डे तु श्रीमदनमोदकम्। सर्वरोगहरं ह्येतत् संग्रह ग्रहणी हरम्। एतस्य सततास्यासाद्वृद्धोऽपि तरुणायते। एतत् कामप्रबृद्ध्यर्थं नारदेन प्रभाषितम्। सारकौमुदी।

tion with long pepper and ginger, under the name of *trikatu* or the three acrids. In fact, as any reader who has gone through these pages must have noticed, very few compound prescriptions are free from the three myrobalans, and the three acrids, which seem to be added often without reason, and sometimes for the sake of rhyme. Black pepper is described as acrid, pungent, hot, dry, carminative and useful in intermittent fever, hæmorrhoids and dyspepsia. Externally it is used as a rubefacient in alopecia and skin diseases.

In intermittent fever, black pepper in doses of about a drachm, is recommended to be given with the juice of the leaves of *Ocimum sanctum* (*tulasi*), or *Leucas linifolia* (*dronapushpi*).[1] It enters into the composition of numerous prescriptions for dyspepsia, piles and indigestion. The following is an example.

Pránadá guḍiká.[2] Take of black pepper thirty-two tolás, ginger twenty-four tolás, long pepper sixteen tolás, *Piper Chaba* (*chavya*) eight tolás, leaves of *Pinus Webbiana* (*tálisa*) eight tolás, flowers of *Mesua ferrea*, (*nágakesara*) four tolás, long pepper root sixteen tolás, leaves called *tejapatra* and cinnamon one tolá each, cardamoms and the root of *Andropogon muricatus*, (*usira*) two tolás each, old treacle two hundred and forty tolás; rub them together. Dose, about two drachms. This confection is given in hæmorrhoids. When there is costiveness and a sense of heat, chebulic myrobalan is substituted for the ginger in the above prescription.

The bald patches of alopecia are recommended to be rubbed

---

1 पीतो मरिचचूर्णेन तुलसीपत्रजोरसः । द्रोणपुष्पी रसोवापि निहन्ति-विषमज्वरान् । भावप्रकाशः ।

2 प्राणदागुड़िका । त्रिपलं शृङ्गवेरस्य चतुर्थं मरिचस्य च । पिप्पल्याः कुडवार्द्धञ्च चव्यायाः पलमेव च । तालीशपत्रस्य पलं पलार्द्धं केशरस्य च । द्वे पले पिप्पलीमूलादर्द्धकर्षञ्च पत्रकात् । सूक्ष्मैलाकर्षमेकन्तु कर्षं त्वगमृणालयोः । गुड़ात् पलानि तु त्रिंशत् चूर्णमेकत्रकारयेत् । अक्षप्रमाणागुड़िका-प्राणदेति च साम्मृता । पूर्व्वं भक्षेत्तु पश्चात्तु भोजनस्य यथाबलम् । मद्यं मांसरसं यूषं क्षीरं तोयं पीवेत्तथा । हन्यादर्शांसि सर्व्वाणि सहजान्यस्रजानि च । वातपित्तकफोत्थानि सन्निपातोद्भवानि च । चक्रदत्तः ।

with some rough leaves as of *Streblus asper* (*sákhoṭa*) and then sprinkled over with powdered black pepper.[1]

PIPER LONGUM, *Linn.*

Syn. Chavica Roxburghii, Miq.

Sans. पिप्पली, *Pippali.* कणा, *Kaná,* कृष्णा, *Krishná.*

Vern. Pipul, Beng. Pipal, Hind.

THE dried catkins and the root of *Piper longum* are used in medicine. They are considered heating, stimulant, carminative, alterative, laxative and useful in cough, hoarseness, asthma, dyspepsia, paralysis, etc. Old long pepper is said to be more efficacious than the fresh article. In the form of *trikatu* or the three acrids (see *Piper nigrum*), it is much used as an aromatic adjunct in compound prescriptions. Powdered long pepper, administered with honey, is said to relieve cough, asthma, hoarseness, hiccup and sleeplessness.[2] A mixture of long pepper, long pepper root, black pepper and ginger in equal parts, is prescribed by several writers as a useful combination for catarrh and hoarseness.[3]

As an alterative tonic, long pepper is recommended for use in a peculiar manner. An infusion of three long peppers is to be taken with honey on the first day, then for ten successive days the dose is to be increased by three peppers every day, so that on the tenth day the patient will take thirty at one dose. Then the dose is to be gradually reduced by three daily and finally the medicine is to be omitted. Thus administered it is said to act as a valuable alterative tonic in paraplegia, chronic cough, enlargements of the spleen and other abdominal viscera, etc.[4]

---

1 हृष्टस्य कर्कशैः पत्रैरिन्द्रलुप्तस्य गुण्ठनम् । चूर्णितैर्मरिचैः कार्य्यमिन्द्रलुप्तनिवारणम् । चक्रदत्तः ।

2 मधुना पिप्पलीचूर्णं लिह्येत्कासज्वरापहम् । हिक्काश्वासहरं कण्ठ्यं प्लीहघ्नं बालकोचितम् । भावप्रकाशः ।

3 पिप्पलीपिप्पलीमूलं मरिचं विश्वभेषजम् । पिबेत् मूत्रेण मतिमान् कफजे स्वरसंक्षये । भावप्रकाशः ।

4 पिप्पलीवर्द्धमानानि । क्रमवृद्ध्या दशाहानि दशपिप्पलिकं दिनम् । वर्द्धयेत् पयसा सार्द्धं तथैवापनयेत् पुनः । जीर्णे जीर्णे च भुञ्जीत षष्टिकं क्षीर-

Long pepper and black pepper enter into the composition of several irritating snuffs. The following is an example. Take of black pepper, long pepper, seeds of *Moringa pterygosperma* (*sveta maricha*) and ginger equal parts; powder the ingredients and rub them together with the juice of the root of *Agaṭi grandiflora* (*vaka*). This preparation is used as a snuff in coma and drowsiness.

Ashṭakaṭvara taila.[1] Take of ginger and long pepper each sixteen tolas, mustard oil four seers, butter-milk thirty-two seers, curdled milk four seers and boil them together in the usual way. This oil is rubbed externally in sciatica and paraplegia.

PIPER CHABA, *Hunter. Sans.* चविका, *Chaviká. Vern. Chai, Beng. Cháb, Hind.* The fruits of this species of *Piper* are considered stimulant, anti-catarrhal and carminative and are much used as adjuncts to medicines for cough, cold and hoarseness.

PIPER BETLE, *Linn.*

Sans. ताम्बुल, *Támbula. Vern. Pán, Beng. Hind.*

THE leaves of this creeper are, as is well known, masticated by the natives of India. The poorer classes make their packet of betle with the addition of lime, catechu and betle-nuts. The rich add cardamoms, nutmegs, cloves, camphor and other aromatics. Betle-leaf thus chewed acts as a gentle stimulant and exhilarant. Those accustomed to its use feel a sense of langour when deprived of it. The ancient Hindu writers recommend that betle-leaf should be taken early in the morning, after meals and at bedtime.

सर्पिषा । पिप्पलीनां प्रयोगोऽयं सहस्रस्य रसायनः । दशपिप्पलिकः श्रेष्ठो-मध्यमः षट्प्रकीर्त्तितः । यस्त्रिपिप्पलिपर्य्यन्तः प्रयोगः सोऽवरः स्मृतः । बृंहणं स्वर्य्यमायुष्यं प्लीहोदरविनाशनम् । वयसः स्थापनं मेध्यं पिप्पलीनां रसायनम् । पञ्चपिप्पलिकश्चापि दृश्यते वर्द्धमानकः । पिष्टास्ताबलिभिः पेयाः शृतामध्यबलैर्नरैः । शीतीकृताह्रस्वबलैर्देहदोषामयान् प्रति । चक्रदत्तः ।

1 अष्टकट्वरं तैलम् । पलाभ्यां पिप्पलीमूलनागराद्दष्टकट्वरः । तैलप्रस्थः समो दध्ना गृध्रस्यूरुग्रहापहः । अष्टकट्वरतैलेऽस्मिन्तैलं सार्षपमिष्यते । चक्रदत्तः

According to Susruta, it is aromatic, carminative stimulant, and astringent. It sweetens the breath, improves the voice and removes all foulness from the mouth. According to other writers it acts as an aphrodisiac.

Medicinally it is said to be useful in diseases supposed to be caused by deranged phlegm and its juice is much used as an adjunct to pills administered in these diseases; that is, the pills are rubbed into an emulsion with the juice of the betle-leaf and licked up. Being always at hand, *pán* leaves are used as a domestic remedy in various ways. The stalk of the leaf smeared with oil is introduced into the rectum in the constipation and tympanitis of children, with the object of inducing the bowels to act. The leaves are applied to the temples in headache for relieving pain, to painful and swollen glands for promoting absorption, and to the mammary glands with the object of checking the secretion of milk. *Pán* leaves are used as a ready dressing for foul ulcers which seem to improve under them.

NAT. ORDER CONIFERÆ.

PINUS WEBBIANA, *Wall.*

Syn. Abies Webbiana, Lindl.

Sans. तालीशपत्र, *Tálisapatra, Vern. Tálispatra Beng. Hind.*

The dried leaves used by Kavirajas under the name of *tálisapatra*, were identified at the herbarium of the Royal Botanic Garden to be the leaves of *Pinus Webbiana.* They are single, spirally arranged all round the branchlets, flat, narrow, linear, one to three inches long, one line broad, narrowed into a short terete petiole, under side with two longitudinal furrows on either side of the raised midrib, upper side shining. The Sanskrit term *tálisapatra* has been hitherto translated by most writers on Botany and Materia Medica, as *Flacourtia cataphracta.* The error originated probably in Wilson's Sanskrit-English dictionary and has since been repeated by subsequent writers. This medicine is regarded as carminative, expectorant and useful in phthisis, cough and asthma.

The powdered leaves are given with the juice of *Justicia*

Adhatoda (*vásaka*) and honey in cough, asthma and hæmoptysis.[1] A confection called *Tálisádya churna* is prepared with *tálisapatra*, black pepper, long pepper, ginger, bamboo-manna, cardamoms, cinnamon, and sugar, and is used in the above mentioned diseases.[2] These leaves enter into the composition of numerous complex prescriptions.

PINUS LONGIFOLIA, *Roxb.*

Sans. सरल, *Sarala, Vern. Chir, Saral, Hind.*

THE aromatic wood of *Pinus longifolia* is used in Hindu medicine. The tree yields an oleo-resin called *sarala drava, srivása* and *kshira* in Sanskrit. In the vernacular it is called *gandhabirozá*. Dr. Royle remarked, "The *chir* exudes or yields to incisions a very fine turpentine. This is chiefly valued by the natives for its resin, and as the latter is only obtained by exposing the turpentine to heat, the oil, the more valuable product is dissipated to procure the resin; but by adopting a very simple still, the resin was obtained as good as ever for the purposes of the natives, while the oil of turpentine which distilled over was pronounced on being sent to the General Hospital of Calcutta, to be of very superior quality." Turpentine is now distilled by the natives in the Panjab but the distilled oil is not mentioned by Sanskrit writers.

The wood of *Pinus longifolia* is considered stimulant, diaphoretic and useful in burning of the body, cough, fainting, and ulcerations; it is generally used in combination with other medicines.

---

1 तालीशचूर्णसंयुक्तः पेयः क्षौद्रेण वासकस्वरसः। कफपित्ततमकश्वासस्वरभेदरक्तपित्तहरः। चक्रदत्तः।

2 तालीशाद्यं चूर्णम्। तालीशं मरिचं शुण्ठीपिप्पलीवंशलोचना। एकद्वित्रिचतुःपञ्चकर्षैर्भागान् प्रकल्पयेत्। एलात्वचोस्तु कर्षार्द्धं प्रत्येकं भागमावहेत्। द्वात्रिंशत्कर्षतुलिता प्रदेया शर्करा बुधैः। तालीशाद्यमिदं चूर्णं पाचनं रोचनं स्मृतम्। कासश्वासज्वरहरं छर्द्यतीसारनाशनम्। शोषाध्मानहरं प्लीहग्रहणीपाण्डुरोगजित्। पक्वां वा शर्करां चूर्णे क्षिपेत् स्याद्गुटिका ततः। शार्ङ्गधरः।

The oleo-resin or crude turpentine is used in the preparation of plasters, ointments, and pastiles for fumigation. It is applied to buboes and abscesses for promoting absorption. The following is an example of a pastile containing crude turpentine. Take of crude turpentine, bdellium, wood of *Aquilaria Agallocha* (*aguru*), and resin of *Shorea robusta*, and make into pastiles. These are used for fumigating unhealthy and painful ulcers.[1]

CEDRUS DEODARA, *Loud.*

Pinus Deodara, Roxb.

Sans. देवदारु, *Devadáru. Vern. Deodár Hind.*

THE aromatic wood of this elegant pine is considered carminative, diaphoretic, diuretic and useful in fever, flatulence, inflammation, dropsy, urinary diseases, etc. It is chiefly used in combination with other medicines. The following is an example of a diuretic mixture containing this drug. Take of *devadáru* wood, root of *Moringa pterygosperma* (*sigru*), and *Achyranthes aspera* (*apámárga*), one drachm each and reduce to a paste with cow's urine. This composition is given in ascites.[2]

NAT. ORDER PALMACEÆ.

COCUS NUCIFERA, *Linn.*

Sans. नारिकेल, *Nárikela, Vern. Nárial, Hind. Nárikel, Beng.*

THE numerous economical uses of this valuable tree are fully detailed in standard works. I will refer only to such of them as are mentioned in Sanskrit medical works. The water of the unripe fruit is described as a fine-flavoured, cooling, refrigerent drink useful in thirst, fever and urinary disorders. The tender pulp of the fruit is said to be nourishing, cooling and diuretic. The pulp of the ripe fruit is hard and indigestible but is used medicinally. The terminal bud of the tree is esteemed as a nourish-

1 श्रीवासगुग्गुलुसर्जनिर्यासधूपिताः। कठिनत्वं व्रणा यान्ति नश्यन्त्युग्राश्च वेदनाः। चक्रदत्तः।

2 देवद्रुमं शिग्रुमयूरकञ्च गोमूत्रपिष्टामथवाऽश्वगन्धाम्। पीत्वाशु हन्यादुदरं प्रवृद्धं क्रिमीन् सशोथानुदरञ्च दुष्यम्। चक्रदत्तः।

ing, strengthening and agreeable vegetable. The same remark applies to the tops of the *tál* palm and date trees. The root of the cocoa-nut is used as a diuretic as also in uterine diseases. Cocoa-nut oil is said to promote the growth of hair. It is much used as a hair-oil by the lower classes of native women. For this purpose it is scented by steeping in it a number of fragrant vegetable substances sold in packets under the Bengali name of *Máthághasá*. The ashes of the leaves are used in medicine. They contain a great deal of potash. The fresh juice of the tree is considered refrigerent and diuretic. The fermented juice constitutes one of the spirituous liquors described by the ancient writers. The cleared shell of the nut or portions of it are burnt in a fire and while red hot, covered by a stone cup. The fluid deposited in the interior of the cup is rubefacient and is an effectual domestic remedy for ringworm.

Narikelakhanḍa.[1] Take of the pounded pulp of cocoa-nut, half a seer, fry it in eight tolas of clarified butter, and afterwards boil in four seers of cocoa-nut water till reduced to a syrupy consistence. Now add coriander, long pepper, bamboo manna, cumin seeds, nigella seeds, cardamoms, cinnamon, *tejapatra*, the tubers of *Cyperus rotundus* (*mustaka*), and the flowers of *Mesua ferrea* (*nága-kesara*) one tolá each in fine powder and prepare a confection. Dose, two to four tolas, in dyspepsia and consumption.

BORASSUS FLABELLIFORMIS, *Linn.*

Sans. ताल, *Tála*, तृणराज, *Trinarája. Vern. Tál, Beng. Hind.*

THE properties of the various parts of this noble palm are described in detail in Sanskrit works. The root is cooling and restorative. "The saccharine juice obtained by the excision of the spadix or young flowering branch," is when freshly drawn, cooling,

1 नारिकेलखण्डः। कुडवमितमिह स्यान्नारिकेलं सुपिष्टं पलपरिमितसर्पिः पाचितं खण्डतुल्यम्। निजपयसि तदेतत् प्रस्थमात्रे विपक्वं गुडवदथ सुशीते शाणभागान् क्षिपेच्च। धन्याकपिप्पलिपयोदतुगाद्विजीरान् शाणं त्रिजातमिभकेशरवह्निचूर्णं। हन्त्यम्लपित्तमरुचिं क्षयमस्रपित्तं शूलं वमिं सकलपौरुषकारि हारि।

चक्रदत्तः।

sweet and useful in inflammatory affections and dropsy. The fermented juice called *tári* or toddy is intoxicating. The yellow pulp surrounding the seeds of the ripe fruit is sweet, heavy and indigestible. It is extracted by rubbing the seeds over a wooden scratcher, and with the addition of a little lime, it settles into a firm jelly which is a ready mode of taking the pulp. It is also made into cakes with flour and other ingredients. The young seeds contain a clear watery fluid which is very refreshing and cooling. They form one of the edible fruits of the country and are sold in the markets in large quantities when in season. The natives after extracting the pulp from the fibres surrounding the ripe seeds, preserve them for some months. When the embryo begins to germinate and enlarge, the seeds are cut open and the expanded embryo is extracted and eaten. It is cooling, sweet and palatable. The terminal bud or top of the *tál* tree is regarded as nutritive, diuretic and tonic. The leaves of this palm tree were used for writing on by the ancient Hindus. The letters were engraved upon the leaves by a pointed iron instrument. This system of writing is still followed to a considerable extent in Orissa where boys in the indigenous patsálás write with iron pens on palm leaves. In Bengal the leaves are written upon with pen and ink as on paper. The ashes of the flowering stalk are said to be useful in enlarged spleen.[1]

ARECA CATECHU, *Linn.*

Sans. गुवाक, *Guváka*, पूग, *Puga*, क्रमुक, *Kramuka.*

Vern. Guá, Supári, Beng. Supári, Hind.

THE chief consumption of betel-nuts is as a masticatory, alone or in conjunction with betle leaf. The unripe nuts are said to be laxative and carminative. The fresh nuts when not yet dry in their interior, have intoxicating properties and produce giddiness. The dried nuts are masticated. They are said to sweeten the breath, strengthen the gums, remove bad tastes from the mouth, and produce a stimulant or exhilarant effect on the system. The burnt nuts are used as a tooth powder.

1 तालपुष्पभवः क्षारः सगुडः प्लीहनाशनः । चक्रदत्तः ।

Medicinally betel-nuts are used in urinary disorders and as an aphrodisiac. The Bhávaprakasa gives a preparation called *Rativallava pugapáka.* It is a confection made of betel-nuts boiled in milk, with the addition of a number of aromatic and stimulant substances supposed to have aphrodisiac properties. Sometimes *datura* seeds and the leaves of *Cannabis sativa* are added to this confection when it is called *Kámesvara modaka.*

PHŒNIX SYLVESTRIS, *Roxb. Sans.* खर्जुर, *Kharjura. Vern Kejur, Beng. Hind.* The *Phœnix sylvestris* is indigenous to India and is cultivated for the sake of its sweet sap which is manufactured into *gur* or *jagari.* The imported fruits of *Phœnix dactylifera* are used medicinally as demulcents and expectorants.

NAT. ORDER HYPOXIDEÆ.

HYPOXIS ORCHIOIDES.

Syn. Curculigo orchioides, Gaërtn.

Sans. मुषली, *Mushali,* तालमूली, *Tálamuli. Vern. Mushali, Hind.*

THE tuberous roots of this plant are considered alterative, tonic, restorative and useful in piles, debility and impotence. They enter into the composition of several medicines intended to act as aphrodisiacs and restoratives. The following in an example. Take of the root of *Asparagus racemosus* (*satávari*), *Sphœranthus mollis* (*munḍitiká*), *gulancha,* seeds of *Butea frondosa* (*hastikarna*), and the tuberous roots of *mushali,* equal parts ; powder and mix. Dose, about a drachm with honey or clarified butter, in the debility of old age.[1] The Rája nirghantu mentions two varieties of *mushali,* namely, white and black. The properties of the white variety are said to be inferior to those of the black which is preferred for use as an alterative tonic. The roots of *Bombax Malabaricum* and *Asparagus racemosus* are sometimes sold by the native druggists

---

1 शतावरी मुण्डितिका गुडुची सहस्तिकर्णी सह तालमूली । एतानि कृत्वा समभागयुक्तान्याज्येन किंवा मधुनावलिह्यात् । जरारुजाक्रान्त विमुक्त देहो भवेन्नरो वीर्य्यबलादियुक्तः । विभाति देवप्रतिमः सनित्यं प्रभामयो भूरिविवृद्धबुद्धिः । भावप्रकाशः ।

of Calcutta under the name of *suffed musli*. These articles have however separate names and are not designated by the name of *suffed musli* in any native medical work. On the contrary a white variety of *tálamuli* or *musali* is, as already noticed, mentioned in the Rája nirghantu.[1] The tubers of *Curculigo orchioides* become when dry, trans lucent like ambar. The dried roots were probably considered a separate variety, namely, the white by the ancients.

NAT. ORDER AROIDEÆ.

ACORUS CALAMUS, *Linn.*

Sans. वचा, *Vachá*, षड्ग्रन्था, *Shadgranthá*. *Vern. Bach, B. H.*

THE aromatic rhizome or root-stock of *Acorus Calamus* is considered emetic in large doses, and stomachic, carminative and nervine in smaller doses.

As an emetic it is administered in doses of about eighty grains with half a seer of tepid salt-water.[2] The following is an example of a prescription for dyspepsia containing this drug. Take of *Acorus Calamus* root, assafœtida, *átis*, long pepper, black pepper, ginger, chebulic myrobalan and *sonchal* salt equal parts; powder and mix. Dose, about half a drachm.[3] As a stimulant or nervine it is used in combination with other medicines in low fevers, epilepsy and insanity.

AMORPHOPHALLUS CAMPANULATUS, *Blume.*

Syn. Arum campanulatum, Roxb.

Sans. सूरण, *Surana*, ओल्ल, *Olla*. *Vern. ol, Beng. Hind.*

THE *Amorphophallus campanulatus* is cultivated for the sake of its tubers, which are cooked and eaten by the natives like yams or potatoes. The tubers contain an acrid juice which should be got rid off by thorough boiling and washing, otherwise the vege-

1 मुषली च द्विधा प्रोक्ता श्वेता चापरा संज्ञका। श्वेता स्वल्पगुणोपेता अपरा च रसायनी। राजनिर्घण्टः।

2 वचालवणतोयेन वान्तिरामे प्रशस्यते। चक्रदत्तः।

3 मूलीविबन्धकोष्ठोऽग्निरप्यामिभूर्ध्विताः पिबेत्। हिङ्गुमतिविषाव्योषवचा सौवर्चलाभयाः। चक्रदत्तः।

table is apt to cause troublesome irritation in the mouth and fauces. Medicinally, *surana* is considered serviceable in hæmorrhoids; in fact one of its Sanskrit synonyms is *arsoghna* or the curer of piles. It is administered in this disease in a variety of forms. The tuber is covered with a layer of earth and roasted in a fire; the roasted vegetable is given with the addition of oil and salt.[1] Several confections are described such as the *Laghusurana modaka*, *Vrihat suraṅa modoka*, *Surana pindi*, *Kánkáyana modaka* etc. These are all confections made of the tubers of *Amorphophallus campanulatus* with the addition of treacle and various aromatics and acrids.

Svalpa or Laghu surana modaka[2] is thus prepared. Take of black pepper one part, ginger two parts, plumbago root four parts, tuber of *surana* eight parts, treacle sixteen parts, mix together and prepare a confection. Dose, about a tolá every morning, in piles and dyspepsia.

SCINDAPSUS OFFICINALIS, *Schott. Syn. Pothos officinalis, Roxb. Sans.* गजपिप्पली, *Gajapippali. Vern. Gajapipul, Beng. Hind.* The sliced fruits of this plant pass by the name of *gajapipul*. They are considered aromatic, carminative, stimulant and useful in diarrhœa, asthma and other affections supposed to be caused by deranged phlegm. They are chiefly used as an aromatic adjunct to other medicines.

ALOCASIA INDICA, *Schott.*

Syn. Arum Indicum, Roxb.

Sans. मानक, *Mánaka, Vern. Mánkachu, Beng. Mánkanda, Hind.*

THE underground stems of *Alocasia Indica* constitute a valuable and important vegetable of native dietary. The stems

---

1 सौरणं कन्दमादाय पुटपाकेन पाचयेत्। सतैललवणस्तस्य रसश्चार्शोविकारनुत्। शार्ङ्गधरः।

2 स्वल्पसूरणमोदकः। मरिचमहौषधचित्रकस्य सूरणभागा यथोत्तरं द्विगुणाः। सर्व्वसमो गुड़भागः सेव्योऽयं मोदकः प्रसिद्धफलः। ज्वलनं ज्वलयति जाठरमुन्मूलयति स्मूलगुल्मगदान्। निःशेषयति श्लीपदमर्शांसि नाशयत्याशु। भावप्रकाशः।

sometimes grow to an immense size, from six to eight feet in length and can be preserved for a considerable time. Hence they are of great importance in jail dietary when fresh vegetables become scarce in the bazar or jail garden. They thrive best in shade under the eaves of huts or buildings and beside fences.

Medicinally *mánaka* is said to be useful in anasarca, in which disease it is used in the following manner. Take of the powdered meal of *Alocasia Indica* eight tolás, powdered rice sixteen tolás, water and milk, forty-eight tolás each, boil them together till the water is evaporated. This preparation called *Mánamanḍa*, is given as diet.[1] No other article is allowed in addition to it except milk. A *ghrita* is also ordered to be made with a decoction and paste of *mánaka* but it is not in vogue.

NAT. ORDER SCITAMINEÆ.

ZINGIBER OFFICINALE, *Roscoe.*

Sans. आर्द्रक, *A'rdraka*, शृङ्गवेर, *Sringavera.*

Vern. A'dá, Beng. A'drak, Hind.

GINGER is described as acrid, heating, carminative and useful in dyspepsia, affections of the throat, head and chest, piles, rheumatism, urticaria, dropsy, etc. It is much used as a carminative adjunct along with black pepper and long pepper under the name of *trikaṭu* or the three acrids. The dried root is called *Nágara*, *Sunṭi* and *Mahaushadha* in Sanskrit. In addition to possessing the properties of ginger it is said to be laxative.

Ginger with salt taken before meals, is highly praised as a carminative. It is said to purify the tongue and throat, increase the appetite and produce an agreeable sensation. Ginger forms the active ingredient of several medicines for dyspepsia and hæmorrhoids.

Samasarkara churna.[2] Take of cardamoms one part, cinna-

---

1 पुराणं मानकं पिष्ट्वा द्विगुणीकृततण्डुलम्। साधितं क्षीरतोयाभ्यामभ्यसेत् पायसं ततः। हन्तिवातोदरं शोथं ग्रहणीं पाण्डुतामपि। सिद्धोभिषग्भिराख्यातः प्रयोगोऽयं निरत्ययः। चक्रदत्तः।

2 समशर्करं चूर्णम्। शुण्ठीकणामरिचनागदलत्वगेलं चूर्णीकृतं क्रमविवर्द्धित-

mon two parts, flowers of *Mesua ferrea (nágakesara)* three parts, black pepper four parts, long pepper five parts, dried ginger six parts, sugar in quantity equal to all the other ingredients; powder and mix. Dose, about a drachm in dyspepsia, loss of appetite and piles.

Saubhágya sunṭi.[1] Take of clarified butter, sixteen tolás, milk four seers, sugar six seers and a quarter, dry ginger one seer; boil them together so as to make an electuary. Then add coriander twenty-four tolás, fennel seeds forty tolás, *báberang* seeds, cumin seeds, nigella seeds, long pepper, black pepper, ginger, tubers of *Cyperus rotundus*, leaves called *tejapatra*, flowers of *Mesua ferrea (nágakesara)*, cinnamon and cardamoms each eight tolás in fine powder, and stir with a ladle till cold. This confection is much used as a carminative tonic in dyspepsia and in disorders of the alimentary canal in females after confinement.

Sunṭi ghrita.[2] This is a preparation of ginger made with a decoction and paste of the root, clarified butter and *kánjika* in the usual proportions. It is said to be useful in rheumatism.

A'rdraka khanḍa. This is a confection made with ginger, clarified butter, milk and sugar with the addition of a number of aromatics in small quantities. It is used in urticaria.

In cephalalgia and other affections of the head, ginger juice

---

मूर्छमन्त्यात् । खादेदिदं समसितं गुदजाग्निमान्द्यकासाऽरुचिश्वसनकण्ठहृदामयेषु । भावप्रकाशः ।

1 सौभाग्यशुण्ठी । आज्यांशात् पलयुग्ममत्र पयसः प्रस्थद्वयं खण्डतः पञ्चाशत् पलमत्र चूर्णितमथो प्रक्षिप्यते नागरम् । प्रस्थार्द्धं गुडवद्विपाच्य विधिना सुश्वित्वयं धान्यकात् मिश्याः पञ्चपलं पलं क्रिमिरिपोःसाजाजिजीरादपि । व्योषाम्भोदद्वोरगेन्द्रसुमनस्त्वगद्राविड़ीनां पलं पक्वं नागरखण्डसंज्ञकमिदं तत्सूतिकारोगहृत् । तृट्छर्दिज्वरदाहशोषशमनं सश्वासकासापहम् । प्लीहव्याधि विनाशनं क्रमिहरं मन्दाग्निसन्दीपनम् । भावप्रकाशः ।

2 सर्पिर्नागरकल्केन सौवीरं तच्चतुर्गुणम् । सिद्धमग्निकरं श्रेष्ठ मामवातहरं परम् । भावप्रकाशः ।

mixed with milk is used as a snuff.[1] The fresh juice of ginger taken with honey relieves catarrh, cough and loss of appetite.[2]

Saindhavádya taila.[3] Take of dry ginger forty tolás, rock-salt, long pepper root and plumbago root, sixteen tolás each, marking nuts twenty in number, fermented rice water sixteen seers, sesamum oil four seers, boil them together and prepare an oil in the usual way. This oil is rubbed externally in sciatica and other forms of rheumatism.

ZINGIBER ZERUMBET, *Roxb. Sans.* स्थूलग्रन्थि, *Sthulagranthi, Vern. Mahá bari bach, Hind. Beng.*

ZINGIBER CASSUMUNAR, *Roxb. Sans.* वनार्द्रक, *Vanárdraka, Vern. Banáda, Beng.*

ALPINIA GALANGA, *Linn. Sans.* कुलिञ्जान, *Kulinjána. Vern. Kulinján, Beng. Hind.*

The aromatic tubers of these three species are occasionally used as carminative or fragrant adjuncts in complex prescriptions, but they have nothing peculiar in their properties or action.

CURCUMA LONGA, *Roxb.*

Sans. हरिद्रा, *Haridrá,* निशा, *Nisá. Vern. Halud, B. Haldi, H.*

The turmeric plant is extensively cultivated for the sake of its tubers which are an essential ingredient of native curry powders. Turmeric pounded into a paste and mixed with oil, is rubbed on the skin to improve its appearance and prevent skin diseases. The rubbing of turmeric and oil is an essential part of the Hindu marriage festival as well as of some religious ceremonies. Medici-

---

1 नागरकल्कमिश्रं क्षीरं नस्येनयोजितं पुंसाम्। नानादोषोद्भूतां शिरोरुजां हन्ति तीव्रतराम्। चक्रदत्तः।

2 आर्द्रकस्वरसःक्षौद्रयुक्तोश्लेष्मवातनुत्। श्वासकासारुचिं हन्तिप्रतिश्यायं व्यपोहति। शार्ङ्गधरः।

3 सैन्धवाद्यं तैलम्। द्वे पले सैन्धवात्पञ्चशुण्ठ्याग्रन्थिकचित्रकात्। द्वे द्वे भल्लातकास्थीनि विंशति द्वे तथाढके। आरनालात्पचेत्प्रस्थं तैलमेतैरपत्यदम्। गृध्रस्यूरुग्रहार्शोर्त्तिसर्ववातविकारनुत्। चक्रदत्तः।

nally turmeric is used chiefly in skin diseases both externally and internally. Turmeric paste with the addition of a little lime is a popular application to sprains and bruises. A decoction of turmeric is used as a cooling wash in ophthalmia; cloth steeped in it is employed as an eye-shade. A paste of turmeric and the leaves of *Justicia Adhatoda* (*vásaka*), with cow's urine is rubbed on the skin in prurigo.[1] Several other combinations of the sort are in vogue, such as turmeric and *nim* leaves, turmeric and the ashes of the plantain tree, etc. Turmeric is also given internally with cow's urine in prurigo and eczema.[2]

Haridrákhanḍa.[3] Take of turmeric sixty-four tolás, clarified butter forty-eight tolás, milk sixteen seers, sugar twelve tolás, and boil them together over a gentle fire in an earthern pot. Then add black pepper, long pepper, ginger, cinnamon, cardamom, *tejapatra*, *báberang* seeds, root of *Ipomœa Turpethum* (*trivrit*), the three myrobalans, flowers of *Mesua ferrea* (*nágakesara*), tubers of *Cyperus rotundus* (*mustaka*) and prepared iron, each eight tolás in fine powder, and prepare a confection. Dose, one tolá every morning in prurigo, boils, urticaria, etc. A cure is said to be effected in seven days.

The term *haridrádve*, or the two turmerics, signifies turmeric and the wood of *Berberis Asiatica*. They are often used together in compound prescriptions both for external and internal use and their properties are said to be analogous.

---

1 कोमलं सिंहास्यदलं सनिशं सुरभिजलेन संपिष्टम् । दिवसत्रयेण नियतं क्षपयति कच्छुं विलेपनतः । चक्रदत्तः ।

2 हरिद्राकल्कसंयुक्तं गोमूत्रस्य पलद्वयम् । पिबेन्नरः कामचारी कच्छुपामाविनाशनम् । चक्रदत्तः ।

3 हरिद्राखण्डः । हरिद्रायाः पलान्यष्टौ षट्पलं हविषां तथा । क्षीराढकेन संयुक्तं खण्डस्यार्द्धपलं तथा । पचेत् मृद्वग्निना वैद्यो भाजने मृन्मये दृढे । त्रिकटु त्रिजातकञ्चैव क्रिमिघ्नं त्रिवृतां तथा । त्रिफलाकेशरं मुस्तं लौहं प्रतिपलंपलं । संचूर्ण्य प्रक्षिपेत्तत्र कर्षमेकन्तु भक्षयेत् । कण्डूविस्फोटदद्रूणां नाशनं परमौषधं । प्रतप्त काञ्चनाभासो देहो भवति नान्यथा । शीतपित्तोदर्द्दकोठान् सप्ताहादेव नाशयेत् । हरिद्रानामतः खण्डः कण्डूणां परमौषधं । भैषज्यरत्नावली ।

CURCUMA ZEDOARIA, *Roscoe.*

Syn. C. Zerumbet, Roxb.

Sans. शटी, *Saṭi, Vern. Saṭi, Beng. Kachur, Hind.*

THE rhizomes of this plant possess an agreeable camphoraceous smell and warm, bitterish, spicy taste. They are considered carminative and useful in fever and skin diseases arising from impure or deranged blood. They are generally used in combination with other medicines as also in the preparation of medicated oils. "The dry root powdered and mixed with the powdered wood of the *Cæesalpinia Sappan* makes the red powder called *ábir* by the Hindustanis, and *phág* by the Bengalis. It is copiously thrown about by the natives during the *Huli* or Hindu holidays in the month of March."

CURCUMA AROMATICA, *Salisb. Syn. C. Zedoaria, Roxb. Sans.* वनहरिद्रा, *Vanaharidrá. Vern. Banhalud, Beng. Jedwar, Hind.* The rhizomes of this plant are of a pale yellow colour and have an agreeable fragrant smell. The Bhávaprakása describes them as useful in skin diseases and disorders of the blood. They are sometimes used in combination with other medicines in these diseases.

CURCUMA A'MA'DA', *Roxb. Sans.* कर्पूरहरिद्रा, *Karpuraharidrá. Vern. A'mádá, Beng.* The Bhávaprakása mentions this plant under the name of *karpuraharidrá*, but the term is not to be found in standard lexicons. The fresh root possesses the smell of green mango and is used as a condiment and vegetable. Medicinally it is described as cooling and useful in prurigo.

ELETTARIA CARDAMOMUM, *White et Maton.* Also *Amomum subulatum, Roxb. Sans.* एला, *Elá. Vern. Eláchi, Hind. Gujráti elách, Beng.* Cardamoms are largely used as aromatic adjuncts but have no peculiarity deserving of special notice.

NAT. ORDER MUSACEÆ.

MUSA PARADISIACA, *Linn.*

Variety of *Musa Sapientum Linn.*

Sans. कदली, *Kadalí,* रम्भा, *Rambhá. Vern. Kalá, Beng. Kelá, Hind.*

THE economical uses of this most valuable plant are too well-known to need any notice here. I will refer only to one of them.

The leaves and leaf-stalks when burnt yield alkaline ashes which can be used instead of country soap or fuller's earth, in washing clothes. In the Noakhally jail, the old leaves are collected, dried and burnt to ashes. The ashes being placed on a piece of cloth supported on four posts, water is made to percolate through them into an earthen vessel. The alkaline water thus obtained is used for steeping clothes intended to be washed. As the stems of the plantain are cut down soon after the fruit is gathered, there is always a large quantity of leaves and stalks available in all gardens where it is cultivated. They can be readily economised in the simple method above described, if not manufactured into cloth or paper.

The unripe fruit, called *mochaka* in Sanskrit, is considered cooling and astringent ; it is much used in diabetes in the form of a *ghrita* prepared as follows :—

Kadalyádi ghrita.[1] Take of plantain flowers twelve seers and a half, watery juice of the root-stock of the plantain tree sixty-four seers; boil them together till reduced to one-fourth and strain. To the strained decoction add four seers of prepared clarified butter and the following substances in the form of a paste, namely, unripe plantains, cloves, cardamoms, red sandal wood, wood of *Pinus longifolia*, (*sarala*), *jatámánsi* root, the three myrobalans, *Raphanus sativus* (*mulaka*), and the fruit of *Feronia elephantum* (*kapittha*) in equal parts, one seer in all, and prepare a *ghrita* in the usual way. This medicine is generally given along with some preparation of tin or other metallic medicine in diabetes. Dose, about two tolás.

NAT. ORDER ORCHIDACEÆ.

VANDA ROXBURGHII, *R. Br.*

Syn. Cymbidium tessaloides, Roxb.

Sans. रास्ना, *Rásná*, गन्धनाकुली, *Gandhanákuli. Vern. Rásná, B. H.*

UNDER the name of *rásná*, the roots of *Vanda Roxburghii* and *Acampe papillosa*, are both indiscriminately used by

[1] कदल्यादि घृतम् । कदलीकन्दनिर्यासे तत्प्रसूनतुलां पचेत् । चतुर्भागा-वशेषेऽस्मिन् घृत प्रस्थं विपाचयेत् । चन्दनं सरलं मांसी कदलीमूलकन्तथा ।

native physicians. They are very similar in the appearance of their roots and leaves, though they differ much in their flowers and fruits. One native physician whom I consulted, pronounced both these plants to be *rásná* ; when however I showed him the different flowers and fruits of the two species, he was puzzled. He had never looked to the flowers before, but only knew the roots and leaves. These epiphytes are very common on mango trees.

Rásná root is said to be fragrant, bitter and useful in rheumatism and allied disorders, in which it is prescribed in a variety of forms.

Rásnápanchaka.[1] Take of *rásná*, *gulancha*, *devadáru*, ginger, and the root of the castor oil plant in equal parts, and prepare a decoction in the usual way. This is apparently a popular prescription for rheumatism, being mentioned by most writers.

Rásná guggulu.[2] Eight parts of *rásná* and ten of bdellium are beaten into a uniform mass with clarified butter. Dose, about a drachm, in sciatica.

Rásná enters into the composition of several medicated oils for external application in rheumatism and diseases of the nervous system, such as the *Mahámásha taila*, *Madhyama Naráyana taila*, etc.

NAT. ORDER LILIACEÆ.

ALOE INDICA, *Royle.*

Sans. घृतकुमारी, *Ghritakumári*, कन्या, *Kanyá.*

Vern. Ghritakumári, *Beng. Ghikumári*, *Hind.*

Aloes (called *mushabbar* in the vernacular), though now used in native medicine, was unknown to the Sanskrit writers. They

---

शैलालवङ्ग त्रिफला कपित्थफलमेव च । कल्केनानेन संसिद्धं सोमरोगनिवारणम् । मूत्ररोगानशेषांश्च प्रभूतान् शुक्रपिच्छलान् । प्रमेहान् विंशतिञ्चैव मूत्राघातांस्त्रयोदशान् । बहुमूत्रं विशेषेण मूत्रकृच्छ्रं तथाश्मरीम् । कदल्यादि घृतं नाम विष्णुना परिकीर्त्तितम् । राढ़ीयसारसंग्रहः ।

1 रास्नापञ्चकम् । रास्नामृतामहादारु नागरैरण्डजं शृतम् । सप्तधातुगते वाते साभिसर्वाङ्गजे पिबेत् । शार्ङ्गधरः ।

2 रास्नायास्तु पलञ्चैकं कर्षान् पञ्चगुग्गुलोः । सर्पिषा वटिकां कृत्वा खादेद्गृध्रसीहराम् । चक्रदत्तः ।

mention only the fresh juice of the leaves which is regarded as cathartic, cooling, tonic and useful in fevers, enlarged lymphatic glands, spleen and liver, eye diseases, etc. The fresh juice is much used in making up various sorts of pill-masses and more particularly those of a purgative character, as for example the preparation called *Taruna jvarári rasa*, described under Mercury (see page 32). In glandular enlargements and spleen disease, the juice of the leaves is given with the addition of powdered turmeric.[1]

ASPARAGUS RACEMOSUS, *Willd.*

Sans. शतावरी, *Satávari*, शतमूली, *Satamuli.*
Vern. *Sàtamuli, Beng. Satávari, Hind.*

The Sanskrit name *sàtamulí* (that is possessing a hundred roots), is in allusion to the numerous fusiform tubers of this plant. These are regarded as cooling, demulcent, diuretic, tonic and aphrodisiac, and are used both internally and in the preparation of several medicated oils. The tubers are candied and taken as a sweet-meat. This preparation however has scarcely any other taste or flavour besides that of the sugar. The fresh juice of the root is given with honey as a demulcent in bilious dyspepsia or diarrhœa.[2] As an aphrodisiac tonic, it is used in a variety of forms. A *ghrita* is prepared as follows.—

Satávari ghrita.[3] Take of clarified butter four seers, juice of *Asparagus racemosus* four seers, milk forty seers, boil them together and prepare a *ghrita*. This is given with the addition of sugar, honey, and long pepper.

Phalaghrita. This is prepared with four seers of clarified butter, and sixteen seers each of the juice of *Asparagus racemosus* and cow's milk, with the addition of a number of other medicines in small quantities, in the form of a paste. Its use is said to increase the secretion of semen, to cure barrenness in women and to remove disorders of the female genitals.

---

1 निशाचूर्णयुतःकन्यारसः प्लीहाऽपचीहरः । शार्ङ्गधरः ।

2 शतावर्य्याश्च मधुनापित्तशूलहरोरसः । शार्ङ्गधरः ।

3 शतावरीघृतम् । घृतं शतावरीगर्भं क्षीरे दशगुणे पचेत् । शर्करापिप्पलीक्षौद्रयुक्तं तद्वृष्यमुच्यते । चक्रदत्तः ।

As a diuretic, it is prescribed in combination with other medicines of its class. The following is an illustration. Take of the roots of *Asparagus racemosus*, *Saccharum spontaneum* (*kásá*), *Poa cynosuroides* (*kusa*), *Oryza sativa* (variety called *sálidhánya*) and *Saccharum officinarum* (*ikshu*), *Batatus paniculatus* (*vidári*), *Scirpus Kysoor* (*kaseruka*), and *Tribulus terrestris* (*gokshura*) equal parts, and prepare a decoction in the usual way. This decoction is administered, with the addition of sugar and honey, in scanty urine with heat and ardor urinæ.[1] The chief use of the drug however consists in the preparation of several popular cooling and emollient medicated oils for external application in disorders of the nervous system, rheumatic affections and urinary diseases.

Náráyana taila,[2] popularly known as *Madhyama náráyana taila* is made by taking of the bark of *Ægle Marmelos* (*vilva*), *Premna spinosa* (*agnimantha*), *Calosanthes Indica* (*syonáka*), *Stereospermum suaveolens* (*páṭalá*), *Erythrina Indica* (*páribhadra*), *Pæderia fœtida* (*prasárani*), *Withania somnifera* (*asvagandhá*), *Solanum Jacquinii* (*kantakári*), *Solanum Indicum* (*vrihati*), *Sida cordifolia* (*balá*), *Sida rhombifolia* (*atibalá*), *Tribulus terrestris* (*danshṭrá*) and *Boerhaavia diffusa* (*punarnavá*), each twenty tolás, water sixty-four seers, and boiling down till reduced to one-fourth and straining. To the

---

1 शतावरी काश कुश श्वदंष्ट्राविदारीशालीक्षुकशेरुकाणाम् । क्वाथं सुशीतं मधुशर्करान्तं पिबन् जयेत्पैत्तिक मूत्रकृच्छ्रम् । चक्रदत्तः ।

2 नारायणं तैलम् । विल्वाग्निमन्थश्योणाकपाटलापारिभद्रकः । प्रसारण्यश्वगन्धा च वृहतीकण्टकारिका । बलाचातिबलाचैव श्वदंष्ट्रा सपुनर्नवा । एषां दशपलान् भागान् चतुर्द्रोणेऽम्भसः पचेत् । पादशेषं परिस्राव्य तैलपात्रं प्रदापयेत् । शतपुष्पा देवदारु मांसीशैलेयकं वचा । चन्दनं तगरं कुष्ठमेलापर्णीचतुष्टयम् । रास्ना तुरगगन्धाच सैन्धवं सपुनर्नवम् । एषां द्विपलिकान् भागान् पेषयित्वाविनिक्षिपेत् । शतावरीरसञ्चैव तैलतुल्यं प्रदापयेत् । आजं वा यदि वा गव्यं क्षीरं दत्त्वा चतुर्गुणम् । पाने वस्तौ तथाभ्यङ्गे भोज्ये चैव प्रशस्यते । अश्वो वा वातसंभग्नो गजो वा यदि वा नरः । पङ्गुलः पीठसर्पीच तैलेनानेन सिध्यति । अधोभागेच ये वाताः शिरोमध्यगताश्च ये । दन्तशूले हनुस्तम्भे मन्यास्तम्भे गलग्रहे । यश्च शुष्यति चैकाङ्गं गतिर्यस्य च विह्वला । एतत्तैलवरन्तेषां नाम्नानारायणं स्मृतम् । तगरं नतमत्रस्यादभावेशोयलिकोपडः । चक्रदत्तः ।

strained decoction add four seers each of the juice of *Asparagus racemosus* and prepared sesamum oil, sixteen seers of cow's or goat's milk and the following substances, namely, fennel seeds, wood of *Cedrus Deodara* (*devadáru*), *jatámánsi* root, liquid storax, *Acorus Calamus* (*vachá*), sandal wood, *Limnanthemum cristatum* (*tagarapáduká*), *Aplotaxis auriculata* (*kushṭha*), cardamoms, *Desmodium gangeticum* (*sálaparni*), *Uraria lagopodioides* (*prisniparni*), *Phaseolus trilobus* (*mudgaparni*), *Glycine labialis* (*máshaparni*), *Withania somnifera* (*asvagandhá*), *Vanda Roxburghii* (*rásná*), *Boerhaavia diffusa* (*punarnavá*) and rock salt, four tolás each in the form of paste and prepare an oil in the usual way. When ready, boil again with fragrant substances as directed in the introduction under the head of Medicated oils. This oil is much used by native physicians in rheumatism, diseases of the joints, stiff neck, hemiplegia and other diseases of the nervous system.

Vishnutaila. This is an oil much used in nervous diseases. It is prepared with sesamum oil, cow's or goats' milk, and the juice of *Asparagus racemosus*, with the addition of a number of substances in small quantities in the form of a paste.

Prameha mihira taila. This oil is prepared with the juice of *Asparagus racemosus*, sesasum oil, decoction of lac, whey and milk, with the addition of a number of substances in the form of a paste. It is rubbed on the body and more particularly over the pubic region in chronic gonorrhœa, stricture of the urethra, and other diseases of the urinary organs.

ALLIUM SATIVUM, *Linn.*

Sans. रशुन, *Rasuna*, लशुन, *Lasuna.*

Vern. Rasun, Beng. Lasun, Hind.

GARLIC is described as carminative, stomachic, alterative, tonic and useful in affections of the nervous system, flatulence, hysteria, etc. During its use, the diet should consist of wine, meat and acids.

Decoction of garlic.[1] Take of garlic thirty-two tolás, water

---

1 साधयेच्छुद्धशुष्कस्य लशुनस्य चतुःपलम् । क्षीरोदकेऽष्टगुणिते क्षीरशेषञ्च पाययेत् । वातगुल्ममुदावर्त्तं गृध्रसीविषमज्वरम् । हृद्रोगं विद्रधिं शोषं शमयत्याशु तत्पयः । एवन्तु साधिते क्षीरे स्तोकमप्यत्रदीयते । चक्रदत्तः ।

four seers, milk four seers, boil together till the water is evaporated and strain. This decoction in milk is given in small doses in hysteria, flatulence, sciatica and heart disease.

Svalparasuna pinḍa.[1] Take of garlic twelve tolás, assafœtida, cumin seeds, rock salt, *sonchal* salt, ginger, long pepper and black pepper, each one-eighth of a tolá; powder them finely and mix. Dose, about twenty-two grains every morning with a decoction of the root of the castor oil plant, in facial paralysis, hemiplegia, sciatica, paraplegia and convulsive affections. This medicine should be continued for a month.

Garlic juice slightly warmed is used as a local application in otalgia. A bulb of garlic is sometimes introduced into the meatus for relief of pain in the internal ear.[2]

GLORIOSA SUPERBA, *Linn.*

Sans. लाङ्गलीका, *Lángalíká*, अग्निशिखा, *Agnisikhá*, कलिकारि, *Kalikári*.
Vern. *Bishalánguli*, *Beng.* *Karihári*, *Hind.*

"THE *Gloriosa Superba* is a native of the forests of India. It appears during the rainy season in Bengal, and is one of the most ornamental plants any country can boast of." Its bulb is one of the seven minor poisons of Sanskrit writers (see page 7). One of its Sanskrit synonyms is *Garbhaghátini* or the drug that causes abortion, but I am not aware of its being used as an abortive for criminal purposes. The root, powdered and reduced to a paste, is applied to the navel, supra-pubic region and vagina with the object of promoting labour pains.[3] In retained placenta

---

1 स्वल्परसोनपिण्डः । पलमर्द्धं पलञ्चैव रसोनस्य सुकुट्टितम्। हिङ्गु जीरक-सिन्धूत्थैः सौवर्च्चलकटुत्रयैः। चूर्णितैर्माषकोन्मानैरवचूर्ण्यविलोड़ितम् । यथाग्नि भक्षितंप्रातोरुवूकाथानुपानतः। दिने दिने प्रयोक्तव्यम् मासमेकं निरन्तरम् । वातरोगं निहन्त्याशु अर्द्दितं सापतन्त्रकम् । एकाङ्गरोगिणेचैव तथासर्व्वाङ्गरोगिणे। ऊरुस्तम्भे च गृध्रस्यां क्रिमिकोष्ठे विशेषतः । कटीपृष्ठामयं हन्यादुदरस्य विशेषतः

चक्रः ।

2 लशुनाद्रक शिग्रूणां स्वरसः श्रेष्ठः कदुष्ण कर्णपूरणे । चक्रदत्तः ।

3 पाठा लाङ्गलिसिंह्यास्य मयूरकजटैः पृथक् । नाभिवस्तिभगालेपात् सुखं नारीप्रसूयते । चक्रः ।

a paste of the root is applied to the palms and soles while powdered nigella seeds and long pepper are given internally with wine.[1] This root enters also into the composition of some complex prescriptions for internal use, as for example the *Lángali guṭiká* described in the Bhávaprakása.

NAT. ORDER SMILACEÆ.

SMILAX CHINA, *Linn.*

Sans. चोबचिनि, *Chobachini. Vern. Chobchini. Hind.*

FLUCKIGER and Hanbury state that "the use of this drug as a remedy for syphilis was made known to the Portuguese at Goa by Chinese traders about A.D. 1535." If this statement, which is given on the authority of Garcia d'orta, is correct, the history of this drug will enable us to fix the approximate age of the latest and most comprehensive treatise on Sanskrit Medicine, namely, the Bhávaprakása. In this work China root is described under its vernacular name of *chobchini*, as a root like *Acorus Calamus*, brought from a foreign country and useful in rheumatism, epilepsy, insanity and particularly in syphilis.[2] It is used in modern Hindu medicine as an alterative along with *anantamul* and other drugs of reputed efficacy in syphilis and rheumatism.

NAT. ORDER CYPERACEÆ.

CYPERUS ROTUNDUS, *Linn.*

Sans. मुस्तक, *Mustaka. Vern. Muthá, Beng. Mothá, Hind.*

CYPERUS PERTENUIS, *Roxb.**

Sans. नागरमुस्तक, *Nágaramustaka, Vern. Nágarmuthá, Beng. Hind.*

THE tubers of these two species of *Cyperus* are much used in Hindu medicine. *Cyperus rotundus* is the most common variety

---

1 मूलेन लाङ्गलिक्याः संलिप्ते पाणिपादे च। क्षमरापातनं मद्यैः पिप्पल्यादिरजः पिबेत्। चक्रदत्तः।

2 चोबचीनि। द्वीपान्तर वचा किञ्चित् तिक्तोष्णा वह्निदीप्तिकृत्। विबन्धाध्मान शूलघ्नी शकृन्मूत्रविशोधिनी। वातव्याधिन पस्मारमुन्मादम् तनुवेदनाम्। व्यपोहति विशेषेण फिरङ्गामयनाशिनी। भावप्रकाशः।

* The *Cyperus pertenuis* of Roxburgh can hardly be maintained as a species; it is a variety of the *C. rotundus* of Linnæus. G. K.

and is used internally. Its tubers are about the size of a pigeon's egg and of a dark brown colour externally; internally white, and fragrant. Those growing in moist soil are preferred for use. The root of *Cyperus pertenuis* is somewhat tuberous with many dark coloured villous fibres. It grows in low wet places and is chiefly used in the preparation of medicated oils. The properties of both are said to be identical. They are considered diaphoretic, astringent, stomachic and useful in fever, diarrhœa and dyspepsia. The tubers of *Cyperus rotundus* are extensively used as an aromatic adjunct to numerous compound medicines.

Shaḍanga páníya.[1] Take of the tubers of *Cyperus rotundus*, red sandal wood, root of *Andropogon muricatus*, (*usira*), *Oldenlandia herbacea*, (*parpata*), *Pavonia odorata* (*bálá*) and dry ginger each one drachm, water two seers; boil down to one seer. This decoction is given as a drink for appeasing thirst and relieving heat of body in fever. It may be taken *ad libitum*.

NAT. ORDER GRAMINEÆ.

SACCHARUM OFFICINARUM, *Linn.* ETC.

Sans. इक्षु, *Ikshu. Vern. A'k, Beng. Uk, Hind.*

THE sugar-cane and its products sugar and treacle were known to the Hindus from a very early age. From the Sanskrit term *sarkara* are derived the Arabic *sakkar*, Latin, *saccharum* and English sugar.* Twelve varieties of sugar-cane are mentioned by

---

1 षड़ङ्गपानीयम् । मुस्तपर्पटकोशीर चन्दनोदीच्यनागरैः । शृतशीतं जलं दद्यात् पिपासाज्वरशान्तये । चक्रः ।

* In the Pharmacographia by Fluckiger and Hanbury it is stated; "Candy as sugar in large crystals is called, is derived from the Arabic *kand* or *kandat* a name of the same signification. An old Sanskirt name of Central Bengal is *Gura* whence is derived the word *Gula* meaning raw sugar, a term for sugar universally employed in the Malayan Archipelago, where on the other hand, they have their own names for the sugar-cane, although not for sugar. This fact again speaks, for Ritter's opinion that the preparation of sugar in a crystalline state is due to the inhabitants of Bengal." The Arabic *kand* is apparently derived from the Sanskrit *khanda*, that is treacle candied into white sand-like grains. Again the Bengali term *Gura* is derived from the Sanskrit *Cuda* which is mentioned by such ancient writers as Charaka and Susruta. The manufacture of sugar therefore was evidently understood in Upper India before it was known in Bengal, at any rate there is nothing to shew that sugar was first prepared in Bengal.

Sanskrit writers, but these can not all be identified at present. The products or preparations of the sugar-cane, as described by Sanskrit writers, are as follows:—

1. इक्षुरस, *Ikshu rasa* or sugar-cane juice.

2. फाणित, *Phánita* or sugar-cane juice boiled down to one-fourth. It can be drawn out in threads.

3. गुड़, *Guḍa* or sugar-cane juice boiled to a thick consistence, that is treacle.

4. मत्स्यण्डिका, *Matsyanḍiká* is sugar-cane juice boiled down to a solid consistence but which still exudes a little fluid on drawing.

5. खण्ड, *Khanḍa* is treacle partially dried or candied in white sand-like grains.

6. शर्कर, *Sarkara* or white sugar.

7. सितोपला, *Sitopalá* or sugar candy.

8. गौड़ी, *Gauḍi* or fermented liquor obtained from treacle.

9. सीधु, *Sidhu* or fermented liquor obtained from sugar-cane juice.

The properties of these preparations are described separately, but it is scarcely worth while to reproduce these details here. The root of the sugar cane is considered demulcent and diuretic. Sugar and treacle are very largely used in Hindu Medicine. Old treacle is preferred to new for medicinal purposes.

Trinapancha mula.[1] Under this name the roots of five sorts of grasses are used in combination. They are as follows .—

1. इक्षु, *Ikshu. Saccharum officinarum, Linn.*

2. शर, *Sara. Saccharum Sara, Linn.*

3. काश, *Kása. Saccharum spontaneum, Linn.*

4. कुश, *Kusa. Poa cynosuroides, Linn.*

5. दर्भ, *Darva. Imperata cylindrica, Beauv.* Some practitioners substitute the root of *Andropogon muricatus* for that of *Imperata cylindrica.* A decoction of these roots is considered demulcent and diuretic and is largely prescribed as an adjunct to metallic medicines in gonorrhœa, strangury and suppression of urine. The following coufection is also much used in these diseases.

---

1 तृणपञ्चमूलम् । कुशः काशः शरो दर्भ इक्षुश्चेति तृणोद्भवम् । मूत्रकृच्छ्रहरं पञ्चमूलं वस्ति विशोधनम् । भावप्रकाशः ।

Kusávaleha.[1] Take of the five roots above mentioned, eighty tolás each, water sixty-four seers, boil down to eight seers and strain. Then add sugar four seers, and reduce to the consistence of a thick syrup. Remove the syrup from the fire and add to it the following substances, namely, liquorice root, cucumber seeds, the seeds of *Cucumis melo* (*karkati*), bamboo-manna, emblic myrobalan, *tejapatra* leaves, cardamoms, cinnamon, bark of *Cratæva religiosa* (*varuna*), *gulancha*, seeds of *Aglaia Roxburghiana* (*priyangu*), and the flowers of *Mesua ferrea* (*nágakesara*), two tolás each in fine powder; stir them well with a ladle and prepare an electuary. Dose one to two tolás.

ORYZA SATIVA, *Linn.* ETC.

The following varieties of food grains belonging to this important natural order, are mentioned by Sanskrit writers:—

धान्य, *Dhánya. Oryza sativa, Linn. Vern. Dhán, Beng. Hind.*
गोधूम, *Godhuma. Triticum vulgare, Linn. Gam, B. Geṇhu, H.*
यव, *Yava. Hordeum hexastichum, Linn. Jab, Beng. Jow, Hind.*

These three are considered the best of grains. The following varieties pass by the name of कुधान्य, *Kudhánya* or inferior grains and क्षुद्रधान्य, *Kshudra dhánya* or minor grains.

यावनाल, *Yávanála. Holchus Sorghum, Linn. Joár, Hind. Beng.*
कङ्गु, *Kangu. Setaria Italica, Kunth. Vern. Kángni, B. Korá, H.*
चीन, *China. Panicum miliaceum, Linn. Chiná ghás, B.*
श्यामाक, *Syámáka. Panicum frumentaceum, Roxb.* Shyámádhán, *B.*
कोद्रव, *Kodrava. Paspalum scrobiculatum, Linn. Kodoádhán, Beng.*
नीवार, *Nivára.* Wild variety of *Oryza sativa, Linn. Uridhán, B.*

---

1 कुशावलेहः। कुशः काशो वीरणश्च तथेक्षुः खगडस्तथा। एषां दशपलान् भागान् जलद्रोणे विपाचयेत्। अष्टभागावशिष्टन्तु कषायं तत्र गालयेत्। खण्डप्रस्थं समादाय लेहवत् साधु साधयेत्। अवतार्य्य ततः पश्चात् चूर्णानीमानि दापयेत्। मधुकं कर्कटीबीजं कर्कारुत्रपुषं तथा। शुभामलक पत्राणि त्वगेलानागकेशरं। वरुणामृताप्रियङ्गुश्च प्रत्येकमक्षसम्मितं। प्रमेहान् विंशतिं हन्ति मूत्राघातांस्तथाश्मरीः। वातिकान् पैत्तिकान् चैव श्लेष्मिकान् सान्निपातिकान्। हन्त्यरोचक मत्युग्रं सर्व्वपुष्टिकरं परम्। भैषज्यरत्नावली।

गवेधुका, *Gavedhuká*. Some species of *Coix*, *Gargaredhán, Beng.*

रागी, *Rági. Eleusine corocana, Gaertner. Maruá, Beng.*

देवधान्य, *Devadhánya, Andropogon Saccharatus, Linn. Deodhán, B.H.*

वेणुज, *Venuja.* Seeds of *Bambusa arundinacea, Willd.*

चारुक. *Cháruka.* Seeds of *Saccharum Sara, Roxb. Sarabij, B.*

ORYZA SATIVA. Rice is the principal and often the only food of the great mass of the Indian population. *Dháyna* the Sanskrit name of paddy, means the supporter or nourisher of mankind. It is regarded as the emblem of wealth or fortune. On a thursday in the month of Pausha (December, January) after the new paddy has been reaped, a rattan-made grain measure called *rek* in Bengali, is filled with new paddy, pieces of gold, silver and copper coins, and some shells called *cauries*, and worshipped as the representative of the goddess of fortune. This apparatus is preserved in a clean earthen pot and brought out for worship on one thursday in each of the following Hindu months, namely, Chaitra, Srávana, and Kártika. Such is the form of the domestic goddess of wealth of an agricultural people living chiefly on rice.[1]

The three principal classes of rice are *Sáli* or that reaped in the cold season, *Vrihi* or that ripening in the rainy season, and *Shashṭika* or that grown in the hot weather in low lands. This last is reaped within sixty days of its sowing. The varieties of each of these three classes of rice are numerous and confounding. *Rakta sáli* popularly known as *Dáudkháni* is the variety of rice that is considered superior to all others and suited for use by sick persons. The preparations of rice used in sick diet and described in Sanskrit medical works are as follows :—

यवागु, *Yavágu* or powdered rice boiled with water for the use of the sick and convalescent. It is made of three strengths, namely, with nine, eleven and nineteen parts of water, called respectively *Vilepi*, *Peyá* and *Maṇḍa*. Sometimes, instead of water, a decoction of medicinal herbs is used in preparing *yavágu*.

1 पौषे च दशमी यस्या चैत्रके पञ्चमी तथा। नभस्ये पूर्णिमा ज्ञेया गुरुवारे विशेषतः। आढकं धान्य सम्पूर्णं नानाभरण भूषितम्। सुगन्धि शुक्ल पुष्पेण शुक्ल पक्षे प्रपूजयेत्। कालचन्द्रिका।

Thus for example if it is ordered to give the patient *yavágu* made with ginger and long pepper, the process adopted in preparing it is as follows. Take of dry ginger and long pepper, one tolá each, boil in four seers of water till reduced to two and strain. Now take nine, eleven or nineteen parts of this strained decoction and one part of powdered rice for making *yavágu* of the strength ordered.

लाजा, *Lájá*, (*Vern. Khai*), is paddy fried in a sand bath. The husks open out and the rice swells into a light spongy body. It is considered a light article of diet suited to invalids and dyspeptics.

भ्रष्टतण्डुल, *Bhrishṭa tandula*, (*Vern. Muri*) is rice fried in a sand bath. This is also a light preparation of rice and is given to sick persons as a substitute for boiled rice. It is also much used by the poorer classes for tiffin and early breakfast.

पृथुका, *Prithuká*, (*Vern. Chura*). To prepare this, paddy is moistened and lightly fried. It is then flattened and husked. This preparation of rice is given with curdled milk (*dadhi*) in dysentry. It is well washed and softened in water or boiled before use.

पायस, *Páyasa* is a preparation of rice with nine parts of milk.

तण्डुलाम्बु, *Tanḍulámbu* is water in which unboiled rice has been steeped. This sort of rice-water is sometimes prescribed as a vehicle for some powders and confections.

The products of the acetous fermentation of rice and other grains have been already described in the introduction.

TRITICUM VULGARE, *Linn.* Three varieties of wheat are mentioned in the Bhávaprakása, namely *Mahágodhuma* or large grained, *Madhuli* or small grained[1] and *Nihsuki* or beardless, that is without awn. The first variety is said to come from the west and the second to be indigenous to the middle region comprising the modern provinces of Allahabad, Agra, Delhi, Oudh, etc. Wheat is considered the most nutritive of the food-grains, but less easily digested than rice.

HORDEUM HEXASTICHUM, *Linn.* Barley though less esteemed than wheat is more employed in the dietary of the sick. It is chiefly used in the form of *saktu* or powder of the parched

---

1 मधूलकः स्वल्प गोधूमः इति सटीक द्रव्यगुण: ११७ ।

grains. Gruel prepared with *saktu* is said to be easily digested and to be useful in painful dyspepsia.

ZEA MAYS, *Linn.* called *makkái* in the vernacular has no Sanskrit name. It is indigenous to America but is now largely cultivated in Behar and Upper India.

The minor food grains are not of any importance in a medicinal point of view. They are used as food by the poorer classes or for cattle.

Old rice is preferred to new as being lighter and more easily digested, but new wheat and barley are considered superior to old. These are said to loose in flavour and taste by long keeping.

Poultices made of rice, barley or wheat flour, with the addition of oil or clarified butter, are applied to abscesses for hastening suppuration.[1]

ANDROPOGON MURICATUS, *Retz.*

Sans. उशीर, *Usira*, वीरण, *Virana*,

Vern. *Bená*, *Beng.* *Khas*, *Hind.*

The root of this plant is well known as the *khas khas* root of which *tátis* or door screens are made for watering during the hot weather. It is described as cooling, refrigerent, stomachic and useful in pyrexia, thirst, inflammation, irritability of stomach, etc. It enters into the composition of several cooling medicines, as for example the preparation called *Shaḍanga páníya*, (see *Cyperus rotundus*). A weak infusion of the root is sometimes used as a febrifuge drink.

Externally it is used in a variety of ways. A paste of the root is rubbed on the skin to relieve oppressive heat or burning of the body. This use of the drug appears to have been popular with the ancients. Kálidássa in his drama called Sakuntalá alludes to it as will appear from the passage quoted below.[2]

---

1 तैलेन सर्पिषावापिताभ्यां वा सक्तुपिण्डिका । सुखोष्णः शोथपाकार्थमुपनाहः प्रशस्यते । चक्रः ।

2 स्तनन्यस्तोशीरं प्रशिथिलमृणालैकवलयं । प्रियायाः साबाधं तदपिकमनीयं वपुरिदम् । शकुन्तला ।

An aromatic cooling bath is prepared by adding to a tub of water the following substances in fine powder, namely, root of *Andropogon muricatus*, *Pavonia odorata* (*bálá*), red sandal wood, and a fragrant wood called *padma káshṭha.*[1] The same medicines are reduced to a thin emulsion with water and applied to the skin.[2]

ANDROPOGON SCHŒNANTHUS, *Linn. Sans.* भूस्तृण *Bhustrina, Vern. Gandha bená, Beng.*

ANDROPOGON IWARANCUSA, *Roxb. Sans.* लामज्जक, *Lámajjaka. Vern. Lámjak, Hind. Karankusá, Beng.*

These two fragant grasses are occasionally used as aromatics and refrigerants like the roots of *Andropogon muricatus. A. schœnanthus* is common in Bengal, being cultivated in gardens for the sake of its fragrant leaves. *A. Iwaruncusa* is "a native of the skirts of the Northern mountains of India." Its virtues seem to reside in the larger roots marked with annular cicatrices.

BAMBUSA ARUNDINACEA, *Willd.*

Sans. वंश, *Vansa. Vern. Báns, Beng. Hind.*

The siliceous concretion found in the joints of the female bamboo is called वंश रोचन, *Bansa rochana* in Sanskrit, and is described as sweet, cooling, tonic, aphrodisiac and useful in cough, consumption, asthma, fever, etc. It enters into the composition of numerous compound prescriptions for affections of the lungs. The following is an illustration.

Sitopaládi churna.[3] Take of bamboo-manna eight parts, long

---

1 ह्रीवेरपद्मकोशीर चन्दनक्षोदवारिणा । संपूर्णमवगाहेत द्रोणीं दाहार्दितो नरः । चक्रदत्तः ।

2 प्रदेहाः परिषेकाश्च शस्यन्ते पञ्चवल्कलैः । पद्मकोशीर मधुक चन्दनैर्व्वा प्रशस्यते । चक्रदत्तः ।

3 सितोपलादिचूर्णम् । सितोपला षोडश स्यादष्टौ स्याद्वंशलोचना । पिप्पली-स्याच्चतुःकर्षाच्चतुर्द्वैलास्याद्द्विकार्षिकी । एककर्षस्त्वचःकार्य्यश्चूर्णयेत्सर्वमेकतः । सितोपलादिकं चूर्णं मधुसर्पिर्युतं लिहेत् । श्वासकासक्षयहरं हस्तपादाङ्ग दाहजित् । मन्दाग्निं सुप्तजिह्वाश्च पार्श्वशूलमरोचकम् । ज्वरमूर्ध्वगतं रक्तपित्तमाश्वपोहति । शार्ङ्गधरः ।

pepper four parts, cardamoms, two parts, cinnamon one part, sugar sixteen parts; powder the ingredients and mix. Dose, about a drachm with honey and clarified butter. This preparation is given in phthisis with pain in the sides, hæmoptysis, loss of appetite and burning of the hands and feet.

CYNODON DACTYLON, *Pers. Sans.* दूर्वा, *Durvá. Vern. Durbá, Beng. Dub, Hind.* This elegant and most valuable grass, like many other useful vegetables, has a niche in the temple of the Hindu religion. Medicinally the fresh juice of the leaves is considered astringent, and is used as a snuff in epistaxis.[1] The bruised grass is a popular application to bleeding wounds.

PRODUCTS OF FERMENATION AND DISTILLATION.

WINES AND SPIRITS.

All fermented and distilled liquors causing intoxication, are called *Madya* or *Madirá* in Sanskrit. The following varieties are mentioned by the later writers.

माद्धिक, *Máddhika*, or spirit distilled from grapes.
खार्जूर, *Khárjura*, do. do. dates.
गौड़ी, *Gauḍi*, do. do. treacle.
शीधु, *Sidhu*, do. do. sugar-cane juice.
सुरा, *Surá*, do. do. rice.
कोहल, *Kohala*, do. do. barley.
मधूलिका, *Madhuliká*, do. do. wheat.
पैष्टी, *Paishṭi*, do. do. from different sorts of grain.
मधूकपुष्पोत्थ, *Madhuka pushpottha*, do. do. the flowers of *Bassia latifolia* and treacle.
जाम्बव, *Jámbava*, do. do. ripe fruits of *Eugenia Jambolana*.
कादम्बरि, *Kádambari*, do. do. flowers of *Anthocephalus Cadamba*.
वल्कलि, *Valkali*, do. do. belleric myrobalan and treacle.

वारुणी, *Váruni* is the fermented juice of the palm and date trees.

---

1 नस्यं दाडिमपुष्पोत्थो रसो दूर्वाभवोऽथवा । आम्रास्थिजः पलाण्डोर्वा नासिकास्रुतरक्तजित् । भावप्रकाशः ।

Some of these spirituous liquors have several varieties. Thus two varieties of *sidhu* are mentioned, namely, that produced from boiled sugar-cane juice and that from the unboiled juice. The liquor distilled from rice receives different names according to its consistence. The clear transparent fluid which floats on the top is called *prasanná* ; that below it, is called *kádambari* ; *jagala* is a thicker fluid than *kádambari; medaka* in the thickest and weakest of all. The forms of medicated spirituous liquors have been already described in the introduction, (see page 31).

Spirituous liquors are described as stimulant, sedative, agreeable, heating, intoxicating, digestive and nourishing. They are easily assimilated but injurious to health in hot climates. New wine is disagreeable to the taste and smell, unpleasant in its effects, not easily assimilated, laxative, heating and injurious to health. Old wine is agreeable, light and appetizing. It promotes the circulation of the fluids in the vessels and renders the senses acute. In amiable and virtuous men, wine promotes mirth and a desire for musical entertainments. In passionate men it gives rise to rashness and evil actions. Used at the proper season, in proper doses and with suitable food, wine acts like nectar. If taken to excess it induces a host of diseases. Medicinally, spirituous liquors are said to be useful in emaciation, debility, anæmia, urinary diseases, dyspepsia, chronic bowel complaints, chronic fever, deficient secretion of milk, etc.

A mixture of ginger, cumin seeds, treacle, wine and warm water is given in ague with prolonged cold stage.[1] In chronic intermittent fever with debility, spirit distilled from rice, together with the flesh of fowls is recommended to be given as diet by most writers, but their advice is not followed in the present day. Several preparations of spirit distilled from treacle with the

---

1 शुण्ठी जाजी गुड़ं पिष्टं पीतमुष्णेन वारिणा । जीर्णमद्येन तक्रेण पीतं शीत ज्वरं जयेत् । भावप्रकाशः ।

2 सुरां समण्डां पानार्थे भक्षार्थे चरणायुधान् । तित्तिरींश्च मयूरांश्च प्रयुञ्ज्याद्विषमज्वरे । चक्रः ।

addition of various medicinal and aromatic substances are used in different diseases. The following is an example.

Mritasanjivani surá.[1] Take of new treacle eight hundred tolas and steep it in thirty times its weight of water. Add to the mixture the following substances in the form of a paste, namely, ginger sixteen tolas, bark of *Acacia Arabica* two seers, of *Ziziphus Jujuba* (*kola*) two seers, of *Symplocos racemosa* (*lodhra*) half a seer, betle-nuts as many as desired; stir in a large earthen vessel, and keep the mixture for twenty days in a covered jar. After this period remove the fermented fluid to a distilling apparatus, and add to it, the following aromatic substances, namely, betle-nuts, cloves, sandal wood, cumin seeds, *ájowan*, black pepper, ginger, nutmegs, cardamoms, cinnamon, *tejapatra* leaves, fennel seeds, nigella seeds, the fragrant substances called *elaváluka*, *padma-káshṭha* and *granthiparni*, *devadáru* wood, *khas khas* root, zedoary root, *jatámánsi* root and the tubers of *Cyperus rotundus* (*mustaka*), each eight tolás, in coarse powder, and distil. This distilled liquor is used as a tonic, astringent and invigorating drink.

---

1 मृतसञ्जीवनीसुरा। नूतनं गुड़संगृह्य शतमेकं पलं तथा। जलं चाष्टगुणं देयं स्थापयेत् मृत्भाजने। बाबरीत्वच संग्राह्य बदरीत्वचमेवच। प्रस्थं प्रस्थं प्रदातव्यं पूगंदेयं यथोचितं। लोध्रञ्च कुड़वं दत्वा आर्द्रकञ्च पलद्वयं। गुड़ं संगोलकं कृत्वा दापयेत् बुद्धिमान् भिषक्। प्रथमे आर्द्रकं देयं द्वितीये बाबरी त्वचं। तृतीये बदरी दत्वा गोलयित्वा भिषग्वरः। मुखे शरावकं दत्वा यत्नं कृत्वा च बन्धनं। मुखसंबन्धनं कृत्वा स्थापयेद्दिन विंशतिं। मृण्मये शौण्डिका पात्रे मयूराख्योपयन्त्रके। यथाविधि प्रकारेण मन्द मन्देन वह्निना। चुल्लिमध्ये विधातव्यम्मृत्तिका दृढ़ भाजने। तदौषधञ्च तन्मध्ये उद्धरित्वा विनिक्षिपेत्। कुम्भमध्ये निधातव्यं पूगञ्च शैलवालुकं। देवदारु लवङ्गञ्च पद्मकोशीर चन्दनं। शत पुष्पा यमानी च मरिचं जीरक द्वयं। शठी मांसी त्वगेलाच जातिफलं समुस्तकं। ग्रन्थिपर्णी तथा शुण्ठी मेथी मेषीच चन्दनं। एषां चार्द्धपलान् भागान् कुटयित्वा विनिक्षिपेत्। यथाविधि प्रकारेण चानलं दापयेत् सुधी। बुद्धिमान् शोधनं कृत्वा उद्धरेत् विधिवत्सुरां। एतन्मद्यं पिबेन्नित्यं यथाधातु वयक्रमात्। आरोग्यं देह दार्ढ्यत्वं बलपुष्टिकरं सदा।

उद्धृत पाठः।

THE

MATERIA MEDICA

OF THE HINDUS

PART III.

ANIMAL MATERIA MEDICA.

THE LEECH.

LEECHES have been employed by the Hindus from a very remote period. Susruta gives a detailed account of their varieties habits, mode of application, etc. His account of leeches has been translated in full by Dr. Wise. Pundit Madhu Sudan Gupta had also furnished a note on the subject for publication in the Bengal Dispensatory. I will not therefore attempt a new translation but will give an extract from Dr. Wise's work. "There are twelve varieties of leeches, six of which are venomous, and six useful. The venomous leeches are found near putrid fish or animals in foul stagnant and putrescent water. Such leeches are consequently to be avoided. The good leeches are found in clear and deep pools of water which contain water lilies, and are surrounded with sweet smelling plants. The middle sized leeches are the best. These leeches are to be caught on a piece of leather or cloth, and placed in a new water pot in which some clay and pure water has been put. Some grass or leaves of aquatic plants are to be placed in the pot for them to lie upon, and the roots of water lilies and dry flesh are to be given them for food. The water is to be changed every third day, and the water pot every seventh day. If the leeches do not fix quickly, apply a drop or two of milk or blood to the part, or make one or two very slight scarifications, which will induce them to fix themselves more readily. When the leeches are sucking, sprinkle a few drops of cold water upon their bodies. When the leeches have removed the necessary quantity of blood, sprinkle a small quantity of salt upon their heads to make them drop off. Put the gorged leeches upon some dry bran, put a little oil and salt upon their mouths and then strip them. Put them next in fresh water and, if they are lively, they will live and may be used again; but if they are languid, they will soon die and they should therefore be at once thrown away. The part upon which the leeches have been is to be smeared with honey, cold water and astringent substances. In other cases poultices may be applied."

LAC.

Sans. लाक्षा, *Lákshá Vern. Lákh, Hind. Gálá, Beng.*

THE lac insect (*Coccus lacca*), has been known to the Hindus from a very ancient period. The *Butea frondosa* is called *Lákshá taru* or lac plant in Sanskrit, this being the principal tree in which lac is said to be produced. The fluid lac-dye obtained by dissolving the crushed stick-lac in water is called *A'lakta*. It is used in colouring silk. Cotton coloured with this dye and pressed into flat circular pieces is sold in the bazars under the name of *A'ltá* and is used in painting the hands and feet of Hindu females. Shell-lac is used in the preparation of sealing wax, varnish for carpenters and ornaments for women. A decoction of shell-lac is much used in the preparation of several medicinal oils, such as *Lákshádi-taila, Chandanádi taila, Angáraka taila*, etc.

Lakshádítaila.[1] Take of shell-lac two seers, water sixteen

1 लाक्षादि तैलम्। लाक्षारस समं तैलं तैलान्मस्तु चतुर्गुणम्। अश्वगन्धा निशा दारु कौन्तीकुष्ठाब्दचन्दनैः। समूर्व्वा रोहिणी रास्ना शताह्वा मधुकैः समैः। सिद्धं लाक्षादिकं नाम तैलमभ्यञ्जनादिना। सर्व्वज्वरक्षयोन्माद श्वासापस्मार वातनुत्। यक्ष राक्षस भूतघ्नं गर्भिनीनां च शस्यते।

भावप्रकाशः।

seers, boil till reduced to four seers and strain. To this decoction of shell-lac add four seers of prepared sesamum oil, sixteen seers of whey, and two tolás each of the following substances, namely, *Withania somnifera (asvagandhá)*, turmeric, *devadáru* wood, root of *Sanseviera Zeylanica (murvá)*, *Pandanus odoratissimus* (*ketaki*), *Vanda Roxburghii* (*rásna*), dill seeds and liquorice root in the form of a paste and prepare an oil in the usual way ; lastly add four tolás of camphor. This oil is much used for innunction in chronic fever and consumption. The other oils containing lac are prepared in a similar way, with the addition of various medicinal substances in the form of paste.

HONEY AND WAX.

Sans. मधु, *Madhu*, माक्षिक, *Mákshika*.

Vern. Madhu, Beng. Shahad, Hind.

Eight sorts of honey are described by Susruta, namely :

1. *Mákshika* or the honey collected by the common bee called *madhumakshiká*.

2. *Bhrámara*, or the honey collected by a large back bee called *bhramara*.

3. *Kshaudra*, or honey collected by a sort of small bee of tawny colour, called *Kshudra*.

4. *Pauttika*, or honey collected by a small black bee resembling a gnat, and called *puttika*.

5. *Chhatra*, or honey formed by tawny or yellow wasps which make their hives in the shape of umbrellas.

6. *Argha* or wild honey collected by a sort of yellow bee like the *bhramara*.

7. *Audálaka* is a bitter and acrid substance like honey found in the nests of white ants.

8. *Dála* or unprepared honey found on flowers.

Of these varieties the first four only are described by recent writers and the first alone is used in medicine. New honey is considered demulcent and laxative. Honey more than a year old is said to be astringent and demulcent. Old honey is preferred to new. It is much used in the preparation of confections and electuaries, and as an adjunct to decoctions, pills and powders.

Wax, called *siktha* in Sanskrit, is used in the preparation of ointments and *ghritas* for external application.

SERPENT POISON.

Sans. सर्पविष, *Sarpavisha,* गरल, *Garala.*

Serpent poison has been used in Hindu Medicine since a very recent period only. Even the Bhávaprákasa which is not more than three centuries old does not mention it. Prescriptions containing it are found in such modern compilations as the Bhaishajya ratnábali, Sárkaumudi, etc.

The poison of the black cobra (*Naga tripudians. Vern. Keute sáp, Beng.*) is used. It is collected by making the reptile bite on a piece of stick or wood when the poison is poured out and received on a piece of plantain leaf. It is preserved in two ways. The liquid poison is allowed to congeal and dry in a cup or it is rubbed with a fourth part of mustard oil and spread out on a piece of plantain leaf. Thus treated it rapidly coagulates into a granular agglutinated mass of a yellowish-brown colour. When allowed to dry spontaneously, serpent poison coagulates into shining, crystalline yellowish white granules. It is used in complicated fever in combination with arsenic, aconite and other medicines. Numerous formulæ containing this poison are given in recent compilations. The following are a couple of examples.

Suchiká bharana rasa.[1] Take of mercury, sulphur, prepared tin, aconite and cobra poison, equal parts, mix them together and soak the mixed powder in the bile of *rohitaka* fish (*Cyprinus Rohita*), wild boar, peacock, buffalo and goat successively and make into a pill-mass. This medicine is administered in doses

---

1 सूचिकाभरणोरसः । रसगन्धकनागञ्च विषं स्थावरजङ्गमम् । मत्स्यवराहमायूरच्छागपित्तैश्च भावयेत् । सूचिकाभरणो नाम भैरवेण प्रकीर्त्तितः । सूचिकाग्रेण दातव्यः सन्निपातकुलान्तकः । भैषज्यरत्नावली ।

that can be taken up by the point of a needle, hence it is called *suchikábharana.* It is given in remittent fever with cerebral complications.

Kálánala rasa.[1] Take of black cobra poison, sulphur, white arsenic, aconite, black pepper, long pepper, ginger, borax, mercury, prepared iron and copper equal parts ; soak them in the five kinds of bile mentioned above and make into one-grain pills with the juice of *datura* root. These are given in fever with coma, delirium and drowsiness.

MUSK.

Sans. मृगनाभि, *Mriganábhi*, कस्तूरी, *Kasturi.*

THE Bhávaprákása describes three varieties of musk, namely, *Kámrupa*, *Nepála* and *Káshmira* musk. *Kámrupa* musk is said to be of black colour and superior to the others. It is probably China or Thibet musk brought via Kamroop. *Nepála* musk is described as of bluish colour and intermediate quality. *Káshmira* musk is of inferior quality.

Musk is regarded as stimulant and aphrodisiac and is used in ow fevers, chronic cough, general delibity and impotence. In low lfevers with prostration, two grains of musk with two of *Makaradhvaja* are given every three hours with the addition of honey.

Svalpa kasturi bhairava.[2] Take of cinnabar, aconite, borax, nutmeg, mace, long pepper, black pepper and musk, equal parts

---

1 कालानलः रसः । अमृतं गरलं गन्धं लौहताम्रञ्च टङ्कणं । रसं गन्धं त्र्यूषणञ्च पञ्चपित्तैर्व्विभावयेत् । मातुलुङ्गद्रवै भाव्यं वटिका यवमानतः । चौद्राद्र्क रसयानु दापयेत् सान्निपातिके । अति तीव्र ज्वरं हन्ति सर्व्वोपद्रव संयुतं । हरिद्रा तैल संमिश्रं मर्द्दयेत् तीव्रतापिनं । तथा स्नानान्तरे गाढ़ं लेपयेत् गन्धचन्दनं । दध्यन्नं दापयेत् पथ्यं द्राक्षादिचाम्ल दाड़िमं । कालानल रसो नाम्ना गोप्यः परमदुर्ल्लभः । रसरत्नाकरः ।

2 स्वल्पकस्तूरि भैरव रसः । हिङ्गुलञ्च विषं टङ्कं जातिकोष फलन्तथा । मरिचं पिप्पली चैव कस्तूरीच समांशिका । रक्तिद्वयं ततः खादेत् सन्निपाते सुदारुणे । रसेन्द्रसारसंग्रहः ।

and make into four-grain pills. These are given in remittent fever of low type.

Mrigandvyádyavaleha.[1] Take of musk, cardamoms, cloves, cinnamon and dates, equal parts and make into a linctus with honey and clarified butter. This is given in hoarseness and loss of speech.

Vasantatilaka rasa.[2] Take of prepared gold one part, talc and tin two parts each, iron three parts, the preparation of mercury called *rasasindura* and calcined pearls and coral, four parts each; mix them together, soak for seven days in the juice of sugar-cane, of the fruits *Tribulus terrestris* (*gokshura*) and of other strengthening vegetables. Enclose the mass in a covered crucible and roast it in a sand-bath for three hours. Lastly add to it four parts of camphor and four of musk and make into four-grain pills. These are given as an alterative tonic in a variety of diseases, but more especially in chronic affections of the lungs supposed to be caused by deranged phlegm.

CIVET CAT.

Sans. गन्धमार्जार, *Gandha márjára. Vern. Khátási, Beng.* The pouch of the civet cat (*Viverra Zibetha, Linn.*) contains an unctuous odorous secretion which is extracted and used in perfumery. The

---

1 मृगनाभ्यादिरवलेहः । मृगनाभि सूक्ष्मैला लवङ्गकुसुमानि च । त्वक्क्षीरी चेति लेह्योयं मधुसर्पिः समायुतः । वाक्स्तम्भमुग्रं जयति स्वरभ्रंश समन्वितम् । भावप्रकाशः ।

2 वसन्ततिलकरसः । हेम्नोभस्मकमभ्रकं द्विगुणितं लौहास्त्रयः पारदाः चत्वारो नियतन्तु वङ्गयुगलं चैकीकृतं मर्द्दयेत् । मुक्ताविद्रुमयो रसेन समता गोक्षुरवासेक्षुणा सर्व्वं वस्त्रकरेण तेन सुदृढ़ं तत्तत् पचेत् सप्तधा । कस्तुरी घनसारमर्द्दितरसः पश्चात् सुसिद्धोर्भवेत् । कासश्वास सपित्त वात कफजित् पाण्डुक्षयादीन् हरेत् । शूलादिग्रहणीं विषादिहरणं मेहाश्मरीं विंशतिं । हृद्रोगापहरं ज्वरारुचिशमनं हृष्यं वयोवर्द्धनं श्रेष्ठं पुष्टिकरं वसन्त-तिलकं सत्य कृयेनोदितम् । रसेन्द्रसारसंग्रहः । अयमपि मारात्मक-कफरोगे प्रसिद्धः ।

pouch together with the secretion contained in it, are used by native physicians in scenting medicated oils.

HARTSHORN. *Sans.* मृगशृङ्ग, *Mrigasringa.* The antler of the deer incinerated in closed vessels is used in painful affections of the heart, pleurodynia, sciatica and lumbago. It is given in doses of about twenty-two grains with clarified butter. Burnt hartshorn leaves 57·5 per cent of phosphate of lime.[1]

MILK AND ITS PRODUCTS.

The properties of the milk of various animals are described in great detail by Sanskrit writers. Milk in general is considered cooling, nutritive, strengthening and vitalizing. Cow's milk is pleasant to take and very wholesome. It promotes memory, strength and longevity and increases the secretion of semen. Buffalo's milk is said to be sweeter, heavier and more cooling than cow's milk. It induces sleepiness, spoils the appetite and brings on cold. Goat's milk is sweet, cooling and astringent. It promotes the digestive power and is useful in hæmorrhagic diseases, phthisis, bowel complaints, etc. Ewe's milk is saltish, disagreeable and not easily digested. Mare's milk is saltish, acidulous and easily digested. Ass's milk is saltish, easily digested, and useful in debility and urinary complaints. Camel's milk is light, sweet, saltish, laxative and useful in dropsical affections. Human milk is light, cooling, nutritive, strengthening and useful as a collyrium or wash in eye diseases. All milk except human milk should be taken boiled. Warm milk just as it comes out from the teats is said to be like nectar.

As an article of diet, milk is considered demulcent, laxative, and especially adapted for children, old men, consumptive people or those reduced by debauchery, for women who are suckling and for patients suffering from chronic fever, mental diseases, dyspepsia,

---

1 शरावसंपुटे दग्धं शृङ्गं हारिणजं पिबेत्। गव्येन सर्पिषापिष्टं हृच्छूलं नश्यति ध्रुवम्। शार्ङ्गधरः। दग्धमनिर्गतधूमं मृगशृङ्गं गोघृतेन सम्पीतम्। हृदयनितम्बजशूलं हरति शिखीदारुनिवहमिव। चक्रः।

diarrhœa, urinary complaints, ascites and anasarca. A pure milk-diet to the exclusion of every other article (not excepting even salt and water) is often prescribed in the later stages of anasarca, ascites and chronic bowel complaints. Along with this milk diet, some sort of medicine, such as *Dugdha vaṭi, Svarnaparpaṭi*, or *Mána maṇḍa*, is usually prescribed.

तक्र *Takra* or butter-milk. Four sorts of butter-milk are described, namely *ghola* or pure butter-milk without admixture of water, *takra* or butter-milk with one-fourth part of water, *udasi* or that mixed with half its bulk of water, and *chhachchhiká* or very dilute butter-milk. The second form called *takra* is used in medicine and as an article of sick diet. It is regarded as astringent, light, cooling, appetizing, nutritive, tonic, and useful in diarrhœa, dysentery, dyspepsia, urinary diseases, ascites, poisoning, etc. It is not suited to the weak, or consumptive nor to those suffer- from fever and nervousness. The habitual use of butter-milk is said to be conducive to health and a preservative against disease.

दधि *Dadhi* or curdled milk is prepared by adding some acid or a little curdled milk as a ferment to milk previously boiled. In the course of twelve hours the whole of the milk thus acted upon is changed into a more or less thick, acidulous, jelly-like mass. It is considered agreeable, digestive and cooling, and is much used as an aricle of diet by all classes of natives. Taken to excess it causes biliousness and catarrh. It is useful in fever, diarrhœa, dysentery, urinary disorders and disinclination for food.

मस्तु *Mastu* or whey is said to have properties similar to those of curdled milk. In particular it is said to favour the circulation of the animal fluids and to be useful in constipation.

किलाटक *Kiláṭaka* or curd of milk (*Vern. chhená, Beng.*) is hard of digestion, but is nourishing, tonic and suited to persons with strong digestive powers.

सन्तानिका *Santániká* or cream is also hard of digestion but nourishing, agreeable and demulcent.

नवनीत *Navanita* or butter is tonic, astringent, invigorating, stomachic and useful in phthisis, piles, facial paralysis, etc. It agrees best with the old and young.

घृत *Ghrita* or clarified butter is much used both as an article of diet and in pharmacy. Clarified butter obtained from cow's milk is considered superior to that prepared from the milk of the buffalo and is preferred for medicinal use. Clarified butter is considered cooling, emollient and stomachic. It increases the fatty tissues and mental powers, improves the voice, beauty and complexion and is useful in eye diseases, retained secretions, insanity, tympanites, painful dyspepsia, ulcers, wounds, etc. It is the basis of a form of medicinal preparation called *ghritapáka* already described in the introduction, (see page 14).

पुराणघृत *Purána ghrita.* Clarified butter more than ten years old, passes by this name.[1] It has a strong pungent odour and the colour of lac. The longer this old butter is kept the more efficacious it is said to prove as an external application. Clarified butter a hundred years old is often heard of. The richer natives always have a stock of old *ghrita* of this description which they preserve with care for their own use as well as for distribution to their poorer neighbours. I have seen some specimens of old clarified butter which were quite dry and hard and nearly inodorous. They looked more like some sort of earth than an animal substance. Old clarified butter is used externally. It is first repeatedly washed with cold water, and then rubbed with it till it is reduced to a soapy frothy fluid which is used as a liniment. It is regarded as cooling and emollient and is much used in nervous diseases such as insanity, epilepsy, neuralgia, paralysis, cephalalgia and asthma, in rheumatic affections, stiff joints, burning of the body, hands or feet, affections of the eyes, etc.[2]

The following treatment is recommended for reducing the temperature of the skin in strong fever. The patient's body should be anointed with an emulsion of sandal wood and of old clarified butter that has been washed a hundred times in cold

1 उन्मादघ्नतो दशा: वा पुराणं वैकृतं घृतम्। उग्रगन्धं पुराणं स्याद्दशवर्षस्थितं घृतम्। लाक्षारस निभं शीतं प्रपुराणमत:परम्। चक्रः।

2 शतधौत घृताभ्यङ्गः शीतवातादि सेवनम्। शीतस्पर्शाश्च संसेव्याः सदा-दाहार्त्ति शान्तये। चक्रः।

water. He should then enter a tepid bath for a short while. His bedding should be made of the leaves of *Nelumbium speciosum* (*kamala*).[1]

BILE.

Sans. पित्त, *Pitta.*

The bile of the buffalo, wild boar, goat, peacock and *rohitaka* fish (*Cyprinus Rohita*), is used in medicine, either singly or in combination under the designation of *Pancha pitta* or the five biles. Bile is considered laxative and is chiefly used in soaking powders intended for being made into pill-masses.

Udakamanjari rasa.[2] Take of mercury, sulphur, calcined borax, and black pepper each one part; sugar and the bile of *rohitaka* fish, four parts each; rub them together for three days and make into six-grain pills. These are given with ginger juice in recent bilious remittent fever. If there is much heat of head, cold water should be applied to it. For other preparations containing bile, see under serpent poison, page 278.

गोरोचना *Gorochaná*, or the concretions found in the gall-bladder of the ox, are considered cooling, aromatic and useful in abortion and diseases supposed to be caused by evil spirits. *Gorochana* is sometimes given to infants in small doses as a laxative, It enters into the composition of some medicines for skin diseases.

URINE. *Sans.* मूत्र, *Mutra.*

THE properties of the urine of various animals, such as the cow, buffalo, goat, sheep, horse, elephant, ass, and camel are minutely described. Of these, cow's urine is much used both internally and externally, in the purification of various metals and in the

1 शीताम्बुः सान्तुशतशश्च विलोडितेन गव्येन चन्दन युतेन घनेन दिग्धा । दाहज्वरी सकमलोत्पलमात्मधारी क्षिप्रं विशेत् सलिलकोष्णमनल्पकालं । काञ्जिकार्द्र पटेनावगुण्ठनं दाहनाशनम् । दर्पणः ।

2 उदकमञ्जरीरसः । सूतं गन्धटङ्कणः सोषणश्च सर्व्वैस्तुल्याः शर्करा मत्स्यपित्तैः । भूयोभूयो मर्द्दयेत् त्रिरात्रं वल्लोदेयः शृङ्गवेर द्रवेण । तोयेशीतं वीजनैस्तक्रभक्तादन्ताकाद्यं पथ्यमेतत् प्रदिष्टं । च्यङ्गैवोग्रं हन्ति सद्यज्वरन्तु पित्ताधिकं मूर्द्ध्नि तोयञ्च दद्यात् । रसप्रदीपः ।

preparation of oils, decoctions, etc. It is described as laxative, diuretic and useful in constipation, suppression of urine, colic, anasarca, jaundice, leprosy and other skin diseases. Goat's urine is sometimes given internally as for example in the prescription quoted under *Nardostachys jatamansi*. In congestive fever with constipation, flushed face and headache, an ounce of fresh and warm cow's urine is given as a domestic medicine. It is sometimes given as the vehicle for administering castor oil, (see page 231). Cow's urine is used in the preparation of various medicines for jaundice, anasarca and allied diseases. The following is an illustration.

Punarnavá mandura.[1] Take of *Boerhaavia diffusa* (*punarnavá*) *Ipomœa Turpethum* (*trivrit*), ginger, long pepper, black pepper, *báberang* seeds, *devadáru* wood, plumbago root, *pátchak* root, the three myrobalans, turmeric, wood of *Berberis Asiatica*, (*dáruharidrá*) root of *Baliospermum montanum*, (*danti*), *Piper Chaba* (*chaviká*), *indrajava* seeds, root of *Picrorrhiza Kurroa* (*katuki*), long pepper root and the tubers of *Cyperus rotundus* (*mustaka*), equal parts; iron rust in weight equal to twice that of all the other ingredients; mix them together and boil the mixed powder in eight times its weight of cow's urine till the watery part is evaporated. Dose, about twenty-two grains, in jaundice, ascites, anasarca, enlargements of the abdominial viscera, painful dyspepsia, etc.

Marichádya taila. Take of mustard oil four seers, cow's urine sixteen seers, aconite eight tolás, orpiment, realgar, black pepper, milky juice of *Calotropis gigantea* (*arka*), root of *Nerium odorum* (*karavira*), root of *Ipomœa Turpethum* (*trivrit*), colocynth root, *Aplotaxis auriculata* (*kushtha*), turmeric, wood of *Berberis Asiatica* (*dáruharidrá*), *devadáru* wood, and red sandal wood, each

---

1 पुनर्नवामण्डूरम्। पुनर्नवात्रिवृच्छूण्ठी पिप्पलीमरिचानि च। विडङ्गं देवकाष्ठञ्च चित्रकं पुष्कराह्वयम्। त्रिफलां द्वे हरिद्रे च दन्तीञ्च चविकन्तथा। कुटजस्य फलं तिक्तापिप्पलीमूल मुस्तकम्। एतानि समभागानि मण्डूरं द्विगुणं ततः। गोमूत्रेऽष्टगुणे पक्त्वा स्थापयेत् स्निग्धभाजने। पाण्डुशोथोदरानाह शूलार्शःक्रिमिगुल्मनुत्। भावप्रकाशः।

four tolás, and prepare an oil in the usual way. This oil is said to be useful in leucoderma, chronic prurigo and other obstinate skin diseases.[1]

ANIMAL FLESH.

In describing the properties of the flesh of various animals, Sanskrit writers divide them into two classes, namely जाङ्गल *Jángala* or land, and अनूप *Anupa* or water animals : Animals living on land are sub-divided into eight orders as follows :—जाङ्गला *Jángalá* or animals living in the wilderness as deers, antelopes, etc.

विलस्था: *Vilasthá*, or animals living in holes under ground, as serpents, lizards, porcupines, etc.

गुहाशया:, *Guhásayá* or animals living in caverns, as tigers lions, bears, etc.

पर्णमृगा:, *Parnamrigá* or animals living on trees, as monkeys sqirrels, etc.

विष्किरा:, *Vishkirá* or birds which take their food after tearing or scattering it, as peacocks, quails, partridges, etc.

प्रतुदा:, *Pratudá* or birds which strike with their beaks, as pigeons, wag-tails, cuckoos, etc.

प्रसहा:, *Prasahá* or birds of prey, as the hawk, falcon, etc.

ग्राम्या:, *Grámyá* or domestic animals, as ox, goat, horse, sheep, etc.

Animals living in water or marshy lands are sub-divided into five classes as follows :—

कुलेचरा:, *Kulechará*, or animals grazing in marshes, as buffalos, yak, rhinoceras, etc.

प्लवा:, *Plává*, or birds which swim in water, as geese, ducks cranes, etc.

कोषस्था:, *Kosasthá*, or animals enclosed in shells, as conch-shells, bivalve-shells, etc.

पादिन: *Pádina*, or footed aquatic animals as tortoise, crocodile porpoise, etc.

---

1 मरिचाद्यं तैलम् । मरिचालशिलाह्वार्कपयोश्वारिजटालिहृत् । शकृद्रस-विशालारुङ्निशायुग्दारुचन्दनैः । कटुतैलात्पचेत्प्रस्थं द्व्यक्षैर्विषपलान्वितैः । सगोमूत्रं तदभ्यङ्गाद्दद्रुश्वित्रविनाशनम् । सर्व्वेष्वपिच कुष्ठेषु तैलमेतत् प्रश-स्यते । चक्रदत्तः ।

मत्स्य *Matsya* or fishes.

Of these classes, *Jángalá* or animals living in the wilderness, and *Vishkira* or birds which scatter their food are considered superior to the others in an alimentary point of view. The different properties of the meat of various animals are desribed by Sanskrit writers in great detail. The flesh of the goat, domestic fowl, peacock and partridge is said to be easily digested and suited to the sick and convalescent. The meat of the deer, sambar, hare, quail, and partridge is recommended for habitual use. Fish, beef and pork are considered hard to digest and unsuited for daily use.

The flesh of various animals is used in medicine chiefly in the form of *ghrita* or *taila páka*. The following is a list of the more important and commonly used *ghritas* and oils made with the flesh of different animals.

Hansádi ghrita, prepared with the flesh of geese, and used in cephalalgia and nervous diseases.

Kukkutádi ghrita, prepared with the flesh of fowls, and used in chronic cough.

Sivá ghrita, prepared with jackal's flesh and used in insanity.

Chhágaládi ghrita, prepared with goat's meat, and used in nervous diseases.

Sámbukáditaila, is an oil prepared with the flesh of snails and used externally in ear diseases.

Nakuládya ghrita is prepared with the flesh of the mungoose and used in nervous diseases.

The following are two illustrations of preparations with animal flesh.

Chhágaládya ghrita.[1] Take of goat's meat six seers and a quarter, the ten drugs called *dasamula* six seers and a quarter in

---

1 छागलाद्यं घृतम् । छागं चर्म्मविनिर्मुक्तं त्यक्तशृङ्गखुरादिकम् । पञ्चमूलीद्वयञ्चैव जलद्रोणे विपाचयेत् । तेन पादावशेषेण घृत प्रस्थं विपाचयेत् । जीवनीयैः सयष्ट्याह्वैः क्षीरञ्चैव शतावरी । छागलाद्यमिदं नाम्ना सर्व्ववातविकारनुत् । अर्द्दिते कर्णशूले च बाधिर्य्ये मूकमिन्मिने । जड़गद्गद पङ्गूनां खञ्जे गृध्रसिकुब्जयोः । अपतानेऽपतन्त्रे च सर्पिरेतत् प्रशस्यते । अत्रयष्टि मधु भागद्वयमिति शिवदासः । भैषज्यरत्नावली ।

all, water sixty-four seers; boil till the latter is reduced to one-fourth and strain. Take of clarified butter, milk and the juice of *Asparagus racemosus* (*satamuli*), four seers each ; and the following substances in the form of a paste, namely, *Tinospora cordifolia* (*guruchi*), bamboo-manna, *Withania somnifera* (*asvagandhá*), *Hemidesmus Indicus* (*sárivá*), berries called *kákoli*, bulbs called *kshira-kákali*, pulse of *Phaseolus trilobus* (*mugáni*), and of *Glycine debilis* (*masháni*), *Cœlogyne ovalis*, (*jivanti*), and liquorice root (one seer in all) ; boil them together and prepare a *ghrita*. This preparation is given in facial paralysis, deafness, loss of voice or indistinct speech, convulsions, hysteria, sciatica, paralysis and other diseases of the nervous system.

Máshataila.[1] Take of goat's meat eight seers, water sixty-four seers; boil together till the latter is reduced to sixteen seers. Take of the pulse of *Phaseolus Roxburghii* (*másha*), *linseed*, *barley*, root of *Barleria Prionites* (*kuranṭaka*), of *Solanum Jacquinii*, (*kanṭa-kári*), *Tribulus terrestris* (*gokshura*), bark of *Calosanthes Indica* *syonáka*), *jaṭámánsi* root, seeds of *Mucuna pruriens* (*ka-pikvachchhu*), each one seer, water sixty-four seers; boil down to sixteen seers. Take of cotton seeds, seeds of *Crotolaria juncea* (*sana*), *pulse* of *Dolichos uniflorus* (*kulattha*), dried pulp of *Ziziphus Jujuba* (*kola*), each two seers, water sixty-four seers ; boil down to sixteen seers. Take of ginger, long pepper, dill seeds, root of *Ricinus communis* (*eranḍa*), of *Bœrhaavia diffusa* (*punarnavá*), *Pœderia fœtida* (*prasárani*), *Vanda Roxburghii* (*rásná*), *Sida cordifolia* (*berelá*), *Tinospora cordifolia* (*gulancha*) and *Picrorrhiza Kurroa* (*katuki*) equal parts ; in all one seer, and reduce them to a paste. Boil the above mentioned decoctions and the paste with four seers of sesamum oil in the usual way. This oil is rubbed externally in convulsions, paralysis, wasting of limbs and other diseases of the nervous system.

---

1 माषतैलम् । माषातसी यवकुरण्टककण्टकारी गोकण्टटुण्टुकजटा कपिकच्छुतोयैः । कार्पासकास्थि शणबीज कुलत्थकोलक्वाथेन वस्तपिशितस्य रसेन चापि । शुण्ठ्या समागधिकया शतपुष्पया च सैरण्डमूल सपुनर्नवया सरण्या । रास्ना बलामृत लता कटुकैर्विपक्वं माषाख्यमेतदवबाहुहरञ्च तैलम् । अर्द्धाङ्गशोष मपतानक माढ्यवातमाक्षेपकं सभुजकम्पशिरः प्रकम्पम् । नस्येन वस्तिविधिना परिषेचनेन हन्यात् कटीजघन जानुरुजः समीरात् । भैषज्यरत्नावली ।

A GLOSSARY

OF INDIAN PLANTS

MENTIONED IN SANSKRIT MEDICAL WORKS

WITH BENGALI, HINDI AND LATIN SYNONYMS.

SANSKRIT.	VERNACULAR.	SCIENTIFIC NAMES.
Áchchhuka	Ách, B.	Morinda citrifolia, Linn. and
आच्छुक	Ál, H.	Morinda tinctoria, Roxb.
Áḍhaki	Arhar, B.	Cajanus Indicus, Spreng.
आढ़की	Tor, H.	*Syn. Cytisus Cajan, Linn.*
Ádityabhaktá	Hurhuriá, B.	Cleome viscosa, Linn.
आदित्यभक्ता	Hurhur, H.	*Syn. Polanisia icosandra, W. and A.*
Agasti		See Vaka.
अगस्ति		
Agnimantha	Ganiári, B.	Premna serratifolia, Linn.
अग्निमन्थ	Arni, Agetha, H.	*Syn. Premna spinosa, Roxb.*
Agnisikhá		See Lángaliká.
अग्निशिखा		Aquilaria Agallocha, Roxb.
Aguru	Agar, B.	
अगुरु	Agar, H.	
Ahinsrá	Kántágurkámái, B.	Capparis sepiaria, Linn.
अहिंस्रा		
Ahiphena	Áphim, B.	Papaver somniferum, Linn.
अहिफेन	Áphim, H.	Opium poppy.
Ajamodá	Ajmad, H.	Pimpinella involucrata, W. and A.
अजमोदा	Rándhani, B.	*Syn. Apium involucratum, Roxb.*

SANSKRIT.	VERNACULAR.	SCIENTIFIC NAMES.
Akarákarabha	Ákarkará, B. H.	Anacyclus Pyrethrum, DC.
अकराकरभ		Pellitory root.
Ákásamánsi आकाशमांसी		A small variety of Jatámánsi said to be produced in the Kedár mountain.
Ákásavalli	Ákásbel, B.	Cassytha filiformis, Linn.
आकाशवल्ली	Amarbeli, H.	
Ákhukarni आखुकर्णी		See Mushikaparni.
Ákshoṭa आक्षोट	Ákhrot, H. B.	Juglans regia, Linn.
Alábu	Láu, B. Lauká, H.	Lagenaria vulgaris, Sering.
अलाबु	Mithi tumbi, H.	*Syn. Cucurbita lagenaria, Willd.*
Alarka	Svetákand, B.	Calotropis gigantea, or procera, R. Br.
अलर्क	Mádár, H.	The varieties with white flowers.
Ámalaki	Ámlá, B.	Phyllanthus Emblica. Linn.
आमलकी	Áṇolá, H.	*Syn. Emblica officinalis, Gaert.*
Ambashṭhá अम्बष्ठा		See Páṭhá.
Ambuvetasa अम्बुवेतस	Barabet, B.	Calamus fasciculatus, Roxb. ?*
Amlaloniká आम्ललोनिका	Ámrul sák, B. H.	Oxalis corniculata, Linn.
Amlána अम्लान	Lál gulmakhmal, B.	Gomphrena globosa, Linn.
Amlavetasa अम्लवेतस		See Chukra.

* Roxburgh gives *ambuvetasa* as the sanskrit for *Calamus fasciculatus*, but *ambuvetasa* means rattan growing in water, while Calamus fasciculatus grows in woods and not in marshes. The translation is therefore doubtful. I have not been able to procure the plant.

SANSKRIT.	VERNACULAR.	SCIENTIFIC NAMES.
Amra	Ám, B.	Mangifera Indica, Linn.
अम्र [haridrá	Ám, H.	The Mango tree.
Ámragandhi-	Ámbahaldi, H.	Curcuma reclinata, Roxb.
आम्रगन्धिहरिद्रा		
Ámrátaka	Ámrá, B.	Spondias mangifera, Pers.
आम्रातक	Ámbrá, H.	Hog plum.
Amritaphala	Náshpáti, H.	Pyrus communis, Linn.
अमृतफल	Nák, Punj.	The pear-tree.
Anantá	Anantamul, B. H.	Hemidesmus Indicus, R. Br.
अनन्ता		*Syn. Asclepias pseudosarsa, Roxb.*
Anjira	Ánjir, H.	Ficus Carica, Linn. in Bengal,
अञ्जीर		Psidium pomiferum is called anjira in Sanskrit.
Ankoṭa	Dhalákura, B.	Alangium Lamarkii, Thwaites.
अङ्कोट	Dherá, H.	*Syn. A. Hexapetalum, Roxb.*
Apámárga	Ápáng, B.	Achyranthes aspera, Linn.
अपामार्ग	Laṭjirá, H.	Also A. bidentata, Bl.
Aparájitá	Aparájitá, B.	Clitoria Ternatea, Linn.
अपराजिता	Visnukránti, H.	
Áragbadha	Sondháli, B.	Cassia fistula, Linn.
आरग्वध	Ámaltás, H.	*Syn. Cathartocarpus fistula, Pers.*
Aralu,		See Syonáka.
अरलु		
Árdraka	ÁdáB.	Zingiber officinale, Rosc.
आर्द्रक	Ádrak, H.	Common ginger.
Arimeda	Guábáblá, B.	Acacia Farnesiana, Willd.
अरिमेद	Gandbábul, H.	*Syn. Mimosa Farnesiana, Roxb.*
Arjuna	Arjun, B.	Terminalia Arjuna, Bedd.
अर्जुन	Kahú, H.	*Syn. Pentaptera Arjuna, Roxb.*
Arkamulá	Ishermul, B.	Aristolochia Indica, Linn.
अर्कमूला		
Arka	Ákand, B.	Calatropis gigantea or procera, R. Br.
अर्क	Mádár, H.	*Syn. Asclepias gigantea, Willd.*

SANSKRIT.	VERNACULAR.	SCIENTIFIC NAMES.
Arkapushpiká	Arkahuli, B.	Gynandropsis pentaphylla, DC.
अर्कपुष्पिका	Sádáhurhuriá, B.	*Syn. Cleome pentaphylla, Linn.*
Arushkara		See Bhallátaka.
अरुष्कर		
Asana	Piásál, B.	Terminalia tomentosa, W. and A.
असन	Asan, H.	*Syn. Pentaptera tomentosa, Roxb.*
Ashtavarga*		
अष्टवर्ग		
Asoka	Asok, B. H.	Saraca Indica, Linn.
अशोक		*Syn. Jonesia Asoka, Roxb.*
Asthisanhára	Hárjorá, B.	Vitis quadrangularis, Wall.
अस्थिसंहार	Harsankari H.	*Syn. Cissus quadrangularis, Linn.*
Asvagandhá	Asvagandhá, B.	Withania somnifera, Don.
अश्वगन्धा	Asgandh, H.	*Syn. Physalis flexuosa, Roxb.*
Asvakarna	Sál, B. H.	Shorea robusta, Gaertn.
अश्वकर्ण		
Asvattha	Asvattha, B.	Ficus religiosa, Linn.
अश्वत्थ	Pipal, H.	*Syn. Urostigma religiosum, Gasp.*
Atasi	Masiná, B.	Linum usitatissimum, Linn.
अतसी	Tisi, H.	
Atibalá	Pitbalá, B.	Sida rhombifolia, Linn.
अतिबला		

* This is a collective name for eight medicines, six of which are not available at present. Their names and the articles substituted for those that are not procurable, are as follows:—

Medá, मेदा. Asvagandhá is used in stead.
Mahámedá, महामेदा. Sárivá, ,,
Jivaka, जीवक. Guḍuchi, ,,
Rishabhaka, ऋषभक. Vansalochana, ,,
Riddhi, ऋद्धि. Balá, ,,
Vriddhi, वृद्धि. Mahábalá, ,,
Kákoli, काकोली. See under this name.
Kshirakákoli· क्षीरकाकोली. Do. Do.

SANSKRIT.	VERNACULAR.	SCIENTIFIC NAMES.
Ativisha अतिविष	Átis, H. B.	Aconitum heterophyllum, Wall.
Átmaguptá आत्मगुप्ता	Álkusi, B. Kiwanch, H.	Mucuna pruriens, DC. *Syn. Carpopogon pruriens, Roxb.*
Avalguja अवल्गुज		See Somaráji.
Ávartani आवर्त्तनि	Átmorá. B. Mararphali, H.	Helicteres Isora, Linn. *Syn. Isora corylifolia, Schott et End.*
Bádáma बादाम	Bádám, H. B.	Amygdalus communis, Linn. The almond tree.
Badara बदर		SeKo la.
Bahuvára बहुवार	Bahuá·i, B. Lasorá, H.	Cordia Myxa, Linn. *Cordia latifolia, Roxb. Bara Lasrá.*
Balá बला	Berelá, B. Khareṭi, Bariár, H.	Sida cordifolia, Linn.
Bálá बाला	Bá'á, H. Sugandha Bálá, H.	Pavonia odorata, Linn.
Bandhuka बन्धुक	Bándhuli, B. Dopohoriá, H.	Pentapetes phœnicea, Linn.
Bhadramunjá भद्रमुञ्जा	Rámsar, B. H.	A variety of Saccharum Munja, Roxb.
Bhadravalli भद्रवल्लि	Háparmáli, B.	Vallaris dichotoma, Wall. *Syn. Echites dichotoma, Roxb.*
Bhallátaka भल्लातक	Bhelá, B. Bhiláwá, H.	Semecarpus Anacardium, Linn. The marking nut tree.
Bhánḍira भाण्डीर	Bhánt, B. H.	Clerodendron infortunatum Linn. *Syn. Volkameria infortunata, Roxb.*
Bhangá भङ्गा	Siddhi, B. Bháng, H.	Cannabis sativa, Linn. var. Indica. Indian hemp.
Bhantáki भण्टाकी		See Vártáku.

SANSKRIT.	VERNACULAR.	SCIENTIFIC NAMES.
Bháradváji भारद्वाजी		See Vanakárpási.
Bhárgi भार्गी	Bámanháṭi, B, Bhárangi H.	Clerodendron Siphonanthus, R. Br. *Syn. Siphonanthus Indica, Lamk.*
Bhavya भव्य	Chálta, B.	Dillenia Indica, Linn. *Syn. Dillenia speciosa, Thunb.*
Bhringarája भृङ्गराज	Bhimráj, B. Bhánrá, H.	Wedelia calendulacea, Less. *Syn. Verbesina calendulacea, Willd.*
Bhumichampaka भूमिचम्पक	Bhuichámpá, B.	Kæmpferia rotunda, Linn.
Bhumijambu भूमिजम्बु	Bhuijám, B.	Premna herbacea, Roxb.
Bhumikushmáṇḍa भूमिकुष्माण्ड	Bhuikumrá, B.	Batatas paniculata, Chois. *Syn. Convolvulus paniculatus, Linn*
Bhumyámalaki भूम्यामलकी	Bhuiámlá, B. Jarámlá, H.	Phyllanthus Niruri, Linn.
Bhunimba भूनिम्ब		See Kirátatikta.
Bhurjapatra भूर्जपत्र	Bhurjapatra, B. Bhujpatar, H.	Betula Bhojpattra, Wall.
Bhustrina भूस्तृण	Gandhabená, B.	Andropogon Schœnanthus, Linn.
Bhutakesi भूतकेशी	Bhutkesi, B. H.	Corydalis Govaniana, Wall.
Bráhmanayasṭiká ब्राह्मणयष्टिका	Bámanháṭi, B. Bhárangi, H.	Clerodendron Siphonanthus, R. Brown. *Syn. Siphonanthus Indica, Lamk.*
Brahmi ब्राह्मी	Brihmi sák, B. Barambhi, H.	Herpestes Monnieria, H. B. K. *Syn. Gratiola Monnieria, Linn.*
Chakramardaka चक्रमर्दक	Chákundiá, B. Panwar, chakaund, H.	Cassia Tora, Linn. *Syn. Senna Tora, Roxb.*
Champaka चम्पक	Champá, B. H.	Michelia Champaca, Linn.

SANSKRIT.	VERNACULAR.	SCIENTIFIC NAMES.
Chanaka	Chholá, B.	Cicer arietinum, Linn.
चणक	Chaná, H.	Gram or chick-pea.
Chandana	Chandan, B.	Santalum album, Linn.
चन्दन	Safed Chandan, H.	White sandal wood.
Chandriká		See Chandrasura.
चन्द्रिका		
Chandrasura	Hálim, H.	Lepidium sativum, Linn.
चन्द्रसूर		
Chángeri	Ámrul sák, B. H.	Oxalis corniculata, Linn.
चाङ्गेरी		
Chaviká	Chai, B.	Piper Chaba, Hunter.
चविका	Chavi, H.	*Syn. Chavica officinarum, Miq.*
Chhikkani	Nákchhikni, B. H.	Centipeda minuta, Benth.
छिक्कणी		*Syn. Artemisia sternutatoria, Roxb.*
Chichinḍa	Chichingá, B.	Trichosanthes anguina, Linn.
चिचिण्ड	Cháchenḍa, H.	
China	Chiná ghás, B.	Panicum miliaceum, Linn.
चीन	Chena, Chin, H.	
Chitraka	Chitá, B. H.	Plumbago Zeylanica, Linn.
चित्रक		
Chobachini	Chobchini, H.	Smilax China, Linn.
चोबचिनि		
Chorapushpi	Chorkánṭá, B.	Andropogon acicularis, Retz.
चोरपुष्पी		
Chukra	Chukapálang, B.	Rumex vesicarius, Linn.
चुक्र	Chukeká sák, H.	Country sorrel.
Dáḍima	Dálim, B.	Punica Granatum, Linn.
दाडिम	A'nar, H.	Pomegranate tree.
Dadrughna	Dádmardan, B. H.	Cassia alata, Linn.
दद्रुघ्न		
Dahu	Mádár, B.	Artocarpus Lakucha, Roxb.
डहु	Dahu, H.	

SANSKRIT.	VERNACULAR.	SCIENTIFIC NAMES.
Damanaka दमनक	Doná, B. Daoná, Marwá, H.	Artemisia vulgaris, Linn. *Syn. Artemisia Indica, Willd.*
Dandálu दण्डालु	Khámálu, B.	Dioscorea alata, Linn.
Dandotpala दण्डोत्पल	Dánkuni, B.	Canscora decussata, Roem. et Schult. *Syn. Pladera decussata, Roxb.*
Danti दन्ति	Danti, B. H.	Baliospermum montanum, Mull. Arg. *Syn. Croton polyandrum, Roxb.*
Darbha दर्भ	Ulu, B. Dábh, H.	Imperata cylindrica, Beauv. *Syn. Saccharum cylindricum, Lamk.*
Dáruharidrá दारुहरिद्रा	Dáruharidrá, B. Dáruhaldi, H.	Berberis asiatica, DC. Also B. aristata, DC.
Dárvi दार्व्वी		See Dáruharidrá.
Devadáru देवदारु	Debdáru, B. Deodár, H.	Cedrus Deodara, Loud. *Syn. Pinus Deodara, Roxb.*
Devadhánya देवधान्य	Deodhán, B. H.	Sorghum saccharatum, Pers. *Syn. Andropogon saccharatus, Roxb.*
Devatáda देवताड़	Detára, H. B.	Andropogon serratus, Retz.
Dhanvana धन्वन	Dhámani, B. H.	See Dharmana.
Dhánya धान्य	Dhán, B. H.	Oryza sativa, Linn. Common rice plant.
Dhányaka धन्याक	Dhane, B. Dhaniá, H.	Coriandrum sativum, Linn. Coriander plant.
Dhárákadamba धाराकदम्ब	Kelikadamba, B. Haldu, H.	Adina cordifolia, Benth. and Hook. *Syn. Nauclea cordifolia, Roxb.*
Dharmana धर्म्मन	Dhámani, H. B.	Grewia elastica, Royle.
Dhátaki धातकी	Dháiphul, B, Dhai, H.	Woodfordia floribunda, Salisb. *Syn. Grislea tomentosa, Roxb.*

Sanskrit.	Vernacular.	Scientific Names.
Dhava	Dháoyá, B. H.	Anogeissus latifolia, Wall.
धव [ká		*Syn. Conocarpus latifolia, Roxb.*
Dholasamudri-	Dholsamudra, B.	Leea macrophylla, Roxb.
ढोलसमुद्रिका		
Dhustura	Dhuturá, B.	Datura metel, Linn.
धुस्तुर [ká	Dhaturá, H.	Also Datura fastuosa, Linn.
Dirghapaṭoli-	Dhundul, B.	Luffa cylindrica, Roem.
दीर्घपटोलिका	Ghiátorai, H.	*Syn. Luffa pentandra, Roxb.*
Drákshá	Angur, B. H.	Vitis vinifera, Linn.
द्राक्षा		Dried fruits called Kismis.
Dronapushpi	Halkasá, B.	Leucas linifolia, Spreng.
द्रोणपुष्पी	Gumá, H.	*Syn. Phlomis Zeylanica, Roxb.*
Dugdhiká	Khirai, B.	Oxystelma esculentum, R. Br.
दुग्धिका	Dudhiálatá, B. H.	*Syn. Asclepias rosea, Roxb.*
Durálabhá	Jawásá, H.	Alhagi Maurorum, DC.
दुरालभा	Duralabhá, B.	*Syn. Hedysarum Alhagi, Linn.*
Durvá	Durbá, B.	Cynodon Dactylon, Pers.
दूर्वा	Dub, H.	*Syn. Panicum Dactylon, Linn.*
Elásukshma	Gujráṭi eláchi, B.	Elettaria cardamomum, W. et Maton
एलासूक्ष्म	Chhoṭa eláchi, B.	Also Amomum subulatum, Roxb.
Elabáluka	Eluá, H.	A red powder sold under these
ऐलवालुक	Láluká, B.	names ; the seed of some plant.
Eraká	Hoglá, B.	Typha angustifolia, Linn.
एरका	Paṭer, H.	*Syn. Typha elephantina, Roxb.*
Eranḍa.	Bherendá, B.	Ricinus communis, Linn.
एरण्ड	Erand, H.	Castor oil plant.
Erváru.	Phooṭ, H.	Cucumis Melo, Linn.
एर्वारु	Phuṭi, B.	*Syn. Cucumis Momordica, Roxb.*
Gajapippali.	Gajapipal, B. H.	Scindapsus officinalis, Schott.
गजपिप्पली		*Syn. Pothos officinalis, Roxb.*
Gambhári	Gámári, H.	Gmelina arborea, Linn.
गम्भारी	Khambhári, H.	

SANSKRIT.	VERNACULAR.	SCIENTIFIC NAMES.
Gandagátra गण्डगात्र	Átá, B. [H. Sharifá, Sitáphal,	Anona squamosa, Linn. Custard apple.
Gandharája गन्धराज	Gandharáj, B.	Gardenia florida, Linn.
Gandhatrina गन्धतृण		See Bhustrina.
Ganikáriká गणिकारिका	Ganiári, B. Arni, H.	Premna serratifolia, Linn. *Syn. P. spinosa, Roxb.*
Gardhabhánda गर्द्दभाण्ड	Parespipal, B. Gajahanda, H.	Thespasia populnea, Corr. *Syn. Hibiscus populneoides, Roxb.*
Garjara, गर्जर	Gájar, H.	Daucus Carota, Linn.
Gavedhuká गवेधुका	Gargaredhán, B.	Some species of Coix.
Ghantápátali घण्टापाटली	Ghantápárul, B. H.	Schrebera swietenioides, Roxb.
Ghantáravá घण्टारवा	Jhanjhania, B.	Crotalaria sericea, Retz.
Ghritakumári घृतकुमारी	Ghritakumári, B. Ghikumár, H.	Aloe Indica, Royle. *Syn. Aloe perfoliata, Roxb.*
Godhápadi गोधापदी	Goálilatá, B.	Vitis pedata, Vahl. *Syn. Cissus pedatus, Lamk.*
Godhuma गोधूम	Gam, B. Genhu H.	Triticum vulgare, Linn. Common wheat.
Godumbá गोडुम्बा	Gomuk, B.	Cucumis Melo, Linn. [*Roxb.* *Syn. Cucumis madraspatanus,*
Gojihbá गोजिह्वा	Gobhi, H. Gojiálatá, B.	Elephantopus scaber, Linn.
Gokshura गोक्षुर	Gokshura, B. Gokhuru, H.	Tribulus terrestris, Linn. *Syn. T. lanuginosus, Linn.*
Granthiparna ग्रन्थिपर्ण	Gántiálá, B. Thivan, H.	A sort of gall caused by an insect on some tree.

SANSKRIT.	VERNACULAR.	SCIENTIFIC NAMES.
Grishmasunda-	Gimásák, B.	Mollugo Spergula, Linn.
ग्रीष्मसुन्दर [ra		*Syn. Pharnaceum Mollugo, Linn.*
Guḍatvaka		See Tvacha.
गुड़त्वक		
Guḍuchi	Gulancha, B.	Tinospora cordifolia, Miers. [*Willd.*
गुडूची	Gurach, H.	*Syn. Menispermum cordifolium.*
Guggulu	Guggul, B. H.	Balsamodendron Mukul, Hooker.
गुग्गुलु		Also B. pubescens, Stocks.
Gundra	Gand paṭer, H.	Panicum uliginosum, Roxb.
गुन्द्र		
Gunjá	Kuṇch, B.	Abrus precatorius, Linn.
गुञ्जा	Chirmiṭi, Gunj, H.	
Guváka	Supári, H.	Areca Catechu, Linn.
गुवाक	Guá, B.	The betle nut tree.
Hallaka	Raktakambal, B.	Nymphæa Lotus, Linn.
हल्लक		*Syn. N. rubra, Roxb.*
Hapushá	Habush, H.	Black stalks like those of black pepper; aromatic.
हपुषा		
Harichandana	Pitchandan, B.	Yellow variety of sandal wood.
हरिचन्दन		
Haridrá	Halud, B.	Curcuma longa, Roxb.
हरिद्रा	Haldi, H.	
Haritaki	Haritaki, B.	Terminalia Chebula, Retz.
हरीतकी [lása	Har, H.	Chebulic myrobalan.
Hastikarnapa-		Butea superba, Roxb.
हस्तिकर्णपलाश		
Hastisunaḍá	Hátisurá, B.	Heliophytum Indicum, DC.
हस्तिशुण्डा		*Syn. Heliotropium Indicum, Linn.*
Hemapushpiká		See Suvarnajuthiká.
हेमपुष्पीका		
Hijjala	Hijjal, B. H.	Barringtonia acutangula, Gaertn.
हिज्जल		*Syn. Eugenia acutangula, Linn.*

Sanskrit.	Vernacular.	Scientific Names.
Hilamochiká	Hinchá, B.	Enhydra Heloncha, D C.
हिलमोचिका	Harhuch, H.	*Syn. Hingtsha repens, Roxb.*
Hingu	Hing, H. B.	Ferula Assafœtida, Linn.
हिङ्गु		
Hingupatri		The subacid leaves of Balanites
हिङ्गुपत्री		Roxburghii, Planchon, are so called.
Hintála	Hentál, H. B.	Phœnix paludosa, Roxb.
हिन्ताल		
Hrivera	Bálá, B.	Pavonia odorata, Willd.
ह्रीवेर	Sugandha bálá, H.	
Ikshu	Uk, H.	Saccharum officinarum, Linn.
इक्षु	Ák, B.	
Indravàruni	Indráyan, B	Citrullus Colocynthis, Schrad.
इन्द्रवारुणी	Mákál, H.	*Syn. Cucumis Colocynthis, Linn.*
Indrayava	Indrajab, H. B.	Seeds of Holarrhena antidysenterica, Wall.
इन्द्रयव		
Ingudi	Hingan, H.	Balanites Roxburghii, Planchon.
इङ्गुदी	Inguá, H.	*Syn. Ximenia Ægyptiaca, Roxb.*
Jalapippali	Pánikánchirá, B.	Commelyna salicifolia, Kunth.
जलपिप्पली	Jalpipari, H.	
Jambira	Jambir nebu, H.	Citrus medica, Linn.
जम्बीर	Goránebu, B.	Citrus acida, Var. 3. of Roxb.
Jambu	Kála jám, B.	Eugenia Jambolana, Lamk,
जम्बु	Jáman, H.	*Syn. Syzygium Jambolanum, W. & A.*
Jaṭámánsi	Jaṭámánsi, B. H.	Nardostachys Jatamansi, D. C.
जटामांसी	Báluchar, H.	*Syn. Valeriana Jatamansi, Jones.*
Játi	Chameli, H.	Jasminum grandiflorum, Linn.
जाती	Játi, B.	
Játiphala	Jayphal, B. H.	Myristica officinalis, Linn.
जातिफल		The nutmeg tree.
Javá	Jabá, B.	Hibiscus Rosa-Sinensis, Linn.
जवा	Gudhal, H.	Shoe-flower plant.

SANSKRIT.	VERNACULAR.	SCIENTIFIC NAMES.
Jayanti जयन्ती	Jayanti, B. H.	Sesbania aculeata, Pers. *Syn. Aeschynomene sesban, Roxb.*
Jayapála जयपाल	Jayapál, B. Jámalgoṭá, H.	Croton Tiglium, Linn. Croton oil plant.
Jhávuka झावुक	Jháu, B. H.	Tamarix gallica, Linn. *Syn. T. Indica, Willd.*
Jhingáka झिङ्गाक	Jhingá, B. Torái, H.	Luffa acutangula, Roxb. *Syn. Cucumis acutangulus, Linn.*
Jhinṭi झिण्टी	Jháṇṭi, B.	Barleria cristata, Linn.
Jingini जिङ्गिनी	Jiol, B. Jingan, H.	Odina Wodier, Roxb.
Jiraka जीरक	Jirá, B. H.	Cuminum Cyminum, Linn. Cummin seeds.
Jivanti जीवन्ती	Jibai, B. Jiba ság, H.	Cælogyne ovalis, Lindl.
Jyotishmati ज्योतिष्मती	Nayáphaṭki, B.	Cardiospermum Halicacabum, Linn.
Kachchi कच्ची	Kachu, B. H.	Colocasia antiquorum, Schott. *Syn. Arum Colocasia, Roxb.*
Kadali कदली	Kalá, B. Kelá, H.	Musa sapientum, Linn. Var. Musa Paradisiaca, Linn. [Hook
Kadamba कदम्ब	Kadam, B. H.	Anthocephalus Cadamba, Benth, and *Syn. Nauclea Cadamba, Roxb.*
Kairáta कैरात		See Bhunimba.
Kákádani काकादनी	Káliakará, B. Káṇṭágurkámái, B.	Capparis sepiaria, Linn.
Kákadumbar काकोडुम्बर	Toṭmilá, H. Kákḍumar, B, H.	Ficus hispida, Linn. fil. *Syn. Ficus oppositifolia, Roxb.*
Kákajanghá काकजङ्घा	Kákjanghá, H. B.	Leea hirta, Roxb.

SANSKRIT.	VERNACULAR.	SCIENTIFIC NAMES.
Kákali काकली	Kákoli, H. B.	A root said to be brought from Nepal or Morung.
Kákamáchi काकमाची	Gurkámái, B Mako, H.	Solanum nigrum, Linn.
Kákatinduka काकतिन्दुक	Mákrá kendu, B.	Diospyros melanoxylon, Roxb. Also Diospyros tomentosa, Roxb.
Kákatuṇḍi काकतुण्डी	Kowáḍoḍi, H.	Asclepias Curassavica, Linn. ?
Kakkolaka कक्कोलक	Kákalá, B. H. Sitalchini, H.	Berries containing a black aromatic waxy substance.
Kálakuṭa कालकुट		A sort of Aconite.
Kalambi कलम्बी	Kalmi sák B.	Ipomœa reptans, Poir. *Syn. Convolvulus repens, Willd.*
Kálánusárivá कालानुसारिवा	Shiulichhop, B. Tagarmul, H. B.	Limnanthemum cristatum, Griseb. *Syn. Menyanthes cristata, Roxb.*
Kálasáka कालशाक	Narchá, B. Ghinalitá, B.	Corchorus capsularis, Linn. Jute plant.
Kaláya कलाय	Maṭar, B. H.	Pisum sativum, Linn. Common pea.
Kamala कमल	Padma, B. Kamal, H.	Nelumbium speciosum, Willd. The sacred Lotus.
Kámalatá कामलता	Tarulatá, B.	Quamoclit vulgaris, Choisy. *Syn. Ipomœa Quamoclit, Linn.*
Kampillaka कम्पिल्लक	Kamaláguri, B. Kamilá, Kambilá, H.	Mallotus Philippensis, Mull. Arg. *Syn. Rottlera tinctoria, Roxb.*
Kánana eraṇḍa काननैरण्ड	Páhári eranḍ, H. Bágbherendá, B.	Jatropha Curcas, Linn. The physic nut tree.
Kánchana काञ्चन	Kachnár, H. Kánchan, B.	Bauhinia acuminata, Linn.
Kánchanáḍa काञ्चनाड़	Rakta Kánchan, B. Kachnár, H.	Bauhinia variegata, Linn.

SANSKRIT.	VERNACULAR.	SCIENTIFIC NAMES.
Kanchaṭa	Káchrádám, B.	Commelyna Bengalnsis, Linn.
कञ्चट	Kánchará, B.	
Kangu	Kangu, korá, B.	Setaria Italica, Kunth.
कङ्गु	Kangni, H.	*Syn. Panicum Italicum, Linn.*
Kanṭakári	Kanṭakári, B.	Solanum xanthocarpum, Schrad.
कण्टकारि	Kaṭái, Kaṭeli, H.	*Syn. Solanum Jacquinii, Willd.*
Kapikachchhu	Álkusi, B.	Mucuna pruriens, D. C.
कपिकच्छु	Kiwach, H.	*Syn. Carpopogon pruriens, Roxb.*
Kapittha	Kathbel, B.	Feronia Elephantum, Corr.
कपित्थ	Kaith, H.	The wood apple tree.
Karamardaka	Karamchá, B.	Carissa Carandas, Linn.
करमर्द्दक	Karaunḍá, H.	*Syn. C. congesta, Wight.*
Karanja	Dahar karanja, B.	Pongamia glabra, Vent.
करञ्ज	Kiramál, H.	*Syn. Galedupa Indica, Lamk.*
Káravella	Karalá, B.	Momordica charantia, Linn.
कारवेल्ल	Kareli, H.	*Syn. M. muricata, Willd.*
Karavira	Karabi, B.	Nerium odorum, Soland.
करवीर	Kaner, H.	Sweet scented oleander.
Karira	Karil, H.	Capparis aphylla, Roth.
करीर		*Syn. Capparis Sodada, R. Br.*
Karkaṭaka	Kákrol, B. H.	Momordica mixta, Roxb.
कर्कटक		
Karkaṭasringi	Kákrá sringi, B.	Rhus succedanea, Linn.
कर्कटशृङ्गी	Kákar singi, H.	*Syn. R. acuminata, DC.*
Karkaṭi	Kákur, B.	Cucumis Melo, Linn.
कर्कटी	Kákri, H.	*Syn. Cucumis utilissimus, Roxb.*
Karmaranga	Kámrángá, B.	Averrhoa Carambola, Linn.
कर्म्मरङ्ग	Kamarakh, H.	Carambola tree.
Karnikára	Kanakchampá, B.	Pterospermum acerifolium, Linn.
कर्णिकार	Kaniár, H.	
Kárpási	Kárpás, B.	Gossypium herbaceum, Linn.
कार्पासी	Kápás, H.	Cotton plant.

Sanskrit.	Vernacular.	Scientific Names.
Karpura कर्पूर	Karpur, B. Kápur, H.	Cinnamomum Camphora, Nees et Eber. Camphor.
Karpuraharidrá कर्पूरहरिद्रा	Karpurhaldi, H. Ámádá, B.	Curcuma Amada, Roxb. Mango ginger.
Karuná करुणा	Karuná nebu, B.	Citrus medica (variety of).
Kása काश	Kás, B. H.	Saccharum spontaneum, Linn.
Kásamarda कासमर्द	Kálkásundá, B. Kásaundá, H	Cassia Sophora, Linn. *Syn. Senna Sophora, Roxb.*
Kaseruka कशेरुक	Kesur, B. Kasuru, H.	Scirpus Kysoor, Roxb.
Kásmari काश्मरी		See Gambhári.
Kataka, कतक	Nirmali, B, H.	Strychnos potatorum, Linn. Clearing nut tree.
Kaṭphala कटफल	Káyaphal, B. Káephal, H,	Myrica sapida, Wall.
Kattrina कत्तृण	Rámkarpura, B. Rohish, H.	A fragrant grass.
Kaṭuká कटुका	Kaṭki, B. Kuṭki, H.	Picrorrhiza Kurroa, Royle.
Kaṭutumbi कटुतुम्बी	Tikta láu, B. Tumbi, H.	Wild variety of Lagenaria vulgaris, Sering.
Kemuka केमुक	Keu, B. Keuá, H.	Costus speciosus, Linn.
Kesarája केशराज	Kesuria, B.	Eclipta alba, Hassk. *Syn. E. prostrata and erecta, Linn.*
Ketaki केतकी	Keyá, B Keorá, H.	Pandanus odoratissimus, Linn. fil.
Khadira खदिर	Khayer, B. Kat, H.	Acacia Catechu, Linn. *Syn. Mimosa Catechu, Linn.*

SANSKRIT.	VERNACULAR.	SCIENTIFIC NAMES.
Khaggara खग्गर	Khágrá, B.	A large variety of Saccharum spontaneum, Linn.
Kharjura खर्जूर	Khejur, B. Khajur, H.	Phœnix sylvestris, Roxb. Wild date palm.
Kharvujá खर्व्वुजा	Kharbujá, H.	Cucumis Melo, Linn.
Kinsuka किंशुक		See Palása.
Kirátatikta किराततिक्त		A name for chireyta. See Bhunimba.
Kodrava कोद्रव	Kodoá dhán, B. Kodo, H.	Paspalum scrobiculatum, Linn.
Kokanada कोकनद	Rakta kamal, B.	Nelumbium speciosum, Willd. Red variety.
Kokiláksha कोकिलाक्ष	Kanṭakulika, B. Kuliákhárá, B. Tálmakháná, H.	Hygrophila spinosa, T. Ander. *Syn. Ruellia longifolia, Roxb.*
Kola कोल	Kul, B. Baer, H.	Zizyphus Jujuba, Lamk.
Kosámra कोशाम्र	Koshám,	Mangifera sylvatica, Roxb.
Koshátaki कोशातकी	Ghoshálatá, B. Karwitarui, H.	Luffa amara, Roxb.
Kovidára कोविदार		See Kánchanara.
Krishnachuḍá कृष्णचूड़ा	Krishna churá, B.	Cæsalpinia pulcherrima, Sw. *Syn. Poinciana pulcherrima, Linn.*
Krisnajiraka कृष्णजीरक	Kálájirá, B. H. Magrelá, H.	Nigella sativa, Linn.
Krisnakeli कृष्णकेलि [ti	Krishnakeli, B.	Mirabilis Jalapa, Linn.
Kshetraparpa- क्षेत्रपर्पटी	Khetpáprá, B. Daman papar, H.	Oldenlandia herbacea, DC. *Syn. Oldenlandia biflora, Roxb.*

SANSKRIT.	VERNACULAR.	SCIENTIFIC NAMES.
Kshirakákoli क्षीरकाकोली		A bulb of the onion tribe brought from the Himalaya.
Kubjaka कुब्जक	Kujá, B. Kujái H.	Rosa moschata, Mill. (variety of.) *Syn. Rosa pubescens, Roxb.*
Kuchilá कुचिला		See Vishamushṭi.
Kukubha कुकुभ		See Arjuna.
Kukuradru कुकुरद्रु	Kukursungá, B. Kukkurbandá, H.	Blumea lacera, DC. *Syn. Conyza lacera, Burm.*
Kuláhala कुलाहल	Koksimá, B.	Celsia Coromandeliana, Roxb.
Kulanjana कुलंजन	Mahábarivach, B. Kulinján, H.	Alpinia Galanga, Linn. *Syn. Galanga major, Rumph.*
Kulattha कुलत्थ	Kulthi, B. H.	Dolichos uniflorus, Lamk. *Syn. Dolichos biflorus, Roxb.*
Kulika कुलिक		See Kokiláksha.
Kumbhiká कुम्भिका	Tákápáná, B. H. Jalkumbhi, H.	Pistia Stratiotes, Linn.
Kumkuma कुङ्कुम	Jáfrán, B. H.	Crocus sativus, Linn. Saffron.
Kumuda कुमुद	Sáluk, B. Koi, H.	Nymphæa Lotus, Linn.
Kunda कुन्द	Kuṇdphul, B. H.	Jasminum pubescens, Linn. also Jasminum hirsutum, Willd.
Kunduru कुन्दुरु	Kundarkhaṭi, H.	Boswellia serrata, Colebr. *Syn. B. Thurifera, Colebr.*
Kupilu कुपीलु	Kuchilá, B. H.	Strychnos nux vomica, Linn.
Kuruṇṭaka कुरुण्टक	Káṇṭájáti. B. Kaṭsareyá, H.	Barleria Prionites, Linn.

SANSKRIT.	VERNACULAR.	SCIENTIFIC NAMES.
Kuruvaka	Raktajhinṭi, H.	Barleria cristata, Linn.
कुरुवक		Red variety.
Kusa	Kus, B. H.	Poa cynosuroides, Linn.
कुश		
Kushmáṇḍa	Kumrá, B.	Benincasa cerifera, Savi.
कुष्माण्ड	Peṭhá, H.	*Syn. Cucurbita Pepo, Roxb.*
Kusumbha	Kusamphul, B.	Carthamus tinctorius, Linn.
कुसुम्भ	Kusum, H.	Safflower.
Kushṭha	Kur, B. Páchak,	Saussurea auriculata, Bth. et Hf.
कुष्ठ	Kuṭ, H.	*Syn. Aplotaxis auriculata, DC.*
Kuṭaja	Kurchi, B. H.	Holarrhena antidysenterica, Wall.
कुटज	Kureyá, H.	*Syn. Echites antidysenterica, Roxb.*
Lajjálu	Lájak, B.	Mimosa pudica, Linn.
लज्जालु	Lajjávati, H.	The sensitive plant.
Lakucha	Mádár, B.	Artocarpus Lakoocha, Roxb.
लकुच	Barhal, Dahu, H.	
Lámajjaka	Lámjak, H.	Andropogon Iwarancusa, Linn.
लामज्जक		
Lángaliká	Bishalánguli, B.	Gloriosa superba, Linn.
लाङ्गलिका	Karihári, H.	
Latákasturiká	Latákasturi, B.	Abelmoschus moschatus, Moench.
लताकस्तूरिका	Mushkdáná, H.	*Syn. Hibiscus Abelmoschus, Linn.*
Lavali	Loná, B.	Anona reticulata, Linn.
लवली		
Lavanga	Lang, H.	Caryophyllus aromaticus, Linn.
लवङ्ग	Langa, B.	Cloves.
Lavangalatá	Langphul, B.	Luvunga scandens, Ham.
लवङ्गलता		*Syn. Limonia scandens, Roxb.*
Lavani.	Noári, B.	Phyllanthus distichus, Mull.
लवणी	Harfarauri, H.	*Syn. P. longifolius, Roxb.*
Limpáka	Pátinebu, B.	
लिम्पाक		Variety of Citrus acida, Roxb.

Sanskrit.	Vernacular.	Scientific Names.
Lodhra लोध्र	Lodh, B. H.	Symplocos racemosa, Roxb.
Loni लोणि	Chhotaluniá, B. H. Baraluniá, B. H.	Portulaca oleracea, Linn. Also P. quadrifida, L.
Madana मदन	Madan, B. Mayin, H.	Randia dumetorum, Lamk. *Syn. Posoqueria dumetorum, Roxb.*
Mádhavi माधवी	Mádhavilatá, B. H.	Hiptage Madhablota, Gaertn. *Syn. Gaertnera racemosa, Roxb.*
Madhuka मधूक	Mauá, B. H.	Bassia latifolia, Roxb.
Madhuriká मधुरिका	Mauri, B. Soụf, H.	Fœniculum vulgare, Gaertn. Fennel seeds.
Ṃadhválu मध्वालु	Mauálu, B.	Dioscorea aculeata, Roxb.
Mahábalá महाबला	Svet berelá, B. Sahadebi, H.	Sida rhomboidea, Roxb.
Mahákála महाकाल	Mákál, B. Indráyan H.	Trichosanthes palmata, Roxb.
Mahánimba महानिम्ब	Ghoránim, B. Bakáin, H.	Melia Azedarach, Linn. *Syn. Melia sempervirens, Sw.*
Makhánna मखान्न	Makháná, B. H.	Euryale ferox, Salisb. *Syn. Anneslea spinosa, Roxb.*
Makushṭaka मकुष्टक	Maṭ, H. Banmudga, B.	Phaseolus aconitifolius, Jacq.
Málati मालती	Málati, H. B.	Aganosma caryophyllata, G. Don. *Syn. Echites caryophyllata, Roxb.*
Malliká मल्लिका	Malliká, B. Bel, H. B.	Jasminum Sambac, Ait.
Mánaka मानक	Mán kachu, B. Mán kand, H.	Colocasia Indica, Schott. *Syn. Arum Indicum, Roxb.*
Mandára मन्दार		See Párijáta.

SANSKRIT.	VERNACULAR.	SCIENTIFIC NAMES.
Manḍukaparni	Thulkuri, B.	Hydrocotyle Asiatica, Linn.
मण्डूकपर्णी	Brahmamanḍuki, B.	
Manjishṭá	Manjishṭá, B.	Rubia cordifolia, Linn.
मञ्जिष्ठा	Manjiṭ, H.	*Syn. R. Munjista, Roxb.*
Maricha	Golmarich, B.	Piper nigrum, Linn.
मरिच	Kálimarich, H.	Black pepper.
Márisha	Natiyá ság, B.	Amaranthus oleraceus, Linn.
मारिष	Marsá, H.	
Másha	Máshkalái, B.	Phaseolus Roxburghii, W. A.
माष	Urid, H.	*Syn. P. radiatus, Roxb.*
Máshaparni	Másháni, B.	Teramnus labialis, Spreng.
माषपर्णी	Máshoni, H.	*Syn. Glycine debilis, Roxb.*
Masura	Masur, B. H.	Vicia lens, Benth.
मसूर		*Syn. Cicer lens, Roxb.*
Mátulunga	Chholanga nebu, B.	Citrus medica, Linn. var. acida.
मातुलुङ्ग		
Mayurasikhá	Lál murgá, B.	Celosia cristata, Linn.
मयुरशिखा	Kokan, H.	
Mendiká	Mendi, B.	Lawsonia alba, Lamk.
मेन्दिका	Hená, H.	*Syn. L. inermis, Linn.*
Meshasringi	Merásingi, B. H.	Gymnema sylvestre, R. Br.
मेषशृङ्गी		*Syn. Asclepias geminata, Roxb.*
Methiká	Methi, B. H.	Trigonella fœnum-græcum, Linn.
मेथिका		
Misreyá	Sulpha, B.	Peucedanum Sowa, Bth. & Hf.
मिश्रेया	Sowá, H.	Dill seeds.
Muchukunda	Muchkand, B. H.	Pterospermum suberifolium, Lamk.
मुचुकुन्द		and P. Heyneanum, Wall.
Mudga	Moong, B. H.	Phaseolus Mungo, Linn.
मुद्ग		
Mudgaparni	Mugáni, B. H.	Phaseolus trilobus, Ait.
मुद्गपर्णी		

SANSKRIT.	VERNACULAR.	SCIENTIFIC NAMES.
Mulaka	Mulá, B.	Raphanus sativus, Linn.
मूलक	Muli, H.	Garden radish.
Munḍitiká	Murmuriá, B.	Sphœranthus hirtus, Willd.
मुण्डितिका	Gorak munḍi H.	*Syn. S. mollis, Roxb.*
Munja	Munj, B. H.	Saccharum Munja, Roxb.
मुञ्ज		
Murvá	Goráchakra, B.	Sanseviera Zeylanica, Willd.
मूर्वा	Murvá, B.	*Syn. S. Roxburghiana, Schult.*
Mushikaparni	Indurkáni, B.	Salvinia cucullata, Roxb.
मूषिकपर्णी		
Mushkaka	Ghanṭá párul, B.	Schrebera swietenioides, Roxb.
मुष्कक	Banpalás, H.	
Mustaka	Muthá, B.	Cyperus rotundus, Linn.
मुस्तक	Mothá, H.	
Nágabalá	Gorakcháuliá, B.	Sida spinosa, Linn.
नागबला	Gulsakari, H.	*Syn. S. alba, Linn.*
Nágadamani	Nágdoná, B.	Artemisia vulgaris, Linn.
नागदमनी	Nágdoni, H.	*Syn. A. Indica,̇ Willd.*
Nágakesara	Nágkesar, B. H.	Mesua ferrea, Linn.
नागकेशर		
Naganá		See Jautishmati.
नगना [taka		
Nágara mus-	Nágarmuthá B. H.	Cyperus pertenuis, Roxb.
नागरमुस्तक		
Nágaranga	Kamlá nebu, B.	Citrus Aurantium, Linn.
नागरङ्ग	Nárangi, H.	The sweet orange.
Nágavalli	Pán, B. H.	Piper Betle, Linn.
नागवल्ली		*Syn. Chavica Betle,. Miq.*
Náktamála		See Karanja.
नक्तमाल		
Nákuli	Nái, B. H.	This is said to be a variety of Rásná (Vanda Roxburghii) which is substituted for it in prescriptions.
नाकुली		

SANSKRIT.	VERNACULAR.	SCIENTIFIC NAMES.
Nala नल	Nal, B. Narkul, H.	Phragmites Karka, Trin. *Syn. Arundo Karka, Retz.*
Náli नाली	Mestápáṭ, B. Nálitá, H.	Hibiscus cannabinus, Linn.
Naliká नलिका	Nalipaṭári, H.	A red bark used in scenting medicinal oils.
Nandi vriksha नन्दीवृक्ष	Tun, B. H.	Cedrela Toona, Roxb.
Náḍika नाड़ीक	Páṭ, B. H.	Corchorus olitorius, Linn. Jute plant.
Nárikela नारिकेल	Nárikel, B. Nárial, H.	Cocos nucifera, Linn. Cocoa-nut palm.
Navamáliká नवमालिका	Nabamalliká, B. Motiá, H.	Jasminum Sambac, Linn. Double flowered Jasmine.
Nidigdhiká निदिग्धिका		See Kanṭakári.
Nila नील	Nil, B. H.	Indigofera tinctoria, Linn. Indigo plant.
Nilakamala नीलकमल		Blue Lotus ?
Nilotpala नीलोत्पल	Nilsáplá, B. Nilofar, H.	Nymphœa stellata, Linn. var. cyanea, Hf. & T.
Nimba निम्ब	Nim, B. H.	Melia Azadirachta, Linn. *Syn. Azadirachta Indica, Juss.*
Nimbuka निम्बुक	Kágjinembu, H. B.	Citrus medica, Linn. var. acida.
Nirgunḍi निर्गुण्डी	Nisindá, B. Sambhálu, H.	Vitex Negundo, Linn.
Nirvishá निर्विषा	Nirbishi, B. H.	Kyllingia monocephala, Linn.
Nisá निशा	Halud, B. Haldi, H.	Curcuma longa, Linn. Turmeric plant.

SANSKRIT.	VERNACULAR.	SCIENTIFIC NAMES.
Nishpáva निष्पाव	Barbaṭi, B. Lobia, H.	Vigna catjang, Endl. *Syn. Dolichos sinensis, Linn.*
Nivára निवार	Uridhán, B.	Wild variety of Oryza sativa, Linn.
Nyagrodha न्यग्रोध		See Vata.
Olla ओल्ल	Ol, B. H. Jimikand, H.	Amorphophallus campanulatus, [Blume. *Syn. Arum campanulatum, Roxb.*
Padma पद्म	Padma, B. H.	Nelumbium speciosum, Linn.
Padmachárini पद्मचारिणी		See Sthala padma.
Padmakáshṭa पद्मकाष्ठ	Padmakáshṭa, B.H.	A fragrant wood resembling toon brought from Malwa or Southern India.
Palánḍu पलाण्डु	Piáj, B. H.	Allium Cepa, Linn. Common onion.
Pálanki पालङ्की	Pálang ság, B. Pálanki, H.	Beta maritima, Linn. *Syn. B. Bengalensis, Roxb.*
Palása पलाश	Palás, B. Dhák, H.	Butea frondosa, Roxb.
Panasa पनस	Káṇṭál, B. Kathar, H.	Artocarpus integrifolia, Linn. Indian jack-tree.
Párasikayamá-[ni पारसीकयमानी	Khurásáni jamáni, [H.	Seeds of Hyoscyamus niger, Linn.
Párijáta पारिजात	Pálitá mandár, B. Pharhad, Pangrá, H.	Erythrina Indica, Lamk. Coral tree.
Párisa पारिश	Palás pipal, B. Pares pipal, H.	Thespesia populnea, Corr. *Syn. Hibiscus populneoides, Roxb.*
Parkaṭi पर्कटी	Pákur, B. Pakhar, H.	Ficus infectoria, Willd.
Parpaṭa पर्पट		See Kshetraparpaṭi.

SANSKRIT.	VERNACULAR.	SCIENTIFIC NAMES.
Parusha	Phalsá, B.	Grewia Asiatica, Linn.
परुष [dana	Pharsá H.	
Páshánabhe-	Háthájori, B. H.	Selaginella imbricata, spring.
पाषाणभेदन		*Syn. Lycopodium imbricatum, Roxb.*
Páshánabhedi	Páthor chur, B. H.	Coleus Amboinicus, Lour.
पाषाणभेदी		*Syn. C. aromaticus, Benth.*
Páṭalá	Párul, B.	Stereospermum suaveolens, DC.
पाटला	Pár, H.	*Syn. Bignonia suaveolens, Roxb.*
Páṭha	Ákanádi. B.	Stephania hernandifolia, Walp.
पाठा	Nemuká, B.	*Syn. Cissampelos hernandifolia, Linn.*
Pathyá		
पथ्या		See Haritaki.
Paṭola	Paṭol, B.	Trichosanthes dioica, Roxb.
पटोल	Palwal, H.	
Pattanga	Bakam, B.	Cæsalpinia Sappan, Linn.
पतङ्ग	Pattang, B.	
Phenila	Riṭhá, H B.	Sapindus trifoliatus, Linn.
फेनिल		*Syn. Sapindus emarginatus, Vahl.*
Pilu	Pilu, B. H.	Salvadora Persica, Linn.
पीलु		*Syn. Salvadora Indica. Wight.*
Pinḍakharjura	Pinḍakhejur, H. B.	Phœnix dactylifera, Linn.
पिण्डखर्जुर		The date palm.
Pinḍálu	Chupriálu, B.	Dioscorea globosa, Roxb.
पिण्डालु		
Pinḍára	Pinḍára, H.	Trewia nudiflora. Linn.
पिण्डार	Piṭáli, B.	
Pippali	Pipul, B.	Piper longum, Linn.
पिप्पली	Pipal, H.	*Syn Chavica Roxburghii, Miq.*
Piyála	Piyál, B.	Buchanania latifolia, Roxb.
पियाल		The nuts are called Cheraunji.
Plaksha		
प्लक्ष		See Parkaṭi.

40

SANSKRIT.	VERNACULAR.	SCIENTIFIC NAMES.
Práchinámalaka प्राचीनामलक	Paniálá, B. Pániámlak, H.	Flacourtia cataphracta, Roxb.
Prapaundarika प्रपौण्डरीक	Panderiá, H.	Root-stock of Nymphæa Lotus, Willd.
Prasárani प्रसारणी	Gandhabhádultá, B. Khip, Gandháli, H.	Pæderia fœtida, Linn.
Prikká पृक्का	Piring sák, B. Chini, H.	See Sprikká.
Prisniparni पृश्निपर्णी	Piṭvan, H. Chákulia, B.	Uraria lagopodioides, DC. *Syn. Doodia lagopodioides, Roxb.*
Priyangu प्रियङ्गु	Priangu, B. H.	Aglaia Roxburghiana, W. A.
Puga पूग		See Guváka.
Punarnavá पुनर्नवा	Punarnabá, B. Sánṭ, H.	Boerhaavia diffusa, Linn. *Syn. B. procumbens and erecta.*
Punḍarika पुण्डरीक	Svetpadma, B. H.	Nelumbium speciosum, Willd. white variety.
Punnága पुन्नाग	Punnág, B. Poláng, Oorya.	Calophyllum inophyllum, Linn.
Pushkaramu- [la पुष्करमूल	Pohokarmuly, H.	This root is not available ; the root of Aplotaxis auriculata is substituted for it.
Putiká पूतिका	Puisák, B. Poi, H.	Basella rubra, Linn.
Putikaranja पूतिकरञ्ज	Náṭá, B. Kaṭkaraunj, H.	Guilandina Bonducella, Linn. *Syn. Cæsalpinia Bonducella, Flem.*
Putranjiva पुत्रञ्जीव	Jiáputa, H. B.	Putranjiva Roxburghii, Wall. *Syn. Nageia Putranjiva, Roxb.*
Rági रागी	Maruá, B. Manḍuá, Rági, H.	Eleusine corocana, Gaertn.
Rájádani राजादनी	Khirkhejur, B. Kshiri, H.	Mimusops Indica, DC. *Syn. Mimusops hexandra, Roxb.*

SANSKRIT.	VERNACULAR.	SCIENTIFIC NAMES.
Rájakoshátaki	Dhundul, B.	Luffa cylindrica, Roem.
राजकोषातकी	Ghiátarui, H.	*Syn. Luffa pentandra, Roxb.*
Rája másha	Barbaṭi, B.	Vigna sinensis, Savi.
राजमाष	Lobiá, H.	*Syn. Dolichos sinensis, Linn.*
Rajanigandhá	Rajanigandha, B.	Polyanthes tuberosa, Linn.
रजनीगन्धा	Gulshabbá, H.	Tube-rose.
Rájasarsapa	Ráisarisá. B.	Brassica juncea, Hf. and T.
राजसर्षप [na	Rái, H.	*Syn. Sinapis ramosa, Roxb.*
Raktachanda-	Raktachandan, B.	Pterocarpus santalinus, Linn.
रक्तचन्दन	Lálchandan, H.	Red sandal wood.
Raktachitraka	Lálchitá, B. H.	Plumbago rosea, Linn.
रक्तचित्रक		
Raktálu	Rángálu, B.	Dioscorea purpurea, Roxb.
रक्तालु	Ratálu, H.	
Raktotpala	Raktakambala,. B.	Nymphœa Lotus, Linn.
रक्तोत्पल		*Syn. N. rubra, Roxb.*
Randá		See Mushikaparni.
रण्डा		
Rásná	Rásná, B. H.	Vanda Roxburghii, R. Br.
रास्ना		*Syn. Cymbidium tessaloides, Roxb.*
Rasonaka	Rasun, B.	Allium sativum, Linn.
रसोनक	Lahasun, H.	Garlic.
Renuká	Renuká, B.	Piper aurantiacum, Wall.; probably.
रेणुका		
Rohitaka	Tiktaráj, B.	Amoora Rohituka, W. and A.
रोहितक	Harinhará H.	*Syn, Andersonia Rohituka, Roxb.*
Rudráksha	Rudráksha, B.	Elæocarpus Ganitrus, Roxb.
रुद्राक्ष [ya	Rudrákh, H.	
Sailaja, Saile-	Chharilá, H.	A species of Lichen.
शैलज शैलेय		
Saivála	Seyálá, B.	Blyxa octandra, Rich.
शैवाल	Sivál, H.	*Syn. Vallisneria octandra, Roxb.*

Sanskrit.	Vernacular.	Scientific Names.
Sáka शाक	Segun, B. H.	Tectona grandis, Linn. fil. Teak tree.
Sákhoṭaka शाखोटक	Syáorá, B. H. Siorá H.	Streblus asper, Lour. *Syn. Trophis aspera, Retz.*
Sála शाल	Sál, B. H. Sákhu, H.	Shorea robusta, Gaertn.
Sálaparni शालपर्णी	Sálpáni, B. Sarivan, H.	Desmodium gangeticum, Burm. *Syn. Hedysarum gangeticum, Linn.*
Sálincha शालिञ्च	Sánchi, B.	Alternanthera sessilis, R. Br. *Syn. Achyranthes triandra, Roxb.*
Sallaki शल्लकी	Salái, B. H.	Boswellia serrata, Colebr.
Sálmali शाल्मली	Simul, B. Semal, H.	Bombax Malabaricum, DC. *Syn. B. heptaphylla, Cav.*
Sáluka शालुक	Sáluk, B.	Roots of different species of Nymphæa.
Sami शमी	Sáiṇ, B. Chhikura, H.	Acacia Suma, Ham. *Syn. Mimosa Suma, Roxb.*
Sana शण	San, B. H.	Crotalaria juncea, Linn. Indian hemp.
Sanapushpi शणपुष्पी	Bansanui, B Sanhuly, B.	Crotalaria verrucosa, Linn.
Sankhálu शङ्खालु	Sáṇkálu, B.	Prchyrhizus angulatus, Rich. *Syn. Dolichos bulbosus, Linn.*
Sankhapushpi शङ्खपुष्पी	Dánkuni, B. Sankhahuli, H.	Canscora decussata, R. et. Sch. *Syn. Pladera decussata, Roxb.*
Saptachhada सप्तच्छद	Chhátin, B. Chhátián, H.	Alstonia scholaris, R. Br. *Syn. Echites scholaris, Roxb.*
Sara शर	Sar, B. Rámsar, H.	Saccharum Sara, Roxb. Pen reed grass.
Sarala शरल	Chir, Saral, H.	Pinus longifolia, Roxb.

SANSKRIT.	VERNACULAR.	SCIENTIFIC NAMES.
Sarapunkhá शरपुङ्खा	Sarphoṇká, B. H.	Tephrosia purpurea, Pers. *Syn. Galega purpurea, Linn.*
Sárivá शारिवा	Syámlatá, B.	Ichnocarpus frutescens, R. Br. *Syn. Echites frutescens. Roxb.*
Sarpagandhá सर्पगन्धा	Chandrá, B.	Ophioxylon serpentinum, Linn.
Sarpákshi सर्पाक्षि	Gandhanákuli, B. Sarahaṭi H	Ophiorrhiza mungos, Willd.
Sarshapa सर्षप	Sarisá, B. Sarson, H.	A common name for mustard seeds.
Sarvajayá सर्व्वजया	Sarbajayá, B.	Canna Indica, Linn. Indian shot.
Satamuli शतमूली	Satábari, B. Satávar, H.	Asparagus racemosus, Willd.
Satapatri शतपत्री	Seuti, H. B.	Rosa moschata, Mill. *Syn. R. glandulifera, Roxb.*
Satapushpi शतपुष्पा		See Misreyá.
Saṭi शटी	Karchur, H. Saṭi, B.	Curcuma Zerumbet, Roxb.
Satilá सतीला	Maṭar, H. B.	Pisum sativum, Linn.
Saureya शौरेय	Suklajhinṭi, B.	See Jhinṭi.
Selu शेलु	Bahubára, B Lasorá, H.	Cordia Myxa, Linn.
Sephálika शेफालिका	Seuli, B Harsingár, H.	Nyctanthes arbor-tristis, Linn.
Seva सेव	Seb, B. Sev, H.	Pyrus Malus, Linn. The apple tree.
Sevati सेवती		See Satapatri.

SANSKRIT.	VERNACULAR.	SCIENTIFIC NAMES.
Sigru शिग्रु		See Sobhánjana.
Silhaka सिल्हक	Silha, Siláras, B. Nágorigond, H.	Liquidamber orientalis, Miller. Liquid storax.
Simbi शिम्बी	Sim, B.	A name for several species of Dolichos.
Sindhuvára सिन्धुवार	Nishindá. B. Sambhál, H.	Vitex Negundo, Linn.
Sinsapá शिंशपा	Sisu, B. H.	Dalbergia Sissoo, Roxb.
Sirisa शिरीष	Siris, B. H.	Albizzia Lebbek, Benth. *Syn. Mimosa sirissa, Roxb.*
Sitalapatriká शीतलपत्रिका	Muktápáṭi, B. Sitalpáṭir gách, B.	Maranta dichotoma, Wall. *Syn. Phrynium dichotomum, Roxb.*
Sitali शीतली		See Kálánusárivá.
Snuhi स्नुही	Mansá sij, B. Thohar, H.	Euphorbia neriifolia, Linn. *Syn. E. ligularia, Roxb.*
Sobhánjana शोभाञ्जन	Sajiná, B. H. Sahinjan, H.	Moringa pterygosperma, Gaertn. *Syn. Hyperanthera moringa, Willd.*
Somalatá सोमलता	Somlatá B. H.	Sarcostemma brevistigma, W. A. *Syn. Asclepias acida, Roxb.*
Somaráji सोमराजि	Somráj, B. Bákuchi H.	Vernonia anthelmintica Willd. *Syn. Serratula anthelmintica, Roxb.*
Sprikká स्पृक्का	Piring sák, B. Lankáyiká H.	Trigonella corniculata, Linn.
Sribása श्रीवास	Gandhabirajá, H. B.	Resin of Pinus longifolia, Roxb.
Srigálakanṭaka शृगालकण्टक	Siál káṇṭá, B.	Argemone Mexicana, Linn.
Srigálakoli शृगालकोलि	Siákul, B.	Zizyphus œnoplia, Mill.

SANSKRIT.	VERNACULAR.	SCIENTIFIC NAMES.
Sringáṭaka शृङ्गाटक	Pániphal, B. Singhárá H,	Trapa bispinosa, Roxb.
Sringi शृङ्गी		See Karkaṭasringi.
Sriphala श्रीफल		See Vilva.
Sthalapadma स्थलपद्म	Sthalpadma, B. Sthalkamal, H.	Hibiscus mutabilis, Linn.
Sthauneya स्थौनेय		See Grinthiparni.
Sthulailá स्थूलैला	Baraeláchi. B. H.	Amomum subulatum, Roxb.
Sudarsana सुदर्शन	Padma gulancha.B.	Tinospora tomentosa, Miers. *Syn. Menispermum tomentosum, Roxb.*
Sunandá सुनन्दा	Ishermul, B.	Aristolochia Indica, Linn.
Sunisannaka सुनिसन्नक	Sunsuniá, B. Chaupatte, H.	Marsilea quadrifolia, Linn.
Surana सूरण	Ol, B. H. Jimikand, H.	Amorphophallus campanulatus, [Blume. *Syn. Arum campanulatum, Roxb.*
Surjamani सूर्य्यमणि	Surjamani, B.	Hibiscus phœniceus, Willd.
Surjávarta सूर्य्यावर्त्त	Hurhuriá, B. Hul hul, H.	Gynandropsis pentaphylla, DC. *Syn. Cleome pentaphylla, Linn.*
Sushavi सुषवी	Shiá jirá, H.	Carum Carui, Linn.
Sushavi सुषवी	Uchchhe, B. Karelá, H.	Momordica Charantia, Linn. *Syn. Momordica muricata, Willd.*
Svarnajuthiká स्वर्णयुथिका	Svarnajui, B.	Jasminum revolutum, Sims. *Syn. J. chrysanthemum, Roxb.*
Svarnakshiri स्वर्णक्षीरी	Chos, Chok, H.	Cleome felina, Linn. f. *Syn. Polanisia felina. DC.*

Sanskrit.	Vernacular.	Scientific Names.
Syámáka	Syámá dhán, B.	Panicum frumentaceum, Roxb.
श्यामाक	Samak, H.	
Syámalatá	Syámalatá, B.	Ichnocarpus frutescens, R. Br.
श्यामलता		*Syn. Echtes frutescens, Roxb.*
Syonáka	Soná, B.	Calosanthes Indica, Bl.
श्योनाक	Arlu, H.	*Syn. Bignonia Indica, Linn.*
Tagara	Ṭagar, B.	Tabernæmontana coronaria, Linn.
तगर	Chándni, H.	
Tála	Tál. H. B.	Borassus flabelliformis, Linn.
ताल		
Tálamuli	Mushali, H.	Hypoxis orchioides, Kurz.
तालमूली	Tál muli, B.	*Syn. Curculigo orchioides, Gaertn.*
Tálisapatra	Tálispatra, B.	Pinus Webbiana, Lindl.
तालीशपत्र		*Syn. Abies Webbiana, Loud.*
Tamála	Tamál, B. H.	Garcinia Xanthochymus, Hook. f.
तमाल		Also a name for Cinnamomum Tamala, Nees.
Támbula	Pán, B. H.	Piper Betle, Linn.
ताम्बुल	Támbuli, H.	*Syn. Chavica Betle, Miq.*
Támrakuṭa	Támák, B	Nicotiana Tabacam, Linn.
ताम्रकुट	Támbáku. H.	Tobacco plant.
Tanḍuliya *	Chámpá naṭiá, B,	Amaranthus polygamus, Willd.
तण्डुलीय	Cholái, H.	
Tankári	Tekári, B.	Physalis Peruviana, Linn.
टङ्कारी	Tepuriá, B.	*Syn. P. edulis, sims.*
Taramburja	Tarmuj, B.	Citrullus vulgaris, Schrad.
तरम्बुज	Tarbuz, H.	*Syn. Cucurbita Citrullus, Roxb.*
Taruni	Seuti, B.	Rosa alba Linn.
तरुणी	Svet Goláb, B.	The Indian white rose.
Tejapatra	Tejpát, H. B.	Cinnamomum Tamala, Nees.
तेजपत्र		*Syn. Laurus Cassia, Roxb.*

* Some Bengali physicians use the Amaranthus spinosus, Linn. under the name of Tandulia.

SANSKRIT.	VERNACULAR.	SCIENTIFIC NAMES.
Tila	Til, B. H.	Sesamum Indicum, Linn.
तिल		*Syn. S. orientale, Linn.*
Tindisa	Dheras, B.	Hibiscus esculentus, Linn.
टिण्डिश	Rámtarui, H.	*Syn. H. longifolius, Roxb.*
Tinduka	Gáb, B. H.	Diospyros Embryopteris, Pers.
तिन्दुक		*Syn. D. glutinosa, Kœnig.*
Tinisa	Sandan, H.	Ougenia dalbergioides, Benth.
तिनिश	Tinis, B.	*Syn. Dalbergia oojeinensis, Roxb.*
Tintiri	Tentul, B.	Tamarindus Indica, Linn.
तिन्तिड़ी	Imli, Amli, H.	Tamarind tree.
Trapusa	Khirá, H.	Cucumis sativus, Linn.
त्रपुष	Sasá, B.	
Tráyamáná	Balábahulá, B.	Ficus heterophylla, Linn. fil.
त्रायमाना	Balálatá, B.	
Tripuṭi	Khesári, H. B.	Lathyrus sativus, Linn.
त्रिपुटी		
Trivrit	Teori, B.	Ipomœa Turpethum, R. Br.
त्रिवृत	Nisoth, Turbud, H.	*Syn. Convolvulus Turpethum, Linn.*
Tuda, Tula	Tut, B. H.	Morus Indica, Linn.
तूद तूल	Tutri, H.	*Syn. M. parvifolia, Royle.*
Tulasi	Tulsi, B. H.	Ocimum sanctum, Linn.
तुलसी		
Tumburu	Tumru, H.	Zanthoxylum alatum, Roxb.
तुम्बुरु	Nepálidhaniá, B.	*Syn. Z. hostile, Wall.*
Tunna	Tun, B. H.	Cedrela Toona, Roxb.
तुन्न		
Tvacha	Dálchini, B. H.	Cinnamomum Zeylanicum, Breyn.
त्वच	Tvach, H.	
Udumbara	Jagna dumar, B.	Ficus glomerata, Willd.
उडुम्बर	Gular, H.	*Syn. Covellia glomerata, Miq.*
Ushira	Benámul, B.	Andropogon muricatum, *Retz.*
उशीर	Khas khas, H.	The root is so called.

41

SANSKRIT.	VERNACULAR.	SCIENTIFIC NAMES.
Utpala		See Nilotpala.
उत्पल		
Vachá	Bach, H. B.	Acorus Calamus, Linn.
वचा		
Vajri	Tekáṭásij, B.	Euphorbia antiquorum, Linn.
वज्री		
Vaka	Bak, B. H.	Sesbania grandiflora, Pers.
वक	Agasti, H.	*Syn. Aeschynomene grandiflora, Roxb.*
Vákuchi		See Somaráji.
वाकुची		
Vakula	Bakul, B.	Mimusops Elengi, Linn.
वकुल	Maulsari, H.	
Vanaharidrá	Banhalud, B.	Curcuma aromatica, Salisb.
वनहरिद्रा		*Syn. Curcuma Zedoaria, Roxb.*
Vanakárpása	Bankápás, B.	Hibiscus vitifolius, Linn.
वनकार्पास		
Vanamalliká	Banmalliká, B. H.	Jasminum Sambac, Ait.
वनमल्लिका		The single flowered variety.
Vana methiká	Banmethi, B. H.	Melilotus parviflora, Desf.
वनमेथिका		*Syn. Trifolium Indicum, Willd.*
Van árdraka	Banádá, B. H.	Zingiber Cassumunar, Roxb.
वनार्द्रक		
Vanayamáni	Bonjoán, B.	Seseli Indicum, W. A.
वनयमानि		*Syn. Cnidium diffusum, DC.*
Vandáka		See Rásná.
वन्दाक		
Vansa	Báṇs, B. H.	Bambusa arundinacea, Retz.
वंश		
Vansarochaná	Bansa lochan, B.	Bamboo manna.
वंशरोचना	Tabá sir, H.	
Váráhakrántá	Lájak, B.	Mimosa pudica, Linn.
वाराहक्रान्ता	Lajjá vati, H.	The sensitive plant.

SANSKRIT.	VERNACULAR.	SCIENTIFIC NAMES.
Vársiki	Bel, H. B.	Jasminum Sambac, Ait. [see.
वार्षिकी		Also a name for Triyamáná, which
Vártáku	Begun, B.	Solanum Melongena, Linn.
वार्त्ताकु	Bhanṭá, H.	
Varuna	Barun, B.	Cratæva religiosa, Forst.
वरुण	Barná, H.	*Syn. Capparis trifoliata, Roxb.*
Varvara	Bábuitulsi, B.	Ocimum Basilicum, Linn.
वर्वर	Bábul, H.	*Syn. O. pilosum, Willd.*
Vavula	Bábla, B.	Acacia Arabica, Willd.
वव्वुल	Bábul, H.	
Vásaka	Bákas, B.	Justicia Adhatoda, Roxb.
वासक	Arushá, H.	*Syn. Adhatoda Vasica, Nees.*
Vásphiká	Rándhuni, B.	Pimpinella involucrata, Wight.
वाष्पिका		*Syn. Apium involucratum, Roxb.*
Vástuka	Bethuá sák, B. H.	Chenopodium album, Linn.
वास्तुक		
Vata	Bar, H. B.	Ficus Bengalensis, Linn.
वट		*Syn. F. Indica, Roxb.*
Vetasa, Vetra	Bet, B. H.	Calamus Rotang, Linn.
वेतस वेत्र		*Syn. C. Roxburghii, Griff.*
Vibhitaka	Bahera, H. B.	Terminalia Bellerica, Roxb.
विभितक		
Viḍanga	Biranga, B.	Embelia Ribes, Burm.
विडङ्ग	Báberang, H.	*Syn. E. glandulifera, Wight.*
Vidári	Bhumi kumra, B.	Batatas paniculata, Choisy.
विदारी	Biláí kand, H.	*Syn. Convolvulus paniculatus, Linn.*
Vijapuraka	Tábá nebu, B.	Citrus Medica, Linn. var.
बीजपूरक		
Vijayá		See Bhangá.
विजया		
Vikankata	Baiṇch, B.	Flacourtia Ramontchi, L'Hert.
विकङ्कत	Kanṭái, H.	*Syn. Flacourtia sapida, Roxb.*

SANSKRIT.	VERNACULAR.	SCIENTIFIC NAMES.
Vilva विल्व	Bel, H. B.	Ægle Marmelos, Corr.
Vimbi बिम्बी	Telákucha, B. Kunduri, H.	Coccinea Indica, W. A. *Syn. Momordica monodelpha, Roxb.*
Virana वीरण	Bená, B. Khas khas, H.	Andropogon muricatum, Retz.
Visha विष	Sringi bish, B. Dagrá bish, H.	Aconitum ferox, Wall.
Visalyakrit विशल्यकृत्	Hápar máli, B.	Vallaris dichotoma, Wall. *Syn. Echites dichotoma, Roxb.*
Visamushṭi विषमुष्टि		Strychnos nux vomica, Linn.
Vitkhadira विट्खदिर	Guá báblá, B.	Acacia Farnesiana, Willd. *Syn. Mimosa Farnesiana, Linn.*
Vridhadárak वृद्धदारक	Bijtarká, B.	Argyreia speciosa, Swt. *Syn. Lettsomia nervosa, Roxb.*
Vrihati वृहती	Byákur, B. Gurkámái, B.	Solanum Indicum, Linn.
Vrischikáli वृश्चिकाली	Barhanṭá, H. Bichaṭi, B.	Tragia involucrata, Jacq.
Yajnadumbur यज्ञडुम्बुर		See Udumbara.
Yamáni यमानी	Joán, B. Ájwán, H.	Ptychotis Ajowan, DC, *Syn. Ligusticum Ajowan, Flem.*
Yashṭimadhu यष्टीमधु	Ja shṭimadhu, B. Jeṭi madhu, H. Mulhaṭṭi, H.	Glycyrrhiza glabra, Linn.
Yava यव	Jab, B. Jav, H.	Hordeum hexastichum, Linn,
Yávanála यावनाल	Joár, H.	Andropogon Sorghum, Roxb. *Syn: Holchus Sorghum, Linn.*
Yuthiká यूथिका	Juiṇ, B. Juthi, H.	Jasminum auriculatum, Vahl.

INDEX.

The Sanskrit terms in the glossary have not been included in this index as they are already in alphabetical order.

ERRATA.

Page 27, line 28, *for* "Reduced mercury," *read* "prepared mercury."
„ 97, „ 1, *for* "SANSKRIT MATERIA MEDICA," *read* "THE MATERIA MEDICA OF THE HINDUS."
„ 30, „ 13, *for* "Phyllanthus neruri," *read* "Phyllanthus Niruri."
„ 40, „ 19, *for* "Vitex nigundo," *read* "Vitex Negundo."
„ 102, „ 16, *for* "Mugrelá," *read* "Magrelá."
„ 171, „ 12, *for* "Cucumis sativa," *read* "Cucumis sativus."
„ 198, „ 28, *for* "of ous," *read* "of our."
„ 198, „ 31, *for* "about Manbhom," *read* "about Mánbhum."
„ 208, „ 20, *for* "Var. Jacquinis," *read* "Var. Jacquinii."
„ 218, „ 13, *for* "Ghambhári," *read* "Gambhári."
„ 320, „ 3, *for* "Echtes frutescens," *read* "Echites frutescens."

THE END.

NIDÁNA:
A SANSKRIT SYSTEM OF PATHOLOGY.

TRANSLATED INTO BENGALI

BY UDOY CHAND DUTT,

CIVIL MEDICAL OFFICER.

EXTRACTS FROM REVIEWS.

"Nidána is a Sanskrit treatise on Hindu Medicine, compiled by Madhub Kur, a Sudra, who lived many hundred years ago. It was intended for the benefit of the ordinary class of students, who, for certain reasons, had no access to the more learned works of Charaka and Susruta. It may, therefore, be accepted as one of the text-books of the Hindu Medical Schools. It gives a clear and concise account of all the diseases and injuries known to the Hindu physicians up to the time when it was written, including their diagnosis and prognosis. The whole work is evidently based on clinical experience, and, as a didactic record of facts, it is very valuable. But, for the explanations of these facts, they are often interwoven with absurd theories and doctrines which take the place of physiology and pathology. The object of this work was simply to teach diseases, leaving their treatment to be dealt with in a separate book; and it would be a great thing if we could have a similar book composed in Bengali, with the light of modern science, for the use of our vernacular medical students. That is a great want which, however, could only be supplied by oriental scholars like Baboo Udoy Chand Dutt, the learned translator of this work. As it is, the Baboo has done great service to vernacular medicine, and our best acknowledgments are due to him for it.

. . . .

"Being free from barbarous interpolations and foreign words, it is calculated to chasten the language of the new vernacular medical literature. On this account we trust Government will insist on a knowledge of this work by all their licentiates in Bengali or English. In that way alone can a proper taste be created for the careful study of Bengali, the want of which is painfully apparent in many of the recently issued vernacular medical publications."—*Indian Medical Gazette, January*, 1874.

"The author before us belongs to the pre-university era. A good English scholar, a reputed master of the healing art, with an inquisitive turn of mind, and thoroughly alive to the merits of the indigenous system of medicine, he possesses many qualifications for expounding the principles of the Sanskrit system of medicine, and has performed well his self-elected task. In his preface to the work before us he says that it is a literal translation of the Sanskrit treatise on pathology, compiled by Mádhava Kar, and generally known under the name of Nidána. It gives a pretty full account of the diseases known to the ancient Hindus, and it has been the text-book on medicine for native physicians from a long time past. With a view to enable the reader versed in English medicine readily to identify the diseases described in this work, our author, wherever it has been practicable, has given their equivalent English names in foot-notes. This translation is a valuable contribution to Indian Medical Literature."—*Hindoo Patriot, October* 20, 1873.
